The
# PROFESSIONAL
# BACHELR

The

# PROFESSIONAL
# BACHEL♂R

How to Exploit her Inner Psycho

Dr.
BRETT TATE

## like the Ravenous Lion...

The Professional Bachelor doesn't just snarl and flash his teeth at his prey, expecting her to succumb meekly. The attack is done on the sly. He hovers in her vicinity, wins her trust, and then he devours her.

Brett Tate's latest controversial release...
from the author of the wildly popular Bachelor's Sex Bible:

--- THE HEDONIST ---
(ISBN – 09752640-0-1)

Published by
TPB Publishing, LLC

www.theprofessionalbachelor.net

ISBN 0-9752640-2-8
ISBN 978-0-9752640-2-7    Printed in the United States

The Essence of Power in Seduction is controlling the chase. It flows from your inner strength and Alpha confidence, charismatic presence, and dynamic execution of the skills. There's no substitute for being a smooth talker, and having *The Look* that speaks volumes. The Art of the Pickup involves analyzing your target, finding her weaknesses, and role-playing her desires. Sexual Persuasion occurs by triggering her subconscious emotions; you remove her barriers, build trust, and initiate the close. The best Players succeed by acting teasingly cocky, have a cutting sense of humor, and the poise to pull it off with class. This acquired talent will elevate your closing ratio, and attract trophy women you thought to be way out of your league.

Mastering speed seduction sets a premium on controlling your time and money management. It also exploits the advantages of psychoanalysis of your targets. Knowing whom not to pursue is the most valuable tool in dating...and without getting too serious about it, be aware of the Alpha Masculine Image you present. Life is about marketing yourself. People make their decisions about you in the first 30 seconds. Men who ooze confidence and a passion for life radiate sex appeal, energy, and social status. Women are instantly attracted and drawn to their *perceived* success. Turbo-charge your game by mastering your look, style and attitude. Body Language and presence are 80% of the game. When you control the timing, tone and emotions, you control the outcome. Life is not a spectator sport for the Professional Bachelor. No pussies allowed.

Many will approach this as a pickup artist manual, as it can dramatically increase your success with women. Yet it's not about memorizing lines and bending rules to get laid, in an attempt to validate yourself. The hidden dynamics of relationships, and understanding the methods in the Chase, are merely facets of the Game. It is not the end, but the means.

In some aspects, this book's central theme is not about women at all. True masculine wisdom is learning a higher level of self-confidence and attitude are what engineer achieving your life goals. Determine exactly what it is that makes you happy. Set out to get what you want, when you want, without compromise. With success and a ballsy attitude, attracting women like a magnet are a *consequence* of becoming an Alpha Male; it's not about the clothes, dance moves, or cheesy pickup lines. Enjoy the thrill of the chase, but absorb the lessons of success. Let it define your identity and lifestyle, until the game fades away, giving way to who you are.

Remember, when the flat line is approaching, your thoughts will not center on the expensive toys you collected. What matters most are the things that no one can take away from you...the exhilarating experiences, heart-throbbing relationships...the sensual, exotic women...and the Hedonistic approach to squeezing out every last drop of pleasure until the last damn minute of your life. Live life to the fullest. Live it on your terms, and be...

A Professional Bachelor

# Contents

# Chapter III

# Chapter IV

# Chapter V

## Personality Types – How to Profile and Seduce

# Chapter VI
## Bachelor College - Cynical Observations from the Trenches

# Chapter VII
## It's All About the Money

# Chapter VIII

# Chapter IX
## Turnkey Bachelor Party Sex Vacations

# IT'S A MAN'S WORLD

On the depths of our genetic makeup, we were all once Prehistoric Warriors and pure Alpha studs. Eyeing them from the trees bathing in streams, we vigorously pursued women. Flexing our Neanderthal biceps, we swooped in and dragged packs of jungle babes by the hair to the nearest caves, and mounted them like rodeo bulls in heat. In the modern era, as budding young boys we continued our mad hunt for prey. We found out the cute girl next door could touch us in so many ways, most of which got us a considerable whipping. As Freshman year rolls around, you move on to trench warfare, and concoct a brilliant scheme to sabotage a girl's lunch. But as she reaches for her food tray, you realize you've made a terrible mistake. Somehow, you failed to notice that sweet little Nikki has blossomed into a woman, and is packing a killer ass. Her sandwich explodes…and as the mayonnaise drips down her chin, she licks her lips and coyly smiles at you. The visual is in soft focus, and slow motion. At that moment, in a bizarre twist of fate, you discover your destiny. You peer away nervously, and for the first time notice her dork friend has grown luscious puffy nipples, peeking out through her shirt. She gives you a devilish wink, and then Bammm; you go brain dead…overwhelmed by a strange, warm, swelling sensation. Your life will never be the same.

## The hormonal frenzy has begun

Forget the theory of relativity, or the first silicon microchip; nothing has had a greater impact on the future of mankind than that first high school hard on. It's the engine behind capitalism. From that moment on, men live in a testosterone fog, racing to earn cash to impress women and get laid, while plotting ways to rip the clothes off of as many women as possible. The techniques will come slowly. To meet cheerleaders, we hid under the bleachers and peeked up their skirts. In college, we experiment with deep science, and discover the compelling relationship between alcohol and wet panties. Then comes the Porsche bimbo-magnet phase, and the romantic parking lot love. In our peak, some of us actually use *speaking* to get what we want. In our golden years, we finally wise up and just tape a Hundred to our zipper. I suppose the whole lust thing lasts forever. After all, my grandfather still watches young schoolgirls play hopscotch, only now he uses binoculars and wears raincoats. Seems his eyesight must be fading, and he has a fear of getting caught in thunderstorms.

It's a Man's World. It always has been, and it always will be. Human existence has advanced by driven males battling for honor, dignity, and their country. Men are the sacrificers in humanity, fighting for discovery, achievement or redemption to create a just world. Every major invention furthering civilization in the last 200 years is man-made; all modes of Transportation, the Infrastructure, Technology, Medicine, Computers,

1

Agriculture, from Nuclear Energy to Space Exploration. Man created it all.

Our veins pump with ambition and a rage to win. A man started every Fortune 500 Company. Men even dominate the feminine fields; fashion, interior design, cooking, and the arts. Why is this? The male brain is wired different than a woman's. Male decisions are based on statistics, facts and logic, and not evolving emotions. Men have more energy, competitiveness, and we channel our aggression in a success driven methodology. Men have larger brains and higher IQ's. Physically, men are genetically superior to women. More importantly, men have penises; and when we're not creating a complex civilization, we need to use the damn things. All the Time.

Staying a Bachelor in your late thirties and forties is no small task this day and age in the States. The anti-male, sex-negative culture does their damnest to smear anyone proudly masculine; who dares to taste the fruits of invigorating freedom. To the elitist sisterhood, a stress free man with a stimulating lifestyle, and supporting cast of sexy girlfriends is sleazy and contemptible. Staying single and keeping all of your own hard earned money is shamefully selfish. Clearly there must be something wrong with you. If your dates are nineteen and can't keep their hands off you in public, Oprah and her beefy Posse brand you an immature pervert of the worst kind, and a greedy one at that. We're told living uncommitted to marriage and raising children is a meaningless existence. "You're only contributing to the anxieties between the sexes." Hardly. It only creates anxiety amongst women, because the man's wallet is no longer in play. Enjoying life as you please sets a dangerous precedent. A man who women cannot control has no value in their world, and his actions must be silenced. It's a well protected secret this is perfectly normal in any other country.

A happy bachelor drives women nuts, yet it's the most natural thing in the world to want variety and live a fuller life. Let's face the facts. Try to find a guy who married in his early 20's, who wouldn't love to switch places with a successful bachelor in his late 30's. You can't. Ask a gourmet chef if he'd like to eat just one meal for the rest of his life, or risk seizure of 50% of his assets. He'll look at you like you're out of your mind. Then ask him if he likes sex more than food.

It can be tough being single, between juggling your sex schedule, waxing the Ferrari, cleaning out the hot tub, and trying to remember girls' names. But it does have it has its moments; just yesterday I pulled up to a stoplight with my college girlfriend's head bobbing up and down. The scowls from the bitter, chunky wenches in the next car always bring a smile to the face.

Reminds me of the old proverb:

Why do wives hate the missionary position?
*Because they can't stand seeing a man have a good time.*

# The Myth of Monogamy

Monogamy and marriage are not always the appropriate choice. It's a level of responsibility that should be both respected and feared. The rules are cast in stone. You have to throw in the towel and stick with only one woman for the rest of your life, or face losing half your estate. There's no room for error. Personally, I think there should be a law requiring a potential groom to take a week vacation to Rio de Janiero before he proposes. If he returns and can honestly say he only wants one girl for the rest of his life, he's either in love, impotent, or brain dead.

Polygamy may not be the perfect lifestyle choice for everyone, yet we are all genetically predisposed to it. Anthropologist Margaret Mead had the courage to dispel the myth of monogamy, and was heavily ridiculed. She discovered over 90% of human cultures are polygamist, and found almost the entire animal kingdom enjoys the same multi-partner lifestyle. The reality is, Men are biologically wired to lust for many women, and the prettiest, young ones we can find.

For me, I choose to live true to my dominant Alpha genes. In my past life, I was the fastest nympho Lion in the jungle. I patiently hid in the woods for hours on end without moving a muscle, until the freshest, cutest young lioness tip-toed out into the field, in heat for the first time. Then I sprinted out like the beast that I am, and mounted her so hard and long, I broke both her hind legs…and then strolled back to home base and waited for round two. Hell, I didn't even drink a victory beer back then. Men are natural born hunters, and are intended to be on a hormonal safari for years.

Your life goal should be to enjoy as many breathtaking, satisfying experiences you can. Let's be realistic. Which is more exhilarating? The first time with that scorching hot Russian exchange student with the bubblebutt at the gym, or your gargantuan, psychotic wife's latest weight loss program that she quits after a week?

## Peeling away the Panty Barriers

After college, we see our future holding the promise of the ages. Strutting like debonair, swashbuckling warriors, we set out to pursue a life of easy riches and horny bitches. The world is our mating grounds. As we pole vault through nightclubs on our rods, we visualize corralling numerous sexy damsels in distress back to our castle for endless sweaty hours of nympho-pumping lust. Girls have a different vision.

The innocent college schoolgirl peering up at you with her pigtails, big doe eyes, perky tits and miniskirt, is plotting an alternate future for you, most of which involves her power shopping, while you're trapped in a lifetime of servitude in an office cubicle, trying to make the payments on her Lexus, 5-carat ring, and massive credit card debt. It's a struggle of the sexes. The truth be known; we are the pursued. Unless you're wise to a woman's devious charms and seduction motives, unless you learn how to work the system to your advantage, you barely stand a chance. Women are far more emotional than rational, but their survival instincts dwarf the typical man's ability to see through his testosterone fog. Girls possess immense manipulation powers over men via the limitation of the sex supply.

While boys are playing little league baseball and mastering video games, girls are being groomed by Mom, their teachers, and Reality shows on how to persuade, manipulate and control boys. They've practically got their Masters in the School of Sexual Temptation before we've witnessed the mystical third leg growing between our thighs for the first time.

Meeting women is the easy part. Navigating through their self-centered, neurotic behavior, imaginary problems, bitch shields, and surviving the chase unscathed is the real challenge. Any new man introduces change and potential disarray in their orderly lives. No matter how irrational they act, there is a science controlling her feelings and thoughts. It is a necessary evil that you must master your side of the game; perfecting the ability to influence and persuade her emotionally and physically to see the value of wanting you for who you are, and not just for what she can get out of you.

This is why you need your own barrier and screening process to determine if a girl represents seduction or destruction. One percent of women if attracted will sleep with you immediately. Ten percent will pursue a sexual relationship if you generate desire and push the right buttons. The rest will treat you to the full gamut of those wonderful things that define American femininity: childish cock-teasing, guilt tripping, game playing, attention-whoring, gold-digging and emotional terrorism. The most valuable skill in a bachelor's arsenal is knowing which girls **not** to pursue, and to excel at cutting your losses quick. Nothing is worse than discovering you've been played like a fool and didn't see it coming.

You have to tread lightly through the sexual jungle. What is intoxicating and irresistible is often laced with deception. Land twice in the wrong girl's bed, and she'll mark your ass with territorial claims faster than an ambulance chasing attorney in a hurricane's path. Coochie risk assessment is one of the most difficult levels to achieve; having the discipline to say no when you're drunk and in a catatonic state of lust. If a flower is unexpectedly spread open in front of you, pause and evaluate the down side. Don't let temptation get the best of you. Sometimes the *risk* of the plunging into the honey is not worth the *reward* of a cinderblock plunging through

4

your windshield when you don't return her calls. There isn't a psychologist in the world who can fully explain what women think day in and day out, but hopefully you'll learn a thing or two with this book. We can all use a little help. Consider what Sigmund Freud had to say on his deathbed:

"Despite my 30 years of research into the feminine soul, I have not yet been able to answer the great question that has never been answered: What does a woman want?

# The Playing Field has Changed

- "I am most anxious to enlist everyone who can speak or write to join in checking this mad, wicked folly of 'Women's Rights,' with all its attendant horrors …Were women to 'unsex' themselves by claiming equality with men, they would become the most hateful, heathen and disgusting of beings and would surely perish without male protection."
  **Queen Victoria**, 1870

Somehow, after millenniums of smooth interaction, something has gone wrong. Drastically wrong. The whole man and woman partnered forever thing stopped working. The catalyst for the problem even had a cute name for it. *Feminism*. With a catchy marketing blitz, and biased news coverage, they managed to glamorize it. Women wanted to try and be competitive with men. How cute! They even set out to prove it in a huge TV event. The infamous "Battle of the Sexes" pitted the current #1 seeded female tennis player (Billie Jean King) against a 55 yr. old below average male tennis player (Bobby Riggs). By a miracle of the ages, she won. Astounding!

The world tuned in to observe this glamorized celebration of the new Super Babe, the Feminist. With great irony, most felt like they had been had. If it's celebration of the woman, why is it you can barely tell the gender? Billy Jean looked more masculine than Bobby. A confused, sexless identity was born, lead by scowling, butch, beefy man-women in frumpy pantsuits. As for the rest of the world, the whole concept was an embarrassing sideshow. The sensual Latin and European women tradition lived on. The gorgeous, statuesque hotties with hourglass bodies, ass-length hair, and sex on the brain continued pursuing men. They continued flirting, screwing, and loving men, while wearing their thongs, revealing tops, mini skirts and high heels. They stayed, well…feminine. The Outrage.

Billie Jean King went on to become a tennis announcer, where she perfected insulting Anna Kournikova's playing her entire career. (2-time Grand Slam doubles champion). After all, Anna is very bad for the cause. She isn't a scheming feminist. She oozes sex appeal and loves everything masculine. Not only that, Butch Billie has no shot at her pussy. Billie even got the TV crew to stop showing low angle camera shots from behind Anna Hell, that's the only reason men even watch women's tennis.

Feminism was alive and here to stay in the states. In many ways it defied explanation. They're against women acting like women, and against men being men. They oppose both manliness and womanliness. Yet they set out to look and act like men, while trying to feminize men through political correctness. Like we wouldn't notice what sexless, bitter, humorless, confrontational, man-hating cattle they became, and in turn we'd become passive, lisping, limp-wristed, bedwetting wimps sipping decaf lattes with brazed tofu and diet lettuce while discussing the nuances of gender conflict resolution studies. Oh wait, there's millions of these alternative, liberal girly-men now. Been to Seattle, Austin, Greenwich Village or a Starbucks lately? Every one of these sassy sailors is just one drunk, emotional sob-fest away from plopping down and blowing his consoling roommate.

"Thanks dude. Thhhaayy Bruce, doth this mean we're gay? I don't know whatth with me lately. My lunar cycle is tho thensitive to my needs, it's affecting my aura and stuff. Think I should shower this month?"

## The Brain Dead Feminized Media

It's both hilarious and insulting watching the ridiculous fantasyland the feminized media lives in. Despite men creating the entire civilization's infrastructure and business world, they ridicule us every minute they can out of raging jealousy. The Cinema, television, teachers, divorcees, Oprah, and the narcissistic airheads in the "Cosmo" world of print media brainwash young girls from an early age about the *inferiority of men.* It's a huge support group for male bashing; an elitist team of calculating, sassy, you-go-grrrl women built like middle linebackers, with faces that would scare a pit bull. Every sitcom, movie, and commercial we're bombarded by feminist propaganda, portraying white heterosexual men as incompetent, vulgar, buffoons mumbling nonsense while struggling to tie their shoes. The wives are beautiful, thin, successful executives supporting the family. Practically a third of the dudes in sitcoms are sassy gays…gays you'd want to open a can of whoop-ass on, though you wouldn't because they'd probably enjoy it.

I don't know what country this is supposed to portray, but it isn't the United States. The last time I strolled through Wal Mart, the wives I see waddling down the aisles average 200+ pounds, and haven't held a job in a decade. They're barely able to negotiate steering a shopping cart, let alone locate their screaming, out-of-control kids. The whole scene resembles a late night infomercial for **Cows Gone Wild…**

…and there isn't a fag in the whole building.

# The Real Motives behind Feminism

Feminists were very slick in using incrementalism to spread their empowerment disease. They successfully camouflaged their real intentions, and men continued to play along and fall in love, like the romantic fools we are. We trusted women and married them, without giving it a second thought. Soon, the cute little feminists played their Ace card. They invented a neat little thing called "no fault divorce."

-   **Di·vorce (di-vôrs), n.**   from Latin (*divortium*)   -
Ripping a man's wallet out through his testicles.

As it turns out, feminism has nothing to do gender, and everything to do with money and power. The person controlling the relationship is the one most willing to terminate it. The way divorce laws are written, that clearly is the woman. Women initiate almost 75% of divorces in the US, as the outcome often resembles winning the lottery. With the media, liberal attorneys and judges in their back pocket the results are guaranteed. Women have seen the big picture, and found that obtaining wealth doesn't actually require hard work. It turns out they really can compete with men. All it takes is a couple of years of marriage role-playing, and a good attorney. Millions have perfected the art, and can be heard bragging how they "*divorced well.*" Forget white-collar crime, white-panty crime has resulted in the largest money transfer schemes conceived in the 20<sup>th</sup> Century. Women now control an astonishing 80% of the wealth in the United States.

There's nothing cute about that.

This country is filled with men living like battered subservient slaves out of fear of losing everything. There are many problem cases out there. A husband slaves a 12-hour workday and returns home, expecting fun playing with his 2 year old and the dog. Instead, for the crime of being 5 minutes late, he gets whacked over the head with a frying pan and is ordered to mow the goddamn lawn. As luck would have it, like most husbands, he didn't win the lottery. He's now married to an unemployed, screeching, neurotic elephant. The wedding pictures of his once thin, cute, bubbly bride who skipped down the aisle seem almost comical now. He doesn't know whether to laugh or cry. He'd call his married friends and compare notes, but wives eliminate all contact with a man's past. What the hell. The other guys are probably holding an ice pack to their head, if they're not divorced already.

# A Woman's Hidden Agenda

Men don't say a word to women about how they should live their life, but boy how they try to run yours. When they can't control you, the look in their eyes is like holding a crucifix to a vampire. It takes a patient man to dodge the bullets, and find the rare sexy, intelligent, honest, respectful bride untarnished by the poisonous feminist propaganda. Women are in the marriage business, and most have a hidden agenda. Men with money are targets, pursued by con artist babes looking to marry you with the intent to divorce in 3 years…to seize your assets. They pressure you to get hitched and have kids, but it rarely has anything to do with keeping the family name. It may have 30 years ago, but times have changed. Men created the Fortune 500, but women are now the CEO's of the largest business in the United States; the Divorce Industry. Sales are way up, divorcees are living fat and happy, and they want to keep the gravy train running and start round two…or was it four? I mean like who can keep track? As if!

## Trophy Wife Boot Camp

Take for example, the trophy wives. While men are seeking love & family, these cons are training hard for the business of future settlements, alimony, child support, cars, houses, and lawsuits, I mean marriage. If all goes as planned, the Boob jobs, nose jobs, tummy tucks, butt tucks, bleached hair and liposuction may soon pay off. Her dream man is on the horizon. The fantasy life of luxuries provided by a Gazillionaire are a tantalizingly elixir, just as long as the old geezer can get out of his wheelchair without knocking over the damn ventilator.

"One more time, you geriatric prick, and I'm giving you a flat!! "

Trophy wives stay honest to the "marriage institution", and tolerate Daddy Big Bucks for the obligatory 30 months, while plotting their exit.

**Divorce Excuse**: "We grew apart".
**Translation**: "I stayed in the master bedroom trying to crack the safe, while medics perform a suspicious autopsy on poor dear old Mortimer."

The last thing aspiring wives need are distractions when they are this close to pay dirt. Professional Bachelors dating a fleet of college hotties and potential divorce protégés are bad for business. These happy bastards need to be suppressed and hidden from view at all costs.

J. Paul Getty reflected how "Sex is what gives a man his business drive." As the world's first billionaire, that pretty much makes him an expert on women. In fact, in his final days, all 7 of his girlfriends lived with him at his palatial Sutton Place estate. They professed their love for him, and naturally claimed they had no interest in his will. Getty was nobody's fool. He played along with his best naïve, old doddering geezer impression, and left 99.9% of his estate to his Trust. In the end, he handed out parting gifts to each girl of $50,000 to close to a million. In a touching display of romantic gratitude, a few reciprocated by lovingly suing his ass while he was still warm in the coffin. Hell, they probably stapled the subpoena to his forehead.

Women take advantage of men not just because they are taught to, it's because they can. More accurately, sad to say, it's because men let them. There's always another sucker around the corner. Almost any hot babe can spend her budding youth on her back, and eventually own a mansion. We all have friends or relatives stuck in a gut wrenching, sexless life, suffering emotionally and financially at the whim of a woman. There is a better way, and every guy has the means to change this. This culture has allowed woman to accumulate too much power over men.

## It's Time to take the Power Back

This guide reveals how to master seduction using psychoanalysis, strong body language and attitude, and persuasive charm. With this ability to easily influence female behavior, you'll enjoy an exhilarating lifestyle that *you* control with numerous hot women. The guide is also designed to make sure men look at the big picture. If you decide to marry, you must be legally prepared. Face reality…it's a battlefield out there now. The best defense is a good offense. In the modern era, like JP Getty, you need to have an asset protection strategy in place before getting engaged, and have the patience of a saint in choosing your partner. Screw this one up, and you'll end up having to subscribe to the married guy's version of Playboy. Every month the centerfold gets a little bit older, a little fatter, and a lot meaner. You'd love to cancel the subscription, but it would cost you a damn fortune.

With extensive practice in the field, these profiled cases of female insanity will bare no resemblance to your future. When you seal away your assets permanently, you maintain the upper hand in dealing with any seductress coyly slithering around your penis and wallet.

You will always be the King of your Castle

The Professional Bachelor Dating Guide is divided into 8 sections

## Mastering Your Alpha Presentation

**Section One…**
Every Seduction begins with creating subconscious inner attraction and lust before you speak. Using reverse psychology, we analyze what women visually desire in a man's presentation and attitude, and layout the techniques to **Give them what they Want to See**.

— The Universal Foundation of an Alpha Stud —

This covers the many facets of masculinity; from strong body language, a highly confident, borderline-cocky attitude and high social status image. The way you project yourself is 80% of the chase.

## Perfecting the Silky Smooth Conversation

**Section Two...**
Charm their panties off. Mastering the gift of the silver tongue is when you have the delivery down to an art. When you play to their ego, you always leave her wanting more of you, by making her feel wanted and special. She is wanted and special, and she's probably smoking hot too. That's why you're trying to date her, rip her clothes off and pin her ankles behind her ears. In the second phase of seduction, you build on her inner attraction and lust and **Give her what she Wants to Hear.**

Here we dissect in eighteen easy steps how to develop the magical talent of Persuasive Charisma. This allows you to quickly create quality time and comfort levels that reduce her barriers, builds a rapport, and sets up the emotional ingredients needed for the close.

## Speed Dating University

**Section Three...**
Speed dating is the only way to execute the chase. Time is money, and a player who controls each has his game polished. Here we cover the methods of mastering your time and money management; the avenue where 95% of men fail. We cover various quick hit and run qualifying methods used for initial dates. Each is designed to swiftly weed out the game players, cons, and selfish whiners, while concentrating on the higher quality targets.

## Role Playing Techniques

**Section Four...**
By finding her weaknesses, beliefs and desires, with persuasion conversation skills you create the proper mood to satisfy her wants and needs. This phase we **Give her the Emotions She Wants to Feel.** This section covers a dozen different role-playing techniques to use in seducing the appropriate targets. Women all role-play to lure in men. For many girls their whole life is one big story. Allow Brett Tate to return the favor and divulge some highly effective role-playing strategies to seduce the ladies.

> Be all you can be. In fact, go beyond that.
> Be someone else.

Mastery of Seductive role-playing allows the average looking guy to be just as proficient at having a revolving door of girlfriends. It will help you conquer any fears in approaching women you've previously thought were way out of your league. After you master the advanced conversation skills, you'll soon host the hot new late night series:

> How to Win Friends and Influence Pussy

# Personality Profiling the Miniskirts

**Section Five...**

Psychoanalysis fine-tunes and accelerates the chase. Concentrate your focus solely on finding the right type of girls for you; it's your most powerful tool in dating. Swiftly size up women and pick the winners, while successfully dodging the emotional tampons, money leeches and psychos. Learn how to spot their nonsense, and master the art of avoiding them. Dating and marriage can either be an exhilarating experience, or it can be a living hell. Men waste extraordinary amounts of time and money dating and tolerating the wrong women in relationships. This is a numbers game. There are plenty of female targets. Align your scopes, and choose wisely.

# Bachelor College

**Section Six...**

Cynical Observations and Field Techniques spelled out in classic rants, slams, raves and zingers, honed from years of execution in the Trenches.

# Follow the Money

**Section Seven...**

If there is anything you get out of this book, this chapter should be it. The marriage industry has failed because the laws provide women a financial incentive to destroy it. There is nothing more powerful than eliminating the ability of women ruining your life financially in a divorce. He who controls the money, controls his life. With today's divorce laws bordering on male castration, before making any long-term decisions with a woman, you need a proactive **Asset Protection Plan** in advance. Legally shelter all your money from potential litigation in layers of trusts and entities. The process is very easy, affordable, entirely legal, and is near bulletproof protection from litigation. Vow to stay single until you near 40. Keep all of your wealth from your top earning years, and seal it away permanently. Spoil yourself rotten with your own money instead of handing it over to Satan's daughter, Mrs. Wrong in a divorce. Want to find out what a woman's true intentions are? Want to know the answer to the age-old question...is she marrying you for Love or Money? There is no faster way to find this out, than to *remove all of your* assets prior to marriage.

Imagine this little scene. You're parked in your mansion driveway, with your trophy babe in the Ferrari Convertible. The Moonlight glistens down, silhouetting her flowing golden locks across her angelic face. As her breathing accelerates, a shiny bead of sweat slides lower between her heaving breasts. She strokes your upper thigh, unzips your fly, and gazes at you licking her lips. As she lowers her head downward, she starts quietly purring about all the advantages of you marrying her. You reach for your 8th Vodka Red Bull, slam it, and crank up the Metallica CD.

*"Sssshhhgreat idea Buffy, Tiffany, whatever. By the way, there's this little thing I forgot to mention. You know all these luxuries we're enjoying right now? The mansion, the sports cars, boats, vacations, and endless cash flow. I don't own any of it!! Layers and layers of impenetrable Trusts control them all. The assets are untouchable. If we divorce, you won't see dime one. Just thought you should know...now this doesn't have any affect on your wedding intentions, does it? **Hey, watch the teeth.**"*

In today's litigious society, with female divorce fraud and identity theft so prevalent, every man needs to take advantage of the legal options in protecting his money. In straightforward language, learn the ins and outs of asset protection, and create a legal shield between your assets and any unbalanced divorces, frivolous lawsuits, judgments, bloodsuckers and ambulance chasers.

What you don't own can't be taken from you

# The Holy Grail is Overseas

**Section Eight...**
When the allure of the chase fades, you become anxious to discover the best options in life for exotic women, sports and adventure. Many bachelors venture out to explore the wilder side of life, and take jet-setting vacations around the globe, dating insatiable exotic women from other cultures. There are places to satisfy your animal lust at levels beyond anything you can imagine. Pure hedonistic lust 24/7. Many expats, myself included, spend most of the year out of the country; and have a lifestyle and revolving parade of hot young girlfriends that perhaps King Hefner would envy.

If you want to catapult your game to the Major Leagues and truly live **The Professional Bachelor** lifestyle, feast your eyes on this section. A time and money saving guide to the best tropical paradises in the world, where the babes compete for *you*. In some cities it requires ZERO talent. Your only limitations are your Viagra prescription and sperm. Hell, you don't even have to speak the language. There are tens of thousands of scorching hot girls who smother you with attention just a flight away. It's complete role reversal. You feel like a Swedish Supermodel strolling through a fraternity party. So kick back, enjoy the ride, and be a master of the game.

You know... at the only game that actually matters.

" It really doesn't matter what people think as long as you've got a young beautiful piece of ass."

**DONALD TRUMP,** *in 1991*

# Chapter I

# MASTERING YOUR ALPHA IMAGE

Creating Sexual Attraction and Desire

# The Alpha Gladiator

**A**nything you passionately desire takes a commitment. It's a line that one crosses. This pertains to all things in life. Once you cross it, there is no turning back. When you make the decision to cross that line, the only way to live is within that commitment; 100% of the time. Failure comes to those who look for excuses not to honor or respect that line. Success comes to those who know where they have been prior to crossing, where they are going once they cross, and where they expect to be: the reason for crossing.

For the Professional Bachelor, this means mastering an intelligent Speed Dating Model, fine tuning your image and personality, and practicing execution in the field. In researching the art, you'll understand the overwhelming advantages of seeing men from a woman's point of view. By knowing what women look and lust for, you can absorb the traits into your identity until you're effortless at the presentation.

Women role-play to attract and manipulate men into relationships, and once he's hooked change personalities from day to day. Men just act natural. Turn the tables, and learn how to use subtle role-playing to attract, and adapt these new skills into your natural personality. You'll generate an immediate emotional attraction, giving you the edge. Study and absorb what makes women tick, and carefully choose the right women you want playing with your ticker. No drama allowed. Analyze men who are successful at the game, and mirror your actions after those who are where you want to be. Remove the naysayers from your life. Evaluate what works, what doesn't work, and adapt to the terrain like a horny Zen master.

Laugh and learn from your failures, humbly enjoy your conquests, and don't take any of this too serious. Seduction is a timeless art. Ladies crave a man who controls all the moves with panache. It relieves them of any responsibility and potential guilt from the mind. Just the way they like it. When her panties end up on your ceiling fan, she'll brag she loved every minute of it. Repeat and/or referral business will flow like a Saturday Night fraternity tap. The rewards of being a smooth player will create experiences and field reports that will have your friends shaking their heads in disbelief. Glasses will be raised, toasts will be made, and people will slurring at your funeral with tears in their eyes....

"The crazy bassstarrrd worked hard and played harder. If dat
sssschhoolgirl wasssn't blowing him when the Ferrari hit
the tree, they'd have bronzed hissssshhh rod.
He wassshhh one of the great oneesshhh. "

# The Seduction Master Plan

**Step 1**: **Creating Desire and Sexual Attraction**
The Alpha Foundation – Your Presentation
**Step 2**: **Building Rapport, Comfort and Trust**
Charismatic Conversation - Role Playing
**Step 3**: **The Close**

The modus operandi in every pickup involves a smooth, well thought out process, with a beginning, middle, and end. Each phase has it's own reasoning and purpose, and must occur in the proper order. What keeps an average player from rapidly level-jumping to the hot babes is the inability to understand and respect the process. Slow down your hormonal frenzy and recognize what creates the proper mood for the pickup and close. Most guys simply cannot control their testosterone. They eliminate their chances of long term relationships by using the nightclub one-night stand approach, going for 1$^{st}$ or 2$^{nd}$ date closes without signals that she's ready. It works with young, naïve, or drunk girls looking for a quickie. But this guide is for advanced players, and our goal here is countless nights of sex with 9s and 10s. If you're looking to land a hot and heavy relationship with classy trophy women, you need patience and a more developed strategy of pursuit. Within reason, the longer the seduction takes, the greater her desire and lust.

Sexy women are propositioned dozens of times a week. It's hard for a guy to imagine how tedious and annoying this must be. To remain sane, they master blowing off guys in a heartbeat. To impress a woman, you should approach with style, attitude and cutting humor. Talk to them like you're simply in the mood to talk, and they happen to be in your space, not like you're a caveman out on a sportfucking expedition. First step, create value and desire in your presentation. Next, over the course of a few dates, using smooth, persuasive conversation, pay attention to her wants, beliefs and needs, and create the perception of providing solutions to her weaknesses. As you accumulate quality face time, you create attraction and a comfort zone. Then you increase your value by being in demand and unavailable.

**Reality Check**: Beautiful women can have sex with anyone, anytime; it's no big deal for them. You're spinning your wheels if you think your sexual prowess has some alluring power over her. Your wallet may for a while, but that's playing a losers hand unless it's Pay for Play. Even if the girl is initially attracted, she still needs to warm up to you and develop a feeling of security and trust before getting involved physically. The first few dates, you will need to establish in her mind why she should drop her resistance. Show her the reasons you are attracted to her, and that doesn't mean getting hammered and complimenting her blowjob lips. As you allow each phase of the seduction to play out in the proper time and order, your closing ratio and quality of targets increases dramatically. When she's ready, you'll know it.

As for the closing booth, don't just sit there. Girls want you to be manly and sexually aggressive. Attack with style, and in teasing fashion. Two steps forward, one step back. Repeat. Make her laugh, make her moan, and make sure you get her name right before you leave.

## Let the Games Begin

Let's dissect the techniques great pickup artists use, analyze what works best from a woman's point of view, and combine the two. This gives us the best approach to giving women exactly what they want in an Alpha Male.

### First Phase of Seduction:
**Give them what they want to see.**

How to create instant attraction and desire just by walking into the room.

# Fine Tuning Your Alpha Image

If you're tall, dark, and devilishly handsome, women will constantly make the moves on you. Yet looks, fame, and fortune will only carry you so far if you have weak game. You'll get a buffet of first dates, but you still have to display a smooth, dominant Alpha image and style to generate longevity. As luck would have it, most natural born studs and trust fund boys are often their own worst enemy. Since they require little effort for getting first dates, they rarely develop the tools and techniques needed to keep the trophy babes in a steady relationship. Many are flat out boring, arrogant, and lack a sense of humor, just like the bimbo babes on the female side. The A-team players are really not to be feared at all, as their playing field bares no resemblance to yours. Like the T Rex, they are only concerned with devouring the quick, easy, high quality meat, and moving on. When you're at the top of the pecking order, you rarely return for seconds. Why would you? It's a tad difficult trying to picture T Rex cowering in the corner while a bloated Momma Rex bops him over the head with a frying pan, while ragging on and on about his lack of emotional sensitivity towards her ever evolving imaginary needs, biological clock ticking, not to mention him forgetting to stop by Wal Mart for tampons, diapers, and size 16 granny white underwear.

For the rest of us bachelors out in the field, to achieve higher status you must project Alpha behavioral patterns that stimulate a woman's initial feelings of attraction. This is the all-important core ingredient of the first phase. **Creating Desire**. Without arousing her senses *before* you meet, it's twice as hard to get past her defenses and talk your way into creating lust. How you carry yourself in public is of vital interest to women.

It signals if you are a Strong Dominant Male who has a clear sense of direction in life; a semi-cocky confident guy with charisma, social status, potential wallet, standards, and a sense of humor.

Fortunately these are acquired skills. This is why when you stroll around the town you see beautiful girls with average looking guys. These guys have figured out the game, and know how the system of attraction works. In some ways, having male model looks can actually work against you. Women immediately assume you are a player, and respond in a guarded, defensive manner. More than anything, they fear being labeled a slut, just another notch in Brett Tate's or someone's belt. If you want to take it up a notch, stack the cards in your favor. A lot of this role-playing stuff will seem funny at first, but if that's what they want to see before shedding their panties, that's what they'll get.

When it comes to picking up women, it doesn't matter whether you are short, bald, or ugly. If your sexual chemistry triggers her inner emotions, and you project value and status, beautiful women will say yes. Why?

It is a natural genetic selection process for women of all species to seek dominant men who appear to be Leaders of the Pack. They want Men who are strong, stable, and competitive; boyfriends who create an environment where women feel safe and secure around them. Not so much physically safe, although that certainly helps. Safe, meaning she is comfortable being alone with you anytime, anywhere. Safe, meaning having she has no fear of introducing you to her family or friends. (of course her posse will still shred you to pieces behind your back). By secure, this means she sees you as very confident in yourself and career, and going places in life. Having a strong first impression, alpha presence, combining mystery about your life, and being distant to unavailable (a challenge) accomplishes this image.

Now in the big picture when they shop for a husband, that's when the inner whore instincts take over. They want to feel stable and "secure" with your assets, income earning potential, carefree spending habits, and willingness to put up with their crap. Your looks and personality are optional at this level. They all dream of a man to finance a Hollywood lifestyle, without having any responsibilities of their own; a beta-male security blanket who they can control. Many of them throw in boning Biff on the side, to "get even" for imaginary problems they project on their husband. Once married, their goal is to quit working, quit the gym, pack on breeding pounds and *maybe* reproduce. Baby or not, they have no intention of reversing the process. In just a few short years, most will look and act like a complete stranger. The fun girl and the great sex become a distant memory. Women never admit to it, but 8 out of 10 wives do this. Not to worry, you'll never admit upfront you have no intention of satisfying her big picture desires.

We all have a dream, honey.

# A Solid Alpha Foundation

The Tools of Seduction begin with studying and mastering a *Solid Alpha Foundation;* a charismatic magnetic presence that appeals universally to women; mastering your attitude, class, smoothness and style. Without the right image, your conversation skills will fail to accent your presentation. The foundation is an overall *perceived* appearance that creates instant attraction and desire in women. People unconsciously pass judgment after a few seconds of glancing at you. We do the same thing with women. When panning a room, we lock on to a couple of hotties, and the rest of the girls are invisible. Fatties could be butt naked juggling flaming bowling pins in the corner and we wouldn't see them. A strong Alpha Presentation accelerates your seduction skills without uttering a word.

A good first impression makes it easy to slide into conversations. Your closing ratio skyrockets if you get their eyes locked on you before you approach them in the first place. Whether the image is accurate, or a work in progress is irrelevant. Showcasing a strong confident persona and look changes the whole terrain in your favor. Here's a list of qualities that women visualize as most desirable in their man, traits that immediately create subconscious inner attraction and lust.

[1] The Alpha Look
[2] Strong Body Language
[3] High Self—Confidence
[4] High Self–Esteem
[5] Social Status – Leader of the Group
[6] A Challenge - Creating Intrigue
[7] The Experienced Player
[8] Intelligent and Passionate
[9] Lack of Insecurity
[10] Never Seeking Approval
[11] High Standards
[12] Credibility - Trustworthiness

All of these characteristics are easily recognized *visually*, as they are action based. It shows a man in complete control, and secure with himself; a man who has a clear defined direction, who leads a successful, busy life and is noticeably well on his way to going places. One glance and a woman sees a man who carries himself with poise and stability, who oozes self-assurance and coolness, and is completely unconcerned with other people's opinions. More than anything, what you need to display is a **Confident Attitude.**

Hollywood has several characters that portray this alpha image in picture perfect fashion. In Oceans Eleven, pay close attention to the characters played by George Clooney, Andy Garcia and Brad Pitt. Of course, the epitome of smooth and strong is James Bond. Each of these roles exudes extreme alpha confidence. The body language is silky smooth, classy, and never intimidated…almost to the point of seeming slow motion at times. Before attempting to tackle this image, it might help if you're at least the second generation upright in the family tree.

The roles sound like a lot to pull off at first, but here's a little insight. Actors play these roles. I repeat. The images you see and experience are played by people **acting**. The scenes are rehearsed over and over and over until the correct image, presence and emotion desired are captured on film. Clooney, Pitt, and The Bondsmen were not born with these traits; they developed them through rigorous practice. These guys had more than their share of uncomfortable, dork moments with women in their high school years.

As actors, they consciously learned to master the specific nuances needed to make the parts they play seem real. In doing so, the more they practiced it, the more natural they became at conveying the appropriate image. Eventually, like many actors, the roles that they play emulate a lifestyle and identity they choose as their own in real life. The game slowly fades away, until the identity becomes who they are. Sound familiar?

## Analyzing the Acting Techniques:

1. **Physicality**: the expressive use of Body Language to generate emotions without speaking. A physical demeanor and look that conveys a believable character for the audience, used in the appropriate fashion for the scene.

2. **Voice**: Tone, clarity, pronunciation, articulation and style to project a character's feelings, thoughts, and emotions. Includes proper breathing, volume, dynamics, and voice inflections.

3. **Words**: the intuitive choice of words, their hidden meaning and emotions they create, and how they shape and control the other characters, as well as the outcome of the scene.

4. **Attitude**: body language combined with dialogue shapes the actor's personality. It creates the mood that best personifies the feelings and attitude for the character. To add intrigue, they often send conflicting signals to aid plot development, and add mystery and unpredictability.

Learn to be consciously aware of your first impression when you meet someone. Create a ten second check off sheet in your mind if it helps. Disconnect from yourself, and establish the difference between how people actually see you, compared to your imagined self-image. Turn the ego off and be honest. Picture yourself from the boss' point of view watching you walk and talk in a job interview. Find your areas of weakness and adapt.

It's perfectly alright to laugh at yourself, and learn from the analysis. It's a one-time learning process. Rent the movie "Dirty Rotten Scoundrels" and watch how Michael Caine teaches Steve Martin to carry himself with class and sophistication. They exaggerate it for laughs, but the lesson is perfect for showing how anyone can make subtle adjustments and dramatically alter their initial impression and accelerate their game. The level of mastery in each of the 4 techniques determines your skill at an alpha presentation.

On the surface, your first thoughts will be "*this is all so corny and phony.*" Of course it is! Think of how ridiculous the Tie is; a piece of cloth wrapped around your neck that chokes you somehow means high social status! Face it; humans are just sophisticated animals with a lot of technology. Like every other species, the males are reduced to stupid rituals to attract the opposite sex. It could be worse; think of the peacock. The female peacocks are butt ugly, and sit around in mud refusing to put out until the male "peacocks" their stuff. Reminds me of the Asbury Park beach scene at the Jersey shore. In peacocks, it's the male with the beauty. They flaunt their feather colors ranging from iridescent blue-green to all the shimmering hues of the rainbow. (said with a lisp). The male proudly sticks his butt up high in the air, spreads his plumage and shakes his gorgeous tail feathers, seeking female approval to get laid. Imagine if the male peacock could speak;

"Look at the goddamn humiliation these bitches puts me through, I mean, I might as well be in the San Francisco Ballet or a gay fruitcake parade."

Mastering your alpha presentation furthers your career and income, elevates your quality of life, and attracts a higher quality and quantity of women. So have fun with all of this; it's the results that matter.

# Smooth Talking Manipulation

The world is a stage. Our days are filled with smooth talking manipulation, be it commercials, business, politicians, or the media. The advertising and sales fields very existence relies on the ability to seduce you, to lure you into spending money while under their spell. Those who excel at it are masters of creating moods. They find your weakness, and then with leading words and images they shape how you look, see, and feel about the benefits of what they have to offer, until the desire to own it becomes overwhelming. Like or not, every time someone is speaking to you, they are trying to influence you in some manner; whether they are selling you a product, a service, or themselves. Understanding how seduction works is a double-edged sword. You can either go through life playing the victim, or educate yourself on using the tools to your advantage. The knowledge of how the game works helps you defend yourself when it's used against your will. The dating world is full of role-playing women who devote their whole lives to manipulating men, using cosmetic to surgical disguises, bullshit personalities and scams. They give you a piece, and then once you're hooked, they bleed you dry when you try to keep tasting the goods. By being cynically astute, it's great fun spotting how they camouflage their intentions with fake smiles, while dangling *possible* sexual favors in your direction in order to vacuum your wallet, or to toy with you for sport.

## Bachelor Code 5
### Amendment 6,subsection 3b
**When a woman is speaking, believe half of what you see
and none of what you hear, until proven otherwise.**

It takes skills and practice in the field to have the silver tongue. Most men having a lousy pick up ratio due to the inability to turn their ego off. They spend their time trying to sell themselves with words; bragging, and trying to *convince* a girl she needs him. This is the anti-seducer approach. True seduction is a soft sell; it creates feelings and emotions subconsciously, and elevates your target's desires without you speaking. You want her to see the benefits of what you have to offer, without showing any self-interest. Give her attention, but bust her chops and play mind games with her insecurities. Create sexual tension. Act only mildly interested to indifferent, since your life is busy without women. You build value by creating the image of being successful, desired, unavailable, and in demand. They all want what they can't have. Once you master your presentation, it's just a simple matter of learning the basics of charisma and seductive conversation.

You can sit around being afraid to approach women, or you can take action and learn. There are winners, losers, and nothing in between. Role-playing puts you in the driver seat, and will quickly take your dating success to the next level. Just like the actors in Ocean's Eleven, we are simply choosing to master the alpha traits that women want to see in a man, until the image becomes our lifestyle. As a guideline to flaunting the desired masculine image (Alpha Foundation), let's make it simple. **Be a Man**. Strut your masculinity and be a confident sexual hunter like your caveman ancestors. Do the exact opposite of what Cosmo, Oprah and the whole limp-wristed, bed wetting, PC crowd suggests. Remember your grumpy, stubborn old grandpa? He would be a stud today with that attitude. Be a ballsy individual who does what he wants, when he wants, without fear of backlash. Last time I checked, there is only one person in your casket.

Who cares what other people think about you? Don't get caught dead wasting your time and money desperately seeking a girl's approval, or sucking up to women. If a new girl isn't interested in an alpha male, dump her immediately and date half dozen others. Dating is just a numbers game.

Make early success in business your number one goal. When you achieve success, the women will find you. Build a lifestyle full of challenges in work, hobbies and sports. Set goals to learn new skills. By adding a variety of new activities in life, you keep yourself mentally and physically engaged. You want to reach a point where you ooze confidence in yourself. By making this your reality, you erase the desperation emotion and approval seeking that women smell a mile away. Women should be just one thing you enjoy out of many. When you lead a fulfilling lifestyle, you learn to really not give a damn when a chick you dig turns you down. There are dozens of new targets in your life each week; it's just a matter of knowing where to look and how to work them.

- - - - -

Now let's examine how to display the characteristics that make up each of the Universal Alpha Foundation traits.

- - - - -

## The Look – Secrets of Sexual Body Language

Nothing like watching a girl's eyes move rapidly up and down as each new man enters a room. It's like a red dot from a sniper's scope. With great consistency, you'll see they all inspect the same traits in the first glance; your smile, your eyes, your shoes, your clothes, your posture and physique, your watch, your body language, and the size bulge of your wallet. Latin girls are different. They look right at your crotch while licking their lips. So you plan your look accordingly. Hopefully, this stuff is basic knowledge you already know. Dress appropriately for whatever club or venue you are going to. For the latest hip fashion, look at other well-dressed men for the appropriate style in each target area. Your look should include:

- Well dressed, clean, new clothes without overdoing it
- New, high gloss polished shoes. *(Very Big)*
- Nice trimmed groomed haircut, and shave
- White teeth, (get whitening bleach if necessary)
- Cologne (dab it, don't bath in it)
- Breath mints before speaking
- Clean nails

**Body Language**: convey confidence and strength, but at the same time you should appear very relaxed. If confused, revisit any James Bond scene.

1.  Have a strong handshake. Use a two hands over grip with woman. Eye contact should be maintained with a half smile.

2.  Erect tall stance, shoulders back, and keep your chin high. This signals you are self-assured, have confident social status, and you're healthy, No peering at the ground while walking or talking. This makes you appear submissive. Slouching is a big turnoff. It signals lack of confidence, low self-esteem, laziness, and even depression. Sit up straight. No crossing of your arms. This signals impatience.

3.  Walk like you have a purpose or destination in mind. Too slow, you are seen as lazy and going nowhere. To fast, you are nervous, late, and carry no clout. No rapid nervous head turns; no stalking eye glances, no dragging your feet, bopping along, or speed walking. No skipping or hopscotch, or peeing in your pants.

4.  Practice strong wide-open fixed-eye contact with everyone. (Bring Visine if you've had a few.) The longer the eye contact, the more honest you appear, and the more intimate she feels the conversation is. Shoot for 70% of the time. When speaking to women, never look below the shoulders. No wandering eyes observing other women in the room in her presence.

5.  When answering a question, keep your eyes locked on hers for the first 5 to 10 seconds. If you look away immediately, it is assumed that you are lying.

People of high status and confidence have eyes that stay focused and attentive, without moving their head around. Weak, nervous, and dishonest people have eyes that dart and shift every which way while you speak to them. You can't overemphasize eye contact. Give all your attention to someone when they are speaking. Don't worry; you won't seem too serious; just keenly interested in what they are saying. Add in occasional small smiles, slow eyebrow raises and head tilting to appear more curious during certain statements. Be slow motion and smooth during everything. There's a ritual in Latin cultures about this; when a woman stares you down, whoever breaks away last is the more powerful. When you win, you own her. She will be at your side in minutes. It's strange, but very effective.

6.  When speaking to a woman, do not "box her in" by standing face to face. Stand at a slight angle to her, and move in closer if she signals interest. During conversation, lean away, with occasional moments leaning in, like you're divulging a secret, or getting mildly intimate.

7.  When listening, the opposite applies; lean in to listen, and then lean out as you react to the statement. Don't crowd her space. As she

warms up to you seeking approval, she'll touch your arm. Then move a step or two in, while doing the same routine. Occasional smiles to let her know you're listening and playful. Avoid the goofy constant smiling. You look weak and phony.

8. Keep your body and hands loosely firm. Important: Don't wave them around nervously while speaking, and stop the nervous combing of hair, or any in and out of the pockets fidgeting moves like children do. You want your body to be quiet.

9. Make some type of body contact after a few minutes, and then lean away. Touch her arm, half hug, touch tip of her nose. Something subtle that tells her you are sexually intrigued, yet not desperate to get laid. Worst move? Holding her in public for dear life after the slightest touch of approval from her. Gag.

## Silver-Tongue Charm School

1. Speak slowly, and clearly pronunciate, Practice lowering your pitch a half octave; it shows more command. Like a Radio DJ. A calm, soothing voice makes people around you feel more comfortable in your presence. The Worst Approach? Nervous, rushed, high-pitched voice coupled with insecure laughter after your own statements. This screams of weakness. Avoid the dreaded "errs, umms" and mispronouncing words. If they think you're dumb, the label sticks.

2. Be conscious of keeping your voice steady, deep and softer. Lower your volume, even in crowded loud rooms. You want her leaning in towards you, not recoiling in fear as you scream and spit in her face while drooling down her shirt.

3. Be conscious of the pace that she is speaking, and adjust to the same speed. People who speak very fast are uncomfortable with slow speakers, as they feel they are unintelligent. Slow, deliberate talkers often think fast speakers are untrustworthy or nervous. Listen closely to the pace and volume of your listener and mirror it. It creates a common energy.

4. Be a very patient listener. Don't interrupt. Let her get out her entire thought and pause before responding. Always wait a bit longer than you normally would.

5. Speak very relaxed and confident, with a smooth cadence. No wild or exaggerated voice inflections. No yodeling.

6. Act like you're only speaking to her because you feel like talking, not like you want to get laid in 10 minutes. After 5-15 minutes pick up the pace and go for the number close, the kiss close, or the parking lot love close. For first kiss, lean in, point to your cheek..

7. Make your stories interesting and short, and have a point. Be approachable and infectious.

8. Remember: Small people talk, Big People listen. Don't feel the need to answer every sentence with a response. Just smile and nod. This can make her feel insecure, which is good. You want her to speak about her favorite topic nonstop - herself. Get her to sell herself to you. You want her to feel the need to try and win you over. Once the target is already showing you interest, if you're speaking, you're losing.

9. Keep your hands off her until she's ready, or, if you're overseas, at least wait until the money has been exchanged.

## How to Ooze With Self-Confidence

Self-confidence is created through achievement. It begins with studying a problem, exercising great patience and discipline, and dedicating hours to repetitive work. The result is knowledge and expertise at mastering the specific skill. Whether we're talking about the A-team Players, or successful businessmen, the results of attaining the achievement mindset applies the same. Once you master one skill, you gain the confidence to move on and conquer others. You become a skilled problem solver. You gain a proficiency in learning more skills, with each battle being won quicker. The levels of difficulty become less daunting each time. This creates inner strength knowing you can do anything you put your mind to.

When you concentrate on attaining success outside of dating, the skills will flow over and make seduction feel more natural. Another result of self-confidence is it creates higher self-esteem. Once you have a high level of self-confidence, life becomes easy. You develop an aura, and it shows all over your face. Nothing intimidates you. This gladiator attitude creates a magnetic presentation; a lightning rod for attracting gorgeous women who previously seemed out of reach.

As a self-confident man, when you are around women, your persona should be somewhat cocky, self-assured, relaxed, and yet distant. In conversation you are always upbeat, charismatic, playful, and interesting. You never even come across as hitting on them; you're just having fun on a rare night out. The vibe is the exact opposite of needy and seeking approval. People seek YOUR approval. You tend to be the guy everyone else wants to be around. When you're confident, you approach dating like any other skill to conquer. You know that dating is not a spectator sport; it's a numbers game. The only way to perfect dating skills is extensive practice in the field. You never concentrate on just one girl. You focus on both quantity and quality. Confident men go for exactly what they want. They are not desperate to get laid, and dump the game players and time wasters the minute they act up.

A confident man oozes success, and women see it the minute they lay their eyes on you. There's just something about you they can't put their finger on, but it's clear that you must be "somebody", because you obviously don't give a damn what anyone thinks of you. A strong confident alpha male attracts women. Period. It's no accident girls avoid the nice guys of the world and are drawn to the bad boys. It's their tough, aggressive overconfidence that gives them presence, not the badness people assume.

A highly self-confident man loves spontaneity, and never hesitates. The minute a hot girl makes eye contact *twice*, he walks straight up to her with no fear. He aggressively pursues his targets knowing he'll most likely succeed. A confident man is the Teflon man, and never fears rejection. Instead, he laughs it off, takes mental notes on what happened, and learns from it, if he made a mistake. He never makes the same mistake twice.

The confident attitude helps develop an extremely high closing ratio. It also provides you with great discipline and the patience of a saint. You avoid lesser targets till the right one appears. No matter how much effort it takes to get a trophy girl in bed, her barriers of resistance never offend a confident man. It's just part of the chase, and he knows to sleep with her he may have to deal with it. Know the value of a longer, drawn out seduction.

A Confident man is willing to take risks, and changes his plan of action as the terrain changes. He knows sitting around complaining about something never accomplished anything. When people are driven to succeed at something, it is easy to spot their passion. They show complete faith in their abilities. They are persistent, and never quit. Women eat this up.

## Creating Desire with Attitude and High Self-Esteem

When you let women walk all over you, or continually date lesser targets, you place a small value on yourself and what you have to offer. Going ugly early for the easy lay may seem the lesser of two evils, but the word of your garbage dick tendencies spreads quickly amongst women. You become known as an easy lay and having no standards. You lower yourself several points in women's minds. This limits your chances of landing high quality babes in the future. To them it screams of low self-esteem. If you don't value yourself highly, why should a woman show you a higher level of respect? When you have high self-esteem, it subconsciously creates natural interest and attraction in women. You present a positive impression of being a leader in life, of someone doing exactly what he wants in life. This confidence in your abilities projects an image of higher self-worth, which makes women want to find out more about you. Women all want to attach themselves to the guy with the higher social status. You project an aura of desirability. Self-esteem must be based in reality. If you're a phony, it's a dead giveaway. You can't be in hock up to your ears and living under a bridge and have it. It is an inner feeling you wear in your walk, talk, and presentation. It enables you to forget about the ever-higher goals you pressure yourself with, forget about the stress, and enjoy the current moment. When you are doing well in life and are free from worry, you have a glow about you. By allowing yourself to feel great about your place in life and your future potential, you shine on the outside without trying.

## High Social Status – Leader of the Pack

Each of the Alpha Foundation traits adds its own flavor and variation to the overall presentation. Displaying High Social Status is the most visible characteristic. This is the guy who has an overabundance of confidence, self-esteem, success, and focus. But what separates this trait from the other approaches is that he is blessed with the silver tongue. He is a vivacious extrovert. He attracts attention with his energy, his ultra smooth quick-witted speaking, and his inner attention whore genes. The High Status guy comes across as the most successful guy in the room, often the funniest, the most outgoing, and people all assume the top dog is most likely wealthy. Where there is money, there are women competing for it. Every girl wants him, and he knows it.

It may seem like we're all individuals, but really there are very few innovators and even fewer social circles. People pick their clique, (Gen X, Jocks, GQ, etc.), and then everyone within it mimics each other in attire, lingo, and attitude. Everyone wants to be part of the cool inner clique within the given social circles. Each clique establishes a leader or two within the pack. The Leader's (High Social Status) act could be a work in progress, but that doesn't matter. He knows exactly how to look and act around women without trying. People then start to mimic his approach hoping to score with the feeder fish women on the outer edges of his conquests.

Some guys like to play the mysterious Antonio Banderas approach, some guys are the soft–spoken edgy Bruce Willis T shirt type; the leader wants to be on the center stage, as he has the right combination of cahones and the gift of gab. His job could be a Type A salesman, entrepreneur, a litigator, stockbroker, real estate agent, whatever it is, the guy knows how to sell. He could play any part he wants. He could lay back and be cool like the rest, but it would bore him to tears.

A leader has a very busy life, with numerous interests, hobbies, and passions. He has the innate ability to steer a seduction, and stir a woman's emotions into following his path. He attracts. His personality is magnetic, and he draws attention without bragging or vainly selling himself. He is the consummate charmer, and has a seemingly effortless influence over women. A leader gets what he wants. Sex is great, but it is not the most important thing in his life. Successful businessmen have a tremendous sex life, but men who devote all their time pursuing a tremendous sex life are rarely successful businessmen. A leader knows to partition his time more towards business. The more successful he is at business, the more women he attracts. A leader goes out of his way to make himself visible. He creates the center of attention aura, while appearing to have no self-interest. He never concentrates on just one girl, or waits for girls to come for him. He uses every opportunity to meet, greet and flirt with good-looking women.

**So how can we show leadership qualities?** Dress well, have strong body language, high self-esteem and confidence, and master the Gift of Gab. The gift of gab is nothing more than practice makes perfect. By approaching ten times more women than the average guy, you're just practicing your style by repeating the same lines over and over till it becomes effortless.

More than anything; high social status means you are playfully fearless. The more babes you flirt with, the more you improve your chances. There is always safety in numbers. The most successful players in the game meet 10 to 20 new girls a week in everyday life; at work, the supermarket, the gym, restaurants, post office, and public places. If you club 3 nights a week, you'll meet another 10 or 20. Even with landing a mere ten percent ratio, your still getting 3 to 5 new dates each week. It's just a numbers game, the more hot women you talk to, the more dates you'll get.

Be a platonic friend with the hottest women you can find, meet their friends and become a peripheral part of their clique. It doesn't take more than a few minutes each time you see one of them. Soon, everywhere you go you will be seen talking to good-looking women by other good-looking women. The fastest way to meet women is to be seen with other attractive women. Being seen with numerous babes creates intrigue and curiosity in women's minds. You become an object of desire by increasing your visibility, as it creates competition. Eventually you start picking off the hottest girls in the group one by one. Repeat and referral business soon follows.

A High Status player guards his reputation, but at the same time appears to care less what others think of him. When women label him a player he laughs. He knows it's not an insult, but really a statement of success. Women are attracted to success stories, not the whiney thumb suckers of the PC world. A leader knows his desires, and sets out with a precise plan of action to obtain them. If he wants to date a model, he will do a bit of research on her first before diving in headlong. He becomes a platonic friend of the target's girlfriends, and gets the inside scoop on her true personality. Plus, the referral through her girlfriend lowers the barriers of access. If he hooks up with her and discovers she's insecure, high maintenance, or has the slightest bit of attitude and disrespect, he calls her a cab and removes the problem. No discussion is necessary. He always cuts his losses quick, and lets the "profits" ride. When you see a gorgeous girl alone, and in the back of your mind hear that old saying; *some guy is tired of fucking her*...the leader is that guy. He values his time, and has too many other options on the table to put up with any bullshit; he simply can't sleep with them all. There is always another girl around the corner to replace her.

Time is a valued commodity, so he always qualifies his targets before approaching. He will plan a specific seduction technique, and have alternate strategies at his fingertips. He analyzes his results regularly, and is always ready to change his techniques or style if it presents an advantage. Patience is one of his strongest points. He is never impulsive, never flies off the cuff or dates too many women at once. He has a clear course, and enjoys taking risks if the reward justifies it. He keeps his ideas private, except to a select few confidantes, and only seeks advice when he needs it. When it comes to important information, he is a listener, not a talker.

Women want what they can't have, and the man who is the center of attention has an alluring quality. Who is this guy? What does he do? What does he have? Why is he so popular? Intelligence and visible respect from your peers are like magnets to women. Their senses are heightened; the hormones and desire are pumping, without even knowing a thing about him. While women stare and gawk at his presence, for all they know, the four girls surrounding him could be his cousins from out of town. Other girls will see his power and move in, trying to be his preferred choice of the group. As he is seen around town surrounded by women, the ending is known before the scripts are handed out. The girls will compete for his attention. The one who puts out first gets to brag that she hooked up with him, which elevates her status in her clique and boosts her ego. She won. Whore Protocol 101.

When you're at the top, people try to make themselves feel important by giving you unsolicited advice and foolish opinions, in an attempt to feel smarter. The High Status player ignores the envious and ignorant. He is not teetering on the brink of a nervous breakdown when jealous people badger him with counterproductive cynicism. A leader never blindly trusts anyone, since people are always after what he has. He surrounds himself with movers and shakers, and men who are as smart if not smarter than him. He never dwells on bad things, and can see a silver lining in every situation. He gets others to do his dirty work, while taking credit for it. This attitude and approach creates the image of being inaccessible; getting to know him well seems difficult, which creates a sexual urgency in women. He is their ultimate target. They want to vacuum his wallet something fierce.

# Creating Intrigue – Be A Challenge

All of the Alpha Foundation characteristics overlap in some aspect. What the challenge trait adds to the mix is mystery, intrigue, and being original and provocative. You give off the appearance of being unknown and unavailable. The beginning of every chase is driven by fantasies. Don't spoil the magic by rushing things and shoving reality at her too quickly. Play with her. Give a seductive tease of flashing aggression, and then pulling away when she shows interest. Generate attraction while hiding your personal details and information. Master the ability to keep it all inside, and let women struggle to find out your "secrets."

By being challenging and distant, you create desire. Just sit back and laugh at the silly insecure dudes bragging about their menial accomplishments to try and get laid; the sea of $30,000 a year millionaires you see in every club. Why brag? There's more power in saying nothing and hanging back in jeans, a t-shirt; unshaved with a cynical smirk on your face.

It's easy to be in no hurry to pursue any one girl when you're working a fleet of them at the same time. They know you are a player, but still lust for you, to be the one that wins. You of course are aware of this, and simply don't care, because you don't have to. Ironically, women love this mildly disinterested approach. Girls long to be wanted. By not seeking her approval or complimenting her looks she starts to feel insecure, and begins questioning herself…. she is losing the power struggle. She makes it her quest to bed the challenge guy… to win you over…to seize control. Girls live to validate their desirability, and flex their perceived power over you. Act unimpressed, and it turns many women into the aggressor.

### Girls prefer a good chase.

When you speak, offer only limited information about yourself. You want your target to be thoroughly intrigued, and yet frustrated at her lack of progress in controlling or understanding you. By being confusing and keeping her in suspense, you are always on her mind and keep her emotionally attracted. There is nothing about you that is predictable. Your style of dating is never routine, and never repeated.

When asked about your life, don't blather on about your career and life details. Hold back and give hazy details; being mysterious creates greater desire. Ask her vague questions that keep her talking about herself.

- *"Sorry, I'm not giving interviews tonight. Let's just say I invest and do well, and leave it at that. Tell me about you, what goals do you have? Where do you see yourself in 5 years? Where have you always wanted to travel to?*

Never ask questions calling for yes or no answers. Ask dramatic open-ended questions that make her open herself up, while always leaving her wanting to know more about you. Segway all thoughts back to her.

- *"I never learn a thing when I talk about myself. Tell me the things that make your toes curl. What do you really desire more than anything? Tell me something no one else knows about you. What's the most unusual place you've hooked up with a guy? How about with a girl? If you were writing Cosmo tonight, how would you describe your sexual fantasies."*

By giving her the stage, you are letting talk about her favorite topic. Herself! By being a great listener, you create feelings of verbal intimacy she rarely feels. *"He understands me."* Allow her to feel special by sharing your own intimate secrets. If you don't have any good stories to rival hers, read a couple Penthouse letters and memorize the best ones. Make the sexual conquests with strangers in unexpected intimate situations. Stay away from anything involving ex-girlfriends. Watch for reactions (licking lips, playing with hair, nipples popping) at key sex points in the story for clues for sex tricks to exploit on a later date.

Never underestimate the value of scarcity. Time should be a precious commodity for you to arrange hooking up. When people limit availability of anything, it creates the impression of being in high demand. It increases value and desire. Let women know your first priority is business and achieving personal goals. Next are the things that interest you most in life; your hobbies, competitive sports, investments, and your health. Women are just one more thing in your life, and hardly the center of it. To make arrangements to do things with her, you always have to try and juggle your schedule. *"This week is impossible, I'm free next Tuesday and possibly Thursday..."* When a girl makes the moves on you, tell her you're interested, but you're seeing someone or just getting out of a relationship and need a week or two to settle things. You are taken, but things aren't quite working out. By being unavailable, she wants what she can't have. This creates the motivation in her mind to steal you away from the other woman. A challenging guy is high demand.

Make your phone calls short, always be the one who gets off first. Act like you don't need her approval or sex from her. You have a life and your own opinions. If during any discussion she says some nonsense you totally disagree with, never cave in to her viewpoint. Counter with *"perhaps,"* or something totally vague. Never surrender a single point to her. Creating emotions, highs, lows and confusion creates sexual tension. The result of mastering the challenge status is you create a sexual frustrated woman; a condition that can only be satisfied one way. She loses her edge, and makes her decisions blinded by frustration, emotion and lust instead of logic.

**Being a Challenge is about Control**. The essence of power in seduction is controlling the chase, making her come to you. You want her to reacting to *your* moves, not the other way around. Aggressively swinging your dick around pursuing multiple women is exciting, but the results are lousy when the style lacks structure. A hunter doesn't run through the woods screaming and shooting. He sets a well-planned trap, and shows great discipline waiting for the animal to play his game. Set your alpha bait, control your emotions, and use great patience to land the trophy women. The ones that shy away prove they were never interested. The ones that come to you feel inner desire ten times stronger, and the closing ratio is damn near perfect.

# The Cultured Experienced Player Image

Experience extends the other traits, but focuses on the overall aura of being cool, calm and collective. People who are perceived as powerful players display experience, high-class, and a reserved self-confidence. They have nothing to prove in their image, as they ooze firmness and achievement. By contrast, the new wannabe in town who brags, is arrogant and conceited rarely lasts, because he alienates people everyday. He's on a fast track going 2 steps forward and 5 steps backwards. He has no allies and takes unnecessary large risks. The players who last have great people skills. They easily make friends in business and with women, but they remain very choosey in their selection, since they want longevity and only the best.

Experience means you rarely make impulsive or rash decisions in business or with women, as these usually turn out wrong. Be adverse to the temptation of undue risk, and concentrate on the high probability of reward. Women are attracted to experienced men who have been around the block. Experience comes from a high level of Street Intelligence in the field, which translates into higher status amongst peers. Experience means potential for higher incomes, which of course all women want. (*What's your is mine, and what's mine is mine.*) The higher up in the pecking order you are perceived to be, the more desirable you are to women. This doesn't mean you have to be the CEO. What it means is that when a woman meets you, she sees that you are very smart about the inner workings of your field, cool with sexual prowess and image, and confident and self-assured with your skills. Experienced people are very tenacious and driven; big positives to women. Being simple minded and showing no drive or direction ruins your chances.

An experienced player let's a girl know that his time is a valued commodity, as he has a very active, busy life. When your horny, bubble gum chewing, schoolgirl hottie calls, you don't reply *"Wassup. I'm power lounging trying to get rid of this vicious hangover."* You are always busy pursuing business projects and are always analyzing some type of investment. You portray knowledge and success. Remember, that doesn't mean you actually are successful. It means you show you have direction and wits, and know your path to obtaining success. This characteristic works best with the younger targets, girls who want a Daddy figure, girls who are new in town, and those who like it when someone else takes control of everything. The type-A aggressive women are not the girlfriend type for the smart, successful guy in the group. These girls consider conversations a debate and take offense when proven wrong, which they usually are, instead of learning from it.

Self-assurance and humility are some of the best personality traits to show. Whatever is your area of expertise; be it business, a hobby, or a sport, carry it with humility. If you are going places in life, it shows without saying a word. Be above the fray, and steer clear of petty office politics and jabs. Never put another guy in your field down in front of women. Never brag about yourself, or blather on about your life. Let people ask you questions, and then use self-deprecating humor in your answers. Mastery at something shows drive and skill, which usually translate into the ability to do the same at other things in life. Experience shows a woman you get things accomplished in life. When placed in a confrontational situation, you pause and strategize. The superior negotiator uses time, instincts and street smarts to get what he wants. You analyze a situation swiftly, and use your wits and ingenuity to decipher and influence events, instead of your fists. You are nobody's fool. You ooze with the street smarts.

Women want to be around a man who people are naturally drawn to. You become the center of attention not because of vanity or ego, it's because you make things happen in life. People want to deal with you, as you seem more honest and in control, and feel they were get a fairer deal because you seem far more intelligent, rational and fair than the average guy. Women feel completely safe and secure with the man with experience. Women see *you* as the one with the barrier, and set out to be the one to crack it.

## Be Intelligently Passionate and Articulate

Everyone is attracted to people who show a genuine passion for something in life. Controlled enthusiasm draws others in to your energy. People with passion tend to excel and be knowledgeable about the hobby, sport, or job that drives them. Intelligence carries many perceptions, and all are positive attention getters. Intelligent people are perceived to be more emotionally stable, independent, socially adjusted, and have more professional success. They're interesting to listen to. People are drawn to intelligence as they can learn about things. Work this to your advantage. Be an expert at things. Now being smarter about a topic doesn't mean you are brilliant. It means you put in the extra effort to learn more about something than others have. It really just means you can memorize and speak well.

Set out to have a broad base of knowledge on an array of topics. Know more than the next guy. Be somewhat of an information junky. However, you should never let on you're smarter than the cocky uninformed blabbermouth trying to impress the ladies. You shouldn't divulge your success or inside information to another guy in front of women, particularly if they are not at a similar level. Let the other guy blather on about how great he is doing, while you smile and act mildly amused. It is better to be self-deprecating in this situation. Woman love this and can sense it immediately. They can't wait to talk to you in private and ask if some guy was full of shit, or find out what the real story is. There is power in being playfully humble. Being arrogant may bring you a lot of attention initially, but unless you can back it up with success, it is an attraction killer.

## Travel Guru:

Act fascinated and in awe of things you know women like. Be passionate in your explanations of your discoveries. Women are all drawn to things that involve travel; far away trips, exotic locations, and tropical paradises. Make it a pet project of yours to study a wide variety of popular locations. Put real time into it, watch the Discovery Channel to help visualize images to describe, and read books about the topics and places. Take up some more extravagant hobbies. Develop wider interests; go scuba diving in the Caribbean, take the hiking trip down and up the Grand Canyon, go blue marlin fishing in Cabo San Lucas, study hiking and mountain climbing in South America. You only live once, so do some of these excursions. Blow off puking with the guys at spring break, and take some eco-sporting trips. Document them with a digital camera…take action shots, and do your best intense James Bond poses. Smirk, and act like you do this stuff every day, and are having the time of your life in them. Pics are an instant conversation starter. Every girl is fascinated by well-documented travels.

It doesn't take much effort to develop an extensive knowledge of exotic places and events. Why all this effort? Picking up women is a competition sport. Nothing bores a woman more than a guy who drones on about his job, and how important he sees himself there. The guy who never discusses his job, and oozes passion discussing exotic adventures attracts. The Crocodile Hunter is the alpha stud, Orville the office cubicle dork is a lost cause. If you can't afford the trips, study all the details, the ins and outs…let's face it. How can a woman really know in conversation if you've done all these trips, when you're so knowledgeable about them? When you combine your knowledge and passion about these things, you draw attention to yourself, without any vanity or ego; you come across as the debonair cashed up travel stud, whom she hopes will take her on the next adventure.

# Insecurity is for Little Girls

Vanity is a peculiar characteristic that is way overvalued. It's an obstacle to seduction, and has no redeeming quality in reality. What's funny about the trait is how much it affects most people's lives. Every little thought, move, and action that ego driven people make balances precariously on reactions and approval from others. The fear of being judged by others poorly has them paralyzed to do anything. Yet the importance of the whole concept is borderline ridiculous. People's minds are pre-occupied with themselves. For the most part, other people are barely even thinking about you, and every little thing you do. They're worried about themselves, and every little thing they are doing! It's a battle of the effeminate limp wristed worrywarts. Sorry to pop your bubble, but you really are not so important that people are staring at you with baited breath, waiting for your approval of them. Relax. It's how *you* feel inside that matters. By the way, the guys leering in your direction at the gym are not laughing at your technique, they're checking out the ass on the blonde behind you.

Insecurity is a benchmark achievement of the Liberal Media Guilt Police. Equality for women was the feminist sales pitch, but it was just a camouflage for their real intentions. The goal was to castrate men and give woman all the power. Female Equality is retarded socialist brainwashing that preaches Man was not intended to be an aggressive overachiever or stand up for himself. They lecture how you should question everything over and over in your mind from a PC stance of how others will feel about it, until the nuances and fear stop you from committing to do anything. Men should be equally passive and miserable, and allow women to control us.

Insecurity keeps you from making decisions without the endorsement from women; avoid this attitude like the plague if you want pussy. In the modern era, when you're a nice guy or a gentleman, women respond by walking all over you like a spoiled brat. Insecurity will destroy your chances with seducing women. It forces you to make decisions out of desperation; decisions that are not in your best interests. When you are insecure, you are an open season target to predatory woman. They can smell weakness in a man a mile away, and will role-play and quickly assume control of your life and your wallet. Through selective limitation of the sex supply, they tear through your assets until you go broke, or until they bore of the game.

Subconsciously, women all seek a man of strength, as he shows the signs of being a provider. In conversations, show you are not the least bit concerned if you disagree with something, and that you will never kiss her ass. When a woman gets a little emotional, remember that she is testing you. Stand up for yourself, and show her she is dealing with a strong man whose behavior she cannot control. Have your own opinions, without being argumentative. Women love intelligence. If she asks, offer up compelling alternative views and be tad controversial with a smile. Eventually, whether it's a few hours, or a few dates, her bitch shield will come down.

Learn how to avoid falling into the same old patterns and negative mind games you play on yourself. It's easy to be a pussy and make excuses for never trying for the hotter girls that you really want. The typical excuse is thinking you have to been rich to get women. The appearance of having taste does not mean you have to be wealthy by any means. It's not like you are showing women financial statements, portfolios, and promising diamonds. The dating world is full of phoniness on both ends of the spectrum. Rest assured, half the Posers in the Porsche's and Fountain Speedboats are in hock up to their eyeballs with lease payments they can't afford, living the life they wish were true. It's no different than the phony bleach blondes with the boob jobs, tummy tucks, and the expensive car and house paid for by the ex. No excuses allowed. You got to take a lot of swings at the plate before you start connecting like a professional.

## Seeking her Approval is Dating Suicide

Being insecure and seeking approval from women is by nature acting highly feminine. Insecurity discourages success and independence. Like everything else the media suggests men should do, the exact opposite is the right attitude. Yet a majority of men are intellectually tone deaf to the whole concept. They feebly play along at the slightest whiff of potential sex. When you play the castrated metrosexual role, women see it as a big red bulls-eye on your wallet. Plus, they're immediately sexually turned off. If you are doing this approach out of inexperience, snap out of it immediately. Once you give off the slightest hint of insecurity, you're closing ratio plummets, and you become off limits to the type of women you *should* be pursuing.

The strong alpha player knows to avoid this male weakness, and exploits the opposite characteristic to his advantage. Think about it. How can being insecure be an attractive trait? Is insecurity the type of masculine behavior that accomplishes *anything* of value? In business, innovation is defined by being secure in your thinking, and bold in your actions. Without being strong and taking risks, there would be no entrepreneurs in the country, no competitive sports; nothing that requires testosterone and drive would exist. Imagine taking feminism in a time machine back to the 15th century and seeing how it fairs. Try to envision Maximus the Roman Gladiator going into battle with Katie Couric as his leader.

*"Now Max, let's all be nice to the other army, take our Ritalin, and share our feelings in the time out room. Now which one of you silly little boys is carrying my panty shields?"*

How you handle yourself when women test you is important. If your woman tries whining and criticism to get her way, the alpha response is not yelling back or getting defensive. What you should do is laugh that she thinks she has that kind of authority over your life.

*"I told you what I'm doing tomorrow night, I'm not asking for your permission. Funny stuff. What reality show did you learn that from?*

Nobody should have the power to decide what you do in life. To be an achiever in life requires taking action when opportunities arise. The only way you can ever achieve things is to take risks. If you spend your life asking for permission for things around woman, two things will happen. She will say no, and you will simultaneously have handed over all your power to her, and erased yourself from her list.

**Never ask a woman for permission for anything**. Be a man. Make firm decisions to do things, tell her what you are going to do, and invite her along for the ride. If she complains about your choice, the correct answer is *"You don't have to go."* If she gives you more lip about your decision and counters with *"let's go drop a grand shopping so I can make Tiffany jealous,"* ignore the comment. Reply back with *"No big deal, I thought I'd ask you first"* and hang up.

Suppose she decides to join you and ends up dissatisfied with it anyway. It's better taking action and doing something, than fretting about it, getting shot down and doing nothing at all. If she wants an apology, that's a no win situation as well. By apologizing, you are again seeking her approval, and acting insecure. This is playing a losing hand. **Never apologize to women**. Even if you're caught in bed banging her roommate, blame in on the girl. Never feel guilty. You're just doing exactly what women do to men. The female capacity to lie, cheat, deny, and break promises knows no boundaries. They're just emotional statements that she'll rationalize later.

Compare that to the typical beta male making his move on a hard body.

*"If noone is sitting here next to you, do you think I could possibly join you and maybe buy you a drink? You're so beautiful; you must be a model. Would you like to empty my wallet now before you get too bored? "*

When you ask out women, they need to know you have set the proper mix values in your life. You are very busy in business and socially, but that you will set aside some time to be with them because you're attracted, BUT, if they give you any grief about it, it is no big deal. You have to show the ability to walk away from them, no matter how hot looking they are. This is how a secure man acts, and how he attracts women into the lair.

As far as sex, an insecure man is passive and petrified to make the wrong move, and always waits for signals from her before making any physical moves. Bad, bad, bad. Obviously you should wait until you have developed a sufficient comfort zone with her before attacking. If you don't, at best you only get one night stands. But you still have to be a man and make the moves, or she will lose any lust and desire for you.

## Project High Standards and Class

Appearances and reality can often be confused. Your self-confident attitude and personal drive for greatness help women perceive you to having High Standards in Life, even if you aren't there yet. So what traits reflect this? Women want men who have strong moral principles and absolute certainty in themselves. Men who are not looking for sleazy shortcuts and a low budget style of living. Men who pay great attention to detail, are highly self-disciplined, have complete emotional control, and are reliable. A man who is persistent in getting what he wants attracts women, especially if his accomplishments appear to be full of honesty and personal integrity. They all want to hook up with a man who appears to want the best of everything, and latch onto them hoping for the free ride.

As far as the all important materialness that women love, high standards is crucial. Girls like a man who knows the value of the finer things in life. They like guys who are classy, well dressed, and go for exactly what they want, without settling for second best. They like guys who are in control, and are a challenge; men who carry themselves with prestige, and aren't caught dead in the wrong places with the wrong people. They like guys who associate with other high-class men. Women all dream of the Hollywood lifestyle. So as a man, you should have a wide array of knowledge on the High Class things that women like. Restaurants, wines, cooking, the theatre, fancy cars, houses, interior design, the arts, travel, etc. A man who is "cultured" and has High Standards receives a higher level of desirability and value in a girls mind. Why? **Because they think you're going to finance all these things for her!** Now this does not mean that you have to live this highbrow lifestyle and cater to her every whim while you're single. It just means you are smart enough to take the time to educate yourself about all the details, and are prepared to discuss anything with the proper lingo. It certainly means all those midnight runs to the local Strip Clubs after you dump your date off better be done incognito in Navy Seal fashion.

## Scammers Always Get Caught

A few years back a friend new to the game calls and says we have to go to some club to meet his new player friend. *"The guy knows all the hot women. He'll introduce us to any of them."* I play along and we meet the guy at a laid-back, casual dance club. The dude is wearing a ridiculous shiny suit like he's a gangsta.
   (**Flag 1:** way overdressed for the club: possible wannabe poser)

Over the next 30 minutes he does his "Mr. Introduction" act with numerous girls. Following the name exchange and fake smiles, his conversations cease after a sentence. He just stands there all rigid, uncomfortable and businesslike. ("Look girls, I'm wearing a suit.... can't you feel my power?") The girls' eyes are wandering immediately. They aren't digging any of his magic. You can cut the air with a knife counting the seconds.

(**Flag 2:** he has no rap, and makes women nervous)

We all just stand there in deafening silence. I say nothing to help him out, since I love watching a great crash and burn. The girls start painfully searching for a reason to exit the area.

### Situation Analysis:

* Walking up to a girl and saying Hi is not a talent. What happens in the next 30 seconds is what matters. You have to make her smile or laugh with some playful flirting, jokes, teasing, or observation humor. Otherwise, women consider you as interesting as the houseplant in the corner.

Next up was the finale. Looking back, I wish I had given him a spotlight and a drum roll. He starts name-dropping, strutting, peacocking, and telling women he's a soon to be famous movie writer/producer; he's just waiting for **The Call** to head out to Hollywood to start the negotiations.

*Sure pal, right about when I announce my Presidential run.*

(**Flag 3:** insecure, attention whore with vomit levels of BS)

There's the sell signal. We exit the area immediately, before the girls start associating us with this dork. We bolt to the opposite side of the bar and meet up with a couple hotties I know. An hour later we leave the club, only to find the GQ player is standing outside alone. He asks us for a ride. I was surprised he hadn't used a stolen credit card to rent a yellow Ferrari with a "COOCHY-KILLA" vanity license plate.

(**Flag 4:** no car, no money, no friends.)

Out of pity for the wannabe Stud, we drive him to his movie star castle, which turns out to be the shittiest apartments you have ever seen. Get this; there was no roof over the entire building he was living in, just a dirty blue tarp! I start wondering if he cuts a hole in it and brags to women how he gazes at the moon through his remote controlled skylight in the master bedroom. He tells us the reason he needed a ride is he setup his roommate with some model at the club and he left him there. Bogus stories to the end. If he has a roommate, that means he can't afford the $200 rent by himself.

**Moral of the story**: Don't act like this fucking Loser.

His game was ridiculous, transparent and phony. The guy has zero Credibility, plus he is a Zero to boot! What the hell does he expect to accomplish with his fairytale presentation? How can he possibly reconcile his bullshit story with reality on a date? His act would be exposed in all of about two seconds. Word will spread in hours and every woman will know what a joke he is.

**Side note**: I saw him out four more times in the next year; each time he was wearing the same suit, boring women to tears. You da man!

## The Importance of Showing Credibility

To perfect your Alpha Foundation Skills, you must have a reasonable amount of reality behind it, or you end up shooting yourself in the foot. It's vital that when people view your image, it is perceived as an accurate representation of your life. If you're attempting to seduce a woman, she has to believe that what she sees and hears from you is genuine. You can't underestimate the importance of being credible in your presentation. It's the difference between being a high ratio closer, and getting busted and labeled by women all over town in ways that are impossible to overcome.

**You have to be** *perceived* **as Credible and Trustworthy** or you'll never be able to develop any attraction and rapport. Now, if you are only a work in progress, there is nothing to fear. Just make sure you choose a persona and lifestyle that you are currently involved in and intend to excel at. That is why being interesting, informed, *vague and mysterious* works to your advantage. It allows you cover your tracks while you're getting your life together. They can't have lingering doubts about things they don't know.

To show you are the real deal, you must display the following:

1. Knowledge and Expertise
2. High Peer Group Association
3. Be Charming and Easy to Like
4. Calm and Poised
5. Passionate
6. Authentic Appearance for the Role

**Knowledge and Expertise:** Whatever skill(s) you choose to be the dominant traits in your life story, it should be a topic that you are qualified to discuss with authority. Know how to control the conversation and make it interesting to the listener, without bogging them down with details. Have fascinating insights into the inner workings of the skill. Occasionally lower your voice, and give her the inside scoop on things. *"I probably shouldn't tell you this, but…"* It's turns women on when they believe you are passing on inside information. They live for gossip. Say things only a qualified person would know about the field. This doesn't mean you ARE an expert at it, just that a woman will *perceive* you to be. The key word here is perceived. This leaves you plenty of room, and only requires time, effort and discipline to study up and master the role. Show intelligence, energy and self-confidence in talking about your skill. Know the lingo, and play the part. By "your skill" this means your job, hobby, athletic/artistic ability, investments, etc. It's whatever topic you feel will attract women the most. It should be no big deal coming across a convincing expert, since a girl will rarely be an equal at the skill, or be as knowledgeable.

**High Peer Group Association:** Always make a point of befriending people who are well-known, established, higher up players in your field. People are judged by the company they keep. By linking yourself with popular, accomplished men with a solid reputation and integrity, women assume you are a credible player to be reckoned with as well. You take on a higher level of respect and trust just by being seen shaking a few hands, talking for 30 seconds and being noticed in all the right places.

Think about it. Even Babe Ruth had a batting coach. When Ruth was traded to the Yankees, he was already the most dominant slugger in history before the two men met. The batting coach was a marginal hitter in the lesser leagues. He swiftly gained credibility though by default. His advanced knowledge of the skill, and the ability to passionately communicate it made people *perceive* him to be an expert. When sportswriters saw him "counseling" Ruth and Gehrig, they assumed he knew EVERYTHING about hitting. It's not like Ruth needed any help; he routinely hit 500ft bombs out of the park. By utilizing **High Peer Group Association**, the batting coach was presumed to be the master of his trade. In reality, he was just fortunate to be at the right place at the right time. Plus, as long as the batting coach stayed out of Ruth's way, fed him beers on command, and kept a fleet of horny groupies close by, Babe would stick up for him.

**Charming and Easy to Like:** If a girl doesn't like you from the beginning, nothing else matters. With strong body language and being positive, optimistic, witty, and charismatic, you easily turn heads. (see next section). People who do not belong in the right clique are nervous, confrontational, seem out of place, and often brag to try and cover their tracks. When you are charming, distant and fun, you attract and are more believable. By keeping everything light and playful, you are assumed to be part of the *in crowd*. Women like the surround themselves with fun guys who are going places. They want to feel good when in your presence. People who are very fluid speakers when it comes to their skill have a significant advantage in creating the rapport and comfort levels a girl needs to feel, which allows you to hurdle over her bitch barriers.

**Calm and Poised:** When you have high self-esteem and are extremely competent at a skill, there is no reason to showoff or act arrogant. When you brag, you reduce the shock and awe value of the success. You are far more credible when you remain relaxed, composed and immune to challenges from others. No matter how difficult your accomplishments are, always pretend that the hard work and execution are seemingly effortless. Resist the desire to reveal all the practice, worry, and stress that comes with the territory. Even if a near death experience got you where you are today, be nonchalant and casual about it. You have more power when you achieve things gracefully behind the scenes. The posers and wannabes describe all their close calls and failures in great detail, while the doers in life enjoy their success with a smirk and a cocky head tilt in silence. Make sure your body language accents your strength, as it is more important than words. You want a girl to SEE your smooth confidence and abilities, as opposed to TELLING her about them. Hey, it's not every day a guy is promoted to being in charge of fries at McDonalds. Act natural, suave, and debonair. Enjoy the moment, you stud. Maybe put a new coat of wax on your scooter.

**Passionate:** Be excited about what you do. Your intelligence and enthusiasm for your skill will naturally attract women. You create energy about you that every girl can feel. It makes her want to be a part of it. It creates the chemistry needed for turning uptight babes into horny beasts. The more passion you show, the more credibility you lend to your story.

## Preparing for Battle – A Field Study

There you have the breakdown of each of the Alpha Foundation Traits. Take a good look at yourself and create a game plan on how you can display the look and attitude. Don't dive headlong into working your new game skills in the field until it is a fairly accurate portrayal of who you are, or who you are going to be. Start out by watching the guys who are naturals at it. Make friends with a few of them, and analyze their technique. In your field studies, go to different venues and observe how the various cliques of people interact with women; monitor the music, age group, appropriate hip attire, and the different attitudes in each. Get a feel for each venue, and pick out a few that favor your style. Play close attention to the style of women and their attitude in each club; each club will have it's own personality. Gauge the quality of targets, and the ease to seduce. Determine which places you can work the best. If you are Gen X and have tattoos, leave the corporate happy hour clubs to the guys who specialize at that. Find the places a bit off the beaten path. **You want to pick spots where you shine;** where you stand out amongst the competition. Don't frequent places where you are invisible, just one of the 50 other mid level players watching the A-list players picking off everything in sight right in front of you.

# Chapter II

# EXPLOITING HER INNER PSYCHO

The Keys to Seductive Charisma

# Exploiting Her Inner Psycho

The first tool in your alpha arsenal is mastering your Universal Foundation…creating lust, attraction and desire with your confident attitude and strong presentation. **Give them what they want to see.** The next phase in seduction is developing a rapport and building comfort time to remove her bitch shields. When a woman first meets you, you begin with a clean slate. Unless you've screwed her best friend, or she's doing some serious stalking, whatever information she knows or not doesn't know about you is entirely up to you. You are the gatekeeper to your life story. In this phase you learn to slyly maneuver a conversation in the direction you want it to go, and **Give them what they want to hear.** Being a smooth interviewer and attentive listener provides a girl a warm reassurance; it builds up the trust needed to see you're a worthy target. This sets the table to steer her into the closing booth and/or start of a relationship. Skilled conversation also gives you the information you need to fine-tune your target profiling, and maximizing your time management during the chase.

Women gravitate toward men with charisma. Charisma is one of those elusive traits people think you have to be born with. Most feel they have no shot in the world of ever having it. Yet it is a learned trait like anything else. Some of the most successful, outgoing salesmen were once too shy to speak, or even look eye to eye. The speaking skills they attained are readily available for anyone to tap. Charisma is comprised of a few dozen clear-cut speaking techniques and methods that are easily memorized and practiced. So what is it about charismatic people? Charisma is the ability to engage women in warm, fulfilling conversations that leave her feeling respected, intelligent, feminine and desired. She always feels good being around you. It weakens her barriers, and builds a subconscious inner attraction and rapport that keeps her always wanting you more.

Gigolos, actors, public speakers, salesmen, politicians, and televangelists all shine with magnetic charisma. People are naturally drawn to them, and love listening to them speak without knowing why. Jealous bystanders shake their heads and wonder what it is about them. The truth is, if you listen closely they really don't say much of anything. It's how they slyly arrange the questioning to engage the target in an emotionally positive fashion, while creating desire for themselves. They are great listeners. Their conversation effortlessly flows. Since they get what they want from their targets, they're genuinely compassionate and interested in the people who will be rewarding them. They love the chase. The magic lies in how they appear to be giving out vital information, while simply telling you what you want to hear. At best their conversation is vague, and open to interpretation. They take both sides of an issue, and have no real opinion about anything.

Their manipulation skill involves knowing how to play to their audience. They study who they are speaking to, and adjust to their level. A Politician making promises to a farmer in Texas is certainly not going to make an appearance as the fast-talking, slick haired, GQ con artist when he pitches him. Speed talking seems annoying and untrustworthy to the ears of a leisurely southerner with a slow drawl. The politician dresses down into jeans, boots and a hat, alters his speech to the farmer's pace. He uses the lingo of a farmer, to make him feel like he's one of his people. The appeal of all great seducers is their ability to size up the woman, and adjust to her personality style. He finds her desires and weakness, and leads her in a timely manner into making the decision he wants. All this happens while he makes it seem like **she** made the decision. He makes everyone feel good, and want what he has to offer. They are role-players of the first degree.

Likewise, this skill is just as important in business as it is in picking up women. Influencing a sales discussion is quite easy when attempting to sway a man into buying a product. But we are talking about seducing women here. Nothing is more volatile than a woman's mind. The real guts of the discussion phase is skating through her ever-changing emotional needs, wants, problems, dilemmas, tantrums, crisis, split personalities, and bitch barriers…while playing the smooth talking psychiatrist who provides her with the *appearance* of satisfying their needs and solutions to all her imaginary problems.

### Exploiting her Inner Psycho

Every girl wants a guy with a great personality; one who is smart, optimistic, is a good listener, has a great sense of humor, and is warm and compassionate. No one wants to hang out with a boring person. To accomplish this is actually quite easy when you realize what it really comes down to; Reverse Psychology. When you agree with her insights and ideas, she sees you as smart and attentive. When you respond positively to her feelings and emotions (without saying a word about your own), she sees you as a warm, sensitive man. When you laugh at her jokes, you have a great sense of humor. It's really that simple. It's all about her. The whole talent involves masking any information about yourself and playing to her ego. You direct the questioning to put her on the stage, vaguely answering in mild agreement with her, while appearing to have nothing to do with how the direction of the interview is going.

# Creating the Pickup Mood

You've got to be in the right mood in the game of flirting. Go into it having a warm sense of energy and humor. Check your conversational ego at the door, and leave all the worries and stress behind. You're not some nightclub stalker with darting eyes. The correct mindset is not a sexual hunter looking to score at all costs. You're a guy who loves women. Act fascinated meeting new people. Act like you are not out to pick up anyone. You are just in the mood to laugh and talk, and your target happens to be in your general area. You are playfully cocky, funny, adventurous, and genuinely curious in learning about her interests and life. Nothing is about you. Phoniness, bogus flattery and lines are easily spotted, and to be avoided. Just relax and be natural. Be yourself.

Leave all your baggage behind. We all have had plenty of bad experiences with previous women. First impressions of a woman can be easily wrong, so don't prejudge her because of her outfit, career, or some initial comment. Forget about all your old ladies, and forget about the ego queens and game players in the past…don't make any mental comparisons. This is a new girl. Come into the conversation with a clean slate, like she's the first woman you have ever met and you're captivated by her existence. Respect your own abilities at target profiling and talk up as many hot women as you can, in every situation. Concentrate on meeting a ton of women, and slowly narrowing your focus on a few…well, a few dozen.

Smiling and constant eye contact while she is speaking is essential. As she rambles on and on about female nonsense, I mean as she tells you about her interests, don't forget to occasionally tilt your head and nod in agreement. This let's her know you are actually listening to her, and makes her more comfortable with speaking to you. This sounds like simple stuff, but most guys have wandering eyes and don't hear a word women say. You're different. As you start developing a rapport, it's time to mirror her movements. People subconsciously mimic the body language of others when they are attracted to them, and it works in both directions. Lean in when she leans in, if she puts her hand on the table, you copy it. She touches her neck, you touch your neck. This creates an attraction without saying a word. Likewise, you can test if you are developing a rapport with her by doing the initial movements. Do a hand movement, and if she copies it, you're in synch. For example, raise a cupped hand pumping towards your open mouth mimicking a blowjob, and if she copies it, it's hummer time.

# Male Conversation Intent

When men meet a new woman, our discussions involve mostly observation humor, and are completely light; just flirting and playful teasing. The conversation is really just damage control, to make sure you will like her company when you're not having sex. Nothing heavy at all is needed on her part. All men want is the chance to date the nice, gorgeous women of the world; her money is the last thing on our minds. Even when we're pursuing marriage, our needs are not all that dramatic and difficult to meet. Be nice, be horny, & be quiet dammit.

# Anticipating Female Interview Intent

For women, the first conversations take the role of a job interview. What a woman wants to know about you should be obvious. They are interested in your social status and stability, sizing up your assets and earning prospects, and rating your compatibility scale; i.e., how much control you will allow her to have, and how much of her crap you will tolerate. The compatibility trait is actually an issue that leaves women torn. The men who turn women on will not let them get away with anything (alpha studs). But my how they love toying with men who are on the opposite end of the spectrum; the beta male wimps. They are attracted to them for many reasons, and none of them involve sex. They love to play games and feel the attention whore power; the sucking up, endless compliments, ego boosting, and free expensive stuff. Fortunately, these childish, selfish scammers angling to vacuum your wallet are easily spotted by Pro Bachelors and a great source of amusement.

Women in conversation are very, very sly in their questioning. On the surface they will pretend interest in your life story, and gaze at you full of eye contact, smiles and all touchy feely. For a moment, you're the funniest, best-looking, most fascinating man they've ever met. However, if they are looking for anything more than a quick lay, their tactics can be quite calculating. They've been schooled by years of media propaganda until it's built into their genes. They just hate going the distance until you *Show Me the Money*. Like a slippery politician, the info they are really after comes when you least expect it. Ninety percent of her questions are a disguise. The other ten percent of the inquiries come in the form of seemingly offhanded comments, which are the whole purpose of the interview. These questions involve what they really want to know about; your level in business, your assets, your income, and knowing what you will do for her.

Once you perfect seeing thru women, it's great fun kicking back and waiting for the real guts of their interview. It alters the landscape; suddenly talking to women can go from a chore to being quite entertaining! Place imaginary bets in your head on how many sentences she will go before she pries for your financial statement. You get to admire their technique, as they bob and weave before throwing out their zingers, while trying to hide their true intent. The cutting questions are said in the middle of a different inquiry. You're answering her X question, when she subtlety throws in a Y ( $ $ ) question, and then swiftly moves back to X question. What they want is the answer to Y ( $ $ ). The more experienced women, when they ask Y, it will be accompanied with a sexual distraction to throw you off. For example, while asking it they'll play with their hair, or rub their necks, lean forward and show their cleavage, or lick their lips. Loss of eye contact is the norm, as well as a softer voice during the question. Each woman has her own "tell" signal like a poker player. You're job is to wait for the Y question, laugh at her performance, and deflect it however you want.

Face the facts, you are being sized up, and the results of answering straight up is a lose lose scenario. In due time, you'll find the money questions are easily tossed aside with a few vague answers that turn it around to her.

## Creating Intrigue through Mystery

People deal with ego and insecurity issues every day of their lives. In conversation, most everyone will reveal their life story and future plans freely without thinking twice about it. They do it to make themselves feel better. They seek your approval to validate their intentions and ideas. Some people just love to talk and talk and talk, and what better topic can there be than talking about themselves? Pure honesty is a double-edged sword when speaking to women. They will hold every last statement against you if you ever wind up on the wrong side of them in dating. Casually speaking your mind is never a bright strategy for multiple reasons. For one, there is nothing to learn about you if you tell her everything. Where's the excitement, if there is no mystery in the details? Curiosity keeps her interested. Likewise, freely divulging your details leaves you open to being misread. How many times have you said something and they misinterpreted it and used it against you? They can be walking around bottled up for days on end dwelling on some meaningless side comment you made in passing that was totally irrelevant to anything.

## Steering the First Encounter

First few minutes, don't ask her name or her job, or compliment her appearance. Use casual observation humor; crack jokes about people in your vicinity; their clothes or attitude, or the room itself. Cover topical things in the news; light irrelevant stuff. Poke fun of her answers like she's your bratty sister, then mildly agree, then poke fun again. No approval seeking. Act like you're more of a "catch" than she is. Ask about chick topics, and dig 2 or 3 questions deep. Some answers agree and touch her arm, others smirk and move away from her. Find out her hobbies and her travel desires. Ask her favorite vacation. Ask why it was her favorite. What was her life goal in high school vs. today? If you're clicking, ask if she has unfulfilled sexual fantasies. Don't ask what they are. Smile, frown, look curious, and yet mildly bored. Act you are always about to leave any minute. Chicks expect you to hit on them, so pretend you're not interested. She wants power, so as she tries to win you over, you've created sexual energy and chemistry. She's now attracted. When she's speaking, occasionally let her feel witty, smart, interesting, and exciting. Never brag, or kiss her ass. Have no opinions; say *maybe* to everything. Share nervous high school dating stories. Say you seem to have a lot in common. Come across as confident, curious, playful, and semi-cocky. Draw her in by having an air of mystery about you. Divulge few details about your life. You're after building a level of trust, sexual tension, and then exiting before she has time to drill you for information. Get her number, point to your cheek, and have her kiss you goodbye. Two follow up short, upbeat dates with light banter builds a rapport, removes her shields, creates a *connection*, which sets up the close. On dates 2 and 3, always take her to multiple venues every 15-30 minutes; it builds an imaginary bond as though you know each other longer than you have. In sales and in seduction, if you're speaking, you're losing. If you hear yourself saying "I" often, you're doing it all wrong. Let her interview *you*, and deflect inquiries with a smile, without ever giving any opinions or deep answers. Always turn them around into multiple questions.

The secret to creating attraction in conversation is to make a woman feel good about herself when she is with you. Concentrate on listening, teasing, playing with her emotions. The trick is to steer all conversation back to her in an optimistic fashion, without ever saying much about yourself. In fact, the guts of the talent is mostly *what you do not say*, and avoiding the typical confrontational attitudes most guys carry around via their egos. Mr. Smooth is the vague, confident guy they love to have around, because he appeals entirely to their ego. The more mind games you play with her emotions, the greater the sexual chemistry.

## The Teflon Man – Take the High Road

**W**omen love to create controversy. Theirs is a world of obsessing and conflicts. Girls live for prodding you, testing you, and provoking you. They love throwing together endless lingering insinuations, snooping inquiries, sneaky statements, mischaracterizations, pontifications, slams and insults; all of which are filled with dozens of capital letters, exclamation points, and question marks….but never seem to have the all important **period** at the end of it. Like soap operas actresses, they'll even take the opposite side of what they believe in to start a heated exchange, just to see your reaction. The intent is to get you bothered and worked up and build up tension inside, until you eventually explode. Then they use your words against you forever.

Anticipating their strategy in these situations is how you stay one step ahead of them. These are the moments when you must be the Iceman of self-control, and leave your emotions at the door. There is logic to the female madness. Charm attracts women in the beginning, but it becomes a sort of personal battleground to them. Charisma is that magical gift of always being warm, optimistic, and seeing the positive side of people. Everyone feels good around you. That's the surface traits people see. But it's true power lies in the way you remain distant, and above the fray. Nobody really knows much of anything about you, as you express almost no opinions about anything. You control your world. You have an impenetrable armored coat of desire around you. By staying upbeat, fun, and aloof, women can't figure you out. It turns them on, since you are a ballsy challenge. Yet it also frustrates the hell out of them, since they can't figure out your core thinking underneath, and they don't have any power over you.

In the beginning, women enjoy spending time with you. As they spend more time with you though, they can't stop themselves from pecking away bit-by-bit, looking for ways to break down your emotional barrier. Since you know this moment always comes, you listen and wait. At all costs, when it arrives, you simply laugh and dodge at their efforts, tell them to lighten up and enjoy your moments together. Never allow them to get a rise out of you. Let the words bounce of you like pellets.

During tense discussions, most people drop their guard and leak out statements that would otherwise remain hidden. Words are said that are regretted later; many times words are misinterpreted and then women create a whole new controversy to hold against you. Female insecurity has deep roots, dating back to the caveman years when we dragged them by the hair for sport. They start these conversation battles because they're attention whores. They always want to be told their right, and feel they have control over you. They want you to take their side in all situations, slowly lose your own identity, and inject yourself into their life in order for you to settle all their disagreements and problems. It's part of the whole deeper desire of creating co-dependency on your part. They want you to slowly inherit all their responsibilities in life and eventually support them, while they kick back and drain your bank accounts, watch reality shows, get boob jobs, overeat and shop. Men don't really understand the constant female dilemmas, nor do they want to. Why live 24/7 in a perpetual state of worry? With beer, sports and sex everywhere we turn, where's the controversy?

### Now Shaddup and make me a sammich !!

In business and relationships, there are repercussions when you prove a woman wrong. They react to your response from an emotional standpoint, and often take offense to the very truth they are soliciting. On the surface they may agree with your answers, but underneath there are unintended consequences. The short-term gain of winning the point fades into a longer-term resentment she feels of you *"acting superior."* They absorb your failure to relinquish power to them, and start associating you with a negative vibe. With each successive correction of them playing lose with the facts, you lose attraction in her mind. Some may not speak to you for days because they think you are trying to make them look dumb with your *elitist attitude*. All that for correctly answering a question. It's just one more reason why there are only a handful of female CEOs in top US boardrooms.

# Bachelor Code 4
### Amendment 9,subsection 12c

**Women want to be treated as equal to men.
When they can't compete, they demand preferential treatment**

They don't like being treated as an equal when they're wrong. So you provide the illusion they're in control and always right by choosing to avoid the battles. It's a hollow win for them, and a big silent victory for you. Besides, even when you prove a woman wrong with the easily obtained facts, they still won't believe you anyway. Arguing with a woman; are you kidding me? Why waste the oxygen when it's a lose lose situation? If she demands your opinion, don't say a word. Just turn around and kick her cat across the room. She'll figure it out.

Always take the high road; never lower yourself to their level.

- *"I see your point. I don't agree with it, but I understand exactly what you are saying."*

- *"You're a smart girl, my view isn't that relevant here. I'm sure most people will come around to your side of thinking."*

- *"I've never really thought about it, but you're usually right about these situations."*

- *"That's your gig, and I wish you luck with it. I'm not getting involved with it. I have my own projects and demons."*

- *"Whatever you say. Bla bla bla. You're right, I'm wrong. Now where the fuck is my beer?"*

Men are right brain thinkers. We live in a detailed world of stats and logic; facts are in black and white, and there is no in-between. In discussing differences, we stick to the facts and use sound principles of reasoning to reach the correct conclusion. If someone disagrees with us, we say prove it. It they show us the fact from a trustworthy source, we acknowledge it. *"Son of a bitch, you were right. I didn't know that."* Being wrong doesn't bother us; in fact, we often enjoy the situations because we learn something. We love competition.

Women are left Brain thinkers. Their belief system is based on evolving emotions. To them, concrete facts, history, statistics and the truth are a gray area open to interpretation (until you agree with them). In disagreements, they generally cannot be swayed towards facts. *"My mind is made up, quit trying to confuse me with reality."* Sort of like the OJ jury. *"Don't slow me down wit da facts. He don't did it."* Women shy away from competition. The way they see it, why bother with all that hard work studying, when you can get what you want just by wearing kneepads and a see thru top?

If you absolutely need to prove your side of a position to a woman, the smartest approach is to do it with actions, not by engaging in a verbal pissing contest. Use some type of physical proof, or sourced documents that prove your point, and hand it to her *without speaking*. Use concrete data to back your assertions and analysis. Words never change a woman's mind.

# Give her the Stage

Date two or three is the time to create a subconscious emotional attraction, which sets up the close. After she's lowered her bitch shields, bite your lip and be a great listener when she talks. Smile away, and give constant eye contact. Tilt your head and nod frequently. Fight the urge to speak, and concentrate on determining what she really wants. Does she want to be consoled, is she looking for sympathy, does she want to feel smart, is she asking for advice, or just trying to get a rise out of you? Give her space to vent out what she wants, and say as little as possible, while being upbeat. Ask light questions that make her go levels deeper into the thought. This is also when you should be listening to the insecurities she is hiding under the surface. Negatives statements will give you the necessary clues. Look for a constant theme in them to find her weaknesses; ex-boyfriend problems, childhood issues, no daddy figure, bad boy desires, lack of self-confidence, lack of money. There's always something to exploit in the future.

Being charismatic is being vague, and giving positive reinforcement. Avoid the temptation to disagree, criticize, lecture, and inject prejudice or insults. Let her talk. Have no opinion. Keep it simple.

Whatever the topic, never respond from a negative viewpoint, or they associate you with that feeling. When you're upbeat and supportive, they associate you with positive feelings, and think you are a great guy. Offer nothing, unless she specifically requests it.

## Situation Analysis:

Suppose your babe comes over after work and starts bragging about something she did. You hear numerous false statements and feel a case of nausea coming on, listening to her misplaced cocky ego and attitude. What's is the normal guy's natural reaction? The natural reaction is for YOUR ego to get involved, and abruptly correct her blatant inaccuracies. This is the wrong reaction.

As a Professional Bachelor, you should be *future based* in your thinking, and automatically know how to handle these situations. You are not interested in the role of her professor grading her SAT answers. You're looking for endless nights of great sex with this beautiful, confused woman. The correct reaction is to tune out her words, and concentrate on her wet puckered lips, swollen nipples, and curvy bubblebutt. Look at her in soft focus, and try to imagine 80's porn music playing. While she's pontificating comical nonsense, picture her butt naked on all fours. Visualize slowly greasing her up in massage oil from behind, while yanking out your massive love torpedo. Imagine bleachers next to your bed filled with a dozen naked cheerleaders with pom poms chanting your name in unison… demanding a sex show, and the chance to join in. Then, stop the fantasy, and come back to the error filled discussion.

## In this conversation you have two choices

1. Shutting up and getting your way with her that night.
2. Stand on your own soapbox, strut your ego and be really smart, which pops her bubble and removes any access to the coochie.

It's a pretty easy decision when you project ahead. What's more important? Silly little words, or a *"really smart chick giving you a victory BJ?"* Shut up, grab a beer, and go warm up the hot tub.

**Remember... It's all about her.**

# The Keys to Seductive Charisma

Seductive conversation in hookups is learning to effortlessly create sexual chemistry, warm inner emotions and desire, while building a rapport and trust. It is not about kissing her ass and acting effeminate. It's the ability to turn off your ego and competitive desire to be right about everything and stealing her thunder. In other words, learn to avoid controversy and allow her to feel smart, important and wanted. How is this done?

Being a Charismatic speaker is as much about knowing **what you don't say**, as what you do. It's also the skill of knowing *how to say things*. There are a number of habits and negative traits that you must learn to eliminate from your conversations to portray yourself in the best light with women. When in doubt, always resort to being a good listener and using humor instead of being pessimistic or insecurely flexing your ego.

## 1. Never give Unsolicited Advice

There is always the temptation to correct people and give advice. In your mind, you offer it because you want to help people avoid similar mistakes you've seen made. Women defy logic. Even when you are overqualified to give advice, when women hear it directed at them, they subconsciously take it as a put down. They think you're a condescending nagger talking down to them. Resist the urge to help. Women are wackos, so stay in touch with their Inner Psycho. Girls are happiest when they sit around **talking about problems**, instead of seeking solutions. If you give a woman exactly what she wants, she'll say no thanks and get turned off. They don't want your solutions to their imaginary problems. They want a world of emotions, they want all eyes on them, and they want to feel important. (think a spoiled 8 yr. old girl). The truth is they have PMS all 30 days of the month, it just peeks for a few days. So being a good listener instead of offering management skills is the correct route to take 90 percent of the time. Let her vent her silly issues and console her on cue when the time comes to satisfy her attention whore needs. Remember, by rendering advice you unnecessarily involve yourself in the outcome. If her whole situation blows up, she will place part of the blame on you. Let them crash and burn before giving unsolicited tips.

Now, if she does ask for your advice, answer in such a way that you are not involving yourself in the situation. The smartest technique is to speak in third person about ways other people have handled a similar problem.

- *"I've never tried it, but I've heard that a lot of people like to do _____ in that situation…"*

Then follow that up giving her support; and make sure you emphasize that you wish her luck, but what ever decision she makes is entirely up to her.

- *"You always excel in these situations, I'm sure you'll do the right thing."*
- *"I don't know what I would do. Most people would just say go with your instincts."*
- *"This is your specialty, not mine. I'm sure things will work out right for you."*

## 2. Don't be a One-Upper

If she shares a story relating something at work, an observation or an accomplishment, let her enjoy the moment. That's why she is telling it to you. Congratulate her on her success, and get her to talk about her feelings and emotions about it. Put her on the stage and let her relive the moment blow by blow. This makes her feel important, smart and wanted, and she will associate you with those feelings. Let her blab on, just bring earplugs.

You have plenty of time to share things you have done, but this isn't the proper moment. She is not speaking about herself to provide you with material for the chance to one-up her and talk about yourself and your incredible day. If she tells you she saw a nice car today, smile and ask about it. Don't turn around and say you saw a nicer one today and yours is better, or that the one she saw really sucks, because it has a smaller engine and had a lousy review in Consumer Reports. Let her talk, be interested and amazed at everything she says. Let her feel observant and brilliant.

We all feel this temptation to relate our similar experiences. Let her ask you about things on her schedule. Don't automatically segway everything back to how you live in a more exciting world than her, and everything you do is better. Doing so may feel like you are showing value for yourself, but she will take it as being uninterested in her. You are telling her you are superior, and that she is unqualified to know good things. It makes her feel inferior, and resent speaking to you. Bragging doesn't make you look strong. It makes you look insecure. Girls are not attracted to insecure stuck up guys.

## 3. Keep it Simple

When you share a story, keep it short and interesting. Make the listener want to get involved. If you have to, practice telling a 5 minute version of your story, then practice a 2 minute version, then do a 45 second version. You'll soon realize a 45 second one with a lot of teasing gaps leaves the listener wanting and asking for more details.

There's nothing worse than someone blathering on about things you could care less about, or people you don't know, or topics you know nothing about, and smothering you with boring unnecessary details. Stories should be short and sweet. If you're talking and see her eyes wandering, and she is starting to fidget for her cell phone and losing eye contact, you are boring her to tears. You want her to get involved, not be overwhelmed with details without choice. Over talking is unattractive. Don't be an attention whore. Quiet and mysterious is what turns women on.

## 4.  Life is not a Debate
When a girl tells you her viewpoint about something, take a deep breath and listen closely. If she talks about something someone said, or if she tells you about her day, she is doing so to feel good about herself, or feel smart, or important, or interesting. It is just making casual conversation, not a time to get defensive. This is not an invitation for you to pick apart her statements and look for flaws and show your amazing intellectual superiority over her. Doing so will only leave her feeling diminished and hurt.

Conversation with women isn't a battle of the wits. Its purpose is to build a rapport, trust and a comfort zone that leads to sex. Learn how to keep the conversation spiced up by appealing to her female narcissism. Let her talk about her favorite topic: herself! The more times you make her feel good, and the more attention you show her in a discussion, the quicker the bitch shields and panties will fall. The reward of great sex for lending her an ear is a far more important than correcting meaningless statements.

Disagreeing with minute points in every statement makes you look very small and condescending. It shows a glaring lack of self-confidence. Grab a big cup of STFU and let her drone on and on. Get off your soapbox and get rid of the dreaded contrarian gene in your discussion brain. It's annoying as hell to the other person. They will cease all conversation with you if they know you are just going to take the opposite position.

Turn off the competitive mind, and give short upbeat responses. Lighten up. Remember, when you're speaking you're losing, so get her to talk. Ask vague questions to get her to expand on every thought. Look fascinated. Have no opinion. Smile, have piercing eye contact and nod your head in agreement like a retarded bobbing head doll.

## 5.  See Situations from Their Viewpoint
Men only see the details that affect us. We blank out the rest of the world. On a beach, we see nice sets of tits and a lack of beer. Ugly, fat people are

completely invisible. Paying attention to strangers talking to us is next to impossible. We are narrow and focused on our life and targets. We are fine tuned sexual hunters. Women see feelings and emotions in everything. They want to talk about the sound of the ocean waves crashing on the shore, the inviting salt water smell, how the warm waves caressed her body, the passionate pastel colors in the sunset, the songs of the seagulls announcing the seasons change, and that kind of crap.

When a woman goes into storytelling mode, you increase her attraction if your conversation covers all the emotions. Get her to laugh, cry, fidget with excitement, make her alternate between confused, aggressive, turned on, to unsure where she stands. Keep control, and makes her play by your rules.

Don't be Mr. Perfect. Play the Tragedy Stud, with a chink in his armor. Share some BS childhood stories where you felt fear and anxiety. Talk about your poor little puppy with a broken leg. Make her feel the urge to "*save you*". Emotion in conversation creates that all-important "*connection*" that women need to feel with their man. Don't ask questions that only require a yes or no. Fire away, and dig into the heavy details of her stories, and make her relive the feelings. It will feel uncomfortable, feminine and corny, but it always works in your favor. Pussy maintenance 101. If you need incentive, try to imagine the excitement of having multiple exclamation points after everything you say!!! Make her brag how you understand her, and you're such a great listener!!! (gag)

- "Sounds like the whole situation just came at you out of nowhere. Your friends will be so jealous. How does that make you feel? !!! "

- "You're kidding, what makes her so emotional? !!!"

- "I can't believe she had the nerve to do that. What do you think her hidden agenda is? What did she say then? !!!"

- "You've got a lot of guts and great instincts to figure that out in advance. I can tell you are already planning your next move. How do you stay so motivated? How do you think they will react? !!!"

- "Of course he's confused. You really put a lot of time into this project. Besides, you have the sexist perfume on. Poor guy could barely think. How did he feel about your ideas? !!! "

- "You're amazing to be such a deep thinker. Damn what a lucky guy I am. All that and tits too. I never met any girls like you in Harvard Law School. Were you the most popular girl at Redneck Community College before you flunked out? !!! "

- "If I act mesmerized at your boring stories, will you give me a blowjob before ESPN highlights comes on? !!!!"

## 6. Sucking the Life out of People

When a woman is chatting you up, there is nothing worse than sucking the oxygen out of the room. If things aren't going great in your life, work on it internally; don't drag everyone else down with you. You want to inspire a woman, not depress her. Don't turn around each conversation into complaining about your job, or your car, or your constant aching back, your shitty apartment, your three-incher, hating some neighbor or society in general. Nobody likes a whiner. Girls don't want to hear about the problems with your ex-girlfriend, or your lousy relationship with your family or boss. Keep things as positive as possible, no matter how much baggage you are carrying around. Life is a self-fulfilling prophecy. If you only see the world through negative thoughts, you will always be depressed. Worse yet, misery spreads like a disease, and subconsciously creates a co-dependency in others. You bring everyone down with this attitude, until eventually, you isolate yourself from the whole world except for a few miserable drones.

There is nothing worse than responding to each thought in a negative fashion. Girls will run in fear from you if every time they pick up your phone calls, they hear *"you'll never believe what happened to me today..."*

## 7. The Cheap Charlie

If your girl went to a restaurant or department store, or repaired her car somewhere, pay no attention if she overpaid. There is often a lot more to a story that meets the eye. It's none of your business where she does her business. Never question what she pays for things. Don't dive in announcing she got ripped off, and proudly state how your place is better and cheaper. In her mind, you come across as being classless, judgmental, and trying to act superior. Whenever you declare yourself right, she is by definition wrong. Women hold it against you when you tell them they're wrong. Guys who tell girls they are wrong don't get laid. Even if you own a chain of stores in that field and know the business backwards, if she wants your opinion on pricing and service, let her ask for it.

Maybe she likes the place because she has a friend who works there. Maybe they treat her like a queen and she prefers their service to others. Sometimes a simple thing like a restaurant that gives her a better table, or a repair shop giving a ride back to work is all it takes to get her business. It's true that in many businesses unscrupulous men will rip off a woman. But if she knows the value of flirting, any woman, particularly good-looking woman, can get things a lot cheaper than you can. Maybe she's fucking Biff the Mechanic and not only gets free car repairs, she gets his Harley as a loaner. Don't get defensive and be the know it all who corrects her choices. Remember, time has a significant cost. You have to factor in someone's time and comfort levels. It may cost a little more at some places, but higher quality of service combined with ease and quickness of access makes the price worth it;

ask any guy who's been to a High Class brothel. You really cheapen yourself in a woman's eyes if you are the guy who knows the price of everything, but the value of nothing.

## 8. Don't Rush Her

If she is making a point, don't start fidgeting and try to speed up what she is saying. What's your hurry? Let her ramble on as long as she wants. Sneak in to the bathroom every 5 minutes and do JD shots if you have to. Women feel better when they are speaking instead of listening. By showing interest and an appreciation for every little thing she says, you increase your sex appeal. If you want to make an impression, **concentrate on listening**, not speaking. What's so hard about that? The purpose of talking to a woman is not analyzing the words spoken; it's to increase her desire and lust for you by making her feel good. If you're in a talking mood, there's plenty of time after the date to call up a buddy on the way home and get the scoop on the hot new strippers at the local club.

So what's the worse thing you can do with a girl? Constantly interrupting her before she finishes her point. This tells her you are impatient and insecure, and could care less what she is saying. It shows a complete lack of social skills, and is egotistical. It's a power struggle you don't want to get into. We all know how difficult it is to listen to someone when they are clearly wrong in whatever point they are making. Just nod your head, and bite your lip. Wait until she finishes her thought. Take a deep breath first.

Now as far as bitchiness, the rules change. The first time she goes off, even if she is beat red in the face complaining, be quiet and laugh when she is done before speaking. Speak quiet and slow like talking to a child. *"Respect is a 2-way street. If you don't show me respect, you won't get any in return."* If she goes off wailing at you a 2nd time, stand up mid-sentence, open your front door, and tell her to get out. Never argue. Just dump the mouthy bitch. If you're at her place, get the hell out of there and call Bambi for a bootie call. Don't be too late, or you'll end up with sloppy seconds.

## 9. Show Respect to Others

When discussing her friends, or people both of you know, show them respect. No matter how full of BS people are, you elevate yourself in a girl's eyes by avoiding being judgmental. If you can get away with it, limit your statements to something like "She's a piece of work." If more is required, use plenty of tack. At most respectfully disagree with others' statements with a touch of class. It's great fun, because it's what you don't say that makes an insult so effective. Women never catch on you are still blowing out her friends, will appearing to be the consummate gentleman.

- "I'm sure there are plenty of things she knows more about than me. My clients would tell you this topic isn't one of them."
(Stuck up dumb bitch)

- "You may not see things eye to eye with her, but she is entitled to her opinion."
  (Arrogant Wench)
- "Your friend Mary certainly has a wide variety of boyfriends at any given moment. Perhaps she's just a little frustrated with the way her parents raised her."
  (Trailer Park Slut)

- "Peg seems a bit adverse to physical fitness. She must rarely have the time, as she's always with her restaurant reviewing girlfriend, out sampling dishes and making chef's nervous."
  (Freeloading Cow)

The reasoning here is simple. If a girl sees you slamming people the minute they turn their back, she will start assuming that you are giving her the same treatment when she is not around. Also, show you respect her as a woman. Don't smother her with dirty jokes, make fun of her quirky traits or her appearance, and try not to act like she is just one of the guys. Even if she is the biggest tomboy in the world, a girl still wants to feel sexy, and know you desire her. Don't get all gushy about it, just say mild compliments in passing, and touch her just the right way as you are changing the topic.

## 10. Avoid being an Attention Whore

We all know that's a woman's specialty. Why steal the stage from an AW if your chances of getting laid improve by shutting up? The macho guys who thump their chest bragging think they impress the ladies, but are really just telling the world how insecure they are. Arrogant, insecure men are the biggest turnoff to a woman. Some guys are naturals at it. Others turn into one after getting drunk. Make sure to gauge your personality as you get hammered around women. If you get belligerent after a few, stay away from women you are trying to impress. You never get a second chance to make a first impression. The word of your instant a*hole attitude will spread around town before you've even completed your first balance test in the drink tank. If 5 beers equals dickhead, beer 6 end the date and go straight to a Titty bar.

So what's a male attention whore? The guy who puts everyone down, brags about himself, never admits when he is wrong, looks for fights, tells blatantly obvious lies, says he's important or rich, is a chronic name dropper, or other poser nonsense. *"Don't you know who I am?"* People who are very successful and going places, the self made rich, or the quiet studs with black belts, NEVER call attention to themselves. Their silence speaks volumes. Women instinctively know when you've got the goods. It's the basis of the Universal Foundation. Actions speak louder than words. If you haven't figured this out yet and are an attention whore, stay home and STFU until you do figure it out. You're wasting valuable oxygen.

## 11. Compliment her Mind, not her looks

Act like you have a fleet of supermodels competing for your rod. Complimenting a perfect 10's looks is boring, hands over all the power to her, and tells her you value her like a piece of meat. You create desire by complimenting her brilliant mind. (barf) Hotties are bored with flattery, and shocked when you ignore their looks. Mildly bust her chops, make her laugh and tease her, like she's your bratty little sister. She'll get worked up and touch you, but push her away. If she calls you a jerk, you're turning her on. If she challenges your approach, don't say *you're kidding*. Hold your ground and be a challenge. Her insecurities for you not validating her looks will make her eventually start selling herself to you, seeking your approval.

## 12. Never talk about ex-girlfriends

This one should be obvious. When you bring up ex-girlfriends, she thinks the girl is still on your mind. They never let this go, and from then on think that you are heartbroken, and angling to go back to her. Plus, if you say anything bad about an ex, she assumes that's how you are going to talk about her when she's gone. Women don't like to be compared to anyone else. They don't want to be in competition with some babe when they're with you. They want to be the center of your attention; the only girl on your mind. Play along with charade. Oh, when she's over your place, make sure you hide all those size 0 panties the Baby Dolls dancers leave behind. Your pad should have no evidence. Pretend you're still a virgin.

## 13.Stay Clear of Major Issues

When quizzed for your position on an issue, maintain the ability to be independent. You never know which side she holds down. They will dance on both sides of the aisle without ever telling you where they stand. Taking sides on any strong belief system she may have is a losing hand. It is best kept off limits in discussions with women. Choose wrong and you lose. The smart speaker will find positives in both positions, but stand for neither. Support her on whatever her side is, but avoid expressing your own thoughts. Agree to disagree and leave it at that. Tell her you understand her position and pick a new topic. Discussions involving conflicting opinions set the table for someone being right, and someone being told there are wrong. Plus the wrong person in the discussion (the woman) will get all defensive and emotional, which just makes matters worse.

One of the fastest ways to turn off a girl of to have a negative opinion about a major belief she has. Some girls have a total devotion to a single issue or two, and plan their whole lives around the topic. Everything they say and do has to be confirmed with their belief system. Some examples are: Religion, men vs. women issues, abortion, astrology, backdoor love in pickup trucks, and lastly, the lib democrat political issues – environmentalism, feminism, vegetarians, animal rights, equal rights do gooders and all the PC crap.

If you are hot and heavy over one of these girls, there is only one method that will keep you clear of conflicts. Simply say *"Religion* (politics, whatever) *is a private issue for me that I choose not to discuss."* When they push you, just repeat the same; *"I respect your stance, but Religion is a private matter to me."* Refuse to discuss it. It's a no win situation. Alternate technique is to just flip it back at her: *"I've never really thought about that, how do you feel about it?"* No matter how much her ideas and opinions may piss you off, what difference does it really make? What's your goal? Battling irresolvable issues or getting laid? Words are overrated.

## 14. Vocabulary highlights your intelligence

Girls like intelligent men, and your vocabulary is one of the easiest ways to separate yourself from simpletons. Don't overdo it, and sound like a NY Times crossword puzzle. People get intellectually lazy after they finish school. Five minutes a day with a thesaurus with expand your vocabulary. This comes in handy in business as well. If you're discussing a specific trade, know the lingo and clichés; it helps make you sound like you have a clue about what you're discussing. Be honest. Don't fake knowledge of things you know nothing about. Don't wear T-shirts that say COLLEGE.

## 15. Maintain your Cool

Never raise your voice, never fucking swear, and be very conscious of your speaking volume…it's always louder than it need be. All of these bad traits signal an impatient person who is not in control of himself, or the situation at hand. Impatience is a seduction killer. Take a deep breath, and slow it down when there is tension. If the problem involves her ragging your ass, smile and talk quieter and slower, or better yet just bust her chops. By allowing her to get you worked up, she has obtained power of you. When you act as though the whole situation is irrelevant, you diffuse the situation and keep the power. This is the first thing they teach a bouncer in a bar. Hopefully you want to come across as intellectually superior to a bouncer.

## 16. The Image you Project

The image you project determines the level of respect you will receive. If you act like an unpredictable flake, she will think you are undependable, can't pay bills on time, have no control over your life, and certainly can't afford her. If you're negative and crude, women will disdain you, treat you like a low class bum. If you always act wild and slutty, you'll get one-night stands, but no serious relationships. If you play the SNL buffoon, girls will never take you seriously. A mild combination of all of these is great, but use moderation for everything. For any longevity in a relationship, remember that girls have only a small portion of our sense of humor. They want to be able to introduce their man to their family, girlfriends, and business associates. So tone down the lunacy, and before the end of every date, steer back towards the desired stuff; intelligent, high standards, integrity, and being secure in your life. When you set a high price for yourself, women will believe you are worth it.

## 17.  Your Eyes tell the story

Women are suckers for good looks, but equally important is *how you look at her* with your eyes. Staring and glaring is for stalkers. Fawning puppy dog eyes like your worship her body is too weak. Be focused and intelligent with your eyes. Be engaged with her mind. Be concerned and look like your dying to hear whatever brilliant thought she's about to say. Pretend she's a stacked Einstein. Treating her like an intellectual equal is rare to girls.

Most guys they meet try to sell themselves, flaunting their ego at every turn. They talk about me me me, and brag how the world evolves around them, while scanning the room for every hot chick who walks by. The way a girl reads this, you are telling her you're insecure, do not value whatever she has to say, and are looking for a hotter chick.

Be different, and you get her attention. Pretend you're her therapist. Tilt your head and nod, flash your concerned and intrigued eyes, and pretend to be sensitive to her moods, and conscious of her needs. Never take on the role of a therapist trying to actually solve anything, just look deeply curious at her nuanced statements. Is it corny? Fucking AAaayyy. It's borderline ridiculous. But you can do all this just with your eyes without speaking, and make her panties wet with anticipation. You make her the center of attention, and every girl finds the guy who is a compassionate, attentive listener irresistible. How you make a girl feel when she is around you decides everything. Shut up and listen, and look intelligently cool with piercing bedroom eyes while you're doing it.  Simple stuff.

## 18. Personality and Sense of Humor

Girls say they want a guy with a great personality and sense of humor. Someone who is damn happy about the direction of his life, his job, his hobbies, his friends, and most importantly, her. Whether in a business or during seduction, how you come across speaking decides your influence. Be funny, upbeat, passionate, and full of energy. You make them feel better about their day, and themselves. Sure they want a guy going places, a stud in business as well as in bed, but they prefer a guy who doesn't take himself too seriously. Big egos are boring. Act like nothing in the world bothers you, and always have some funny observation humor handy to share with her. Make fun of cocky posers, don't be one yourself. They want a successful guy who never talks about work. A woman is more interested in what you do when you're not working, i.e., how much time can you devote to her whims. They love a guy who is more content playfully teasing her with a witty repertoire. When you're always having a good time, you attract women. It shows you are completely in control and self-confident, which translates into higher social status.

# Chapter III

# SPEED DATING UNIVERSITY

Time and Money Management
Determines your Levels of Success

# Control Determines your Closing Ratio

Dating can be an exhilarating hobby, or a preposterous waste of time and money. It all depends on who is controlling the game. This section provides a guideline on how to fine-tune your pursuit and conquests and enjoy superior results, spending eighty percent less time in the process. An experienced player always places a high value on efficient speed dating, and the importance of time and money management.

Most of us can confess to times we were dating way too many women at one time. It can be as addictive as anything in life, and you get caught up in the moment and lose your perspective. Without following any clear strategy, it takes as many hours as a part-time job. Between the hangovers, waking up in your car upside down in the median, and sleeping in the john at the office, your career suffers for extended periods of time…as in roughly a decade or two. When you're smothered by a time consuming habit, you lose focus. It whittles away at your own power. Everyone is guilty of it at some time or other. It's easy to caught up in the cycle of just going out and hitting the happy hours and hot clubs every other night. You date almost any cute one who smiles at you, and live in a constant world of scheduling nightmares. Most of the girls turn out to be game players, wallet suckers, and a complete waste of oxygen. This lifestyle costs a fortune in time and cash, not to mention lousy productivity hours at work.

At some point we all say *"knowing what I know now, I wish I could turn back the clock and re-live the last decade."* You would eliminate the dozens of hours per week you lost clubbing, schmoozing, gawking and dating the wrong chicks. You could have spent your time more efficiently speed dating, and concentrating on your career. The net result is you'd be far more successful in life. You'd be making a hell of a lot more money, have more confidence and attitude, and attracting hotter looking women way beyond what you are getting now.

It's not just the average looking, inexperienced guys who suffer from lack of skills. There are plenty of good-looking guys who suffer from insecurity and a lack of technique. They strike out every night like fools, and have no one to blame but themselves. They go into a club, head straight to the bar and start slamming shots and drinks. Within 30 minutes they're drunk and obnoxious. Then they spend the rest of the night complaining how all the girls are bitches, because they aren't getting any attention from them. The reason they're not getting any attention, is because they're drunk and obnoxious. It's a self-fulfilling prophecy.

Street smarts can begin anytime you want;
but you have to be willing to commit to it

# Bachelor Code 1

## Men want a sexy girlfriend
Men want a nice, beautiful girl who loves sex,
and can make pretty babies.

-------

## Women want a Hollywood Lifestyle
Women want a Life of Luxury without any responsibility
with a wealthy man they can control.

Men want a girlfriend. Women want a lifestyle. The goals between men and women couldn't be more different. Numerous studies reveal women want both good-looking men with personality, as well as men with money. But if forced to choose between the two, money wins every time. And to think they call us shallow. Let's be realistic. Women certainly are not going to be upfront about what they really want from you. Can you imagine your reaction if they did? So in return, you give them the same treatment. Women offer the possibility of sexual favors, in return for being spoiled rotten. A smart bachelor waves around the possibility of spoiling her rotten, without actually providing anything until she passes his tests and **he gets what he wants**. He gives subtle hints of a high income, assets, and earning potential, without disclosure of anything. It's a chess match relationship based on promises, smoke and mirrors. You simply one up them at their own silly games. Women have to believe there's a chance of you letting her get her way for things to sexually progress. In their minds, the padlock is on the panties, and if you want the key, it's gonna cost you big boy.

### Dream on sister.

Most hot looking women have developed quite the whorish attitude about what used to be an exhilarating mating chase. They are out working angles and schemes to trick men into a subservient marriage, or at the very least get top dollar for their goods and services. This attitude forces men to tolerate mindless charades to attract and test them, while always looking for the quick exit. It takes the sincerity out of dating, and reduces us to playing along with their call girl mentality. Sure, the occasional star appears. But until you master the skills, mostly you end up with a severe case of buyer's remorse, standing at the end of the bed with a clipboard, making sure the delivery of product occurs, and the service justifies the price.

### It Rarely Does

In due time, as you perfect your target profiling this nonsense will rarely happen to you. A Pro Bachelor sees this type of woman a mile away, and never gives her the time of day. Laugh at their self-centered immaturity and prostitute attitude and move on. They're somebody else's problem. Next!

# Bachelor Code 2

## When a woman is on her back, the meter is running

— — — — — — —

Invest wisely. One way or another, you're paying for it. The sooner you face up to it, the quicker you'll learn to put your own self-interests first. That's what women do. Next to personality profiling, the most important skill is managing your dating time and money efficiently. The quick release program should be used without thought or emotion. You're far better off living stress free concentrating on your career, hobbies and health, than dying a slow death playing the walking ATM machine and emotional tampon in life-sucking relationships. If a girl plays the actress to catch you and does a personality change, you immediately move on. Why reward deceptive behavior? This applies not only to the misses, but also the direct hits that go bad after a few nights of sweaty sex.

The Professional Bachelor always gets his needs satisfied first, or he moves on to the next target. He ignores this nonsense of *hoping for results* with high dollar courting. Sorry ladies, the free stuff comes after the sex begins, not before. (dabs eyes with Kleenex) If women desired a man on a human level for who he is, instead of a childish *"what have you done for me lately"* attitude, we'd give them the luxury lifestyle. But they want to cart before the horse. That's the facts, Jack. Plan accordingly.

There's too many fish in the sea to dwell on time wasting game players. While hot looking women tease you with potential sex, they're stringing along 3 to 5 other guys at a time. Why do you think they're on their cell 12 hours a day? The minute you leave the room, they check their cell to see which guys called, and what their *offers* are. These girls are the epitome of classless and rude, and are the mirror image of a prostitute who runs with your money before putting out. Why waste a penny on such blatantly dishonest whores? With three billion women on the planet, there's no reason to get lazy and settle for disrespect. The keepers require near perfection. Never feel guilty moving on to the next woman quickly. After all, we are the ones who are honest about our intentions upfront.

When a girl's flirting is sincere, and the chase leaves you dying of anticipation, you're with the right girl. If not, take those courting dollars and spoil yourself rotten. Go rent a few honest, gorgeous Perfect Ten escorts while you sort out the next batch of prospects. Invest wisely.

# Bachelor Code 3

## A woman is entitled to the same amount of respect she gives you, and not one ounce more

# THE C P F

**I**'m out jogging the other day, and see this new Hummer parking on the side of the road in front a low-rent apartment complex...an odd place for a somewhat pricey vehicle. As the door opens, I can see the driver is clearly a desperate Beta Male trying to buy attention. He comes bounding out, slouching, dressed like a slob, with a big gut exposed under his t-shirt. He plops out and he literally **runs** around to the passenger side with two-dozen roses in his arms. Warning signs immediately trigger in my head. I can size up this situation in two seconds. I slow down, and wait for the humiliation to painfully unfold like clockwork.

Sure enough, his bitch, who knows his arms are full with her roses, is too lazy to open her own door. He opens the door, struggling with the flowers. Out pops some good-looking mid 20's Oriental chick, dressed for royalty. She makes no eye contact. No smile, no thanks honey. Nothing. She completely ignores him, and struts towards the apartment gates. In her hands are four of those huge shopping bags from the most expensive department stores in town. Neiman Marcus was one. (Needless Markup is one of those highbrow places where you spend $250 for a blouse that costs $50 anywhere else). The four bags she's carrying are the oversized three feet deep kind, and they are stuffed...easily a grand or three of crap she doesn't even need. (she'll return the stuff for refunds after she dumps him).

The chick stands impatiently facing the gate, pissed off that he has the nerve to make her carry the bags. The guy shuts the truck door, and **runs** up the sidewalk to open the gate for her. They disappear out of sight. The only thing missing from the scene was for him to get down on all fours, while she lifted her skirt and took a dump on his head. The whole scene makes you want to vomit. I bet he spent the rest of the afternoon begging for sex. She got pissed off, started arguments, ripped up one of the $250 blouses, and screamed that he is treating her like a whore. Finally, after 3 hours, she drops her guard. She lifts her skirt, and he gets down on his knees. He pushes the protruding string to one side, and licks away like a German shepherd vampire, while she makes a couple cell phone calls to other guys. The only Hummer he'll ever have with her is the one he drives up in.

## Bachelor Code 6
### Amendment 2, subsection 23c

**The amount of money you spend on first dates is inversely proportionate to the level of respect you receive in return.**

There's a rule they don't teach at Wharton School of Business. If you spend like a fool, they treat you like a fool. You show little value for yourself, and hand over all the power to her. Being a total pushover who caters to the whims of every woman screams of insecurity. Plus, it's an attraction killer for women. Of course when you screw up like this, they won't tell you to zip up your wallet, but you won't be closing the deal anytime soon, if ever. The most common mistake men make in the beginning is trying to win a girl over by *purchasing her approval*, seeking acceptance with the wallet. The first few dates are pricey dinners, trips and events rivaling the cost of a great vacation. The dinner conversation consists of being a beta male phony, full of insecure agreement with everything she says, desperately seeking a whiff of her endorsement of your status…acting more like her girlfriend. A girl can get a night out like that 7 days a week. It bores her to tears. Her only fun is watching you spend money and kiss her ass.

Whatever level of dating you start out with will be used against you as a benchmark for expenses going forward. They'll expect the gifts and events to become ever more extravagant. This would be no big deal if you were dealing with honest, rational women. Let's be realistic. Nine out of ten girls never make it to the third date. Maybe 1 out of 20 girls ever make it past 6 weeks in your life. Slow your ass down, and quit turning women off by being so easy. The odds are the chick won't be around long term anyway. Keep it light, and manage your time and money until you are damn sure you really want her, and vice versa. Only after the sex relationship begins do you loosen the wallet up. This has nothing to do with money, and everything to do with control and testing her honesty. If you don't show you value yourself and your time, why should she? There is no excuse to let a woman play you like a fool. You're the reward, not your wallet. Spending your time with her and money on her is her reward, and it only comes after she shows you respect, sexual interest, and the right behavior towards you.

# Alpha Dating 101:

Physical attraction is a feeling. It does not have a dollar sign. It is a girl's subconscious physical and emotional response to your masculinity. She admires your strong attitude, cool self-assurance, your look, and the way you make her feel. The purposes of first dates are to build value for yourself in her eyes, create intrigue in her mind, and establish a connection. You give her a mixture of hot and cold emotions. You flirt and act semi-interested, but play hard to get. This increases sexual tension and attraction between you. Seduction is best done slow, as it brings the excitement to a peak. When you nail the presentation correctly, she is filled with desire and lust. You become an idealized target, an image of someone she wants, but can't have. This drives them nuts, and loosens up the buttons on her pants rapidly. You want her to be selling herself to *you,* to the point when she feels like she needs to make a move or *she'll lose you.* Be someone challenging. Be someone she desires both physically and mentally; and she'll be damned if that big titty bitch Tiffany next door is going to steal you away from her. Screw her and the golden tampon she rode in on. Third date, when you land the unexpected slow wet kiss that lasts for days, as they say in Golf, at that point it's just a tap in. Never acknowledge the applause. Signatures will be requested, but never offered. No pictures, please.

# First Dates in the Field:

**Time Management Rules**: phone calls before the first date and between the 1$^{st}$, 2$^{nd}$ and 3$^{rd}$ dates should be five to ten minutes tops. Don't put too much importance into the buildup. Don't get cocky or insecure and feel you have to prove yourself prior to the date. Be upbeat, interesting, funny, mysterious and vague. Always initiate the hang up. Get off the phone before you start boring her with an interview, or being too nice. You'd like to talk more, but you have a busy schedule. Until you're having sex, this rule never changes.

**Dating Time Management**: A smart first date is happy hour for **one drink** at a popular outdoor patio, total time of date is 45 to 60 minutes. You want to quickly lower her bitch shields by showing a casual confident attitude, create a warm rapport, build a comfort zone and exit quickly. The first five minutes will tell you all you need to know. Gauge her body language, sexiness, and attitude towards you. Make a decision to meet again or exit. Again, you have pressing things you must attend to. This creates scarcity and builds value for yourself and your time. It removes all appearances of seeking her approval. This instantly makes you a challenge.

**First Date Location**: A crowded place with a high turnover that offers a lot of people watching. This provides a relaxed, casual environment to protect you from embarrassing scenes, and dead air. It makes the exit easy if you're stuck with a cold fish, a user, an attitude chick, a sexless tease or psycho. It presents numerous opportunities to make funny, casual conversation about the people strolling by. If observation humor is your specialty, you can shine here with little effort. Gaze playfully at other couples, and ask your date questions: *"guess what they are thinking...*or *how do you think they met?...will they work out together? How soon till he checks his watch? How many cell phone calls will she answer before he gets pissed off?"* No high-fives or moonwalks after dazzling her with your brilliant commentary. Make sure to avoid talking about how incredibly important you and your frigging job are, and how the world revolves around you. If she's curious, she'll ask about it. Don't bring it up. Downplay your career and be vague as possible. *"I buy things, I sell things, and keep most of it for myself."* Keep her curious. Mystery works. If she pushes for more info, just brush it aside.

*"Let's just keep it light, stress belongs in the boardroom, not here",* or
*"you can put the calculator away,*
*I'm not releasing any financial statements without a subpoena."*

Stay focused. The date's purpose is determining if she's someone who you'd love being around when you're not having sex. Or, the purpose is to get her hammered and have a sweaty one night stand; some violent, jackhammer sex at her place, followed by a slippery escape out the bedroom window. Then hop in the Porsche and floor it to the VIP room at the Platinum Club. Remember, those Lesbian Shower Shows start at such odd hours these days. How 'bout some consistency Guys, I'm not a mind reader.

Back to the patio date. See if she's a sensual person or not. A frigid workaholic is boring. Successful career women have difficult and unreliable schedules, and they'll selfishly refuse to cancel meetings for those impromptu threesomes you arrange. They often carry around warehouses of baggage with their fantasy gender superiority issues. Exercise your freedom of choice. You want a horny spontaneous companion, not someone who works all hours of the night on a Summary Judgment motion.

Sexual chemistry with women is all about feelings, emotions, and creating a *connection*. Skip boring work questions or her appearance. Get her to open up. Ask about things in recent past, her childhood, her hobbies, her future desires; share stories that generate an emotional response; make her re-live past experiences and feel every sensation; happy, sad, excited, nervous, scared, anxious, and turned on. Ask what does when she isn't at work? Does she have a life, or is she a bar flirt? Where has she traveled, where does she want to visit? Discuss the impulsive, cool things she did in college, and still does today. What has she always wanted to do? Where does she see herself in 5 years? More importantly, does she have a Schoolgirl outfit?

Some girls can actually hold your interest in a discussion, and may even think to ask about your life. Don't volunteer anything, but be prepared to speak. Say nothing about work, and discuss your passions and hobbies you actively pursue. Let her know you have a fulfilling life whether you are dating or not. Be interesting. Throw in comments about some fascinating trips, experiences, or vacations you have taken. If you recently took one, have your camera handy with some action photos that *just happen* to still be on the card. Make sure you look natural and are having the time of your life in the pics; don't be some dork poser. Give off the air that your job means nothing to you in life; it's the impulsive excursions you dabble in that have the most meaning to you. Avoid sex discussions and ex-girlfriend quizzes, as they will use the words against you in the future.

## Display Value, Taste, and High Standards

Discuss your favorite restaurants, vacations, NYC, Vegas shows, events, concerts you'd like to see, and other fun things she knows cost a bit of money. You are not offering them to her, you simply imply you appreciate finer things and can afford them. If she pushes for them, you probably have the wrong girl; play along and say *"we have to see if we get along first,"* as in no money before the honey. You're planting the seed and sub-consciously teasing her, just like she is doing by wearing hip huggers and a midriff with her nipples popping out. It's just a matter of who cracks first.

## Testing her Intentions

Remember, this is a one-drink date for feeling her out; a quick hit and run. Your initial date suggestion with her was *"Let's get together for a drink over at _X_ place."* Naturally, you're looking for a girl who devotes all her attention to you. Look for smiles, constant eye contact, a good sense of humor, is all touchy feely, oozes sex appeal, and is great company. If your chick is not curling your toes and throwing a great vibe, you can be in for some free bonus entertainment. On dates that aren't progressing well, a pretentious babe just can't keep her inner whore instincts under control. She'll spend the whole date with her eyes wandering around, checking her cell phone every five minutes. Suddenly, she'll fake sexual interest and then yank out the menu and try to parlay the one drink date into some expensive meal and a half dozen high dollar drinks she would never pay for herself. Let her grab the waiter and sit there with a smile while she orders. *"Do you mind?"* Just sit back and shrug your shoulders. Then, when the waiter turns to you, hand him cash and close the tab for your one drink. (not hers). Say: *"Gotta run. I sold my business for 8 figures and the closing is in an hour. I can't waste any more time on such trivial matters."* Get up and leave.

Keep your peripheral eye trained and locked on. Some of these bitches can hurl a dinner plate at your head with uncanny accuracy.

The scene makes for a great reaction on their face, similar to a melting candle. On the way out, tip the waiter, and then bet him a buck that she cancels her order after you leave. Better yet, when she tries to cancel, have him tell her it's too late and it'll be out in a minute. After she goes into hysterics, he can get a great laugh and then say *just kidding.*

## Exploit the Alpha Waiter

Find a great place or two for quick patio dates, and take ALL your first dates there. Get to know the friendliest, stud waiter. Make sure he has different taste in women, or he may be a cockblock. Buddy up with the guy, tip well, and get any inside dirt he may have on the girls you bring there. Create your own Groundhog Day sequence over and over. Develop 3rd base coach hand signals between you and him about your dates. Get referrals on other hot prospects in the patio target area. You'd be surprised how often the waiters drop the bomb and inform that you blew it and chose a professional dater, ie., a con-artist broad he's seen with three other dudes in the last week. Flip him an extra fin if he points out which of the hard bodies at the nearby tables are horny married MILFS hiding rings.

# Dinner at your Pad:

For second or third dates, you score major points cooking dinner for her and watching a movie at your place, or doing a stroll in the park and having a wine and cheese picnic. (For strippers, make it a bong and vibrator lunch). These dates show originality, separate you from the wimps, and generate an emotional response. They are far more personal and effective in creating attraction than just showing you can spend money at Club Fat Cat. It displays the coveted "family man" skills, and puts her in the romantic mood. It also puts her physically next to you in the *closing booth*. If you happen to be a prolific 1$^{st}$ date closer, have the bleachers setup and popcorn ready in the bedroom for your buddies. Nothing wrong with sharing the wealth and the view. Quiet on the set. Lights, Cameras, . .and….. Action.

# The Player's TV Setup

Keep a 27 inch TV in the family room, but put the Big Screen in your bedroom. After dinner, it's time to get her plastered and grope, I mean it's time to share a quiet, intimate moment wiping tears away watching a romantic comedy together. "This is such a special moment. Hold me, Buffy." The reverse TV locations work great as it gets her in your bed, while allowing her to make the decision. When it's movie time, say:

> *"I don't care which TV we use. I usually watch TV in bed,*
> *so I put the big screen in there. Which one do you prefer?"*

Of course she'll say the bedroom, unless you keep the castle looking like a dumpster. Being a Professional Bachelor, that would never happen now, would it? The pad is very important, as it is a reflection of your life and character. Girls scrutinize this heavily, just like the shine of your shoes, and the bulge of your wallet. Your place should be designed to show stability in your life, full of photos showing a strong family unit, some education plaques, sports trophies and awards. Naturally you'll be a hip audiophile. You'll have some classy furniture, the token wine rack, cook books, cool lighting and wall fixtures, paintings, etc. Clearly you should hire someone else to create the layout for you. We're not fags after all. As painful as it is, you can always get advice from sassy Bruce, the interior designer at the gym in the pink shorts. You know, the guy who crosses his fingers when he farts. Who knows? He may refuse to give you his opinion until you give him the one drink Groundhog Day patio date with the same waiter.

# Advanced Alpha Pad

When you bring the babes into The Alpha Love Nest, they observe a snapshot of what a classy, well-rounded successful guy you are. That means you need to plan ahead and make some sacrifices. The innocent Lolita blow-up doll. Gone. Ms. 2007 Shaved Cheerleaders calendar on the walls. Gone. That sporty new Turbo-suck Vacuum cleaner you dress up in silk

Lingerie. Gone. Neidermeyer. Gone. Yes, it means you have to take down the Golden Hand trophy on your mantle. You know the one. You got it by smashing the single year record for jar purchases of Vaseline. The illustrious Wanker of the Year distinction. Remember how proud you felt when the CEO handed you the trophy, but refused to shake? Gone. This is all going to hurt at first. No crying in the time out room, big boy. You can keep the keg hidden in the laundry room. I mean we have some standards.

You should have your place decked out with touching memories of your extraordinarily successful childhood. On the fireplace mantel, place your fake Photoshop pictures of you dancing with the Prom Queen, you scaling Mt. Everest, you meeting the Pope and the President, and the family photos showing your ties to both Bill Gates and the Michael Dell. Have up plaques for all the Ivy League scholarships you got, certified letters for your numerous Valedictorian awards, the 7 figure starting salary job offer letters in gold-plated frames. Pay attention to detail, and only buy the quality sports trophies at the Local Pawn shop. The Heisman Trophy you won should not be made of cheap silver that dents easily. Get the dates right for the Olympics medals too; this prevents wasting valuable sex time trying to explain how you were silver medallist for the Decathlon at Berlin in '36.

*"I had to fuel up the DeLorean flux capacitor for that one honey,
I couldn't qualify in Sydney..."*

## The Closing Booth

When it comes to the closing booth, you can't ask permission for a kiss, fondling, groping, and eventually sex. Trying to convince a girl with words to sleep with you is usually a deal breaker. She has to want it physically and emotionally, and has to welcome the moves. Sex is not a thought-based process; it takes lust and feelings, or 6 martinis; whichever comes first.

Monitor the situation, get a good feel, and take action. Stay a gentleman, but **you** have to make the moves, (while accusing her of moving too quickly). Take it two steps forward, one step back, repeat....tease her, step back, peel some clothes off, then lean away from her. Build anticipation until it drives her crazy. Most girls will mildly test you in the closing booth if you move too quickly. Give the impression that it's no big deal if she doesn't want sex. Back off and re-group. If she still wants it, she'll start things up again. Once she's naked, you arrive at the best time to give compliments. Girls are always insecure about some part of their body. The big egg yoke nipples, a tiny cellulite area on the back of their thighs, giant labia resembling a pink catchers mitt, a sewer pussy with an echo. Pick out a potential spot you think she may dislike, and fire away: *"God I love your tight little ass,"* or *"I love your musky dumpster scent...I love your musky dumpster scent."* Lie if you have to; in these situations you can't go wrong. Don't overdue it, just one or two compliments and leave it at that.

Now, if you have pushed forward too quickly, it can be a deal breaker for multiple reasons. Be attentive. Don't fret about it, or come across as needy. Just stop, kiss her, pull back and listen. It may be a minor test. Women don't like to feel like a conquest, and always fear being labeled a slut. Worst scenario; if she has no sex drive, she'll let you know. If that's the case, nail her roommate when she's out of town. Then she'll be forced to listen to how incredible you are in bed. Next!

## The Movie Date Close

Back to the movie date at your pad. Let's say you're watching the Big Screen TV in bed. After a little while, start putting up a bogus fight. Tell her she's treating you like a piece of meat, and putting on the moves too fast. Play hard to get, but make sure all your body language angles accidentally include having your crotch inches from her face. If necessary, swing from the twirling ceiling fan butt naked pleading with her until she blows you. Eventually she'll give you a sympathy hummer, just to stop the painful back cracks and screams you unleash. If that doesn't work, threaten to impersonate Neil Diamond. During the BJ, try to balance the remote or your beer on her head while she's bobbing. Tell her she's growing a huge bald spot on top, just like her sister.

By the way, the Cheap Charlie approach is only for the first few dates, the feeling out period. After you start officially dating and bonking, she's earned your trust. Then you start doing the fun, more expensive dates together. That's why you work, to enjoy the good life the income affords you. She earned the right to enjoy the ride by being honest upfront about her interest in you, and not your wallet. Time to throw all caution to the wind and Super size her meals.

## Weeding out the Con Artists

The main reason to invite a girl over your place on the 2$^{nd}$ or 3$^{rd}$ date is to accelerate the Speed Dating Chase, and find out if she is sincerely attracted to you. The approach swiftly weeds out the scammers, I mean the self-proclaimed "high class" girls. They never, *ever* accept a dinner date at your place, since sex is the last thing on their mind. To the inexperienced man in the field, these girls will appear to be the infamous **Trophy Women**. The ones who demand to be wined and dined like royalty for zero return. For target sighting, here's some pointers. The virgin TWs are seen winking at every guy walking by them while they window shop at Tiffany's, and expensive department stores. The amateur gold diggers (GDs) are found hovering in the VIP rooms in nightclubs. Look for ten pounds of makeup, 30 pound suitcase sized gold purses; watch for chicks plastered on martinis, constantly rubbing their coke-stained noses. The shameless veteran GDs are seen in front row floor seats at NBA playoff games asking their 60 yr old date if the white referee is Shaq. The Pro Trophy Cons can be found blowing freshly widowed Gazillionaires at funerals and in old folks homes. One telltale sign for spotting all of them; you will never actually see them paying for anything in life. The motion of reaching into a purse and handing over currency has been known to cause heart attacks. If you're in a hurry to find the GDs, put on a huge shiny fake Rolex in a nightclub, and rapidly swing the arm with the watch left to right ten times. Look for cross-eyed silicone bleach blondes falling off their heels with motion sickness.

# Conclusion:

By concentrating on zeroing in on the sexy, honest targets utilizing the low CPF, effective Speed Dating eliminates eighty percent of the time and money wasted courting the wrong women. It keeps you in complete control. You increase their desire because you play hard to get, and are nobody's fool. It cuts to the chase, and requires women to be completely sincere about their intentions; a very scary proposition for most of them. Most guys think the way to impress a girl is to spend more and more. Wrong, wrong, wrong.

The initial dates are a dry run to see if you dig her company. Judge a girl by her actions, not her words. Focus entirely on how she treats you. Pay close attention to her body language. Does she show you respect and ooze genuine interest? Do her eyes shine, and face glow when she looks at you? Does she constantly smile and run her hands all over you? Or is she is merely tolerating and testing you? Does she announce certain things you say or do appear on her negative check off list? Do you see calculating coal black eyes without a soul, and feel strange itching sensations after she touches you? Learn to spot this stuff a mile away. It's a number game; cut your losses quick, and move like a cheetah till you find a few keepers.

Dates are as much a time for her to be proving herself to *you,* as you to her. Forgot draining your bank account. It's far more effective to concentrate on your presentation than your wallet. They want to see how you carry yourself…your confidence, attitude, direction in life, and a sense of humor.

**Create scarcity** for yourself by being busy; give the impression you're always about to leave, and that she needs to do things that you like to keep your attention. **Create value** by showing high social status; show the ability to spend, but that you won't be manipulated. Dress well, cologne, shiny shoes, nice car, be a gentleman; but the first dates should be short; a movie, a coffee, a drink somewhere. Skip the 5 star restaurants or big expenses, whether you have ten dollars or ten million dollars. In fact, a low CPF shines best when she knows you make a lot of money. This way you are a huge challenge. On the first date, if she goes into the attention whore princess routine, or in your car acts like a rude prostitute, answering cell calls from other guys, take her to the nearest 7-11, send her in for beer, condoms, and a Hustler, and leave her sorry ass there.

# What's the  C  P  F ?

I suppose you're wondering what **The CPF** is. It's a running joke I tell quantifying how much money spent on a new girl before the first lay. The Cost-per-Fuck. It's stood the test of time across the globe; the lower the CPF, the fewer the scammers, the higher probability closing ratio, the better the sex, and the better the relationship. Why? Because everything is based on honesty upfront.

Any guy who calls me up for a field report and asks "So how was she?", a normal reply would be *"Her body was an 9, the helmet a 7.5, performance was a strong 8.5. The CPF got a little out of hand though, it nearly hit double digits."* I've had many $0 CPF's with some scorching, young knockouts. Last month I had a smoking hot Brazilian bombshell appear out of nowhere and do me for 9 straight days for something like a $8 CPF per date. (booze and movie at home). There was no reason to take her anywhere; she said she just wanted to stay home and rape me. (on day 10, her fiancée returned from an extended business trip, and she disappeared into the sunset. I was used like a piece of meat. *I faked the orgasms beeotch!*

It's all psychology in this aspect. It has nothing to do with money. You will find a low CPF has uncanny success with girls who are used to being spoiled rotten by fool's spending the family inheritance trying to impress them. You're different; you're the international man of mystery.

# Me So Horny Crash Course

By the way, back to the original story about the dork and the Gold Digger Filipina. This is an area of expertise of mine. Here's some advice. You have to watch the hot ones from Thailand, Viet Nam, or the Philippines. These countries have poverty that make our "poor" look like millionaires. A college graduate's income there is $600 a month, less than half of what our so called poor get for free from our government in handouts, in return for voting democrat. (*Vote for Freebies* should be the Dem platform.) Overseas, many girls work family rice farms for Zero dollars a year. When they turn eighteen, millions of girls are encouraged to leave home and earn a living to support the family. This means only one thing. Many of them end up working in "full service" strip clubs. It's morally accepted behavior, as it's one of the few jobs available. Contrary to the media lies about sex slaves, the bargirls volunteer for the job and consider themselves overwhelming fortunate to have found such an easy career path to "fame and fortune." Most girls love the job, as they party all night with their friends, instead of the 18-hour work days of hard labor they left back home. The vast majority are mature adults who willingly continue to work in the sex industry not out of need, but out of greed. Some of the hotties make an equivalent of five hundred to thousand dollars a days. Some of them take limos to work.

# Me Wuv You Long Time

In the US, girls from Thailand, Viet Nam and Filipinas will be one of three types. **The first type** are the sweetest, shyest, most subservient girls you've ever met. Date them the minute one bats her eyes at you. Most of them are scooped up and married quickly. The **second type** of these girls are smart, hard working, successful businesswomen. They're usually self-employed, and get ahead quickly because they never pay a penny in taxes. The **last type** are pure hustlers. These girls are usually gorgeous, dress to kill, and are totally untrustworthy. They are often ex-prostitutes who worked near American naval bases overseas. When the aircraft carriers pull in, the hottest girls at the clubs do a dozen or two men a day. A lot of these girls pay a military guy a few grand for a bogus marriage, get their green card, and move here and divorce. They are born nymphomaniac con artists.

If you are in the US and you meet a Thai, VN, or Filly who drives a Mercedes but has no visible means of support, you have spotted the wrong type. They have five to ten Sugar Daddies at a time, and are incapable of telling the truth about anything. I wouldn't believe one if they told me what time it is. However, I'm all for the nympho trait. I have several Asian girlfriends who are married, and whenever they are in my area, they stop by and give me Hall of Fame blowjobs. It's like breathing to them. Great for me, but I wouldn't want to be the guy on the other end not knowing.

The guy in the Hummer story really takes the cake. His girl looked exactly like this sexy Filipina whore I know, but wouldn't touch. She points her nose to the sky and is one of the biggest gold-diggers in town. She will literally tell you upfront *"you can't afford me, I'm high class"*, meaning she rents her pussy to any dork willing to pay an exorbitant price. Amazingly, there are lonely idiots who believe she just presents a challenge, and set out to prove her wrong. She gets a new sucker every week.

Brett Tate knows her past very well, which is why he turned down her coochie for free. She was a military base whore outside Manila for six straight years. The guys that date her think they have a hot prize. In reality, she should be wearing a T Shirt that says, *"I fucked the entire 7ʰ fleet, and all I got was this T Shirt"*. When she sits and crosses her legs, you hear loud squishing noises. Hell, you could probably put your whole leg in there.

> " We should look upon the female state as it were a deformity,
> though one that occurs in the ordinary course of nature. "

**ARISTOTLE,** *brilliant philosopher*

# NEVER GET PINNED DOWN TOO EARLY

## Q.

*I've got this new babe who's hot to trot for me. We did the one drink first date test, and she seems really cool, interesting, and horny. There may be some potential there, but it's hard to say, since we only spoke for about thirty minutes. I'm a little concerned about one thing, though. I walked her to her car and kissed her goodbye on the cheek. Before I could even turn around, she wanted to know where we stand, what I did last night, where the relationship was going, why I seemed so distant, did I think I was I too good for her, and that I wasn't being responsive enough to her needs, wants, and desires, not to mention her biological clock was ticking.*

*On the bright side, she did appear to have a nice flat head, no teeth, and handlebar ears. I forgot to ask if her Dad owned a strip club.*

## A.

Sounds like you got a Stage 5 Clinger on your hands. This is the type of girl who accidentally brushes into your cock with one hand, while masterfully plucking out your wallet with the other.

### Bachelor Code 7
Amendment 1a, subsection 16f

**Never get pinned down into a relationship too soon.
Hold onto your independence like it's your virginity**

— — — — — —

Woman love to pin you down early on and lay territorial claims on your ass. Scientific tests have proven that an obsessive control freak is a feminine gene. By committing too soon, you're putting a piano on your back for no good reason. This allows her to barrage you with those 20 phone calls a day that last an eternity, and opens the door to her goal of sucking the life out of you with endless demands for your time, attention, and wallet. Have you forgotten? Man wasn't intended to be a groveling slave. We're meant to be in a female pulled Golden Chariot, lounging in the King's chair high above the ground, being fed grapes by insatiable naked nymphs.

Every new girl you go out with, on the first date tell her you are **just getting out of a relationship.** Say you're attracted, but need to take it slow and easy and let things naturally progress. You don't want a rebound fling.

*"Let's just enjoy each other's company for now
and take things one step at a time."*

It's the responsible adult approach, and it protects your freedom. The minute you are her property, you lose all your power over her. You will be more respected by being independent and a challenge. She will be on a quest to be the one who wins you over, which entitles you to her best behavior. Once they own you, it never gets better. They get lazy. So don't worry about damage control by being distant. If she starts becoming less fun and continually complains about *"where do we stand?"*, ie, the slow pace of you accelerating spending money on her, you may have chosen the wrong girl. This is why you chose this approach. It's a built in excuse to get rid of her when her personality changes.

Even if you've had sex half a dozen times, maintain your independence, at least a month or two. If she starts up with commitment demands, remind her you were completely honest upfront about taking it slow and being on the rebound. It takes time to determine if she is a chameleon who's role-playing her way into a relationship under false pretenses. Naturally you dangle the possibility of a commitment, but when you rush into relationships it screams of weakness, and jeopardizes the results. Here are a couple stock lines to help keep your independence:

*"Let's be patient and make sure this really works.*
*I don't want to rush into things and see you get hurt."*

*"Let's not be too impulsive.*
*Sometimes being too anxious ruins a good thing."*

*"I may turn out to be less than what you expect."(yuk, yuk)*

*"I'm still banging three nympho freshmen on the side,*
*and don't want to cut into that action."*

*"The blowjobs aren't that good honey. Trust me, you'd never get hired*
*at a third rate Asian massage parlor with that action."*

*"A relationship, are you fucking nuts?!!!*

# KEEP YOUR EMOTIONS ON ICE

Rushing into a relationship is a sign of insecurity and weakness to women. An expert controls his emotions, and always maintains the upper hand. Stir as much interest as you can, but remain non-committed to a relationship in the beginning. Encourage their advancements and sexual innuendos, act turned on and attracted, but remain detached. Remember. Girls don't like a guy who is an easy lay. Where's the challenge? Holding out and not settling shows high self-esteem, brings you greater respect, and increases your desirability. It becomes each suitor's quest to be the one who conquers you. This creates curiosity, unease, and ever-building sexual tension and desire.

Until you have been with a girl several months, you have to remain distant. The freedom from being controlled by another is a valuable commodity not easily surrendered. Falling too quickly for a girl is a test of your self-discipline and sanity. Women are highly emotional creatures. Being involved on a daily basis sucks you into her girlfriend banter, battles and arguments. In due time, you'll lose your mind being preoccupied with trying to solve her imaginary conflicts and issues. You develop a co-dependency to the perpetual crisis. Life is too short to be an emotional tampon for women. They drag you into things that have nothing to do with you. Not to say you should ignore her daily events. Be compassionate, sympathetic, take her side on everything, but do it from a distance. Tell her she's right, but you can't talk because you have some pressing work you have to take care of immediately. Remember the value of your dating time management. Never get involved in her problems. Ever.

*"Good luck in your battles. Come on over later and we'll watch a comedy to cheer you up. I'll keep the hot tub warm.*
*Don't forget to bring your thong and some beer."*

If your girl is the type who loves to call you up everyday and go straight into smothering you with her hang-ups, or only calls when she needs a favor, from day one you have to shut her down in a hurry. Never get suckered in to that role. It only gets worse.

*"Whoa whoa, put the brakes on honey. I'm not your errand boy, or the guy you call up and dump all your problems on. That's what Moms are for. I'm the fun, party guy you love to hang out with getting drunk and naked."*

# Chapter IV

# ADVANCED SEDUCTION ROLE-PLAYING TECHNIQUES

Create Emotional Attraction by
Satisfying her Weakness

# The Devils Lure in Seducing Women

Role-playing and the conversation tools of persuasion dramatically improve your seduction skills and elevate your closing ratio. In this section, we cover how to **Give her the Emotions she wants to Feel**. As you acquire an understanding of the how and why a conversation brings out a desired outcome, you become more adept at mastering the end game. Women protect their independence with a natural barrier of resistance. Change can be scary. It's always easier for her to say no, even when she is licking her lips picturing you naked. But there are ways to soften her up, and let her attraction and desire overcome her reasoning. Your job is to determine the easiest way to break down her shields and provide her with appearance of potentially satisfying her weaknesses.

Every girl has a weakness, an emotional void missing in her life. A relationship is her attempt to satisfy this need. By analyzing your target's beliefs, desires and needs, it's just a matter of assuming the appropriate role and providing a solution to her dilemma. The answers to her hidden wants can be many things, but it usually starts with a lack of lust, adventure, and excitement. Take a long hard look at your target. Women are chronic worriers. Insecurity is their middle name, no matter how cocky they act.

The sexiest girl who's the center of attention would die if she were suddenly cast aside; the strongest presentation often hides the weakest ego. Likewise, the trophy babe who brags about her job and money craves social status. If she woke up tomorrow unemployed without her Mercedes, the thought of being an irrelevant low class chick would have her crying in a psych office for a year. The rich cocky appearance hides social status insecurity, and probably a pile of debt.

Explore deeper. A girl's exterior presentation and surface personality is often a mask. It's what she believes is the social norm, and what will give her the most attention and best results. But it is not the whole story. It is also a disguise to hide her weaknesses. This makes the job that much easier for the seducer. Face it, it's not like it's difficult to pump a girl's ego. The only talent lies in maintaining your own challenge status and desirability in her mind while doing it. Let's take the lack of adventure weakness. The girls who crave excitement are often the ones you least expect. Many times you'll find the quiet ones, the girl next door dressed down like a tomboy is wildly passionate, as sexual adventures rarely seem to come her way. Dig levels deeper when you analyze their weak points. Listen closely when she speaks about what she fears, is hiding, or wants more than anything. Listen to what she holds dear, and what would hurt her most if she lost it.

What has she lacked in previous relationships? What was she missing in her childhood? Where does she want to be in 5 years? What does her job keep her from doing? Who is she most envious of, and why? Does she desire role-playing herself, and want to be treated the opposite of who people think she is. Does she want a daddy figure, and bad boy, an intellectual, or an adrenaline junkie? Her clothes, her idols, her hairstyle, her music choice, the clues are everywhere; your job is to decipher them in casual interviewing, while appearing only mildly curious. You can jumpstart the process by telling her about your own hidden secrets and desires. By exposing yourself with real or imaginary weaknesses, two things will happen. She'll either counsel you, or share her own.

There are different techniques to satisfy each weakness. After choosing your target, her personality will lead you towards one of the approaches that will work best out in the field when it comes time to seduce her. Watch their reactions, and adjust as necessary. The following chapters are a number of role-playing techniques designed to lower the bitch shields. Each one applies a different remedy. Giving the appearance of satisfying her weakness should be easy to do. The talent lies in your ability to subtly give her the approval she desperately seeks, while still playing hard to get and being the mystery man. Your poise and self-assurance will stimulate her sub-conscious. Your target, without the benefit of knowing the real details of your life, will let her imagination be drawn to your energy, and provide a mental image far more generous than you may deserve. Women desire a man who takes control of what he wants, and if attracted they love to be playfully steered into the player's lair. This relieves her of any guilty feelings of being responsible for her own actions.

## Handling Women testing You

Women will present barriers so as to never appear to be easy. A confident player simply brushes them aside as part of the cat and mouse game, and shows no reaction but a smile. Use reverse psychology. Learn to push her female insecurity buttons with funny teasing comments instead of seeking approval. Be persistent, coy, and a confident jerk. Now if you've gone a few dates and accidentally screw up big time with some irrelevant comment and she becomes eyes bulging furious, cut your losses quickly and let her go. Men are compassionate. When there's sex involved, we forgive and move forward. Not so with women. You can never repair the damage and start fresh with a woman, unless **she** initiates the regrouping. The magic is gone once you enter the damage zone. Every controversy going forward she will eventually bring this moment up again in a rage, as well as every other little imaginary mistake. Women never forgive. That's why you have to always be upbeat, distant, and completely vague in discussing anything with them, so they can't use words as ammunition against you in the future. Until proven otherwise, never assume a girl to be honest or rational.

# Dumb as a Fox

**P**eople occupy their minds with their daily rituals, worries, hobbies, goals, and dreams. An expectation of effortlessly flowing into a new woman's life is ego-driven, and rarely a high probability event. Most women tend to shut others out when being spoken to, unless they hear what they want to hear. To break through the monotony of their self-centered beliefs, they must first *allow you to do so*. Few women consent to an aggressive newcomer invading their space and life, unless he is exceedingly handsome, or rich. Even then, the fresh Boy Toy tends to be rarely more than a passing fancy.

There is always a bitch shield to overcome, not to mention the condescending posse of girlfriends who believe their purpose in life is stop each other from ever allowing a man to have a good time. Women are taught to be cynically skeptical of men, and since they are approached constantly, they have tons of practice blowing them out. To make it worse, most guys mimic one another, and present bad game. It's highly predictable. The pickup attempt is awkward, too forward, and the guy's conversation veers off quickly into sexual innuendos and propositions within moments after the first hello. This is fine and preferred if the tables are turned, but women aren't backed up to the ears with testosterone like men.

## Soften her Ego with Misdirection

The hotter looking a woman is, the more likely you're dealing with an ego superiority complex. Whether it's her looks, social status, or intelligence, she doesn't like to be challenged. Correct her incorrect statement, she thinks you're calling her dumb. Discuss a hot looking ex-girlfriend of yours, she thinks you're calling her less attractive. Her ego will see you as a competitor, not a suitor. Since she wants to win the battle, she will blow you off and not give you the time of day, or worse, she'll lead you on and play the extortion game. The smart Alpha Players use this knowledge to their advantage. Lay low like a sleeping serpent, and keep your cards close to your chest. Play to a woman's ego, don't battle with it. There's always time to play hard to get as the chase evolves.

## The Angle

The approach discussed in this chapter is like walking in backwards into a room. It's complete role reversal compared to the typical male approach. You do what girls do to guys; your intention is to go in with the *Friends First* approach. You earn the trust of numerous women by making no effort to seduce them. You befriend them in a harmless fashion, with an Alpha persona that is interesting, yet uninterested. The purpose is to remove all forms of resistance, and create a comfort zone quickly. You are not the standard enemy combatant they protect each other from. From here you spin your seduction web and slowly lure in the targets.

# The Opening Approach

You enter a social gathering or club and look for the hottest posse of babes in the room. Walk straight up and nonchalantly introduce yourself to all of them. Memorize each name. To each group of girls approached you explain you are the Fresh out of a Relationship Guy.

*"You girls can put your shields away, and no hitting on me. I just got out of a heavy relationship with Satan's daughter, and I just want to meet some new people. I'm sure you've all been there."*

They of course all smile and agree with you. Your persona is the cool, indifferent Alpha male in the background. Rarely speak. When you do, make it light, completely vague small talk, and throw in some observational humor about other people in the club. All girls love shredding people. Smile casually, and nod the head a lot. Have no opinion on anything. Ever. Play the Alpha Flat line Guy.

Your body language is non-aggressive, pointing away from them all. Every time a good-looking guy walks by, grab him and play the Mr. Introduction role to all the girls. Big bonus points if you remember all their names. Since you are providing the girls all the attention and handing over new meat with no work on their part, you move up a few notches quickly in their minds. If you're smart, this strategy works very well with a wingman. However, make sure he is actually somewhat of a Player and not an Anchor, otherwise you lose points. Separate at the door, and when the wingman goes by, pretend you're strangers; grab him and introduce. Now you are both meeting and working the group. Both of you should be exiting within minutes.

# The Casual Cool Distant Look

Do a lot of mild grinning, and occasional winks. Maintain the traditional confident strong posture: chin high, shoulder width stance, and no quick movements. No primping fools here, well-dressed, unshaved with spiked hair. Drink a Red Bull or water instead of alcohol. Explain to the girls you have to get up at 6am. Have a pre-planned high-energy adventurous story/role; in the morning you have to run 10 miles, train for mountain climbing, skydive, fly to Vegas for the poker tournament, or some exotic vacation or business trip. You're a consumed, vivacious, action-oriented guy. (Preferably *you should* be an action guy, it's a great avenue to meet girls) Despite being in a drinking environment, this angle eliminates the impression of being a bar fly drowning his sorrows away. Girls hate drunks.

You are creating mystique in their minds. To pass time, check out the décor of the club like a seasoned museum expert. Talk to yourself out loud, expressing amused discontent at the artwork period chosen. Simulate kung fu moves, imitate bizarre animal noises, and speak Chinese into your cell phone. If asked, translate it as *"Buy, Sell, Buy, Sell. Offer a Billion two, and not a penny more."*

Take inventory of which girls in the group are smiling often in your direction, do a silent *clinking the drink* toasts, without speaking. Your eye contact is sort of the glazed look. You are peering off into the distance in soft focus, like your mind is elsewhere. No glaring, staring, and refrain from getting caught eyeing other girls strutting by in the club. In fact, make no focused eye contact at all. While no one is looking, examine the ladies outfits, and find something unique on the girl(s) who give you the most attention…maybe her shoes or earrings.

Spend just 5 to 10 minutes in the area, and then make a casual exit. *"I see an old friend across the room; it was great to meet you girls. Try to go easy on the guys. You look like you are on the prowl and haven't been fed in a while."* Start to walk away a few steps. Then turn back to the girl who gave you some looks, and tell her *"I really like those high heels on you"*, or whatever item it was you picked out. Then walk away before she comments. This raises the eyebrows and creates some intrigue, as it seemed you were oblivious to them, yet you actually had a keen eye. (Next time you see this group of girls somewhere, do the same thing, and as you leave, throw a parting compliment to a different girl in the posse.)

Move to another area in the bar, do the same thing with more packs of girls. After a half hour, circle back to the first pack and to the girl(s) most receptive, and ask what other clubs they prefer. Start to walk away, and almost as a side thought, turn around and touch her shoulder and say *"I need your number so I can meet up with you girls again. You can show me where all the cool people hang out. "* If you get a no, laugh it off and ask the girl right next to her using *the exact same words*, talking in an ridiculously slow manner. One of them will say yes.

You are showing interest in all of them, and not being aggressive, while singling one out. Get a few numbers from different groups each night, get a lot of names, and leave the club, skipping along in your carefree manner. Work a few clubs a week, just a meet and greet…*"you girls are really cool, blah, blah"* and split. No opinions, no work talk. Nothing but an occasional wink and smirk. Within no time, you have a pocket full of numbers, and will be seeing the same packs of girls elsewhere. You quickly build up comfort zone points with dozens of potential targets.

# Master the Listening Role

Ever had a client call you up for the first time in months or years, and he remembers every little detail about you, your life, favorite sports teams, birthdays, anniversaries, and the specific things you discussed on previous calls. Your first thought is one of amazement of how sharp his recollection ability is. Well, here's the Inside Baseball for you. The movers and shakers of the world remember all these little things because when they are on the phone they are *taking very specific notes.* They have whole file cabinets or laptops dedicated to just this purpose. Every person they come in contact with who has the potential to be involved in his life down the road, they take notes. They ALWAYS have a pen and paper handy. They review the notes prior to calling you, or meeting you somewhere. If they meet you unexpectedly, they will hit the john and review their notes on their blackberry. Also, when they meet you in person, they will be taking notes soon after departing. It is not by accident they are so sharp. This approach gets you places must faster. Personally, Brett Tate is not very good at the phone call note taking. So he puts people on speaker phone, and calls over his ever so hot Latina secretary; "*Honey, come over here and sit in my lap and take some Dicktation.*"

In the Dumb as a Fox role you need to be attentive and quick with the wits, because a steady flow of information for future use will come your way. While pretending to just hang out, you are actually taking inventory on ALL the girls'; names, jobs, life stories, dislikes, and weaknesses. This will be a whole new experience, because *you are actually listening to what girls say.* I know, I know. No crying at the thought. Take deep breaths and relax. There's nothing sneaky about being prepared, or a good listener. Here's what you do. Every 15 minutes or so, excuse yourself to get a drink, or to go say hi to someone across the club. At that point, hit the nearest bathroom stall, call your own answering machine, or pull out your paper and pen and jot down your notes. Don't pull anything else out, while thinking about the girls. We're professionals here, dammit. Keep your writing and the notes private. If you ever get caught, just say you don't want to be rude and make people repeat things, particularly since you just met everyone.

Then you start up again in Round 2 meeting the same girls out. Stay sober, as this role requires an advanced attention span. In a few weeks, you will meet more girls by saying you don't want a girlfriend, than you would in months by trying real hard to get one.

Pick out 3 or 4 of them that show the most interest, and start having ever-lengthening phone calls that start with the *meeting all the girls out* angle, but are more introspective of her life, and the problems she wished some man would solve. Develop more of a friendship over the phone, but always throw in how you are just getting over a relationship and not ready for anything more than friends.

Each successive time you run into the girls around town, it's more of the same. You are never hitting on them, you just pop over for a quick vague chit chat and then move on. You stay a little bit longer with each meeting. Vague, friendly, non-committal comments about nothing. Virtually no depth in any conversation, a few smiles, and then bubbye. It will seem strange at first, like you have an IQ of 50 or something, but the purpose is very subtle and effective. You are building rapport and mystique, while doing virtually nothing.

You continue taking info and determine which girls are more receptive, and get more phone numbers. As you learn the locations the girl frequent and memorize their daily patterns, you keep accidentally running into them, acting completely surprised, of course. In a nutshell, you are slowly but surely becoming part of a posse or three, and have a stack of phone numbers. You never offer up any real information about yourself, and are completely vague when asked anything. You never hit on any of them directly. All phone calls with the girls are short, and upbeat. Never individualize the girls on the phone; act as if you are talking to the whole pack. Throw in a few comments about how you girls are all so cool, and how nice it is to meet such positive, energetic women..."it's so different from your last relationship," blah, blah.

## Halftime Scorecard

You're a complete mystery to all of them. More importantly, as they slowly have become completely secure with you, they grow to be very curious. The bitch shields never even appeared. In the process of the game, they'll notice every time they see you it is with a lot of good looking girls. You continue to be Friends First with every hot girl everywhere you go in front of the posse...but quickly move on. The player persona is slowly sneaking into their mind, but since you've been so innocent in your conversations with them, they won't know what to think. You will become the subject of a lot of debate amongst them. Pretty soon, if you have the look and attitude down just right, there will be a subconscious battle beginning on which girl is going to have you first. You act naïve of the whole thing.

## Advanced Levels

One of the most effective roles to use when your game is really high is to combine this role with playing dumb. You read that right; you are the cocky, fun, dumb Alpha Male. You rarely speak at all. It's also spin-off version of the Classy Bad Boy (see chapter). The strategy works because it combines mixed and conflicting signals. The girls just can't seem to figure you out. You are clearly confident in approaching them from the beginning, but you are not trying to pick them up. By rarely speaking, they don't know a thing about you; **mystery always attracts**. Any questions about work, you dodge with a simple "*I'm an entrepreneur*," and then say "*Sorry, no interviews tonight, let's just let our hair down and have fun.*" You don't ask anything about them. You learn their details by eavesdropping.

As time passes, you will have met out these same packs of girls multiple times. Each time you are "building on something", creating a comfort zone. Steadily you earn their confidence through brief, upbeat conversations, when in fact all you are doing is standing there smiling and looking stupid. Women don't like the feeling of being intimidated when it comes to intelligence, but it happens all the time around men. This leaves a wide open door for the deceptive player to shine in their minds. Nothing strokes a woman's vanity more than complimenting her brilliant mind. When you put yourself down in self-deprecating fashion, and make her feel superior, it's a slam dunk. Granted, it's as difficult as telling a beefy wench how much you love fat, but it's overwhelming effective. Whatever the topic, in a very subtle fashion, you let the girl know that you are not as smart as her. Throw in side comments like...

"Why didn't I see that angle? You're right again."
"You're something else. I never thought of it that way,"
"Buffy, your mind just moves way quicker than mine,"
"Ho de do, who am be you? Einstein?"
"Damn bitch. You fucking brilliant and shit."

Appealing to a woman's intelligence creates a target who is overconfident, and borderline cocky. Sometimes they completely drop their guard because they feel sorry for you. The upbeat dumb guy is endearing to women in almost a childlike fashion. You're just so loveable and cute to have around. (gag). You play the aw shucks role to the T, and act like you're a virgin. Soon they feel like "protecting" you from the bad girls out there, and this can quickly lead to a buffet of sympathy fucks.

It's only a matter of time before the girls will start counseling you on how you need to let go of the bad previous relationship, and start dating again. They will set you up with someone, or compete to go out with you on their own. The seduction is complete. They will have made the move thinking it was their own idea. The last thing they expect is that you owned them from the minute you laid eyes on them.

Some of the most successful A-team players running the field have worked this angle for years. It shows what subtle irony exists in the whole pickup world. Most guys work it too hard. They talk and talk and talk trying to win a girl over. They oversell themselves, overspend, make themselves easily accessible as opposed to scarce, and ultimately get nowhere. It's the guy who slyly puts the least effort into it who gets the best results.

# THE CLASSY BAD BOY

It is human nature for men and women to imitate each other's actions, in compliance with societal norms. From fashion, appearance, conversation and mannerisms, it is a world of predictability in each culture. This generates an orderly environment, a safe haven for the timid followers of the world, and compliant nice guys. It also creates a perfect window of opportunity for the mysterious, untamed bad boy. An avenue is wide open for those who differentiate themselves by being impulsive, brash and undeterred by social restrictions. Rebellion is an aphrodisiac.

It is the dark rebel whose non-conformity reeks of sexual tension. Bad boys are reckless, untamed, and wired with sexuality. Tommy Lee, Clint Eastwood, Brad Pitt, Antonio Banderas, Vin Diesel, Johnny Depp, and rock stars all take advantage of this style. The high-class rebel is a curiosity, and a trendsetter. He is seemingly unconcerned with the restrictions of a moral compass, or what others think of him. This extreme confidence, and a capacity for indifference are magnets for both sexes. This does not require flamboyance or showy attitude; only subtleness. Eccentrically appealing, and yet radically uninterested in giving a damn about anything but what interests him. Mocking the norms is a defiance that is anything but insecure. These are not efforts aimed at trying to please others. No selfish flashy ego, or exaggerated forceful attitude. It's a lure of the forbidden, the challenge of the emotionally untouchable that turns ladies into whores.

He seeks not attention, but attracts it in droves. No matter how much surface jealousy people show, underneath there is always a fascination of the dark figures in society. A self-assured refusal to be conventional is a sexual enticement to any woman, a narcissistic lightning rod to her inner naughty side. To incorporate any amount into your personality is astute. It can't be faked, but it can be mastered and exploited with reckless abandon. It's a pursuit of hedonistic pleasure. It's the ability to speak volumes, without uttering a single word.

## Perception is Reality:

In many a woman's distorted view of life, her understanding of power, money and rebellious affairs comes from the cinema, soap operas, and romance novels. In these twisted forums, there are two dominant male figures that make her toes curl. For untamed, reckless, and oozing with desire, you have the radical bad boys. Then there's the merciless gazillionaire businessman. Both men are sexually aggressive gigolos and objects of pure lust. The mega wealthy business underworld is charged with dangerous men who struggle for domination and control, while surrounding themselves with mansions laden with gold, riches, and self-proclaimed "high-class" bimbos. The fantasy equates the acquisition of wealth with ruthless, conniving madmen driven by maniacal methodologies and greed. (The possibility the money came from basic capitalism, slick advertising, and a great product never crosses their mind).

These dark fantasy men are her dream saviors, and deep down she craves to marry one. The common school of thought is that a woman is attracted because she wants to *change* the guy after marriage. Change him into some subservient, complacent fool who puts his head between his knees and succumbs to her every materialistic desire. Also known as the Pretty Woman dream. The fact that Julia Roberts was a hooker never crosses their mind. Nor does the fact their own prostitute mentality glamorizes the same slutty, get rich quick scheme. (They edited out the real ending of the movie. In the director's version, Gere nailed JR in the limo and dropped her back off at hooker row, then picked up a hotter one. Rinse and repeat.)

My line of thinking on this state of affairs is a tad more realistic. Sure, Gold Diggers wanna reform the guy. For the rest? Nah. I think most girls want to get drunk to forget their imaginary problems, and then have a loud, dirty, turbo fuck in sexual assault fashion by a Neanderthal stud, to satisfy their inner whore fantasies. Then the next day, they deny the whole thing and it's back to the secretarial phone gig; *"Thank you for calling Virgin Angel Ministries. Can I help you?"* The whole point is mute, to downright absurd anyway. The superhero stud is meant to be single. Can anyone really picture James Bond married to some 200 pound screeching old hag swinging a rolling pin at his head for not taking the trash out. Give me a fucking break.

# The Targets

Despite years of denial in PC training and feel good pap, the allure of the rogue desperado draws the weak, easy lays into your web. From Daddy's girl next door, to repressed secretaries, to sugar daddy trophy wives, from models to strippers, the rebel turns normally passive women into Nympho aggressors. Eroticism has a direct correlation between the barriers of access. This is where the nice guys of the world get it all back-asswards. Never be easy, or come across as desperate. The less you care, the more you attract. If she can have her way with you anytime she wants, where's the excitement? But if it's forbidden, untouchable, and full of mystery, her panties get steamier than Georgia asphalt in summer. (You may need to bring extra strength air freshener, you super stud.)

With this knowledge being driven home, it's easy to see why the outlaw persona is a great one to master. You are the no nonsense guy who does exactly what he wants, when he wants, without apology. You're best off to be the bad boy who has a lot of money. Combine stylish clothes with the leather, don't shave, and perfect your Elvis sneer. You are a successful entrepreneur, but you never discuss your endeavors. *"I buy stuff, I sell stuff, and keep most of it for myself... in offshore accounts, of course."*

When we're young, we want be rich. We want the shiny red sports cars, flashy suits, and showpiece girlfriends. We want to flaunt our money without a care in the world. Once you obtain considerable wealth, you discover that's the last thing you want. What becomes most important is a veil of secrecy. Through anonymity, you're unconditionally free to do whatever you want. Being invisible provides a camouflage over any suspicions. The reality of power takes precedent over the appearance of it. Through secrecy, you can invest as a ghost, and freely indulge in the occasional vices, illegalities, and trips to the darker, wild side of life.

## The Approach

In this role you rarely speak. You just give hints of dangerous adventures, without admitting anything. Speak third person, and never say I. Show Zero ego. Speak very slowly, use a deep voice, and practice succinct, clear pronunciation. Sound similar to a radio announcer. Slow hand movements; a stand tall, slow confident walk. No goofy, beaming smiles; control your laughter. This isn't SNL, this is smooth, confident class. Watch old Clint Eastwood movies, or Bad Boy Bruce Willis roles if you're confused. The characters play a perfect example of what we're describing, except perhaps the clothing should be a trace more darkish.

- Don't let her see you pull up to the VIP only nightclub on your "Dumb and Dumber" scooter. When it's time to leave, hail a cab to a Love Motel. No reason to blow your cover and take her back to the vomit-stained polyester couch in your pad above the parents' garage.

You live life on your terms, and can't be negotiated with. You're a take charge, no nonsense guy. You act with authority, and command respect because of the attitude. It helps to put a little fear into her as well.

- *"Last night I took my date to the ballet. We left thru a side door, and I ripped her clothes off and did her right there in the dark alley. Scared the piss out of her. We're talking a lot of piss. It went shooting out all over my pants... it was friggin' ridiculous. Do I look like a sponge? The nerve of dat girl. Where's the respect? I mean people say I'm a big thing around here. "*

# Advanced Levels

Any self-sacrificing actions you take to prove your interest in her will alleviate any doubts of your intentions. Have a wingman man approach your starstruck college hottie while she's making the moves on you. Swipe his arm away and shove him back a few feet. In a deep throaty whisper, threaten to chop his head off and shit on his neck. Slyly pop a ketchup packet in your hand, and grunt to her *"Wass da matter with dat friggin' guy? Where's da respect? You all right?"* Then slowly reach for her face, exposing the bloody hand. Smirk, and leave to go wash it off. Make sure you pretend you don't hear her when she yells at your back, *"Do you want fries with that?"* Careful cleaning up now, we don't want any crying if you stub your hangnail, sailor. Yo, Adriannnnnnnnnnn.

In any relationship, you are seemingly unavailable. You take days to return calls, and never make plans in advance. When you do it's only on your terms. You give off the air that you have an entire secret life they know nothing about. You are mysterious, and you tease heavily. Girls all want what they can't have. They will string along half a dozen guys, until they find a guy who doesn't take her bait. The others are then dumped, and she will put on the full court press to prove that you too will fall for her.

But you never do.

You're emotionally unavailable, and any ultimatum she gives, you laugh and say *"Whatever. You know that's pretty fun stuff, did you write that?"* Independence shows confidence, which commands respect. The whole approach may seem arrogant, but appearing to be not trying to pick up a girl is a far more successful approach. As a bonus, the classy bad boy persona rarely attracts girls looking for longevity; it's a very busy role.

## Bachelor Code 8
### Amendment 11, subsection 27h

- - - - - - -

**In the game of Life, Men Appreciate...
and Women depreciate.**

**Plan accordingly.**

- - - - - - -

# THE ALTERNATE PLANET

There's a certain segment of the female population that flies by the seat of their pants, without a concern in the world. Every facet of her life is oblivious to conventional structure. Traditional schools of thought are considered cynical small world thinking. Everything she learns is viewed as just one of an infinite number of possibilities. She will go impulsively from one phase in life to the next, mesmerized by each new believe system. These secular junctures can last years, or as little as one week. She dives headlong into each fantasy with every ounce of energy. The girl's hair is on fire 24/7.

What separates this target is her constant quest for alternate philosophies and "deep-rooted" thinking. She is naively receptive to any new experience, as her ability to see right from wrong is missing. She will immerse herself into almost anything; the more bizarre or foreign to western philosophy, the more exhilarating. Her deep levels of insecurity and her inferiority complex allow her to believe in fantasies with little skepticism.

Accordingly, her identity is a never-ending work in progress. This winter she could be flying to Mexico to discover if her imaginary ancestors can shed some light on her past life. Next season it's off to a New Age Commune to study 14th century astrology. Each new passion will be pursued as though she has finally discovered the Holy Grail. Impulsiveness eventually becomes reckless overindulgence. As each new potion envelops her, she is never one whom settles for being an innocent spectator along for the ride. She strives to be the leader, and experiences profound emotions and feelings in the first few days.

The standard attempts by men on the hunt in seducing this type of girl will fall flat at her feet. They take feeble stabs at her with the standard temptations of money, power, and sex. She cynically rejects these as being beneath her. After all, she's a worldly thinker! (*barf alert*) Her relationships are one big romance novel. She believes in being swept away by a powerful spiritual man, and surrenders herself to him immediately. Dating serves as a diversionary adventure, but she secretly hopes each guy will be able to show her *The Answer*. She bounces from one relationship to the next with guys sharing little in common. Each new male is her potential rescuer, so he is pursued with impassioned intensity. But the fires quickly fade.

For her appearance, think theatrics. You will see overtly skimpy and flamboyant clothing, to dressing like she's from India. Once you make any impression with her in a conversation, she's an incorrigible flirt. Dr. Tate has dabbled in alternative women more than a few times. If I have baffled them with intellectual artistic BS for a hour or so on a first date, I just flat out say "Wanna get naked?", and usually get a yes answer....in the name of Buddha, of course. These are horny girls with no inhibitions, and no moral limitations. (Now if they would just shave them damn jungle bushes in advance, it would make a better field report... *"there I was..."*)

## Peeling off the Panties

To draw attention in her world, it takes advanced levels of spiritual awakenings and experiences. Your countenance is of a man who is tragically intellectual. You talk about your never-ending quest for spiritual, and emotional mind development. To concentrate on such mundane things as material luxuries, or pagan lust is so Cro-Magnon. You draw her in by flashing mesmerizing cerebral intensity. She wants you for your mind, and loves your willingness to challenge authority.

After vaguely describing some experience of your own, do a quick interview to determine whether she wants someone to mirror her own beliefs, or teach her new viewpoints. There are innumerable alternative lifestyles to draw from. Religious, eastern philosophy, the Occult, meditation, horoscope lunacy, Yoga, New Age crap, vegetarian, tree hugger, drug experimenting, backpacking nomad, past lives and destiny, ESP, Dark magic, Goth nonsense, atheism, paranormal, ETs and UFOs and aliens, dream psychology, mind control, hypnosis, alternative medicine, acupuncture, karma and junk science. The Looney Tune list is endless.

## Advanced Angles

Some girls combine this alternative thinking mindset with adventure sports and travel. Hiking, camping, canoeing, mountain climbing, animal watching in lesser-traveled regions; some attempt to adapt to holistic cultures and simple life in other countries. Another angle; you can reflect how you prefer the life of the 18th century. Hit the cliff notes and review their art, music, tapestries, sculptures, dynasties, and approach. Study their literature, memorize a few sonatas and poems, toss around latin quotes liberally. Segway every thought of hers to reminiscing how *"they were so cultured and sophisticated back then."* This seduction can also encompass many of the techniques in the Artistic Allure strategy. *(see chapter)*

The illusion of being solely interested in expanding the mind and exploring new worlds draws her into your web unrestrained. Spirituality is a perfect camouflage, leaving not the slightly hint of the seductive kill you are setting. If you really feel drawn into the whole rebellious thinker role, move to Seattle, grow a caveman beard, stop bathing, and wander around dazed for days. You'll fit right in at the Microsoft campus.

Teach her an alternate culture from an unknown foreign country. Maybe lure her in by promising enlightenment through some exotic foreign religion that features sexual rituals with multiple partners. Make them rituals that can't be verified, but need to be practiced constantly, *while being filmed.*

## The Approach

Either mirror her current inner world, or offer up your own emotional and spiritual crusade. In the initial conversation, you draw her in by describing all the anguish and torture you felt complying with Western philosophies. Describe how the standard rituals of daily life leave you feeling lost in the wrong culture, and babble on in detail about the inner struggles you felt pulling you away towards *The Answer.* Share the pain, emotion, and immense conflicts you had to battle before you finally made the decision to seek greater enlightenment elsewhere. Wrinkle the brow, sigh a lot, splash visine in your eyes and use her hands to wipe away the tears.

> *"I get so emotional when I see a New Age bubble butt like yours."*

Tell her everyone tried to stop you; family, church, teachers, etc., but your vision and destiny was too strong to fight. You may have alienated yourself from your past, but you have discovered *"there is so much more out there."* Your eyes have opened, and you've witnessed a new beginning. By now, her nipples are popping clear through her silk Eastern blouse, like radio dials tuned to WFUK.

## Halftime Report

You're tear jerking heartbreaker story is exactly what she had to go through. It's what she is always experiencing, as she has no real identity to call her own. You took into the depths of your pain and despair, and rode the holy roller coaster all the way back to the top. The contrasts of emotions are electric for her. She feels as if she lived all the moments and sensations with you, as though they were her own. The bait is set, the line is taut, and it's just a matter of reeling her in. Take your time, the longer the build up, the more powerful the seduction. Be vague, and yet speak volumes of truth. Let her absorb everything and project whatever fantasy she wants. You're the unselfish orator who is enriching her life. Soon, she will rape you numb, and treat like a piece of meat.

Climb up onto your soapbox, and pontificate away diatribes of nonsense in your preacher/philosopher mode. Share with her the new worlds you have discovered. While speaking, look off into the distance like a crowd of one million is listening. Raise your arms slowly, as if to shush the crowds. No pictures or autographs please, just throw panties with phone numbers.

*"My child, it's like our aura and like the stars and like the solar system and stuff have united our paths. You're my Density. We need to align our karma and join in universal bliss as one. So if you can just shift your ass cheeks left of the center console and put your head out the sunroof, we can achieve a spiritual blast of orgasmic fate."*

By bringing her into your world and establishing trust, you will be opening a gate into her hungry soul. She is driven to fresh experiences, and does not want to miss out on anything in life. Thus, her *hunger* for new knowledge that you share will be transferred to you. You show her your superior mind, and she shows you her superior snatch. Have her bow down on one knee. Pull out a $5 plastic Royal Sword you got from the local Halloween shop, and tap it on her shoulder, while she peers up at you in awe…
Lecture out loud about your exalted vision;

- "How I long to be judged worthy enough to drink the fruits of the Gods of Budweiser. Worry not child, your hunger is strong. Thee may dine on my Holy tube steak smothered in underwear."

You are intriguing, passionate, enlightened man in her mind. You will of course have done significant background research on the topics of choice, and have a buffet of worthless historical trivia at your command. One of the easier choices is Eastern Philosophy. Study up on the roots of the beliefs, how it has changed over the years, and spread from continent to continent. Have a substantial amount of token geographical and societal trivia about some foreign country at your command. Dress flamboyantly, and walk somewhat hunched over. Explain that you are only the 2$^{nd}$ generation upright in your family. Assume ridiculous body language positions, and create cultural habits out of thin air that are customary. Two octave Farts, blowjobs in public, etc. *"Our people are so free spirited and sensual."* Fill her home with incense laced with Thai stick, and make sure all those wonderful new foreign fruity drinks you hand her are almost entirely grain alcohol. *"Bless you my child. Another round of gasoline and OJ on the rocks, my dear?"*

Your day-to-day life is engulfed by an alternate culture. Your passions are entirely different than those around you. You constantly question life's meaning, and make your own existence seem inconsequential to the bigger picture. With a dreary sigh, make mortal pronouncements, and express discontent with humanity's current direction. Humbly question your purpose on the planet.

- Why am I here?
- What is it that I am supposed to achieve?
- What is that toxic odor coming from your panties hamper?

- Why am I not ramming you like a jackhammer with your ankles flailing behind your ears?

- Why did I waste 2 weeks of my life in your stupid Eastern philosophy class, only to discover your roommate is a way hotter total nympho?

The spirituality lure carries the common ingredients of the more successful seductions; the combination of positive and negative, highs and lows. You invite her to indulge your engaging insights, and alternative spiritual view of the world. You enter her mind, and then enter her body. The sexual mixture of brainpower and animal lust is overwhelming to the alternative believer. Explain to her that sexual favors are just an extension of the philosophy that you intimately share. Since this is anti-western materialistic culture, we're talking effortless, inexpensive dating. Combine it with earthy adventures. Take weekend camping trips deep into the mountains. Somewhere where she can waltz around naked, while you can pound bongo drums and smoke an ounce of herbal medicine, while chanting Kumbaya.

These earthy, cerebral chicks can be incredible nymphos. In fact, you'll find she will demand spending every minute of the day with her, as she is in such awe of your knowledge and cannot stand being alone. Keep your home and work address unknown, and try to limit the threesomes to occurring only at her place, or in the woods somewhere. Extreme highs can be followed by depression quickly. She always feels she is entitled to more, and can lapse into an abyss of worries with the drop of a dime. Serious drug issues and suicide threats can arise in the problem cases. She will go to great lengths of self-sacrifice for her new man, but one minor indiscretion can bring rage and closure. Dizzying extremes of idealization and rejection, as in borderline schizophrenic. When it goes bad, which it always does, they turn into frightening stalkers. This can permanently resolved if you happen to be in the Orient; point to the Great Wall of China and hand her a slinky.

It's a volatile relationship, full of screaming breakups in public, followed the next day by a 24-hour orgy. Relationships never work because you are placed on an idealized pedestal so high, it's impossible to maintain. That's why you need a buffet of new spiritual beliefs and cultures at your disposal. If you're out of favor, bait her by alluding to a big announcement. For example, tell her you have founded a new inspirational Televangelist lecture series that promises salvation through anal sex. She's got potential to be the Star, but it's going to take a lot of practice and donations on her part.

" Educating a woman is like pouring honey
over a fine Swiss watch.  It stops working."
Kurt Vonnegut, **Author**

# THE TEMPTATION POTION

**S**exual seduction is a game of persuasion. We allow it because the fantasy feels good. It opens us up. It removes the mundane uniformity of everyday life, if only for a fleeting moment. Most every spoiled girl has grown up and had high expectations unrealized and crushed by reality. The disenchantment of lost youthful dreams opens the door for a debonair player to be her allusive savior. The seducer rekindles the fire of potentially fulfilling her fantasy. It releases the shackles of hardened emotions and cynicism. She is uncontrollably consumed inside, rather than mildly entertained on the outer. She is naively ripe for the taking. Game on.

Seductive conversation is the elixir of snake oil telemarketers, CEOs, military leaders, from pickup artists to call girls. The talent has flourished as a highly regarded gift. It has been skillfully utilized by many a woman to coerce both power and money from men for a millennia. Beginning at the Garden of Eden, practiced through the Halls of Caesar, and perfected on Rodeo Drive in Beverly Hills, a skilled seductress can charm her way from peasant life to royalty. The gift requires mastery, as retribution of being caught by nobility used to lead to beheading. (we use duct tape now)

Unfulfilled temptation is the potion needed when hunting the big game. Trophy women have more options than they care for. They find the whole game annoying at best. To succeed requires stirring a deeper interest, being alluring yet distant. Never be perceived as an easy kill. Good looks open doors, but you go from exotic to old news without some mysterious allure or element of surprise. Strategic unpredictability is what creates deep desire. You generate contrasts; a curiosity that calls for deeper inspection. You are her naughty escape from the ordinary; an object of stimulating desire, while being mischievously unavailable. This is where the Machiavellian dance comes in play. A great leader aims to be both feared *and* loved by people. It takes the slow hypnotic disguise to reel her in at just the right moment; it takes the gift of seduction.

This chapter offers up variations of this tried and true technique, creating ever-increasing sexual lust by teasing and temptation. Through the subtle massaging of her ego, and intent listening, you discover her weakness and desires; be it travel, adventure, frail ego, lack of father figure, danger, cheap thrills, etc. There's always something. After finding her weakness, you dangle the prospect of fulfilling this want just out of reach. You offer the hope of satisfying hidden desires, but painfully delay the reward until the target succumbs to your spell. You establish a deep craving in her of wanting you, but you are at the moment distant and unavailable. The timing is off. Eventually, you have her believing she forced *you* to change your behavior in order to meet her wishes. She took control over you. Truth be known, you coyly created the whole dilemma, and pinned her ankles behind her ears. In her mind, she believes the conquest occurred solely through her sheer determination and prowess. You surrendered, and she won. Dammit.

Every man keeps his surface appearance as a mask. For the Pro Bachelor, underneath we all have internal struggles. It's a battle to retain interest in our seven figure careers, and still have time for signing autographs in the Playboy mansion Hot Tub. Fortunately, men are born Greek Gods and warriors... (at least that's what we're told in the VIP section at the Cabaret Royale Saloon.) We survive the 19th hole, Ferraris' notchy clutch patterns, titty bar shift changes, the braces blowjobs, binge drinking blackouts, and still find time for sportfucking like wild rabbits. It's a jungle out there.

Women generally do not enjoy a life of leisure. Life is full of anxieties. They struggle to make ends meet and pay their bills, while trying to throw off the airs of Paris Hilton. Their masks are transparent at best, and this knowledge sets the table for a seducer. Believe not what you see. Women will fight the good fight and show good intentions, at least till they get fired in the first week for theft. Alas, Temptation is everywhere in her life.

## The Interview

Every girl has her weakness. Your discovery process will begin with analyzing her appearance, and body language, and putting the picture together. Make relaxed inquisitive conversation, and assemble the pieces of the puzzle by listening to what's missing. A good indicator is when she tells what went wrong with her relationships, or what her career is keeping her from enjoying. It's always there. Make the conversation light, and easy going. This isn't an interview. No job questions, no opinions, just be smooth and observe the signals. If it seems she is longing for excitement, you adjust. Talk casually about recent adventures you may or may not have taken; have pictures handy if you actually took trips, and watch for her reactions. At all times, scrutinize and take note.... what is it that is missing in her life? What is it that she wants? Whatever she complains about is the key, for example, if you find she keeps returning to the fact that she is bored, you have a slew of options to tease her with..

- **Adventure Role**: backpacking, scuba diving, skydiving, parasailing on X, horseback riding, camping, gangbangs, tattoo parlors, off road bikes, bungee jump, riding a Sybian, windsurfing, mountain biking, rollerblading, sex in public.

- **Travel**: (beaches, NYC, Vegas, Cancun, Bahamas, museums, hiking, Casinos, Mardi Gras, visiting the tomb of the Unknown Bowler, concerts, revisit her childhood city, bong conventions, spring break, motorcycle getaway, national beer pong competitions)

There's many variations. Some girls are born nerds and want to be naughty; some miss a part of their childhood, or want a controlling daddy figure; some just want to be noticed. Some girls want to do something totally out of character, to say how much they feel alive; to be able to brag about it to make others jealous. Every girl has inner child qualities still lingering beneath the surface. These uncontrolled emotions are readily available to tap. Children can be impossible to obey your orders, but dangle a secret surprise in front of them, and they will follow you anywhere You can use this same approach with a bored girl looking for some adventure in her life.

## The Grass is Greener

Most girls suffer from the "grass is greener syndrome.' They want what they can't have. They see privileged lives of others, hear of reckless adventures and want them for their own. Many, in fits of jealousy, will turn on their slut phasers full blast and try to steal another girl's husband or boyfriend. The life of leisure and security is never realized, and reality is full of disappointments and anguish. It can be astonishingly easy to sniff this out in her conversation and actions if you consciously listen. Likewise, the desire works both ways. A Pro Bachelor knows a girl who is separated or fighting with her boyfriend is often a prime target in play. She'll fuck a stranger just to piss the old man off and *show him*. They're often smothered in luxuries, but live with a workaholic or a guy who's predictably bland. Or, he's just tired of fucking her and listening to her whining. These are grass is greener girls as well. A taken girl also wants what she can't have, ie, to have a fling and screw your brains out. Find a girl with a ring staring you down and it's basically a tap in at that point. To work a spoken for girl, you need a buildup. In successive conversations, you move from offended she propositioned you, to semi-interested, to very interested (but unavailable), to yes, but only this one time at a safe-house at an exact time. Either that, or buy her a few martinis and take her out back to your pickup truck for a few hours and see how the shocks hold up. No repeats allowed.

## The Approach

Your initial assignment in the Temptation seduction method is to figure out what it is that she yearns for more than anything. Next comes the most important part of the process. Temptation. You flirt, and tease, and compliment, and touch, and give her all your attention when you briefly see her. But you are never available. This goes on for as long as it seems to be building tension, without her losing interest. An effective approach is to say you're in a serious relationship that has gone bad, and are in the process of getting out of it. You have to help the ex move her things out. You don't want to hurt her feelings in the process, because you did have a lot of great times together…and you get along with her family well. This shows what a caring family man you are, and gives an insight into what a great, compassionate guy you are in a relationship.

If you are just looking to hump the new girl a few times, tell her you're engaged and breaking it off. You bought an expensive ring way beyond what the girl deserved (dangling the carefree spending allure), and now you just want her to leave...

"She can keep the damn thing. I'd love to hook up with you right now, but I'm monogamous. When she's gone, we'll go out. I'm gonna have to put up a hell of a fight; I have the feeling you're gonna try to rip my clothes off on the first night."

# The FFF

If all you want to do is FFF, (Find her, Fuck her, Forget her), tell her you're married to a sexless bitch, but you've never cheated on your wife. However, *"you're so hot I may crack one of these days."* You've set the table for the kill, whether she knows it or not. At the same time, you continually flaunt and tease her with the solution to her above-mentioned wants. Put together a loose idea of how to conquer some of her desires. You dangle the solution in front of her, while keeping it just out of reach. Tormenting her with a smile, reluctantly offering it in the future at some unknown time. (bad timing, I just met another girl, or I've love to do it this weekend, but I'm swamped at work) This creates a double-edged sword of attention. She wants the excitement, she wants to use you to get at it, hopefully she wants to bone you in the process, but none of it is available.

# The Mystery Man

A spin-off is to use the secrecy approach; there's something keeping you astray from her, the timing is just not right to get together. You can't afford to be taking any risks. Be vague; shake your head a lot, while pondering the dangerous implications. Heavy sighs. You can just leave it at that.

If you prefer, play it up, and drop hints...

- *"Let's just say it involves an obscenely large business deal and commission. I could face insider-trading inquiries. "*

- *"I'll deny ever saying it, but rumor has it I launder money for the rich and famous. They say I'm the only financier licensed in Curacao and Switzerland who can pull it off "*

An added option can be to simultaneously play the *Classy Bad Boy* (see chapter). Your target babe in that case should be tragically hot, dumb and naïve bimbo longing danger and excitement; maybe an explosive, neurotic, tattooed, hard body stripper with outstanding warrants, bounty hunters after her ass, and a bong pierced through her nose.

The conversation would go something like this...

- (spoken in whispers) *"Honey, there's a small private plane flying below radar stuffed with duffel bags of foreign currency and a lot of unknown baggage. I think you get the picture."*

- *"There's a pending drop off for a navy seal excursion. They say this one is gonna be a really, really bad one; worse than Nam, worse than Desert Storm. I'm a bit nervous. It's so over the top, it could be more dangerous than the gig supplying kiddy porn for Michael Jackson at Neverland. Pray for me."*

- *"I'm running the Boston Marathon as a body guard for a famous billionaire; the payment is rumored to be a Jaguar, some minor league prospects, and a Playmate to be name later "*

- *"I'm saving up sperm for upcoming porno with Jenna Jameson and Tera Patrick. We could use a horny fluff girl, you any good?"*

"The Souls of Women are so small,
some believe they have none at all."

**John Donne,** *English poet (1573-1631)*

# MISERY LOVES COMPANY

When women land a high-income gig in their desired career, they are more guarded with their emotions. Once a girl is content with her life status, the fears, anxieties and tensions of paying the bills disappear. Being cashed up gives her independence and self-control for once in her life. Worry is replaced by attitude and a gigantic ego. The distressed call for a man to fix her problems flitters away like a strip club flier in the breeze. Her need for a relationship fades from a craving to a rare, fleeting thought. She takes on a new set of desires, and men rarely have anything to do with them. Her goal becomes more money, more status and power, and more batteries for her vibrator. She loses her femininity gene. She becomes a cocky man with tits.

> **" Nothing is more intolerable than a wealthy woman."**
> **JUVENAL** (*A.D. 60-130*)

No matter how much money a woman makes, she will still seek a higher lifestyle from men income levels above her. For a man to catch a high dollar babe's eye and create long term interest, nine times out of ten he must be a *serious* business player, since having sex is virtually the last thing on her mind. They want the bigger better deal, to satisfy their materialistic inner whore tendencies. A potential partner has to be either wealthy, or spends like a millionaire. Regular men assume the role of a recreational amusement, a sideshow to play games with. Her nose sticks so high in the air, she looks like a seal waiting to balance a spinning ball. Her bush grows out like a Brazilian forest, and the silky thongs get tossed for big old granny white underwear. The bitch factor is razed to Def Con 4.

If your desired target is driving a brand new Mercedes convertible and her pad blows yours away, what the hell are you going do for her? You could rent a high class call girl for one tenth the CPF this girl would require, and get 10 times the performance. Sex means nothing to women. They can get it any time they want. No matter how hot she is, no matter how much she flirts with you, unless it's a guaranteed quickie, retreating for a higher probability target is the best tactical option. Never obsess about things you can't have. The only shot you have with high income chicks is to ignore her, laugh at her ego and attitude, and make her come to you on your terms.

## Bachelor Code 9

### The Higher a Girl's Income, the lower her Sex Drive

— — — — — — —

Since being a Professional Bachelor is all about achieving a high success ratio and maximizing your time, there is no reason to consider dating higher income women unless you have a sure thing going in. She has to be ALL

OVER you to even consider putting up with the baggage and lack of respect. Aligning your sights for easier, more desirable targets is the first step to greater success in seduction. There's no reason to force yourself into a low probability outcome. The higher prospects for closing are younger girls just getting their life together; girls in or just out of college, struggling at their first job, new in town, waitresses, personal trainers, broke and horny dreamers, wannabe models and strippers. One night stand paradise.

This chapter is about role-playing to seduce girls who dive into each day struggling with a world of troubles. They are loyal, appreciative, and a far more respectful girlfriend than a wealthy player bitch. Why? Because they don't have the liberty of having numerous options. The clock is ticking for an immediate solution, and you're just the timely stud to provide it. They have constant uncertainty, are emotional roller coasters, and are always questioning their direction. Job issues, money problems, creditors, cars in lakes, bail bondsman, you name it, everything can add up to a feeling of desperation. They lead empty lives living vicariously through other people. The greater the insecurity, the more a girl reaches out for a guy to be her savior. When a hot young girl hits you up, confidence is very high. They're so new at the game, they'd much rather have sex and fun. They'd never think to sit around like the typical American bitch without a boyfriend, shredding men to pieces with their posse, while plotting devious extortion angles. Whether young girls want a father figure, career advice, adventure, or full-blown orgies, they all hunt for a quick fix to their situation. These are the high probability situations you should choose to exploit.

# Target Profile

As always, the first step is target profiling to find out what makes her tick. First up is the body language. What you want to see is an overall lack of self-confidence. Look for a somewhat slouching posture, and little effort at fixing herself up. No dramatic, look at me ego. Her initial glance at you is darting eyes that linger too long, getting all flirty when guys walk by. Extra sensitive is also good. If you return her glance back and her eyes look down at the ground, you have locked on confirmation. The clothes should make no effort to accentuate her body. Often she has one appearance feature she thinks makes her uncompetitive, ie, small tits, big nose, skin issues, small brain, bad hair. The insecurity of being less than perfect has made her cynical and bitter about the whole peacock presentation. There's a lingering self-hate about the whole game. You don't want to see business attire or gaudy gold purses. The overall appearance and attitude says major issues.

The signs of a life in disorder are fairly easy to spot. You can gauge her by the apartment condition and her car. If her apartment is low rent, or overall trashed, this is a reflection of her life. The car is always the deal closer. Shitty, trashed car means she's very open to being rescued and is a prime

**106**

target. A lot of these girls drive cars so trashed they look like they belong in the remotest part of a junkyard, where even the guard dog is afraid to go. Cracked windshield, taped windows, no rear view or side mirrors, dents everywhere, dashboard Jesus, fast food wrappers, empties, diapers, 6 month old expired temp license plate, 4 bald tires angled sharply in. Hell, if a girl's car has no muffler or rear windshield, I get a hard on. Insecurity creates desire for a man. With the right look and lines, these chicks have been known to blown you right there in the parking lot for a couple drinks.

## The Approach

Upon target lock on, we will implement the **Buzzkill Strategy**. This line of attack involves inserting doubts and anxiety in her mind from the beginning. You are a mood killer, and see only the bad things in life, and spread constant negativity. Your initial conversation is concentrated on accentuating her failures. You start out by telling how rotten your day went, and then ask if she ever had X problems? (You already know the answer). Once you get her going into misery land, ask about the worst days of her life; the most unlucky things that have happened to her, how shitty school is/was, ask about recent car wrecks, unexpected bills, recently killed pets or deceased relatives. The options are endless. Look off into the distance, utter how it's amazing that some people have such horrible things happen to them in life that they can't control.

The point here is to create a deep emotional bond with her,
by relating to her on the same misery level.

## Bonus Points

Re-live the most gut-wrenching event that ever happened to you; tell her about the time your entire porn collection was destroyed in an apartment fire. When she asks what else you lost in the flames, scream:

*"It's irrelevant, we're talking I lost the entire Mother load.
Every Hustler subscription every produced. Sticky pages and all!"*

Turn your back, squirt visine in your eyes, and break down in front of her for a minute. Request a trip to the time out room. Segway into other horrible events till she consoles you over; the whole rotten despair routine. Act dejected and uninspired at her condescending efforts. You create sadness, misery, dejection, boredom and pain in her mind. Find out her unfulfilled childhood dreams, and moan how sad it must be for her to see them vanish. Talk about how difficult and irrelevant she must feel about living a passionless life going forward, without hope. Just keep making her talk about it. Pick multiple topics and hit on each, and determine which is creating the biggest trauma. Create unease and plant sad feelings of darkness everywhere. Dig at them like open sores. Answer each statement with even more gloomy analysis; "damn, I didn't realize how tough things must be for you. I don't think I could handle that right now." Like the saying goes, *Misery loves Company*. Once you start getting her going, she instinctively moves into even lower depths, telling tragedy stories, as the ego takes over. She may proclaim she's the unluckiest chick on the planet; she's more depressed than anyone in the history of depression.

Once you've created shared pain bonding between you, she will have dropped her guard and accepted you into her world. At this juncture, you have multiple choices. Maybe you feel comfortable being the negative Killjoy guy all the time. You enjoy playing the role that life is harshly tragic, and you are content as a miserable piece of debris. Create a co-dependency hate-hate relationship with her and work it from there. If this sounds exciting, you should dabble into Internet dating. There's a world of tragedy there. Here's a good ad from Craig's List for you.

-- - - - - --

SWM in dead-end job seeks dumpy neurotic for mutual psychological torture, tepid sex, and co-dependency. I enjoy drinking, smoking, pornography, and self-righteous indignation. I can't stand movies, and the last album I bought was The Marshall Tucker Band's Greatest Hits. I have middling intelligence but try to appear smarter by affecting a world-weary air, memorizing useless facts, and chuckling at my own vicious, agenda-driven jokes. I'm 40, but look 50 and feel 60. You are a whiny, bitter shrew with a misplaced sense of entitlement and unrealistic expectations. In time you will become coolly hostile when I don't fulfill every unmet need you've ever had. Bonus points if you just finished screwing every guy in town and now want to take it slow with me. My perfect night would include getting hammered in a sleazy bar while you flirt with seedy old drunks, followed by an embarrassing screaming match. I would be open to an unsatisfying fling that leaves me filled with regret and dread, but prefer a long-term, soul crushing descent into booze and pills. No friendships. I don't need any goddamn friends. Age unimportant, but I will condescend to women under 30 and rehash mother issues with women over 40. Serious replies only.

-- - - - - --

The first step in any seduction is to establish a comfort zone, and a level of trust. In this case, you've gotten her to open up, to expose her inner self and weaknesses. You have disarmed the target by non-confrontational, vague discussion. She has left herself vulnerable by exposing her problems, and is ripe for you to cure her boredom and needs. Once you have the catastrophe girl feeling fragile, you have a perfect window of opportunity. The feeling of low esteem, and questioning self worth creates a void that is easy to fill.

# Situational Analysis

There are tons of insecure chicks out there working the field that come from single parent families. Without positive reinforcement at home, a girl often starts adult life with a serious of failures. Soon she is prone to seeing bad karma and breakdowns in everything. She lacks self-confidence, motivation, and fears change like the plague. She is a constant worrywart, takes everything out on herself, and creates her own problems in a self-fulfilling prophecy. It is almost painful for her to take the initiative to aggressively pursue any challenge outside her limited realm of experience. She has difficulty making decisions, and rarely indulges her full talents and efforts entirely to anything. Most importantly, they **rarely** express disagreement with others for fear of losing their approval and support.

Once you show her you are on her side, you can easily turn the girl around in any direction you want. They often have a lot of talent, but have never had anyone support their abilities. Playing the Father figure here opens an avenue for you to literally change her life for the better, as well as have a girlfriend completely trustworthy. The best personality match for her is a guy who likes to take control. As she becomes more confident in herself, she may even suggest things that you cannot see for yourself.

# The Transition Phase

The second part of the strategy is to get her over your place and pump her up emotionally and suggest cures for all the bad karma information she just provided you. Be it unfulfilled childhood dreams, career change strategy, new boyfriend, sex, some type of adventure, travel, whatever. You create a temporary solution. You first start up with a lot of mental reinforcement. Point out how her tough situation and the unfulfilled desires aren't her fault. Reflect aloud about positive things that have happened to you when you least expect it. You see the same traits you have in her. You build up her self-esteem. Confide to her your inner secrets. Be humbly embarrassed to admit that you have done exceedingly well for yourself, by learning to overcome similar unexpected obstacles in life. Go full tilt into the Anthony Robbins NLP con job. Become a paper bag full of upbeat words.

**Be all you can be. In fact, go beyond that.**
**Be someone else.**

Say you used to feel like a prisoner and a captive observer to events, but you choose to use them as a challenge to overcome barriers and hardships. In fact, right now you *have a déjà vu feeling good things are going to start coming her way.* You tell her that insecurities are only a mind game that people play on themselves. When you wake up each morning, you can choose to be either positive or negative. You tell her she can do whatever she puts her mind to. You can see the talent inside her. You remove her insecurities, and point out a brighter future is always possible. All of this is vague ambiguous banter, vintage motivational/political mumbo jumbo, but it has a powerful effect. Football coaches, politicians, money managers, preachers, and gigolos all use this approach.

The person projects whatever fantasy they want. They are oblivious to the role-playing you have taken, but are mesmerized that you feel such confidence in them. You have turned the whole conversation and picture around 180 degrees. You took her from despair to fantasy. She experiences an unexplainable emotional bond with you, as her ego is boosted. She loves how you make her feel. If you really dig the girl, do all of these things over the course of a few dates. Pump her up without being a suck up. You have created the image you symbolize a better way, an escape from her worries. Look her deep into the eyes and tell her *she deserves better*. A lot of times a little inspiration does change her life dramatically, and will reap serious bootie benefits by being the catalyst.

If you originally met her in a bar and are only looking for a quick lay, do your cold to hot flattery reversal over a couple of shots. Toast to the two of you being "survivors." She will project a better future for herself just by knowing you. (You will be projecting a better future if she ends up blowing you). Propose the two of you do something totally impulsive together, since you have so much in common. A *What the Hell* crazy time. If the conversation is going well, go for the kill. *"Let's get out of here, and get naked."* Tragedy girls are an easy one-night stand. Once you are back at your place, hide all sharp objects, conceal the valuables, and don't get her too wasted; this type has been known to pee for ten minutes in her sleep.

# THE ARTISTIC ALLURE

Inside every girl lies a set of weaknesses and characteristics she chooses to smooth over. Her life is a product of a few successes, and innumerable attempts and outright failures. For her self-image, she conveniently masks the latter, and projects the former. Nobody wants to dwell on their disappointments and shattered dreams and present them forefront as the selling card of their inner soul. We are all natural born salesman of ourselves. And we are all prone to diversions.

History has shown that women often seek an escape by attaching themselves to fantasies and romantic images. Hollywood exists for this reason; to showcase the ability to dream; to forget about her vulnerabilities and life's mundane predictability. When a woman chooses a man, he is her vehicle to mentally escape. She projects herself into his world, and assumes his lifestyle and characteristics as her own. She assumes his wallet as well.

This field guide chapter shows how to exploit a woman's fascination with the artsy fartsy fantasy life. The Artistic Allure technique is another spin-off of the James Bond international man of mystery projection. The approach can be devastatingly effective, and is fun because it is role-playing that men don't normally do. Some players have been known to adopt portions of the technique permanently into their persona.

The Artistic Allure requires you to confuse her reality with passionate encounters, followed by calculated disappearances. You are not the guy that calls every six hours and discusses everyday life. You don't care if she supersized her Big Mac meal today. You date once every week or two. When you call her, use the vague "away on business often" angle; "*I don't like to discuss work, let's talk about you*". You are allusive, capricious, and teasingly unavailable. (I'm in town a week from Friday). Clever variations can include somewhat different personalities; one day you're the talkative historian storyteller, the next time a tad distant, and vaguely aloof. This creates panic she's losing you, and she'll double her efforts to win you back.

## The Approach

When you are with her, the dates always involve the arts in some fashion. The angle revolves around fantasy, imagery, and emotion, and exploits her weakness for any man who shares her fascination in high culture. Your dates embrace Artsy Events in the form of short vacations, which leave a sentimental reflection of you in their mind. Symphony, Ballet, Operas, Theatre, Plays, a poetic recital, Art Galleries, Museums, flower gardens,

Fashion shows, Belching contests; any of the arts are the perfect setting. The most effective approach; make it an *out of town weekend getaway* to see the ballet, or symphony, etc. It could actually be an in town event, or a nearby town, but you always stay at a hotel. Their hormones go nuts out of town for some reason; maybe since there are no witnesses, they feel no guilt for being such an easy lay. This stuff doesn't have to be elaborate or overly expensive; it's the aura and symbolism that matters. Do your homework and familiarize yourself with the event, and read up on the historical background of the field. Have the ability to provide a peripheral expert analysis on how the event has changed through the centuries.

# The Main Event

*Attention to the romantic details is essential for full effect*

- Plan a sunset dinner at a restaurant with outside patio. Option: have a violinist play a solo at your table. Put Visine in your eyes, dab away with napkin. Tip him $1 wrapped in a wad of Monopoly money. Whisper to date he was out of tune, but had great vibrato.

- Next up, go to your special event, symphony, ballet, whatever.

- After the event, back at the hotel, on the outdoor balcony under the moonlight, give her a small gift symbolic of the trip.

- Throw in a bullshit rose somewhere in there, a few lines from an Italian poem that you translate. This requires practice, as it must be done straight faced without gagging.

- Compliment her often for her appreciation of the finer things, how rare it is to meet a woman of such taste. Allude to it that the whole cultural events are her idea, as she inspired you to broaden yourself. She becomes addicted to the way you make her feel.

- Dress in a suit. Fake Rolex, optional bogus English accent, imaginary Royal heritage, drinks shaken, not stirred. A lot of aristocratic head tilting, poetic pontification, reflections on life and romantic future potential. Get into the whole routine.

The gifts don't have to be expensive, just some little girly romantic crap; a trinket or something with the name of the town or symphony. Most men confuse why a gift is effective with women. Contrary to common thought, it is not the cost of the gift. It is simply the fact that it symbolizes a moment when your thoughts were entirely on her. It's a self-centered, emotional feeling she craves, because it validates her femininity, charms and perceived power over you. Some originality in the gift doesn't hurt either.

A $300 purse is no more effective than a nice card. What matters is the manner in which you give it to her. If she's the type that thinks the cost matters most, you have the wrong girl. Again, make the gift something symbolic of the weekend or the event.

The best is something small that she keeps on her bedroom bureau. An object that when she looks at it, she relives the feelings she felt on the trip, and romantically associates it with you. Whenever she is alone at home, you are subtly are always on her mind. A glance at your gifts on her bureau or hope chest brings back heated memories. You may reach such an illustrious level of importance, that she may nickname her vibrator after you. Added bonus points; send a postcard to her from the hotel at the event, telling her much fun you are having. Get her something from the hotel gift shop. Maybe sneak out at night without her and buy her a T shirt from the local Titty bar.

With all the heartaches in everyday life, the Artistic Allure is very rewarding, as it allows the girl to escape; to fantasize about her man. This is why long distance relationships are magical. In her mind you are a man of high status, a well-dressed noble man of culture. Thus by association, you raise her self-esteem, and overall outlook on life. You rescued her.

Artsy girls are often intensely motivated to experiment with new adventures. They're uninhibited and spontaneous risk takers. She has an endearing ability to detach herself from reality. Almost childlike. Do not overexpose yourself, as that takes the fantasy illusion away. You must keep up the tension. Have her worrying about you. Consumed by you. Intensely fixated on you. *"Is he really mine? Am I good enough for him? Will he go away in the sunset, never to return? What did he mean when he said,*

## "Fuck Diamonds, a good blowjob is forever"

Keep her imagination running overtime, particularly when she is alone. She'll develop an image of you that is larger than life. As long as you pump her up with an idealized image, she is intensely physical. A girl in love with a mystery man is vulnerable, and believes most anything if it's presented well. These artistic events for her are emotional, spiritual memories that leave a lasting impression. Right up there with topless lesbian oil wrestling.

The Artistic dreamer girl has a volcanic emotional view of life and its relation to fantasy. Courting her exposes you to an experience ranging from passionate, to possessive, to frighteningly immature. They can regress from roaring laughter to fits of tears on a drop of a dime. There's no fear of this Borderline personality disorder as long as you see her sparingly and keep it simple. She is a girl intensely motivated to experiment with new adventures, making her very receptive to your getaway romantic interludes. The reward is she is extremely responsive to sensation, experiences, and pleasure. The risk is her impulsive desire often leads to reckless self-indulgence to self-destruction. A virtual Disney World roller coaster ride that is best maintained by keeping a safe distance. She will find emotional significance in everything, and expresses gratitude to devastation with grandiose terminology. She places you on a pedestal with each romantic thought and interlude. *Note to self:* Tread lightly; under the surface she has you balancing precariously with each overanalyzed thought of hers.

In healthier relationships, a woman of the arts has her own creative outlet or talent, and has an interesting historical understanding of life in relation to cultures. She can be quite extremely intelligent, and full of worthless facts. (you can be extremely flamboyant, and go cross-eyed staring at her amazing rack). Stay clear of the smug, elitist, liberal Artsy girl. Besides the lack of sensuality, bland appearance and hygiene issues, you are subjected to her inflated self worth which may force uncontrollable laughter. This may risk you blowing your sophistication cover. How do you keep a straight face dealing with a condescending snobby attitude from a sexless drone with half your IQ? Sorry Blanche, not bathing for a week and having a jungle bush does not make you a revolutionary philosopher.

## Spin-off Version

You can use the exact same approach, and interchange the whole suit guy image to a Antonio Banderas, Bruce Willis biker routine. Bad boys are exciting; the classy bad boy with money image is overwhelming. Although you orchestrate everything, give the impression that you are a spontaneous madcap driven by uncontrollable impulse adventures. You may recall, the movie 9 ½ weeks is a play on this approach as well. The Classy, strange guy who disappears for days, only to return with more outrageous, psycho-sexual dating rituals.

You can start the relationship with a few "by chance" passings by, saying hello and then disappearing. Do some secret admirer notes to her at work before your first "accidental" encounter. A masterful seduction is one that takes place slowly, unexpectedly, and builds into a crescendo; like a Beethoven symphony. Added twists and mind games can include naughty sex games during your romantic artist events; make her wear a mildly see through dress with no panties in the theatre, play hide the flute, have sex in the dark upstairs balcony during orchestral ballads, you get the picture.

# THE GREEK TRAGEDY

**A** dangerous, successful, or artistic persona draws in women like a magnet. Power and strength attract, but a presentation that is too perfect or strong can be dangerously close to a turnoff. Women love to "conquer" a man who is perceived to be a challenge. However, the overly aggressive alpha male can present an experiment for a girl that may seem not worth the effort. Let's do a role reversal moment; think of how many times you spotted 9's and 9.5s, but never considered approaching them out of the fear of rejection. The overachiever or extra-cocky player/bad boy may likewise lose out on his options. He is playing his cards to close to his Neanderthal chest. Women will fear rejection. They fear you only want sex, and they fear being cheated on, or treated like crap. One-sided narcissistic conversations are a big turnoff. Without some level of vulnerability, the turbo stud can be just as lonely a role as being labeled a nice guy.

The advanced path to seduce always embraces creating curiosity through a combination of contrasts and mystery. Predictability is always the death knell to a relationship. For you to create any fantasy image in her mind, she cannot know all the pieces of the puzzle. Ever. For the strong alpha male, by starting so far on one end of the masculine scale, you can easily tilt it back unexpectedly to instill intrigue and desire.

The Greek Tragedy role-playing is designed to inspire more humanness into a strong personality. The most common angle average players use when hitting on a hottie goes as follows. The typical shallow, cocky, insecure man is constantly negative; his conversation centers on insulting the competition, in order to draw attention to himself. He never gives the girl a chance to speak, or hears a word she says. The more advanced, intelligent player shows vulnerability in himself, and is a great listener. When a woman discovers how you are balanced with a gentler side, she is far more attracted. You retain the alpha, but flash the beta. This comes across as being natural and likeable, and women are enticed by the illusion. You are not like the others; a closed emotional wall. You allow her the comfort of dropping her wall of resistance, giving the impression of a target she can conquer. Reverse seduction is a power elixir.

She realizes that she has a possibility to get her hooks in there. You just may be the alpha male stud that she can get to crack. It's common sense that the dichotomy attracts. Who is going to attract more women? The guy who constantly brags about himself? Or the guy who lets his actions speak for themselves, while he secretly confides to her he wishes he could do better. Being humble triumphs every time it is played.

# Bachelor Code 10

**Strength and self-confidence generates attraction.
Add a subtle weakness, and the attraction explodes.**

– – – – – – –

Proper execution requires a delicate touch, as the alpha must remain dominant. The best avenue is to show the soft side involving your most powerful attribute. For example, let's say she's attracted to you because you are an exceedingly successful businessman, or so you told her ;^) . When your career comes up in conversation, explain in a soft-spoken confession that a part of you feels guilty about wiping out the lesser players of the game. You love winning, but are still keenly aware of the financial pain others feel. To alleviate this to some extent, you like to make charitable donations anonymously. You thrive on seeing the change you can make in people's lives firsthand. For example, tell her you perform charity work with youth business groups, or give counsel to up and coming students in your field. The fact you only counsel freshmen babes in schoolgirl outfits sans panties never comes up.

# A Crack in the Armor

Suppose your macho strength, and the feeling of security attracts her. In all likelihood, she is a girl who is somewhat subservient and has dependency or motherly advice tendencies. Explain to her that you have a bad habit of being impulsive and a tad reckless. At times your emotions can swell so quickly, you just can't help but deck the first guy that touches her. This stems from some bad experience you had as a child, or some previous relationship. (Take a long hard look back into your own life; there are always a few situations like this that you wish you handled differently.) Maybe some thugs were beating up a friend, and you either ignored it or beat the crap out of someone.

Maybe you had a drunk relative who beat his wife, and you hate yourself for not stepping in; at the time you were only 14 and scared. Maybe someone pushed you while playing hopscotch in first grade, you stubbed your toe, and secretly have spent two decades stalking him and plotting murder. Confide with her that you will share the tragic childhood stories, as long as she keeps it a secret. This brings her in closer to the real you, and establishes a level of trust and attraction that only you two share. Explain to her how these incidents created who you are today. They have become an inner struggle you always have to deal with. When you finish these stories, show pain and anguish, a lot of side-to-side head shaking. Explain how the whole situation shouldn't have had such a profound effect on you, but inside you know you have to come to terms with it before it happens again. In summary, your greatest strength carries a mortal weakness through a lack of patience. She sees a big window of opportunity of being the solution to your problems.

This opens up the door for her to get involved, and share her motherly advice. Maybe she can help you overcome these brief moments of rage. You explain to her that as a great Greek Warrior, you have only the best of intentions, but at this point in life you can't control your aggressive feelings. (megabarf) By unleashing the vulnerability, you shatter any conflicts she initially felt towards never being able to get close to you. The illusion is very convincing. No one expects that by exposing your weakness, you are manipulating and seducing. When she's done with her counseling, tell her you feel so much better about the whole thing, your going to go out back and unload a hundred AK-47 rounds into your gigantic Rosie O'Donnell mannequin. Make her wear army fatigues, while you slip on a pink frilly skirt, read Cosmo, and suck your thumb. If you really want to scare the piss out of her, suggest sitting through an entire Oprah show.

What you create here is a soft side to aggression, a chink in the shiny armor. You still are the feared alpha male, but you didn't seek the role or the reputation. It somehow seems to find you. By asking for her guidance, you are giving her the upper hand. She will protect you from yourself. It creates an exciting co-dependency. You are a passionate man because you are an attentive listener, and seek her supervision. This puts her in an imagined position of power over you in a subtle fashion. Major bonus points here.

# Advanced Levels

You should mix hot and cold attitudes with this mind game. Just when you seem to be docile with her advice, go off on a violent tangent. Tell her one of those bad situations came up and you lost control. *"You should have seen what I did to his knee with my nose."* Keep the whole thing a big secret; just tell her it was really bad. Get into the act, throw crap around the house, pull an all-night bender with the boys. In the morning, tell her we need to talk. Then get her back into the whole counseling routine again. *"Let's go over how to be patient in the wrong situation again."* Hot, cold, hot, cold keeps the whole power struggle going, and keeps the tensions high enough. She keeps feeling she has to conquer you again; the power struggle continues. If she starts to lose interest, bang her sister a couple of times and start up the whole routine with her.

The Greek Tragedy survives, Long Live Caesar!!

# The Tragic Victim

Another angle is playing the chronic victim syndrome. You keep getting into situations where you were minding your own business, and all hell breaks lose in front of you. You try to break things up. Somehow *you* are always the one who ends up getting blamed for things that you didn't start, and ends up getting arrested. The whole thing just pisses you off and creates a triangulation inside. Should you get involved or not? If she is the type who is not successful at things in life, than you are showing the same weakness that she has. You are both victims. This co-dependency of uncontrollable events is a potent attraction. Remember though; don't linger long with the down in the dumps attitude. You always bounce right back to the successful alpha. You just visit the basement once in a while, wave to her, and then shift back to the Alpha Male in complete control.

# The Obsessive Artist

Suppose the alpha trait that she is most attracted to is a creative one. You are a painter, writer, poet, sculptor, songwriter, guitarist, actor, designer, etc. Getting her to believe she is intimately involved in the creative process is a very powerful elixir. Don't think she won't be bragging about it to her friends when your work or you are being discussed.

## Scenario 1:

Let's go with the obsession scenario. Come up with dilemma that the minute inspiration hits, you stay up 72 hours straight working on it, and skip work and put your life into a tailspin. You need her help in learning how to channel the ideas in a more constructive means. You need her on her side to achieve the optimum creativity process. You display weakness surrounding your strengths, and get her involved with a solution. Maybe give her a title like The Ideas Manager. It worked great with Yoko, just ask Paul & Ringo.

## Scenario 2:

You could be the artist, musician, sculpture who deep down is never satisfied with his own work. You are fanatically insecure about the final product unless it passes your own impossible standards. You ask her help in alleviating this madness of indecision. You show her the finished product (it kicks ass and **is the final product**), but tragically whine about it in a pathetic self-doubting fashion. You beg for her to get involved, as the anxieties of decision are too much for you. If she likes you, she will obviously compliment your work. Through leading questions, you eventually get her to make the pronouncement that the product is perfect just the way it stands. *She* decides when the projects are complete.

"Couldn't have done it without ya, babe. This calls for a celebration. Whattya say we have a threesome with that hot little neighbor of yours."

118

# PIERCING CHARLOTTE'S WEB

Gazing through her exterior disguise is the first step in understanding what makes your target tick. Underneath most girls lies an array of fears and frustration she protectively conceals. Only a thin outer shell conceals her constant insecurity and vulnerability. The psychological barrier that binds her defenses are a combination of ego and pride, a little arrogance and dishonesty, and most important of all; *her snotty support group*. This is her safety net of catty girlfriends, family, co-workers, and daily routines that keep her life in repetitive order. The posse serves to validate each other's actions, and create a security blanket to hide behind, as they advocate a similar mindset and presentation.

Each member of the posse conforms to the accepted group role to receive status and respect, while hoping to avoid rejection and punishment. This applies in business as well as relationships. Everyone wants the benefits of being in the cool clique; there's safety in numbers. Granted, there are leaders and trendsetters within the posse, but they must tread lightly when breaking out, or suffer the possibility of being labeled a skank and getting booted out. Most members of the group mirror each other's actions, to the point of often finishing each other's thoughts and sentences. As long as each person continues to support and accept her compadres' image, the status quo continues. They collectively put non-clique members down to make each other feel better about themselves, like all insecure people.

## The Strategy

The line of attack herein is to completely separate the girl from her safety net for a period of time. The support group can be entirely suffocating to a new suitor of one of the group. Quite often, when you find a girl surrounded by the poison posse, your entire perception of her is colored with distaste, and you reject her. It is by association alone that she is taken out of consideration. Separation from the nest can be difficult to arrange. The more tightly knit the group is, the more difficult the initial division can be. If it's a highly desired target, one easy method is doing an *out of town for the weekend* first date. Don't set a bad first precedent and drop a fortune, just something interesting and inexpensive nearby.

You set out to rapidly alter her comfortably predictable surroundings and shifting her reality. You throw her daily routines into disarray, until they become a distant memory. Determine in the gathering of intelligence mode what fascinates the posse, and what they do to amuse themselves. Create an approach entirely different; alternate manner, dress, music, location and attitude. While tedious uniformity exists and is accepted behavior in the support group, everyone secretly longs for a walk on the wild side. Give her unchartered waters, an approach wholly different; the more exotic and unusual, the better.

Primary goals are to smother her with attention while in the midst of deep conversation. Then, in a sleight of hand, take her out of her world and into yours; physically, intellectually, and emotionally. What's key here is that what attracts you first and foremost is her *intelligence*.

Your modus operandi is a mind reversal. This is a delicate dance, as you're not to become a subservient, brain-dead pussy. You are still the iron fisted dominant alpha male. Although you control the whole seduction; the events, places, things, and topics you discuss, you throw off the allusion that she is actually the dominant one, due to your fascination in her mind. To pull it off, remember you are not changing your view to hers. You express your strong manly thoughts and observations, but you lean in with great interest to her perspective. Never be disagreeable, use leading softball questions, and rephrase her statements in an agreeable response. Concentrate on comparing casual life observances and how they relate to intimacy in relationships, and move the conversation subtlety towards sex. Keep deep eye contact, establishing a verbal rapport. Mirror (mimic) her hand and body movements, thus creating an unconscious sexual tension and bonding.

When expressing your views, speak as vague as possible, to allow her room to be specific. The unspoken mystique lies in the fact that you never actually say she is more correct in her thinking, but create the perception of inclusion of her approach. Speak your thoughts in an authoritative tone, but soften your vocals in reaction to her ingenious responses. Sort of like ramming her cranium into the headboard, while gently complimenting her soft, shiny hair in the process.

Include some non-verbal communication that develops neural sensations while she is speaking. For example, when she replies to a topic, repeat certain body language and touches; stroke her arm, across wrists, maybe a hair touch. This creates a reference point, a tingling association with the touch and the emotion being felt at the exact time of the touch. When you repeat the same subtle movement over and over, she equates it with both an intellectual and physical turn on. When you perfect this movement's usage, you will eventually be able to simply repeat it anywhere, anytime, even when neither of you are speaking, and create an instant emotional feeling. It's her built in Bimbo-meter; sort of a Pavlov's dog trigger.

In honor of Pavlov, when this technique is working big-time, take her upstairs and bang her doggie style. Put on a hat with floppy ears, plop a bowl of water on her ass and lap at it, while pumping her silly with your tongue hanging out. "*Woof*!"

We're not creating the Holy friggin Grail here. For once, someone is paying attention to what she is saying and giving it a level of authority, instead of palming her ass and demanding she barks. (all in due time)

Why does it work? Because very, very few guys can turn off their ego long enough to give two shits about a girl speaking and how she thinks. You are showing a compassionate intellectual value that is refreshingly new to her. In due time, practicing this thinker/listener role-playing will become a powerful tool for the arsenal; a natural stimulator of the senses. Your attentive interaction will help you choose and conquer the more difficult targets, ultimately strengthening your sexual encounters. You'll discover an extraordinary source of increased intimacy via your intellectual persuasion tools. Granted, there's only a remote chance you'll find a hot babe who's an Ivory Tower thinker, but play along. If she has an agreeable background and some schooling, the role is enjoyable to play. If she's smart, she may figure it out and play along; you may notice she's caught on to you and still continue. Sort of like the titty dancer "mind" games; where the dancer lies about being a college engineering student, you know she's lying, she knows you know, and it's still fun to play along. The fact that she's topless and grinding your crotch only suggests she needs an added sales tool to pull off her persuasion. You do not need these sales tools. Although, I imagine if you had a board meeting with perspective clients and surrounded the room with half a dozen gold poles with topless girls swinging around them, the technique could create a few extra sales.

Your listener role-playing can go sour a tad if you choose the wrong target. The girl can take it the wrong way and in response become an elitist condescending "thinker." She may turn out to be a horoscope wacko with the street smarts of a rock who suddenly feels brilliant, but you never let on to this error. You simply adjust your timetable into a FFF. But with the right target, it's a golden approach. In a nutshell, you make her feel more emotionally and intellectually valued than she ever has before, sending a powerful and passionate message of self-importance. Her self-esteem skyrockets, and she's craves the feeling.

You ask her views on everything and embrace their originality. Upon hearing them, you are taken aback by the keen insights and perceptive mind.

*"I never thought of it that way, your friends must jealous that you're so analytical."*

*"Like many people, I guess I suffer from having a very narrow view due to my upbringing"*, and *"hearing your perspective has really helped me better understand other people."* (yuk, yuk)

# Halftime Line of Attack

Mention her thought process has helped you better analyze your current business model, and you're showing greater ease in moving product.

*"You've really added a whole new dimension to my pitch, blah blah."* (keep extra barf bags in driver's door pocket).

Although you plan everything, you display a growing dependency on her perspective and thought process, as if you are her student. By smothering her with emotional feedback, complimenting her mentally, and surrounding her in a whole new environment of places, people, and things, you create a methodical overload of the senses. You provide her with an entirely different way of viewing herself, by living in your world. By keeping her inaccessible to the Posse, i.e., the jealous board of directors, you have her cut off. She is alone, and vulnerable. Once she becomes mesmerized with the way you make her feel, she relinquishes entirely into a co-dependency. You are always on her mind. The need of consent and approval from the posse is gone. She is now easily influenced and culpable to be seduced.

This technique uses the rapid-fire approach. From the first date, you practically never let her out of your sight. Date every day for a week, with the whole schedule and routine planned in advance. See her every day, talk numerous times a day, and make each successive date completely different and a surprise. Within no time you have created an alternate posse, (you), one far more exciting, that envelopes her senses. She becomes hypnotized by your presence in her life, and the importance of her Charlotte's Web of friends becomes rendered insignificant.

# Advanced Role Playing:

You never want to become predictable. Complacency has no place in this role. Once she's trapped in your web, mix up the theme of your events, take her to new places, and periodically shift your moods to keep her uneasy. Pretend you missed your period and feel your biological clock ticking. Cry when you see trees. This creates anxiety and thrusts the need for her to win you over once again. As time goes by and the sex begins, you reverse the tables and slowly become the dominant male again in the relationship. Her world is upside down, and her co-dependency will be in full force. She will need you more than ever to relive the feelings you provided her initially.

" Girls begin to talk and to stand on their feet sooner than boys, because weeds always grow up more quickly than good crops.

**MARTIN LUTHER,** *German religious reformer 1546.*

# THE GOAL LINE STAND

A highly desired target requires a calculated strategy to successfully seduce. Rarely will someone succumb to charms without putting up a goal line stand. For the overanxious infatuated man on the hunt, the ability to operate in a controlled mode of pursuit can be too much. The target's wiggling ass and pouty lips have been known to create temporary blindness. In the more serious cases, a man is barely able to function with such hormonal insanity. Great care must be taken in this fragile state. You'll spend your days walking in a blue balls daze fantasizing about her, with a raging tent-pants hard on. At a desk job you can get away with this. But if you're a kindergarten crossing guard at an all-boys Catholic School and the parents are watching, there may be some explaining to do.

The average guy meets trophy babe, throws caution to the wind, and dives in recklessly. He'll ignore the wisdom of the initial low CPF, and rush forward connecting a few Hail Mary passes. The first 2 weeks of dating, he dazzles and spoils her rotten with every elaborate and expensive trick in his book. He over compliments, and smothers her with aggressive attention, figuring she just *has to see* what an incredibly great guy he is. She responds by taking cell calls from other guys in his face, barely acknowledges him, and rarely returns his messages. While the guy considers taking out billboard space and advertising on blimps to tell her he wants her, she's out dating 4 other guys and barely remembers his name. He's blown his load and gotten exactly squat.

The full court press may have had an impressive kill ratio in the 19th century. With today's self-absorbed neurotic women, the normal response is from boredom to pushing you away. To succeed, you have to show scarcity and build value by presenting yourself as a challenge. If she can walk all over you with little effort, there's no buildup and tension. Being easy is a big turnoff. Never sell yourself short. The more attention you show, the less interest she has. They want what they can't have. Men and women are wired differently. Sex means nothing to women, they can get it anytime they want. It means everything to men. To ignite her interest and retain it, you have to create a sub-conscious emotional interest. In your absence, you should be on her mind, wondering about you, waiting for your return.

## The Value of Distance

It the course of any seduction, you will eventually encounter resistance. Regardless of how sincere your approach is, a woman tends to be guarded and walled off. Sure she'll enjoy the sucking up and watching you submissively reach into your wallet, but she remains unavailable. A few weeks of heavy attention are fine, but at this juncture, the wiser move is to show restraint, particularly if things are not advancing and she has become hesitant. What is occurring can be a number of variables. She may be dating simply because she's bored. She may feel her time and pussy require Paris Hilton pricing. If your approach was lousy, or she's banging the entire fraternity down the street, chances are you're just spinning your wheels. However, if you have been interesting, funny, showed social status, and acted somewhat aloof, you have done the job and made a sufficient dent in her bitch shield.

If she is genuinely interested in you, make sure you don't overexpose yourself. You must be coyly vague in your delivery. Instead of a crotch first direct in your approach, casually retreat to pleasant, but somewhat distant conversation. Phone calls should be ten minutes tops. Continue being friendly, but remove the sexual overtones. Since you have been careful not to divulge all the details of your life, she will spend time thinking, pondering, and idealizing you. Soon, all your little idiosyncrasies and perceived flaws will be smoothed over. Your positive points will be amplified to undeserving levels. You're the one that may get away. Since every move you make is discussed with her posse, she certainly can't face them being dumped. She will immediately question what she has done wrong. No woman's ego can handle losing a guy she wants in this fashion. It would be a blow to her sensual prowess, and she'll put on the heavy moves to win you back.

She may still have lingering doubts about the depth of your intentions, but with a little mystery she will want to find out more. If a girl is interested, she'll let you know. But its up to you to show that despite your attention, you cannot be taken for granted. What you need to do is suddenly have a full calendar; you become unavailable. Go a few days without calling; reschedule a date for another day. You are implying that you are just not as interested as you were the previous weeks. You are not specifically saying you are seeing someone else; you simply have made other plans. Vagueness breeds apprehension. If you have adequately intrigued her, your sudden absences will create doubts in herself. Keep in mind; more often than not the bitch shield that is cocky and cynical is masking insecurity inside.

# Creating Doubt

By displaying hesitation in your game, you are showing you value yourself and your time. You're interested in her, but not attracted to game playing or wasting time. You are not some easy target who doesn't have other options. By engaging this technique, you draw the conclusion to a head. If she is sexually attracted, she will play her hand. The most heated relationships entail *her coming to you* full of hormonal aggression, instead of meekly succumbing to you in the first round. The passive target is a lifeless one, and your awe inspiring porn star performance will be responded to during the session by yawning while doing her nails.

Gauge the result; if she is still keeping a distance from you, she may be busy with other guys. She could be at the salon trying to get the dried sperm out of her hair, while reminiscing about her perfect pickup line from the night before. *"So what team do you guys play for?"* If she isn't sexually attracted, you saved yourself time, money, and eliminated aggravation. She must commit to this new situation; to begin pursuit of you. It's not like it's tough, a simple phone call gets it going again. Next date should be at your place, a dinner and movie at your home. If she won't come on over to your closing booth, you know exactly where you stand.

This is a simple and effective sleight of hand. You set the whole play in action, but she feels she created the ending. Like the saying goes, "if you love someone, set them free. If they come back they're yours; if they don't, they never were."

If she's attracted, she thinks that she may have underestimated you, and that there must be more to you than meets the eye. She's petrified that people will find out she lost you to another woman. This same hot cold diversion is something you see and experience many times in relationships. Ever wonder why couples break up and then get back together, over and over again? When they get back together, the sexual gymnastics reach new levels of excitement and debauchery. Even the East German bitch judge stands up and applauds, flapping her hairy armpits in the breeze. And remember, getting together again gives you yet another opportunity to blow her out in a foul-mouthed public rage again.

When a woman is in hot pursuit, the end result is well worth the effort. Make sure after the conquest you reward her with an autographed picture and a healthy high five. Don't leave her there thinking it was all for nothing. By her seducing the seducer, she's living proof of the age-old adage.

## Bachelor Code 11
### Amendment 6a, subsection5-8g

**Women want what they don't have,
And when they have it, they don't want it.**

– – – – – – –

# Chapter V

# PERSONALITY PROFILING
### YOUR
# TARGETS

Precision Selection of
Targets to Seduce

# Profiling the Miniskirts

Your Alpha Presentation and Role-playing Charisma are vital weapons in attracting and seducing women. With a little practice in the field these things will become second nature. BUT, when it comes time to truly mastering your game, there's a skill of greater importance, and it usually gets lost in the shuffle.

- - - - - - -

## Bachelor Code 12

The most important tool in seduction is
**knowing who NOT to date**

- - - - - - -

Efficiency in profiling your potential targets controls your dating time and dollars. It can mean the difference of years, tens of thousands of dollars, not to mention your sanity. In sales they call it finding the right ear.
*"Never waste your sales pitch on the wrong guy."*

This principle applies tenfold in courting women. As tough as it can be, you really have look beyond a babe's tan legs that go for days and peer into her mind before asking her out. The younger inexperienced studs think they're slaying the field by dating four new girls a week. They mistake aggressive dating for effective speed seduction. After a few years of hangovers and a lousy sex life, they shake their heads wondering where the hell they're going wrong. Looking back, they see their work productivity suffering, they're pissing away money with little return, and their dicks are waving a white flag at the lousy closing ratio. The problem is they forget to profile their targets. Meanwhile, all around them they see the A-players hitting home runs with nines and tens, effortlessly kicking their ass at every turn. The studs are picking off *Lexus* and *Mercedes* from the main stage, while amateurs score with *Yugo* and the crusty old dayshift MILF named Pinto:

*"Don't hit me from behind, I may explode."*

Dating is a school of hard knocks if you don't do your homework. Newbies learn the hard way that the majority of female targets you meet in the singles scene are game players, gold diggers, attention whores, time wasters, and sexless cockteasers. Welcome to Reality. Don't waste your breath complaining about it. We've all been there. Thanks to feminism it's the terrain we operate in. Sooner or later everyone has to learn the value of target profiling and the quick exit. Take action and adapt. There are more than enough quality, sexy girls to conquer. The challenge is to weed through the trash, fine-tune your profiling ability and dazzle them with your magic.

In time, you'll know within minutes if a potential skirt is a keeper or a waste of oxygen. When confronted with yet another con woman, instead of getting pissed off, sharpen your skills and use the situation for research and laughs. Suppose you approach a girl, and in five minutes she makes very little eye contact, and goes straight into sizing you up with the sleazy gold digger routine. *"What do you do, what do you do drive?"*, you know, the typical prostitute mentality. Once you're onto a girl's charade, lead her on a bit. Master recognizing their bullshit lines and spotting their angles…how they tempt you with sexual favors you know will never occur. Try to keep a straight face as she points her nose to the sky flaunting her *"high class image"*, while blatantly trying to sell her pussy to the highest bidder. Have some fun and give her the same BS treatment. Ponder out loud about taking her on weekend getaways to Cancun, Greece, cruises, dinners and shows in NYC or Vegas. As she becomes convinced she has you conned and has a shot at vacuuming your wallet, pay close attention to the body language changes. Watch how she suddenly makes constant eye contact, flips her hair, licks her lips, exposes cleavage, strokes your arm and fakes sexual interest. Then, with a laugh, walk away while she's in mid-sentence.

*"Sorry, I don't date whores. It's cheaper to rent them."*

Target profiling is a fact-finding mission. It's not your job to baby-sit or finance a neurotic woman with a lousy attitude. You're looking for nice, honest girl who respects you, and is sexually attracted. Slow down your game and step out of your testosterone fog. Narrow your selection from the beginning. Start with only the women sending you signals that indicate interest. Then in your meet and greet, just a few minutes of checking her body language will give you additional clues. You'll know if she's attracted to you for a relationship or a quickie, or if she prefers to manipulate and tease. If she passes this test, do a quick profiling of her personality for self-confidence, honesty, sexuality, and character strengths.

## The Female Personality Types

There are roughly ten unique individualized personalities that we can classify people with. It's common to share overlapping characteristics from other types, but there is always one specific type that defines your identity better than any other. You are who you are, and your identity begins early in childhood. People do not change from one personality type to another. Each of the ten personality types is made up of positive and negative traits. People who are *Mentally Healthy* within their personality types are warm in relationships, have strong self-confidence, a clear direction in life, and can get along with anyone. They project the positive traits of their personality type, and are able to keep the negative traits under control. The *mentally unhealthy* person's life is dominated by their negative personality traits. They have difficulty in relationships, and have less control over their minds and their life. Unhealthy people have an buffet of problems, both real and imaginary; lack of self-esteem, nagging and worrying, anxiety and insecurity, alcohol/drug issues, lower IQ's, job or money problems. Many unhealthy girls hide behind childhood issues they create out of thin air (imaginary rape by an Uncle is a popular one). A lot of girls are just naturally born psychos, and are perfectly happy going through life miserable and blaming it on everyone else. The bottom line is the mentally unhealthy chicks fear reality; they'll do anything to avoid taking responsibility for their own life. You've heard the terms Obsessive Compulsive, and Manic Depressive. They're examples of unhealthy classifications of personality styles. So how we use this psych info our dating careers?

In the dating world, a **Professional Bachelor** maximizes his time and money by only dating the *mentally healthy* women of the world. Someone else can baby-sit the irrational life suckers. This brings us to the purpose of this section of the book. **Target Profiling.** Develop a clear understanding of the female personality types. In no time you'll become an expert at knowing which style they are. A smart approach is to pick out in advance the two or three types that appeal most to you. This will efficiently narrow down your partner choices to a target rich environment. Then perfect your skills of seeing how each new target deals with the positives and negative traits of her personality style. Once you become familiar with profiling, you know a new chick's life story a mile away. You'll know how to tell if she's mentally healthy, and you'll know what approach work's best in seducing her. As you reach that point, your dating career leaps to the next level. As a rule of thumb, people with the same personality type are rarely compatible. (for one night stands, the mentally unhealthy are the easier targets)

## The Emotional Rollercoaster

Girls notoriously fluctuate back and forth between healthy and unhealthy as situations change in their life. This is where the phrase **Inner Psycho** comes from. Women can be perfectly warm and rational one day, and raving lunatics the next. Unlike men's fact-based decisions, females base most of their decisions on emotion and insecurity. In doing so, they treat men to witnessing insane fits of jealousy and guilt based on nothing. Every guy has been through bizarre scenes; like being accused of staring at another chick, when you're simply trying to catch the score of the game on the TV above her head. Most times women are not even aware of how schizophrenic they act. Normally they bounce back quickly, and pretend nothing happened. Your job in the relationship is to find ways to navigate through her waves of nonsense and emotion. Learn to deflect the lunacy, and keep her mentally healthy by avoiding the imaginary minefields in her head. The big **Inner Psycho** problems occur when the girl stays unhealthy for an extended period of time. When this occurs, it is a dangerous warning signal. You have to figure out the cause, and make a decision about an exit strategy. Your biggest fear? When you first met her, she may have caught you in a moment of weakness and has been role-playing from the beginning.

# Beware the Chameleon

Women in courting mode are phenomenal actresses. Some should be inducted into the Chameleon Hall of Fame. The month before you meet, she just got out of a relationship, *ie*, a guy dumped her because she gained 35 pounds and turned vicious. When she sees a new monied prospect, after just a few short weeks of snorting blow and living off her kid's baby food, she'll be back in fighting shape. On the first date, a completely new (and false) look and attitude will be presented. She'll be skinny, die her hair, have sexy new clothes, she'll laugh at all your jokes, love your friends, overnight become a sports fan, change religions, even go from a prude to a horny nympho. She'll assume an entirely new personality if you look like *The One* (a gullible rich boy she can control). She'll change anything and everything if she thinks you're going places and will support her in an inflated materialistic lifestyle. Then she'll revert back to her natural state a few months after the marriage. Needless to say, you do not want to get involved with a chameleon. Target Profiling can be crucial to your wallet and sanity.

Rapid unexplainable personality changes into the unhealthy mental state, particularly for any length of time, means you have chosen poorly, and entered the damage zone with the girl. Forget the rescue attempt. There is no turning back from the damage zone. Something has seriously gone wrong in her head, and you can be sure she will blame it on you the rest of the relationship. Cut your losses, and exit the stage. Change your phone number, change your locks, and watch your back.

### Bachelor Code 13
#### No matter how hot a chick is, you have to be willing to walk.

– – – – – – –

The inability to control their Inner Psycho is always the reason. This is why it is of utmost importance to know the healthy/unhealthy traits and a girl's personality type long in advance. It also shows why the smarter guys do a little background research on a girl before dating her. They ask around and find out the dirt on her from an ex, friend, or a co-worker to determine her true personality type and decide if she is a chameleon role-player. At the very least they watch her from a distance for a bit and make a judgment call.

# The Fallen Star Syndrome

As women get older, their looks, confidence, and appeal start to fade away. This creates gradual personality depreciation, resulting in a majority of unhealthy traits. The babes who had superior looks and power over men can't handle losing it. It kills their ego and creates serious mental health decay, as their newfound low social status becomes the norm. There are similarities in ex-stud athletes and musicians. Imagine being a 22 yr. old local rock star who had naked groupies up to the eyeballs, and 15 years later his best options are coyote dates with the crusty old Wal Mart cattle. Imagine what goes through his mind.

The percentage of US women in their late 30's who are still hot and mentally healthy is roughly one half of one percent. Over 40, maybe one tenth of one percent. Why is divorce rate so high? **Women change**. One way or another, as they near forty they've got a screw loose and/or a major league chip on their shoulders. Ask any divorce attorney or therapist; bitter and neurotic would be a compliment for the most of them. Not to mention a large percentage need a forklift to plop onto the bed at night.

# Payback is a Bitch

Age 40 is when the selfish whore mentality of the hottest trophy babes comes back to bite their ass. When they were young and cocky, they only dated trust fund frat hunks, bad boy thugs, and rich older men. Twenty years later when they have two kids, drooping titties, varicose veins, and stretch marks, they expect the nice guys who they blew off in their youth to open their wallets and be a surrogate daddy to someone else's kids. Their power over men vanishes, and options for hooking up with studs are slim to none. When sassy, aggressive "cougars" hit on young alpha studs, the typical guy's reaction is cringing in horror, and disbelief that she thinks she has a chance. The illegal alien who cuts her yard will say *"Chit lady, I don' fuck fossils for free."* Usually the best a crusty old cougar can hope for is the occasional sloppy dry fuck from a local pub drunk, who does her on a dollar bet. He pops her for five minutes with a semi-limp whiskey dick, changes his mind in the middle of it, and runs for his life back to the bar. He may have earned his money for courage, but unless he's sufficiently lubricated and blacks out, the image haunts his brain's hard drive for years to come.

Role reversal highlights the amazing differences in Self Worth and Pride when comparing men and women. If a 23-year-old stud started dating a 50 year-old free-spending millionaire Granny, if anyone found out he'd be ridiculed for life and have to flee the city. Every guy in town would be pointing fingers at him, doubled over in laughter. *"There he is! Licking a senior for cash. Disgusting!"* Yet everywhere you turn, the hottest trophy pieces and Hollywood's most desired women do it on a daily basis AND BRAG ABOUT IT!!!

> "I don't chase women, I just sit on my wallet
> and wait for them to come to me. "
> **Mickey Spillane,** *Author in 1988*

# It's Great to be King

For 40 yr. old men with money, the party is just beginning. Older Men with money have MORE options with girls than ever, and sexier ones to boot. Remember when you were just out of college and broke? The hot young chicks didn't want a thing to do with you. Twenty years later as you near forty all cashed up, the current batch of early 20's hotties see you've got money to throw around, and suddenly you're the funniest, best looking man they've ever met! Prostitution is alive and well in the good ole USA.

"A man's only as old as the woman he feels." *Groucho Marx*

Think long term when it comes to women. The smartest thing to do if marriage is your goal is to wait until you are 40 before making the big commitment. That way, you keep all your own money from your top income earning years, and get the trophy girl you never had a chance with when you were younger and just making end meet. (Obviously you put all your money in an asset protection plan before marrying. – see chapter).

As a Professional Bachelor, remember **The Inner Psycho** mental health guidelines and plan accordingly. It's in your long-term best interests to only date sexy young women with a *healthy* personality, at a preferred age of 18 to 25. That way, if you find a keeper and marry when you're 40, by the time your 25 yr. old wife becomes a deranged worrywart, I mean 40, you'll be nearing 60; her attitude won't mean that much to you. Now if she becomes completely undesirable, not to worry. Inform her of her expiration date, drop kick her out the front door, and trade her in for a new young squeeze. It's not your fault she changed. With your asset protection firmly in place before marriage, it's a smooth transition. Hand her an autographed photo, slap her ass on the way out the door, and say: *"Thanks for playing. Next!"*

Alrighty then, let's move on to a quick class in **Body Language 101**. Then, we move forward with **Target Profiling**, and take a look at the most common personality types you will face in the jungle.

- - - - - - -

# Female Body Language 101

One of the finer techniques in increasing your success ratio with women is learning to read their body language before approaching. Don't advance where you're not appreciated. If she's not interested, you're only wasting time and money on her. When you learn the body movements and signals they are sending, it narrows down the targets. It stops you from needlessly pursuing someone not attracted. (The exception being the trophy pieces, who have so many offers they never approach guys.) Like a third base coach, most girls noticeably flash you visible signals if they want you to approach. These will be suggestive of what she is feeling and thinking about you, and they can either be unconscious or deliberate. The only trick is deciphering these signals aimed at getting your attention. Pay particular attention for the pumping hand to mouth simulated blowjob signal. Likewise, if you misread a signal and moved in guns a blazing, she will let you know if you're not wanted. For example, if a girl hands you her tampon and says *"guess my blood type?"*, you may not be doing so well.

Men tend to be more direct when it comes to interaction with women. To employ game playing, subtle nuanced language and body signals seems like a preposterous waste of time. We know what we want, and we want it now. My best signal is putting a Benjamin on my forehead and unzipping my fly. (for best results and shorter rap sheets, this should only be done in Full Service Strip Clubs or Brothels).

Expecting girls to cooperate would be too simple. Many women find being unattainable and hard to read very important, so they specialize in mastering charades and deception. They go to clubs to boost their ego, and then complain about getting hit on all night, which was the reason they originally went out. Nightclub chicks give off plenty of false signals; it's clearly not the best venue to pickup women anyway, except for sportfucking.

They are plenty of girls who *are* looking to hook up though. By being able to determine which women are available in advance, and gauging her intentions after you meet, your success ratio in scoring will vastly improve. Many studies claim human communication is 80% non-verbal and 20% verbal. The truth is that once you have approached a woman, as you interact, her body positioning, posture, eye contact and gestures will tell you all you need to know without words being spoken. Sure you will make mistakes from time to time. But through trial and error you will be putting your ego less on the line, and getting higher probability results.

# Field Research

After learning the signals, do some field research in restaurants, clubs, and coffee shops to train your eye for the signs. It's fascinating. Soon you'll be looking for signals everywhere you go. Watch the women like the Crocodile Hunter on the prowl. Fine-tune your skills in spotting her body language; is she suggesting sexual interest, monetary interest, or just going through the motions? Most guys are oblivious to the true signals, and are wasting time. The funniest is watching married couples. Most give off signals that they would rather be anywhere on the planet but together at that moment.

After mastering this visual art, when you see a girl giving all the right signals, you'll know it immediately. She wants you to be there. She is focusing all her attention on you; even more so than her vibrator. You want a girl visually and mentally attracted to you. Remember, first impressions mean everything. She will make her decision in the initial 30 seconds whether she will consider sex or a relationship with you. Be confident, a good listener, be cocky, funny and yet distant…and try to stop staring at her amazing rack.

There are three phases to this process. First, is to scan the room and determine which women are sending overall available signals. Second, look for some confirmation signals that she's approachable by you. Third, once you've approached, pay close attention to her body and hand movements. She'll signal whether she wants to ride you cowgirl style, or she'll signal for you to piss off. It's a numbers game. Don't take it too serious if you get shot down. Laugh it off, and move on.

## <u>Female Body Language Signaling She's Available</u>

- Sitting with her legs open
- Smiles at you and licks her lips
- Makes eye contact and holds it
- Preens and twirls her hair a lot
- Standing with one foot behind the other
- Sitting with legs crossed flashing a thigh
- Sitting with one hand touching her breasts
- Wearing a low cut blouse, exposing breasts
- Makes eye contact and looks down and away
- Standing with head tilted at angle, hips forward
- Licking her lips and looking around the bar often
- Standing alone at the bar, looking your direction
- Sexy strut around the bar, glancing both directions
- Separates from her girlfriends and stands at the bar
- Wearing a t-shirt with prices for sex acts clearly marked
- Positions herself close to you, with both her head and legs pointing your way.
- Looks in your eyes, peels off panties and throws them to you

# Signs of Interest During Conversation

- She buys *you* a drink.
- Her entire focus is you
- She ignores her friends
- Hands and palms up is good
- She keeps touching your arm
- She doesn't look around the bar
- She squeezes her tits together
- Smiles constantly, licking her lips
- She laughs too hard at your lousy jokes
- She tilts her head while listening to you
- If she is interviewing you in conversation
- She doesn't answer a ringing cell phone
- She looks at your lips while you're talking
- Changes her voice patterns to mimic yours
- She's rubbing her legs together (turned on)
- She leans in towards you during conversation
- Her hand or thigh brushes against your thigh
- She loosens the neckline to show you her rack
- She returns from the bathroom with a lot of lip gloss
- Sudden protruding nipples that can pop your eye out
- A lot of hair twirls, touches, putting hair behind the ears
- She turns her body, angles her head and legs towards you
- She comments about getting together for a drink or movie
- She unconsciously mirrors your hand gestures and posture
- She's on her knees blowing you, demanding a happy ending
- Sits legs crossed, pointing at you. Bouncing leg is real good
- Plays, fidgets with her jewelry, sign of nervous sexual tension
- Excessive blinking, raises eyebrows up and down then smiles

# Signs of Disinterest during Conversation

- She drinks really fast
- She crosses her arms
- She vomits in your shirt pocket
- She turns down a drink you offer to buy
- She pays attention to everything but you
- She stares at your hand when you touch her
- She ignores you or throws a drink in your face
- She pulls up neckline of shirt to block your eyes
- She ignores or is repulsed by sexual innuendos
- She answers her cell phone while you're speaking
- She keeps checking her cell phone, looking in her purse
- She concentrates on talking to her friends more than to you
- She goes to the bathroom and 2 hours later you're still waiting for her
- She scans the room while you're talking, looking for a timely escape to just about anywhere but near you
- She says her and friends are going to another bar, as in, they want to avoid you

# Body Language by Men that turns Women Off

- Foul mouth conversation
- Bad body odor, bad breath
- Real tacky or wrinkled clothes
- No eye contact while speaking
- Guys who brag about themselves too much
- Strangers who fondle and paw at their body
- Guys who are too pushy, forward or obnoxious
- Scanning the room for other women in front of her
- Stubborn drunk guys who insist on dancing when they say no

Women prefer to be approached respectively, not aggressively. They may be just looking to get laid, but they prefer not to feel like a whore in the pickup. They prefer a well-groomed, well-dressed guy who is funny, and has a strong confident attitude. They dislike drunk, conceited, aggressive men. Now for the all important psychological analysis of potential targets. Time for the Personality Profiling.

# THE SURVIVOR
### (Vigilant –Paranoid Personality)

**Dominant Characteristics:** passion, resilience and independence.
**Her Greatest Fear:** being controlled by anyone.

She has a passionate zest for life, is feisty, full of energy, and vigilant against anyone stopping her from getting her way. She is highly self-confident, and has the instinctive energy and drive needed to achieve most goals. She roots for the underdog, and is the eternal optimist.

## Personality Strengths

1. Self-sufficient, belief in herself
2. Cautious, careful, self-restraint
3. Superior control of her emotions
4. Self-defense, courage, determination
5. Disciplined, hard worker, overachiever
6. Savvy, perceptive and aware, thick skin
7. Serious, responsible, personal integrity.
   High morals, an inner sense of rightness.

This personality type is often the result of some painful psychological issues in early life, a shattered self-identity crisis that she successfully overcame. Her unstable childhood problems may include:

1. Dad always away from home on business trips, constant family arguments and power struggles
2. Dad had multiple jobs transfers – family moves constantly. Numerous schools, no sense of a real home or long-term friends.

### More common are serious internal family issues

3. A sibling (or herself) with a history of drug/alcohol problems, or troubles with the law,
4. Partial abandonment as a child, feelings of inadequacy, humiliation or helplessness.
5. Violent/alcoholic parent(s), or raised by a Single parent.
6. Divorced parents, raised by numerous people.
7. Extreme poverty.
8. Dad likes Yankees, Mom likes the Red Sox,
9. Her brother likes the ballet.
   LiL' Sister likes farm animals.

# Target Profile – What Makes Her Tick

She has overcome painful obstacles and is now winning in life. You can't pull one over on her, and she will not back down from arguments, threats, or challenges. She has very strong opinions, and will use her fists if provoked. She is NOT going back to the life that she came from. Therefore, she is somewhat suspicious of people, and can be difficult to get to know at the outset. She has great self-discipline, guards her feelings, and is very slow to commit. She has a fine tuned emotional intelligence, which helps her get a good read on people's intentions and feelings. If you are the no worries, laid back kind of guy, don't waste one minute trying to seduce her. She only dates the more serious type.

## Typical Careers

- Legal Assistant
- Real Estate Sales
- Advertising Manager
- Marketing Consultant
- Financial Management
- Human Resource trainer
- Medical Equipment Sales
- Graphics Artist/Designer
- Temp Employment Agency Sales
- Entrepreneur – one person business

# Seducing the Survivor Personality

Due to bad childhood experiences, she is highly suspicious of people. She shields her past from others, and protects her independence at all costs. The girl just doesn't know how to relax, and is obsessed with trying to figure out your motives to protect herself. Sweet talk and charm will turn her off, and she'll immediately label you are a player working angles. This type does not seek approval from you. She already knows she is good at things. Her inner core is confrontational, so you need to avoid all verbal controversy with this one. No worries here, speaking with women is overrated anyway.

*Her weakness* is hiding from her past, which is usually quite easy to recognize. It will show in her rapid defense of her current status. **The best targets are the young survivors,** who are only in their first year or two of success, and still feel vulnerable. (21-24yr old).

Often you can spot her past in her appearance; cheaper items of clothing, trying too hard to look sophisticated or rich. You may see excessive makeup or a punkish hairstyle in a corporate environment. Her body language is still a few years from your Bond silky smooth mannerisms. You'll see inappropriate nervousness and defensive responses. The body never lies.

The survivor types often dates men fifteen to twenty years older. They want a gentleman who is rock solid, honest, and straight to the point. It's a rapid level jumping desire for stability, and there are also Daddy issues at play. She is attracted to a guy who is successful, predictable, distant, and non-aggressive towards her. She wants to be treated like a grownup with years beyond her actual street experience.

Utilize the highly confident attitude and seriousness in life approach with her. Do mild flirting at most. Ninety percent of her brain is preoccupied with worries and goals, so don't expect her to fly into your arms. It will take a bit of time. In casual conversation, all girls will do the financial checkup and inquire about your job and social status. Don't volunteer any information. Let her bring it up. Go into the aw shucks humble explanation of your success. Then lower your voice a bit, and let her in on a little secret. Nothing came easy. It took tons of hard work. *"Between you and I, let's just say I came from a really rough upbringing."* **The Tragedy Stud.** Quickly segway out of your past and talk about how she reminds you of yourself in the early years of your career. *"I wish I had your guts and determination at such a young age. I was such a late bloomer."* Look into her eyes and say her future looks quite bright. Remember, she has no idea you easily see through her surface mask and know she has had a troubled past she wants noone to know about. Survivor bonding works like a charm.

Now, other than sharing your past troubles, do not share any of the other personality characteristics of her. Two survivors do not get along together. This is a very aggressive personality that does not allow for competition. If you attempt to change anything in her life, or attempt any control moves, she will start pushing you away. She has no problem identifying your faults, but is unable to see her own, and will never accept blame for anything she did. If you are patient and stick around for the kill, once she drops her bitch barriers, she is extremely loyal, respectful, and will be all yours. The hard part is telling when she gives in. As a bonus, survivors have a great sense of humor when it comes to OTHER people, but tease her and she'll get defensive and take it the wrong way.

She has deep emotional reserves; so don't expect her fawning at your every move. Do not anticipate standing ovations after yet another superior sex performance. Besides difficulty in showing any emotion, she is often overly reserved in the sexual department, since she can't turn her brain off. She is very selfish in bed. Other variations of sex problems can be her barking orders, refusing sex acts and demanding position changes at the wrong time; for example, when you're smashed and grunting while doing simulated body builder poses in the bedside mirror during a violent doggy style romp. For the frigid Survivor Girl, you can try to encourage more sex using caveman physical hints, but verbally there is nothing you can say to change her into a hyperactive hormonal beast. Either she is horny, or she isn't. Make you decision early on if you have the wrong girl. She has one major flaw that is tough to overcome. If you are a player, you cannot get away with having a fleet of girlfriends on the side. She is extremely possessive, suspicious and jealous, and will always find out. Don't be surprised if her girlfriends spy on you in town, or she plants a GPS tracker on your ride; hell, she may imbed one in your rod when you're passed out drunk.

## Inner Psycho Signals – Paranoid Disorder

The older women get, the more insecure and unhinged they become. Keep a sharp eye out for the warning signs on the younger ones. The Survivor has rather alarming tendencies when things go bad, particularly unjustified distrust. She feels threatened and suspicious that people are plotting to exploit or deceive her. Perceives everything has hidden meaning, and is an insult or attack. She reacts with anger and violence. Extraordinarily self-centered. Despite high intelligence, she can no longer handle authority. She becomes cold, belligerent, sarcastic and argumentative about everything. The worst part is she holds grudges; every new delusional problem just adds to previous incorrectly perceived issues and compounds her anger. When this type loses her self-esteem, she projects all her imaginary problems and weaknesses on others. *Everything is your fault.* Deep down she wants dependency, but can't handle the transition. She is petrified of losing her independent survivor status. If paranoid, she is a ticking time bomb.

## Target Conclusion:

We all admire the survivor's youth, energy and spunk. Keep in mind though; you are dealing with a military stiff girl who is a Major Butthead at times. Yes, this type usually works out hard and tends to have sexy little hard bodies. If she's got a great ass and puts out, she will be quite entertaining...until the first blowout argument. But in the long run, let's be realistic. Anger management courses are not a turn on. The uncontrollably suspicious mind and power struggles are difficult to deal with, even when you are getting along well with her. Get in a couple good sessions and find yourself a sensual girl with less attitude.

## One Night Stands

The session should be done at her place, or a secure location. Give her a fake name, glue on a comb-over toupee, and wear track shoes. Doggy style position only. Hum TV Game show theme songs during the pumping. During the happy ending finish, slap her on the ass and call her the wrong name. Dismount, and Run Forest, Run!!!

# Difficulty Level:
## 8.5

There's more satisfaction in dumping a cocky girl than giving her undeserved power, and putting up with her insecurity and arguing

— - - - - - - - - - —

### Successfully dumping her without a police report
+ 5 points.

### Bookmark her Bible with a used condom
+ 8 points

### She spray-paints a cross on the hood of your Porsche
- 20 points

### She spikes your drink, you wake up nude, tied to the mailbox in your driveway. The entire house contents are gone
- 50 points

— - - - - - - - - —

"There's nothing tougher than remembering why you've chased a dame once you've had her."

*Actor* **CLINT EASTWOOD,** *in 1990*

# MOTHER GOOSE

**Dominant Characteristics:** to feel needed in a close relationship.
**Her Greatest Fear:** to be ignored or unappreciated.

## Personality Strengths

1. Honest, Loyal, Sensitive
2. Non-judgmental, Faithful
3. Innocence, Naivety, Humility
4. Sympathetic, Compassionate
5. Generous, Loving, Forgiveness
6. Considerate, Trustworthy, Modest
7. Responsibility, Patience, Persistence

## Target Profile – What Makes Her Tick

You'll recognize this target immediately. In one day, she'll give more compliments, and do more nice things for you than the typical self-centered US girl will do in a year. Maybe a lifetime. Every time you blink she's running an errand for you. It's like dating your Mom. She's so flattering, it almost makes you feel guilty. Naaaaaahhh.

Often she is a sexy girl with the hidden body…the camouflaged girl next-door type wearing baggy clothes. She is not flashy by any means. She knows she can't compete visually with the killer babes of the world, nor would she want to act all cocky, dishonest and slutty like them. Her style of dress is either very professional, or very casual. Her mannerisms are quiet, sensitive, and reserved. She knows her talents and abilities to lure in men, and is very effective at her role. This girl feels she must always be in a relationship, and her rebound to the next guy can take place in a few days. She doesn't like being alone. Whatever you do, don't ruin a good thing and buy her a vibrator.

She surrenders her own desires in return for pleasing her man. She has almost a maternal desire to be self-sacrificing in a relationship. Compassionate and generous with her time, she gets her reward by seeing the happiness she brings to other people. She has great insight into people's feelings and desires, and knows how to push the right buttons to satisfy them. She closely values relationships, and is very forgiving to your faults. She lives to give favors and do good deeds without being reciprocated. The whole thing will feel very, very strange to the Professional Bachelor. When she's around, we don't know whether to put on a dunce cap and suck our thumbs, or grab her and shake her silly till she confesses what angle she's working. *What's da scam, Sista?*

## Typical Careers

- Nurse
- Caterer
- Bookkeeper
- Receptionist
- Social Worker
- Athletic Coach
- Dental Assistant
- Flight Attendant
- Child Care Worker
- Massage Therapist
- Special Ed Teacher
- Professional Volunteer
- Elementary School Teacher

# Seducing the Mother Goose Personality

Numerous quiet passive girls are attracted to jerks, problem child guys, and bad boys. The troubled persona is her preferred target, though he's the hardest catch for her. When a man acts vulnerable and prone to problems, the devoted rescuer is instantly attracted. In the good girls, her reasons are sincere, and multi-faceted. She needs someone to "save" and take care of to feel whole as a person. Showing compassion to your problems, she subconsciously expects you to give back to them. When you give back, she has the relationship she was shooting for. She has a man she can trust, who appreciates her, and who she doesn't have to worry about losing.

To seduce one with ease requires you to be the hard luck guy. You must play up your issues, and bat your crocodile tears in her general direction. Try not to tell her directly about your problems. Actions always speak louder than words. Pretend a NBA Ref just called a bullshit technical foul on you. Let her see you talking to noone in particular, and throwing your hands up in disbelief while shaking your head, etc. Life just isn't fair for you; you never seem to get a break. Why me? Put your head in your hands in an exaggerated fashion. Slam a drink down. Kick a cat, bark at posters on the wall. Fake an injury. Get in an argument with your imaginary friend and lose. You want to create a little scene all by yourself, while pretending you don't know she is present. You want to make her lean in and initiate the move. Even more effective is to include the bad boy image with your weaknesses. You don't want to be the leader of the pack to attract; it's the vulnerable stud sitting all alone in the club, or coffee shop, or bookstore that she looks for. The Rescuer loves a strong, independent, dominant man, and every girl is drawn to a bad boy (within reason). The more you exaggerate your flaws and tough luck in the world, the harder her nipples get.

# In a Relationship

If this is your first time seducing a Rescuer, it can feel a little strange. You'll definitely look like the odd couple if you got the whole bad boy image going. But this girl can be a great victim, as she really does put everything into the relationship. She is dedicated, polite, shows respect and is dependable. She will expect you to be honest and appreciative of her, but will never think to ask for compliments. *"Don't be silly, you don't have to thank me. I love bailing you out of jail for stealing a priest's car and soliciting prostitutes, you bad little boy."* She is perfectly happy letting you be the center of attention, and staying in the background. Warning; the girl takes criticism very hard; keep your comments light. In many ways she's as gentle and submissive as an Asian Lolita. First date she'll cook you a gourmet meal, feed you beers, undress you, massage you, blow you, and hug you like a teddy bear. The only thing missing in your pseudo-Asian relationship will be the jungle bush and sideways snapper. Me so horny!

Rescuers are very giving and subservient, and will do almost anything sexually for the relationship because they fear losing you. If you want blowjobs in the church parking lot, all you have to do is ask. She never says no. But if you don't ask, she won't do it. If you're the aggressive player, a high ratio closer doing five girls on the side, the Rescuer is the wrong girl for you. She will be onto your game, and will not tolerate it. *"Sorry honey, I'll do anything for you, but I don't share."* Get caught once, you're gone.

## Inner Psycho Signs – Dependent Personality Disorder

Unfortunately, Mother Goose's often completely lose their minds. The older they get, the more twisted and insecure their minds become. Even some of the devoted sweethearts start to lose it. When they do, you're in for a frightening transition into a life sucking hell. Pay very close attention to the warning signs. Her problems will overwhelm any fun you once had. Here are some of the signs that alert you to be plotting your exit:

- Petrified of being alone
- Quits job, sleeps all day
- Inability to make a decision
- Anxiety, panic, low self-esteem
- Deep depression, eats like a pig
- Daily panicked breakup questions
- Acts helpless, has imaginary fears
- A sick co-dependency cycle begins
- The blowjobs are a distant memory
- Instills guilt, pathetic hypochondriac
- Big Prescription drug dependencies
- Her ass belongs on a Water Buffalo

The worst is the chick who's two-faced in her niceties. She does things for you for deceitful hidden reasons, not because she's a sweetheart and likes you. She does favors without asking so that **you owe her** something in return. Afterwards, she brings it up in most every disagreement.

In the worst cases, (around year five of marriage), her cup isn't half full, it's friggin' empty, and it's all your fault! She has no control, no desires, no skills, and devotes all her time to detailing everything that's wrong in her life. When you offer rational solutions, she'll discount it and counter with even more problems. And of course, instead of facing up to her own insecurities, she finds it much easier to flail your ass with a torrent of endless droning. Say goodbye to your independence, your pride, and your wallet if you succumb to this type of toxic whining. Eventually just the sound of her voice will send chills down your spine. In the end, you'll be treated to painful silences, a big ass, no sex, whining, and a heavily medicated life sucker.

## The Breakup Line

"I'd really like to stay home with you and compare debts and arthritic back pains, but Tiffany is gonna be on the main stage in 45 minutes, and my bi-nympho girlfriend is waiting for me in the driveway."

--------------

### *Exit Difficulty Level:*
### 7

**Prolonged mind games**
+ **4** *points*

**She files a restraining order, barring you from your own house**
- **8** points

**Subscribe to Hustler in her name**
+ **4** points

**Pee on her cat while she's asleep**
+**8** points

**She catches you in the act**
+ **12** *points*

--------------

" Offend her, and she knows not to forgive;
Oblige her, and she'll hate you while you live."

**ABRAHAM COWLEY,** *English Poet (1618-1667)*

# ALTERNATIVE DREAMER
(Artistic – Solitary Personality)

**Dominant characteristic:** non-conforming attitude towards society.
**Her greatest fear:** being in compliance with society, going corporate, being considered part of a group instead of the autonomous individual.

She's an introspective, free-spirited dreamer who has no interest in seeking other's approval. Quiet and passive, she never surrenders emotionally to anyone. Independent, has few close friends, and is governed by her own belief system. Very passionate and emotional about her creative skills, but withdrawn and lonely about everything else. She leads an eccentric to imaginary lifestyle, and centers herself by following her heart and treating society as unnecessary noise.

## Personality Strengths

1. Alternative, Spiritual
2. Reliable, Trustworthy
3. Focused, Determined
4. Open-minded, Original
5. Highly Artistic, Creative
6. Confident Inner Strength
7. Emotional, Ultra Sensitive

## Target Profile – What Makes Her Tick

This is the girl who spent most of her childhood alone in her room, alienated from all the cool people in school. She often has well-developed creative skills (music/arts) at an early age; she devotes hours a day to her craft. Isolated from the outside world, she has no interest in exploring the highly visible social circles, clubs, chasing boys, etc. Despite her aversion to showing public interest in these things, she is internally consumed with keeping up with reality shows and Hollywood news and gossip. Also, there can be a heavy interest in romance novels, movies, soap operas, and fantasy life stories. Some fantasize about living in another era, romanticizing about being a queen courted in 18$^{th}$ century, living in castles and other nonsense. Some of them even keep their superior artistic skills at their craft hidden from others, and are almost embarrassed to share their abilities. They know they have talent, but they can't handle the emotions and stress involved with exposing themselves naked to world, facing the possibility of not being accepted. She spends her whole life avoiding people because she's afraid of being rejected, yet desires acceptance more than anything. She acts cold and distant in public, thus creating her own non-acceptance from people. The perfect self-fulfilling prophecy. The girl is ripe for the taking.

## Typical Careers

- Poet
- Author
- Singer
- Pianist
- Sculptor
- Psychologist
- Horticulturist
- School Teacher
- Yoga Instructor
- Software Writer
- Clothing Designer
- Impressionist Artist
- Environmental Crusader

# Seducing the Alternative Dreamer Personality

In her appearance, she will downplay her positive features, and hide from wearing anything openly suggestive. Look for subtle attire; no makeup, librarian glasses, college sweater, tomboy shoes, plain haircut; she's often skinny and flat-chested, and slouches. If you look close though, you can always see her hidden sensuality; the full pouty lipped *Hurt me Daddy* face. She has hypnotizing bedroom eyes that tend to look down and away, giving both a sultry and sad look at the same time. She rarely speaks, and has an adorable girly girl persona, like a young teenager.

She's suffering from a seriously low feminine self-esteem, and in many cases for no logical reason. This can be one of the most enjoyable girls to seduce, since you are rescuing her, raising her self-confidence and making her shine. It's a life-changing event for her. She is the opposite of 95% of the good looking girls out there; she is trustworthy, shows respect, and is unconditionally infatuated with you, as opposed to just being interested in vacuuming your wallet like the typical speed dating whore.

This girl confuses reality with fantasy, and still believes in being swept off her feet like in Pretty Woman. Deep down she would love to be more outgoing, but she's petrified and hypersensitive to being put down by catty women. She makes a great fixer upper, and a lot of them can be really hot looking if they want to be. The Professional Bachelor approach is to help her gain the confidence to dress up sexy for us AT HOME. There's no reason to parade around the new and improved babe in public, where others guys may pick her off.

She is usually trapped in a boring relationship with a male version of herself; a plain, stale non-sexual dork. In your initial conversation, listen to what she casually expresses discontent about…the loser boyfriend is usually mentioned in there. Find out what her artistic talent is, and be real casual about it. Before the subsequent follow up call, do research on everything about her talent so you are qualified to discuss it with her. Study up on the history of it, find out who the greats were, and who are the most popular today; find out the names of the more unusual players involved on the outer edges of fame. Learn the lingo. Then express interest in seeing/hearing her work. A lot of these girls are downplaying extraordinary talent accumulated after a decade of practicing. None of your act should be phony; the girl is worth every minute of it. This will add a facet to your own personality, and of course the process will be handy in the future.

Most important is giving her the chance the shine; to flaunt her talents, instead of being embarrassed of them. Flattery will get you everywhere with her. Be humbly overwhelmed at how she is so much more talented than you, and how you wish you had continued pursuing the arts during your childhood. This brings her barriers down, and builds up her self-esteem. The girl wants excitement in her life. Give it to her and she's all yours. Say the right lines and she holds onto you for dear life on the first date. Be Mr. Spontaneous. Try and get her *to change her ways*. Find out all the places she has always wanted to go, and take her there. Also, she usually is into tomboy things as well; hiking, bike riding, rollerblading, water-skiing; the more unpredictable, the more exciting. When she jumps in your arms and bats her eyes at you, you're instantly powerless, trapped in a hormonal fog walking around with tent pants, feeling like a dirty old man. Time to break out the schoolgirl uniform, and make her bend over playing hopscotch.

# In a Relationship

Who doesn't love the hot little girl next door? Even at age 25 she looks underage, and is totally submissive. The perfect little play toy who won't cheat on you. In public, she's extremely shy and totally passive. She may seem distant and aloof, but at home she's warm, open and sensual. She's very cautious in getting to know you, and will guard her emotions tightly. In reality, *she's dying to rip your pants off but is scared out of her mind you'll turn her down.* Ironically, as an avid reader, she is well versed on exotic resorts and foreign countries, but **she's petrified to try anything new.** Take her on a trip and she'll think you're the most romantic man in the world. Be careful, one little misunderstood statement by you can send her quickly into tears. As far as sex, you have to initiate all the moves. Don't expect her to be experienced. This will give you the rare chance to have a girl actually believe you when you explain that a three-incher is considered huge. Forget high maintenance, this girl is no maintenance.

**148**

# A REAL THINKER
## (Conscientious - Obsessive Compulsive Personality)

**Dominant Characteristics:**
Dedicated to good old-fashioned hard work and discipline. Her passion is achievement, getting the job done, doing the right thing.

**Her Greatest Fear:**
Failure, disorganization. Being perceived as unreliable, misinformed, or accused of making a mistake.

### Personality Strengths
1. Responsible, diligent, productive
2. Tenacious, meticulous, cautious
3. Disciplined, Self-control, deliberate
4. Orderliness, Persistent, perseverant
5. Steadiness, rational, sensible, methodical

## What Makes Her Tick

She is the consummate perfectionist, and prefers to do everything her way. She's the mid-level behind the scenes chick with great work ethic. With her intense, focused attention to detail, strong will and self-discipline, you can always count on her getting the project done. She has a strong conscience, and is very clear on right from wrong. She maintains high standards, and pushes herself hard to accomplish things. Organization, tidiness and cleanliness are just as important as achievement. She loves working, and is practical and conventional in her ways. *Down side*: she is very hard on other people if they don't follow her advice and techniques, and is very opinionated when it comes to deviating from her ways. The girl just doesn't know how to relax. She's the type that packs a full briefcase of work on vacations. She's cautious, safe, and thrifty. Hot damn boys; looky see here. Seems we got ourselves a Real Thinker on our hands.

## Typical Careers
- Auditor
- Librarian
- Engineer
- Professor
- Recruiter
- Psychologist
- Data Processing
- Career Counselor
- IT Service Director
- Medical Research

## How to Spot:

You're first thought is *"I'm Hot for Teacher."* Happy hour attire is painted on tight slacks and sleeveless blouse to show off her lean little body. She's the spunky, confident Girl-next-door with a perky butt. She wears very little makeup, heels, and she walks tall and really fast. The latest highlighted haircut, and a rare but sexy smile. She wears those quirky librarian glasses that make you think of squirting milk ( **god I look smart!** )

## Positives:

Reasonably intelligent, and amusingly perceives herself as your mentor. May spend her own money on a date. She is focused, and quite successful at achieving her goals. You can be seen in public with her without embarrassment. When you're together, all the other girls will stare and try to figure out what you've got. They'll plot how to snake her. Your rating goes up simply by appearing with her, and way up when you ultimately dump her. In dating, she's like your Mom, cleans up after you, and does all the shopping and errands.

## Negatives:

The bad ones are bossy, snooty, patronizing, and an emotionless prude. She demands perfection and has zero patience for you, but can't make up her own mind about anything. She gets lost in the details, can't see the big picture. She hasn't done a spontaneous thing in her life. Admitting she's having fun or is horny is painful. Rarely gets drunk.

Hates threesomes and Strip Clubs
**If you see two people talking and one looks bored,
she's the other one.**

She can be quite the anal bitch; incorrectly corrects your every statement. When you speak, she furrows her brow immediately and will quickly interrupt (**you're wrong, but I've got the solution!**) She can even discuss her imaginary stock portfolio with reasonably few foolish statements. The ultimate techie buff (**she reads email!**).

# Target Profile

The conscientious personality characteristic flourishes in most men, due to the superior work ethic required to succeed in the US. Masculinity is almost defined by your high levels of achievement and drive. Men live in a world of facts, and are activity driven. Everything is left brained and analytical. We take pride in creating our destiny, and despise the free lunch. Men don't sit around picking petals off roses. We don't have emotionally charged fantasies, longing for a Sugar Mommy version of Richard Gere to rescue us from Hooker Row. It's what characterizes the difference between the sexes.

# Bachelor Code 14
## Men think. Women emote.
### It's genetic, and women will never admit it.

Now there are some women who share the hard working, high IQ mindset. Now let's not get our hopes up too high here. A sexy, **rational**, intellectual equal on the female side is a very rare commodity; particularly if you want a horny one who treats men with respect. The intelligent, workaholic trait in a woman usually comes packaged with gender conflicts, degrees of feminism poison, and full of a condescending, elitist attitude. She gains the masculine traits, but loses all the toe-curling sensual traits that define femininity. **The Real Thinker** doesn't naturally feel lust or emotion for men. She hides her feelings, and panics when criticized. This is what makes her a great target. There's a gaping hole of pleasure in her life just aching to be filled...

People's surface presentation is often the exact opposite of who they really are. The bad ass karate expert is quiet, soft spoken and reserved. The arrogant, braggart looking for fights usually gets his ass kicked, and inside is nothing but an insecure child. Likewise, the high-minded, cocky chick who tries to talk down to you, underneath is full of insecurity and worries, and is not all that bright. She is a perfectionist, and agonizes over making decisions, out of fear of being wrong. On the outside she is strong and upbeat. Inside she is full of anxiety and stress, and has difficulty enjoying anything. Ya ain't fooling anyone but yourself, sister.

In choosing her dating partners, she will usually take the easy route, and hooks up with a successful, intelligent, dull guy. This protects her from taking risks, and satisfies her condescending "thinker" posse of girlfriends. But the mirror personality of her own doesn't satisfy her sexual desires. She feels trapped in her mental prison, and craves to let herself go and feel pure lust. What she longs for is a cocksure, flamboyant, witty stud who is thoroughly underwhelmed with her elitist attitude. The Universal Foundation always applies. She wants a guy who doesn't seek her approval, and oozes with a self-confident, could give a flying fuck attitude.

## Seducing the Real Thinker

Most guys will approach this girl the wrong way, and flex their ego trying to battle her intellectually. This is a waste of time, and will be nothing but tension and stress for the both of you. She will never admit that she's constantly wrong, so what's the point? Plus, the girl is not attracted to aggressive people who are direct intellectual competitors.

When you first meet her, give her the stage and make her feel brilliant. This creates the initial comfort zone and gives her a superiority power base over you. It helps hide your maneuvering behind the scenes. We'll use the **Dumb as a Fox** angle. (see chapter).

Use the awestruck idiot interviewer role: Since you "don't know squat about anything" in her mind, start with passive short questions that get her to spout out her superiority on topics. For bonus fun, choose a field you're an expert at. It'll provide the most silent laughs when you hear how often she slips up. A lot of nodding and agreeing with everything she says; the open mouth look of astonishment is quite effective.

-- - - - --

" *Stunning, I never thought of it that way.* "

"*That's so bold of you.*
*I wish I had your courage and drive.* "

" *I bet your friends are really jealous of you* ".

"*What's it like to be one step ahead of*
*everyone all the time?* "

-- - - - --

Maybe let her help you with her astute business analysis skills. Tell her how brilliant she is in pointing out the flaws in your failing John Deere Tractor overseas mail order business.

" Ahhh, so it's a shipping problem !!! "

Any brainless ludicrous crap like this will do. Practice at home; see how submissive and dense you can actually be. After a series of conversations like this over a week, you've created a comfort zone, and she likes how she feels when she is around you.

**Phase two**: To begin seducing her, you want to take her out of her world, and assume complete control...but in a playful, macho way. She may not know it, but she prefers a confident, dominant man; a guy completely different than what she faces in everyday life. You want to play to her **physical** attributes, and ignore her intelligence. Likewise, hide your own brainpower, to keep her from getting into any competitive intellectual battles. Yes, she will initiate arguments and power struggles at every turn. It's what she does best, and is how she gets her power. But you anticipate this, and effortlessly swat it aside. You simply tell her you respect her point of view, and stay distant with yours. Remember, she is the details perfectionist, not the outgoing, flamboyant leader. Successful Entrepreneurs leave the details to the little people like her, and concentrate on the Big Picture by staying silently two steps ahead of people…closing mega deals by persuading people with their charm. Enter the Professional Bachelor.

For dates, make the events the opposite of everything she is used to doing. Make her put her hair down, and feel like a cavewoman. Do physical outdoorsy dates, just like you would with the adventure girl. Trips to the beach, hiking, biking, strolling through parks and museums, outdoor concerts, all non-competitive, relaxation based, non-thinking events. Rarely speak. Force her to turn her brain off, and let herself go into your world. When she starts up with controversy, pause…and then look at her up and down with lust. Tell her how cute she looks when she is flustered. Keep her off balance and spinning in ways she has never let herself go before. Flirt, and pull back, tease, and pull back.

Once she lets her guard down, you own her. No one has ever made her feel this way. The girl makes for a great victim, and satisfying partner. She is faithful, responsible, and does all the chores. She's a great cook, irons your shirts, and even cleans up puke.

## The Warning Signs – Obsessive Compulsive

The heavy thinker can go very bad when she loses her confidence and competitive edge. When the signals appear, it's time to discard your damaged goods before she destroys your sanity. Look for these:

- Inflexible about all her beliefs
- Becomes a Psycho Control Freak
- Inability to trust others with any task
- Excessively perfectionist, she can no longer complete tasks due to strict standards
- Unable to make decisions without agonizing
- Devotes 100% of life to work ; anal buzz killer
- Obsessive about cleanliness and orderliness
- Takes out imaginary problems, insecurities on you
- Procrastination, fear of failure, all-or-nothing mindset

## Inner Psycho Exit Signals

Some of these girls camouflage their true selves until you're a few dates deep. A common nightmare is the superiority issue; she thinks she's on a mission from God to fix everyone else's life. She'll want you to put your entire life on hold, while she gives up her precious time in order to repair your miserable existence. She'll question your career, your attire, your friends, "*you call that music ?* " She'll critique your every hobby, thought and move, and put you down in public.

> "You need to quit that silly little job and see my friend Matthew;
> he'll throw you something to keep you busy."

**She may be a serial whiner, but at least she nitpicks...**

She plays the elitist Attention Whore to the hilt. Anyone interrupting her holy instructor mode will throw her into full-blown open mouth panic. Once the men in her town learn her charade, she'll find herself in the most frightening situation of all…no one to counsel, ie, nowhere to hide from herself. What usually follows are the textbook moves; quitting her job, hacking off her hair, buying another car, and moving to a new apartment.

The complete 4-step makeover.

**"That'll show 'em who's in control !"**

# One Night Stands

The Hit and Run is the only modus operandi for the Preaching-in-Your-Face girl. Play along till the conquest and get the hell out of there permanently. You won't be missing much; this type is horrible in bed. She's such an amateur at a blowjob, you're not sure if it's even in her mouth. It's like sticking your dick in a warm bathtub. It kind of feels good for a while; but in the end it just makes you wanna pee.

### *Difficulty Level:*
### 6.2

— - - - - - - - - —

Successful dumping without her committing suicide
**+ 5 points**.

Scream "Psycho Hosebeast from Hell" in her face in front of her boss
**+ 8 points**

Leave a casket in her front yard with a sign…
"What are you waiting for ?"
**+ 15 points**

Fill her cubicle at work with 1000 pounds of ice cubes
**+ 25 points**

You drive by her house and see your Prized Hunting Dog
has turned blue on the ice in the casket…
**- 40 points**

— - - - - - - - - —

"If you let your wife stand on your toe tonight
she'll stand on your face first thing tomorrow morning."
**SIR THOMAS MORE,** *English statesman (1478-1535)*

# THE ATTENTION WHORE
### (Narcissistic Personality disorder)

**Dominant characteristic** is her excessive emotionality and attention seeking; a narcissistic desire for seeking everyone's eyes and approval. She is a flashy, seductive dresser, and her behavior is full of look-at-me dramatics, but in a good way. She only wants to see the positive side of things. She interacts with others in an overly sexual and provocative manner. She is charismatic, infectious, energetic, and highly in tune with her seductive skills. She has an intense, emotionally charged view of the world. Everything she says and does has to be done in extravagant fashion, full of melodrama. There are sexual overtones to everything, and she's quite adept at being an uncontrollable flirt. She's feels invisible unless she is entertaining and impressing people.

**Her greatest fear** is being unattractive, boring or ignored. Without people fawning over her she feels powerless.

## What Makes her Tick

Though fun and outgoing, she is a lost soul inside. Her life is all outward based, reliant on creating interest and desire in men. She wears her emotions and feelings on her sleeve. She lives for meeting strangers and winning them over. Likewise, she loves being in a group of strangers, picking their lives apart, analyze what each likes, and then play the matchmaker. She's engaging and charming throughout the process, and constantly joking. Everyone feels better when she is around and the center of attention. She pursues men's affection at a pace few women can rival. She is working dozens at a time, and is barely aware she is flirting with half of them. It just comes natural. The world is her stage, dammit. *"Worship my coochie."*

**Theme song**: "Doncha wish your girlfriend was hot like me..."

### Personality Strengths
1. Sensitive, Free Spirit nympho
2. Sensual, witty, compassionate
3. Open-minded, horny exhibitionist
4. Agreeable, enthusiastic, gracious
5. Idealistic, motivated, inspirational
6. Creative, artistic, flashy, energetic
7. Spontaneous, engaging, attractive

# Target Profile

The Attention Whore was raised in an emotionless environment. She suffered from a lack of attention and confused parental guidance. Her parents were constantly in heated arguments, and displayed no love between each other. More significant, she had virtually no warmth or relationship with her mother. Mom was passionless, and counseled her that all men were rotten. But the daughter silently disagreed with her, because she always felt a tighter bond with her father and looked up to him. She was Daddy's girl from the beginning. She carried this admiration of men forward, and it accelerates with each year.

She sets out in life to be the complete opposite of her mother, and hopes to prove Mom's views about men wrong. Her subconscious pursuit of men derives from an attempt to overcome her feelings of isolation and inadequacy. She is permanently infatuated with men. She starts out by dating a million guys, hoping to find one as good as her father. Eventually, she tires of trying to find his equal, and instead becomes addicted to the sex and attention. Her sensuality gives her power over men. As she grows addicted to controlling men, her quest for replacing Daddy is long forgotten.

Each man she has sex with validates her shallow self-esteem and existence. Many would argue that her flamboyant appearance, overly dramatic personality, and nympho pursuit of men are an attempt to fill the void left from no maternal love. Perhaps. For the Professional Bachelor, what the hell do we care about her issues? We're not psych doctors, we're horny Alpha Gladiators backed up to the ears with sperm. We're just happy to find that rare breed of US women who actually lusts for men and likes sex more than money.

## Typical Careers

- Singer
- New Age Art
- Poet/Novelist
- Holistic health
- Sex Therapist
- Swimsuit Model
- Clothing designer
- Real Estate Agent
- Fashion consultant
- Dept Store Beautician
- Novelty Sex Shop Sales Rep
- Adult industry sales/content

# Seducing the Attention Whore Personality

This is probably the easiest target to spot in public. Her clothing is provocative, original, a tad slutty, and full of vivid bright colors. All slinky hips, wet lips, and exposed tits. There's always some unusual items she wears to go with the package to be different; stripper high heels, funky hat, huge hoop earrings, pink mini-skirt, etc. Like it or not, the girl has her own style and all eyes are on her. Dressing is a whole occupation for her. If you're out on the town, you can usually *hear* her first. She'll be surrounded by people, and a bit loud. She's a storyteller, and her Hollywood fantasy imagination overwhelms the facts in every tale. Her experiences are related in grandiose language, with descriptions of things and events just over the top ridiculous. It doesn't matter, because she's funny as hell, and is always looking to get laid.

For all the effort she puts into drawing men towards her, she is emotionally immature and subconsciously pushes them all away over time. She's afraid of committing herself fully to anyone. So she seeks out men who are strong, distant, and emotionally unavailable, like herself. The Attention Whore is easily influenced, and takes mild compliments and suggestions to be symbolic of fate and love. When you first meet, give her the stage. Don't be particularly funny or interesting, or she'll be turned off by your competition. Like Andrew Carnegie's book, her goal in life is to Win Friends and Influence People. Be a challenge, and let her pick you up. Show attraction, but be only vaguely curious. Flash interest, but act like you aren't going to lose any sleep over her if she's not attracted. She's just another girl. The distant unimpressed guy makes her blood and loins boil. Most guys fawn all over her, and she isn't used to someone showing such power over her.

Compliments are how you win her over; but you have to do them in such a way that you separate yourself from the pack. Stir some interest in her first with a few side comments about something she's wearing. *"I couldn't help noticing what a hip taste in fashion you have...that hat is so tight."* (barf) Compliment her sense of style, how sexy her shoes are, etc. A little admiration goes miles with her. Also, keep in mind that this one is far more interested in humor and gossip than reality. She may actually subscribe to National Enquirer. Any provocative comment will excite her; *"my horoscope (palm reader, faith healer) told me I'd meet a sexy, dangerous woman this week."* Then pause, and give her a sly, almost dirty up and down look. Rape her with your eyes.

Most girls are offended by direct sexual innuendos when you first meet them. This one lives for it. Give her a teasing line and then move away from her. Keep a distance. For example, *"I bet you're a really good kisser."*

Then smirk, look her up and down a second time, and walk away like your bored. Keep it slow, cool, and casual. Then, go start up a conversation with the first good-looking girl you see. Use observation humor, or anything that will keep you there for a few minutes. Now you have created competition. The Attention Whore is not used to having to try hard to win a man over.

Let her win you over, and the roller coaster ride begins. This type considers everything symbolic, and she latches on to each new guy with great emotional significance. She is convinced that each new guy is *The One*. Her infatuation of you will be profound. However, this idealized image of you will be impossible to maintain over long periods of time. Expect wild, uninhibited passion and attention in the beginning. Also, expect her to cheat on you the 1st week. It goes with the territory. Many AW's will proclaim love at first sight, and then one-night stand your ass. They're the biggest flirts on the planet, and at the same time violently jealous if you say 2 words to another chick in front of them. Enjoy it while it lasts; it never does.

## In a Relationship

If you're dating the dramatic Attention Whore, she needs to be reminded of her beauty, fashion sense, and amazing skills at least once a week. She likes surprises, roses, candy, and the typical romantic crap. We all hate to grovel like this…but you gotta love a girl who comes home with you on the first date, puts her legs behind her ears and gives a double dildo show!!

Her flamboyance and sensuality are enticing, but oh how her fragile ego needs to be fed. She needs spontaneity and excitement, craves newness, and wants to be surrounded by people. She will want to drag you out dancing and clubbing every other day once you start dating. This comes as quite a shock to a seasoned bachelor who prefers a social itinerary of sitting home seven days a week getting head while watching ESPN.

Keep in mind she is all emotion, and has no ability to pay attention to details. She is highly undependable when it comes to schedules, organization, planning, honoring appointments, or being on time. Her life is in total disarray, because she can't commit enough mental energy to anything, like even paying bills on time. She just can't bother with the little things like being trustworthy. If you plan an evening hooking up with her, allow for HOURS of leeway. In her life, "pick you up at 7:15pm" becomes tonight-ish. After she jerks you around once or twice, you'll realize the best approach is to call her up and say *"I'm running late at the office, I'll meet you there."* You will lose your mind waiting around for this bird.

Her inability to concentrate, and endless need for approval seeking attention make it near impossible for her to stay interested with just one guy in a relationship. On the bright side, since she is a certified nympho, and she may bring over a horny girlfriend once in a while. Remember to compliment how sexy the old lady is, not the friend.

## Inner Psycho Signals – Histrionic Disorder

When these girls go bad, you are in for some rough times. As she grows bored in the relationship, she can be quite volatile. She has rapidly shifting and shallow emotions, and no control over them. Her constant flirting with other guys in your face is done to taunt you, to see how much she can get away with. She goes from a childlike excitement to violent fury if you make her mad. In arguments, she will blow you out like a foul mouth drunken sailor. Expect violent breakups followed by ecstatic making up every week. The only way to avoid this is to compliment her a lot, and ignore everything she says. Say nothing controversial. After all, you're dealing with a child who must get her way.

How to make her scream with rage at you? Be possessive, jealous, or suspicious of her. Accuse her of affairs. Try to outshine her in public. Correct her stories. Tell her you don't like her taste in clothes. Demand her undivided attention to you, and not every other guy in the club. She feels your role is to be the responsible one who doesn't try to slow her down. Have a strong opinion different than hers, insult someone or be negative, and she will blow you out in public.

## Conclusion

The Drama Queen is very exciting and sensuous in the beginning. But her approach to dating is designed to fail on purpose, since she prefers multiple partners. Basically, this is the type you want to stay home with and screw all night, but she won't let you. Once she stops romanticizing about you, you become her old man; not her hot new stud. From then on, you can't trust her alone, and when you go out together, she flirts with every guy, and will show you zero respect. It's a no win situation. (But damn the sex is good.)

The rule of thumb is to tolerate her as long as you can until the emotional terrorism becomes overwhelming. If she's seriously hot looking, just being seen with her you will elevate your status and help you meet a lot of future targets. But in the end, this little trophy piece loses her value, and takes her place along side the rest of the wackos. She becomes just another beautiful, intolerable woman. You end up admiring her like a well-manicured lawn. They're both very nice to look at, but you sure as hell don't want to pay for it, let alone have to maintain it.

# One Night Stand
## *Difficulty Level:*
### 5.2

A player working the dating field with skill is an admired and respected stud. When a girl does this, she's a slut. Pro Bachelor's have self-respect. We always dump sluts.

---------------

**Successful Breakup**
without a keyed car
**+ 3 points**

Cruise your Harley around her living room
during your exit out of her life
**+ 6 points**

She talks you into one last fuck and
pulls out handcuffs in the bedroom
**+ 8 points**

She spikes your drink and puts the cuffs on you
**- 10** points

You wake up shackled wearing a diaper in a
Gay Hells Angels dungeon
**- 35 points**

------------------

" Direct thought is not an attribute of femininity.
In this, woman is now centuries ... behind man."
**THOMAS ALVA EDISON,**
*in Good Housekeeping 1912.*

# ADRENALINE JUNKIE
## (Obsessive - Manic Compulsive disorder)

**Dominant Characteristics:** challenge, risk, excitement, adventure.
**Her Greatest Fear:** being alone, safe and bored, without risk.

## What Makes Her Tick:

The girl lives for the here and now. She is always exploring new challenges, high-risk adventures, or men to seduce. She has no fear, and oozes high self-esteem. Wildly aggressive and confident, she loves to take anything and everything to the next level. Apprehension and caution do not exist; she dives headlong from one extreme challenge to the next. A passionate daredevil with a zest for life, she is a non-conformist known to make decisions on a whim. She takes full responsibility for her actions, since they're usually proud accomplishments.

When she enters a room, she lights it up with her charisma and energy. She has a quick mind, cutting wit, and is a very persuasive speaker; though she need not be with that rock hard bubble butt she's packing. Most importantly, she's very in touch with her Inner Whore, and shares the wealth freely with worthy targets.

### Personality Strengths
1. Challenge-seeker, enthusiastic
2. Talented, aggressive, ingenuity
3. High-spirited, tough, no anxiety
4. Sexy, charismatic, spontaneous
5. Disciplined, boldness, high-energy
6. Self-assured, good instincts, hysterical
7. Resourceful, innovative, nymphomaniac

## How to Spot:

Subtle sensuality; tastefully hidden in professional attire in the day, wears hiking boots, ripped shorts and a midriff in the afternoon, and a painted on miniskirt and high heels at night. Underneath, she could compete in the swimsuit competition at a Ms. Fitness Pageant contest. Naturally magnetic, she has a permanent smile, and is surrounded by at least 5 guys at all times...she looks bored when they're speaking, peers over their shoulders at other guys while chugging her fifth drink this hour.

## Habitat:

Ski Mountains, Vegas hot tubs, Vacation Resorts, hiking, competitive sports, in the gym at 5 am doing hour long spin classes or kickboxing, front row seats at concerts, marathons, Skydiving, VIP only clubs talking to gazillionaires, in bed with your best friend.

## Positives:

A genuine passion for living. Confident, resilient, spontaneous, impulsively horny, smart and witty. She lives with her hair on fire, is quick witted, and is more athletic than most guys. Rock hard body, washboard stomach, has favorite porno stars and a doctorate in sex positions. She has no problem with sleeping her way to the top, so she has her own money. She knows the inside scoop about everything going on in town. Been known to have sex in public. If you're her boyfriend, sometimes she does it with *you*.

## Negatives:

The bad ones are greedy, extraordinarily selfish, critical, jealous, and annoyingly hyperactive. Undependable risk taker. She cheats like a fiend. Answers her cell phone during sex. Underneath all her sophistication she can be an insensitive vicious shark. You'll feel exhausted just having a conversation with her. Any attempts to offer constructive advice will bring a rather violent barrage of ferocious, cutting insults that she really means. The kind that you could never forgive. Yet she'll think nothing happened just 10 minutes later.

## Cell Phone Report:

On dates, you'll want to grab her cell and smash it. Rings every three seconds, she answers all of them. Pulls out a calendar and schedules outdoor sport excursions with other guys, flirts with them right in front of you. In a span of one minute, she can go from friendly to you, to annoying beyond description. The Professional Bachelor always dumps this girl when her rudeness escalates. If you're in a restaurant with her post-sex, on the third call claim you're going to the bathroom and just leave her ass there.

## Car Report :

Drives a Porsche Boxster Convertible, license plate reads **"Was His."**

## Typical Careers

- ER Surgeon
- Police Officer
- Ski Instructor
- Personal Trainer
- Commercial Pilot
- Securities Broker
- Litigation Attorney
- College Sports Coach
- Collision Crash Dummy
- Car Show Rent-a-Model
- Multi-Sport Competitive Athlete

# Target Profile – What Makes Her Tick

She's a hyperactive extrovert who loves the constant adventurous search for pleasurable experiences. Most people find approval through other people; this type finds it through physical challenges. People are just an added source of stimulation and pleasure. She lives for instant gratification. (So do men, but do we really need to climb a friggin' mountain just to get laid?) The girl just cannot sit still.

She is a connoisseur of numerous experiences, and loves to tell fascinating animated stories about each. She also has an insatiable desire to learn. She'll learn A-Z about a country and its history before going there. She just likes to learn about things, period. Often has multiple degrees, studies stock financial statements to eastern philosophy. When she walks into a book store for a specific book, she'll leave with ten books. She just can't slow down her busy mind. She tends to be a workaholic, and has an over abundance of drive and persistence to achieve most anything.

She's a voracious socialite, dines at all the best restaurants, appears at every grand opening, never misses a great party, and loves hosting parties. She knows the entire who's who list, and has slept with a lot of the players. Despite discriminating cultural taste, she is often wildly uninhibited when it comes to sex.

# Seducing the Adrenaline Junkie Personality

The adrenaline junkie is a very aggressive woman who channels her drive outward towards physical challenges. To get her attention, you need to have a similar driven characteristic. That means you can't be lazy, needy, seek her approval, or be physically inactive. While every girl is attracted to a success story in business, it's the buff sports adventure guy that makes her toes curl. Your business talents are just bonus points. Never talk about business unless she asks. As far as socializing, she prefers the spotlight. Hang back a bit and let her work the room and shine. Make sure you're not an attention whore, put her down, or segway conversations back to you. Give her the stage. There's plenty of time when you get her home in bed to show her who's really boss.

Despite her serious, driven exterior, underneath is often a somewhat immature little girl…in a good way. The keepers are extremely fun to be around when you are on their good side. The reason is she spent most of her high school and college years competing in sports, instead of hanging out in social circles. She is still a bit emotionally immature, giggly, silly, and playfully engaging. Though a type A powerhouse in her productive skills, she still maintains a childlike innocence and believes in only the good things in life. Use this to your advantage; only appeal to her girly girl side.

To work the sexy athletic girls takes a bit of maneuvering before making your approach shot. Be like the potential trophy wife, and do some quality research (stalking) first. Find out where she trains, where she runs/bikes, happy hours she goes to, and favorite nightclubs. You want to appear in her circle nonchalantly and have her notice you. Find out her gym schedule (days-hours), and make sure you are there before her. Actions speak louder than words. In races, when she crosses the finish line first it turns her on, but so does the athletic bad boy who isn't particularly impressed with her. You are serious competitor, but the last thing you do is take yourself too serious around her. All your conversation should be teasing and cocky, with self-deprecating jokes. By laughing at yourself, you are actually complimenting her in reverse fashion with humor. Seriousness will only bring out her competitive spirit. Lets dub this the Buff Comedian angle.

> If she hovers near you lifting in the gym, ask her to spot you:
> *"Can I borrow you for a minute? If this falls on my head,*
> *you can help me pick up the body parts."*

Don't worry if she lifts more than you, it's your training dedication that will impress her. Make friends with a girl or two in her posse, and then "by coincidence" run in some of the same races she competes in. If you're faster than her, be humble about your performance. For example, when you see her after the finish, pull her close and tell her *"I know it's not polite to brag, but I placed 6th place in the women's 60 and over division."* You get the picture. After 3 or 4 short conversations of teasing, ask her to join you at some athletic event: *"I don't know if you'd be interested but…"* Any chance to show off competitively, or to do something new, she will say yes.

Invite her to an outdoors events where you don't compete against each other; hiking, mountainbiking, whitewater rafting, canoeing, water-skiing, ocean fishing, rollerblading, etc. Keep everything outdoors. Make constant self-deprecating jokes about how you can't keep up and she is kicking your ass. *"If you make me go any faster, you're gonna make me cry."* Put in time and she'll loosen up quickly.

## Mega Bonus Points:
Take it from experience, adrenaline junkie girls can drink like there is no tomorrow. They have an extremely high metabolism. Even at half your weight they may drink you under the table. When they're drunk, they are aggressive as hell, and will fuck your brains out like you're on a deserted island and a meteorite is inbound. When you get a good one, she may not stick around long, but you will remember the experiences for a lifetime. For longevity in a relationship, you need to come up with something new and

"spontaneous" every week. Repeat events don't work with this type. Of course, make sure you show up at all her competitions at the finish, congratulate her, and pump 20 drinks down her in a hurry. Love is grand.

## Inner Psycho Signals – Paranoid Disorder

When their looks and competitive edge start to go, some of the Adrenaline Junkies get insecure and unhinged. She'll either learn to handle it with grace, or become reckless with her whole life. Make sure you exit when you see the target goes bad…it's like watching a plane crash in slow motion.

Her obsession can go from external challenges and experiences to excessive materialistic possessions. The excitement is in the discovery and acquisition of the expensive toys; appreciating the ownership is lost on her. The grass is always greener on the other side. Underneath is a growing fear of depression and anxiety. The constant high level of activities become not so much productive as they are just merely escapism and restlessness. She develops an inability to concentrate, and the levels of high achievement become delusional dreams.

Impulsiveness and hyperactivity can become sheer mania. Rapid career changes, heavy binge drinking, stock options trading, Vegas gambling, sky diving, African Safaris, rapid accumulation of debt, multiple marriage and divorces; nothing is off limits. Her greatest fear is the anxiety of becoming content or bored; not to mention a newfound acute inferiority complex.

Although choosy at first for her adventures, as she conquers each, she quickly becomes obsessed for more, out of fear of missing out on anything great. Soon she is diving headlong with reckless abandon into endless precarious situations without a single discriminating thought. Quantity of adventures replaces quality adventures. And the level of risk must be ever higher. If you question her motives she won't accept it. Expect impatience and a rapid heated debate, flying off into near rage due to her inflexibility. She loses focus and concentration, and has a limited attention span. Great ideas are quickly discarded before being completed. She becomes the jack of all trades, but the master of none.

## One Night Stands

Kick her ass in a race, drink her under the table, and then fuck her under the band stage where they're handing out the race awards above you. After the happy ending, give her a high five and never ask her name. Pop up butt naked and get your trophy from the MC above you, than go back under the stage for round two. It's not like she hasn't done it before.

# Ending the Relationship Cleanly

## *Difficulty Level:*
## 6.5

This type usually breaks up with the guy, not vice versa. Her ego can take quite a hit if you drop the bomb. Of course she has no problem with hitting on ten guys at a time right in front of you.

— - - - - - - - - —

Successfully exit without your windshield smashed
**+ 5 points**

You place an Escort ad for her, and post her work number
**+ 8 points**

Her boss calls it, she makes a quick $300 and gets promoted
**- 10 points**

She places an ad for you in a Gay Biker penitentiary porno mag
**- 20 points**

She files rape charges against you, her dad is the Judge
**- 30 points**

You get life, and are chosen to star in the prison's hot new theatre production, Brokeback Cowboy. For the rest of your life, you'll play the supporting actor. The star of the show is Long Dong Silver
**- 100 points**

— - - - - - - - - —

" Offend her, and she knows not to forgive;
Oblige her, and she'll hate you while you live."

**Alexander Pope**

# THE CONQUEROR
### (Aggressive – Obsessive Personality)

**Dominant Characteristics:**
Competitive, disciplined, success and power
**Her Greatest Fear:**
Weakness, failure, losing, and subordination

## What Makes Her Tick:

She has an insatiable desire for dating and taking advantage of successful bachelors to live a spoiled rich lifestyle she could never afford. This lust for power likewise flows over into her career pursuits. She must dominate and control everything and everyone in her life. Activities must be done her way, because only *she* knows what's best. Anyone who stands in her way must pay a price. The end is always more important than the means. In her dog-eat-dog world, society's rules are a mere inconvenience. She will fuck a superior to get a promotion. She will marry and divorce inside one year if there's a big payout available. She focuses on results, not feelings. Her acquisition of power and material things are more important than relationships, health, and even her own family. She is inflexible and ruthless in getting her way. The Type A chick; if she wants your opinion, she'll give it to you. Picture a cold blooded Drill Sergeant with Tits and a Nice Ass.

### Personality Strengths
1. Energetic, driven, aggressive
2. Dominant, confident, powerful
3. Goal driven, leadership, bravery
4. Crafty, adventurous, competitive
5. Fearless, self-control, achievement
6. Inner strength, responsible, shrewd

## Childhood Issues

This personality type is often the result of a cold dysfunctional home. The mother lacked the ability to show warmth and nurture the child as she grew. In many cases, the mother's greatest pleasure comes from liquor bottles/prescription drugs, extra-marital affairs, and blowing out her husband in irrational tirades. The husband grows tired of the lunatic at home, and works more and more just to stay away from the combative household. Every effort to bond with his daughter is brief, as the wife pushes him away and demands some chore to be done.

The daughter starts life a very sensitive, high strung, happy-go-lucky child enjoying herself freely. She's a tomboy, and competes on an even level with most boys. One day the angry mother snaps at her for no reason. From that moment forward, Mom ridicules the daughter for being a carefree fun loving child and demands more respect and responsibility. The daughter is devastated, and has nowhere to turn. She concludes she is no longer safe showing her feelings and emotions. She grows a protective shell to keep from getting hurt again. She avoids anyone trying to get too close to her, and will only rely on herself in the future. She becomes both aggressively single minded, and emotionally repressed.

## Typical Careers

- Attorney
- Engineer
- Daytrader
- Office Manager
- Corporate CPA
- WWF Wrestler
- Civil Suit Litigator
- Financial Planner
- College Professor
- Editorial/Art Critic
- ER Trauma Specialist

### How to Spot:

Hot, Hot, Hot, but not in a flashy, look-at-me way. She combines classy and seductive in everything she does. When you see drinks being dropped and the *Oh My God* face on every guy, she's just arrived. She owns the room when she enters it; a sophisticated backless dress that tastefully tries to cover her chiseled Sports Illustrated physique. When you see beefy, jealous women scowling in your direction and mouthing *what a whore* comments, she's moving in right behind you and looking smoking hot.

She's a skilled listener, has an infectious laugh, and stage-like charisma. You'll swear you've never met a woman so sensual, quick-witted and intelligent. There's not a topic she can't make more interesting with insider insight and dirty jokes. During her intellectually stimulating comments, she throws in subtle sexual hints; piercing eye-contact while licking lips, twirling her hair, leaning forward to expose cleavage. Your IQ goes to five trying to concentrate. She is the master of her domain, and the domain of every guy in the room for that matter. Keep in mind though, this chameleon persona will only be seen when she's on the prowl. Once she has locked on and acquired her target, at home she is domineering, passionless, belligerent and ruthless.

If you scan the perimeter of the room she is working, you may see a retired Professional Bachelor in the corner who's already screwed her and gotten away cleanly before she could destroy his life. He'll be admiring her technique and style with awe and respect. Raising his glass, he can be heard slurring... *"Ssssshe wasss one of the great onesssssshh."*

## Positive Traits:

Gorgeous, oozing with energy, a captivating upbeat personality. Adrenaline junkie for outdoor sports, Gym rat, self-made successful businesswomen. Spontaneous, invigorating, vivacious, and resilient. Body and face a 9. Quick witted, and uninhibited (till married).

## Negatives:

For the bad ones, it's all an act. Self-centered, cold, ruthless user of men. Feels she never has enough in life, gets quickly bored. Deep down she's empty, lonely, and has erratic mood swings. Flashes her six-pack tummy when you get cocky about your build. Isn't impressed when your first dates are taking her to Drag races, Truck pulls or Redneck Flea Markets.

# Target Profile

This species has a very visible trademark. She comes into your life like a tornado, and leaves in the exact same fashion. She has a very strong need for dominating men. Many, many, men. In order to validate her self worth, she needs to control every guy in her life. This need requires constant reinforcement. She's naturally sensual and flirtatious, and craves a high level of spontaneity. She seduces and quickly loses interest. If you date her, you will find yourself in the midst of very unfamiliar territory...scary territory. The kind where you think you've found *the Perfect Girl*. Only later will you find out she that she was using you as a casual seek and destroy mission.

She is the insatiable Conqueror. As soon as she seduces one guy, she quickly bores of him and seeks out a new challenging mark to control. Without a dashing man in her life, she feels helpless, reduced to lulling in her own irrational anxieties. In every facet of her life she is the same voracious warrior. She excels in every sport, every career move, and even every investment. But nothing can satisfy her. She always wants more. Particularly men.

She drops one and moves onto the next without ever looking back. The guys never see it coming. After practically living together with her for 2 weeks, she'll give you some weak excuse for being busy for a few days. While you're plotting the next event in "your relationship", she's long gone. In fact in her mind, you never even existed. She's off pumping a rock star for a week, and you're sitting there staring at the phone like Pavlov's dog... waiting for her call that never comes...and to think you thought you might be falling in love.

In reality, you barely even know her. She represents one of the sneakiest and most lethal piranhas you'll ever encounter. She's extremely self-centered, has no interest in emotion in her life, and is numb to the consequence of her actions. The welfare of others is a problem someone else can deal with. This is her sport, and you are her prey. Like all women she sizes up your financial statements and future prospects looking for the big kill, but deep down she prefers just moving on. When she finally bags her mega-millionaire husband, within weeks she'll find a huge hole in her life. She misses all her Boy Toys and New Meat, and will soon resent her hubby for falling so easily for her ploy and ending her game.

She then starts up almost immediately dating new victims on the side; all the while she's working on setting up her frustrated confused husband for a quick and ugly divorce. She may work in teams at this level, using a predatory girlfriend for a side affair with her hubby. Soon the Private Eye and the films appear, and the game is over. Her average marriage lasts two years. She typically marries 2 or 3 times.

## <u>Seducing the Conqueror Personality</u>

This is the girl who always gets her way. In order to create attraction and intrigue you have to make it a heck of a chase for her to land you. The casual laid-back guy is not her type. You will need the full blown successful, high self-esteem Bond image to even get her interest in the first place. The girl is impartial to strength, power and perceived large income in a man. You cannot come across as needy or sensitive, or disloyal. The target should not work in the same field as you. This creates too many competitive issues; there can be only one leader in her mind.

Aggressors usually chase aggressors. The person who has the upper hand in the chase is the person who cares least about the seduction. To seduce her and keep her in a relationship, you have to be an exceedingly self-confident, mildly interested challenge. You have to let her know that you are extraordinarily busy, and don't care if she walks. Since she has more of a serious confrontational personality, you should be more cynical and humorous. In any areas of conflict, you need to avoid the clear-cut right and wrong, one winner one-loser solution. Compromise with a smile, but never concede defeat. Emotion is a sign of weakness to her. The girl expects to win, and likes to get the prize in a hurry. So the longer you hold out, the greater her interest. This applies not just to the dating and chase, but the first round of sex as well. Set dates a week to ten days in advance, reschedule a few as they get closer, and you will create the scarcity needed to peak her interest in you. The girl is a very tough one to land, but it must be done on your terms or you'll be kicked to the curb in short notice.

# In a Relationship

Think of the movie 9 ½ weeks, only speed it up to 9 ½ days. Everything seems so perfect, so clear, and so right. It's all happening so fast. Warning signs should be going off everywhere, but they usually don't. Why? Because you're living like a Thoroughbred horse out to stud, and this mare keeps on comin' back for more. Aggressive women have an insatiable sex appetite. She's doing acrobat moves in bed Russian gymnasts never dreamed of. Hell, the East German judge is standing up and clapping... hairy armpits and all. You find yourself looking over your shoulder, fully expecting to see porn stars asking "*What's your secret? You da man!*"

On the 9th day you're totally mesmerized and hooked, and she's already jumped ship to the next victim with a bigger wallet. Every posse of alpha players has seen this scenario played out amongst each other time and time again. One guy will be in the middle of it, and another will be thinking "wonder where Brad is, he hasn't returned a call in a week." Sure enough he'll call up and start talking nonsense.

*"I met this hot chick man, she's unbelievable. I mean this one is different. I keep pinching myself wondering if **she is the one**."*

Like good friends, we don't let him pinch himself. Instead, we slam him over the head with a Bottle of Jack and chain him to a keg for a week. After all, we're Gladiators, not sappy girlfriends.

# Inner Psycho Signs – Sadistic Personality Disorder

When these girls go bad, it's like nuclear war. There are specific signals to look for in dating that will alert you to a defective product. There is no gray area with this girl; she's either good or avoided.

### Here's her Inner Psycho checklist

- Public insults and humiliating scenes
- Constant lying in a pathetic power grab
- Enjoys seeing/inducing pain in others lives
- She doesn't trust you to go anywhere alone
- Vicious attitude and complete lack of respect
- Jealous rage over incorrectly perceived situations
- You become a prisoner to her childish insecurities

- Takes up martial arts, a new fascination with violence
- Forces you to read Cosmo articles, and watch Oprah
- Uses intimidation and threats to get you to do something
- Sex is negotiated; you must first buy her furniture or something. All attempts to hide her call girl mentality cease, plus she puts an absurdly high price on her pussy.

When **The Conqueror** girl is under 28, almost all of these warning signs will rarely appear, unless she spends too much time with her posse. However, women in their mid to late thirties add these nasty traits rather quickly. As their looks start to fade, their pussy power over you leaves proportionately. Soon the mentally unhealthy traits begin to become dominant,. and they are substantial with this chick. A very heavy plate of insecurity, jealous rages, and violent, irrational behavior. In a nutshell, she becomes her Mom; the very thing she vowed she would never be. The Psycho Gene Pool has traveled full circle. Needless to say, as these traits appear, plan your exit immediately.

" Rules are like women. They are meant to be violated."

**DENYS DIONNE,** *Quebec court justice*

# MISS SLOW AND EASY
## (Leisurely – Avoidance Personality)

### Dominant Characteristics:
Tranquil, ultra casual, terminally happy and stress free. Does the bare minimum in everything just to get by. No worries mate, I'll do whatever the hell I want, when I want.

### Her Greatest Fear:
Being controlled, schedules, responsibilities.

## Personality Strengths
1. Relaxed, easy going, mellow
2. Responsible, low key temper
3. Self- assured, modest, rational
4. Patient, stress-free, disciplined
5. Independence, slow and steady
6. Pleasure seeker, humble, stable

## Target Analysis – What Makes Her Tick

She is very self-absorbed and laid back. Her number one priority is having a good time pursing her pleasure seeking at her own pace. Work and relationships are an added little sideshow. She is very easy going, and never in a hurry. Haste makes waste. She is optimistic that things always have a way of working out, so there is no reason to rush a situation or worry. Skipping out of work early and spending the day at Starbucks drinking decaf lattes with her whiny girlfriends, while reading Cosmo and solving world peace are much more important than working overtime to meet a rushed corporate office deadline.

She is the exact opposite of the Type-A aggressive woman. She has no big picture goals or desires, is chronically late, rarely cleans up around the house, and procrastinates about everything till the last second. Tight schedules and being on time are comical annoyances she never considers. Nothing is ever her fault. Doing more than is asked would never occur to her. She will do the bare minimum of what is required of her, and the rest of her free time is all hers…and there is nothing you can do about it.

She has little difficulty saying No. She's not a bitch about it, or self-centered. You simply cannot influence her. A rare treat; as her ego is tiny, and she's not an attention whore. She's content with having little and saying the world isn't fair. Her street smarts are non-existent. If she stumbles on success, she is humble about her accomplishments.

## Typical Careers

- Cooking
- Teacher
- Secretary
- Child Care
- Receptionist
- Floral Displays
- Postal Worker
- Union Employee
- Bookstore chick
- Starbucks chick
- Dental Assistant
- Government Employee
- Worker's Rights Activist

# Seducing the Leisurely Personality

She is slow and deliberate in removing her bitch barriers, but once she softens up to you she is very warm and respectful. She expects to be taken care of, and freely starts new relationships when the approach meets her style. The seduction angle is simple; whatever she likes, you like. Mirror her habits, routines and thoughts, but compliment her on thinking/doing them first. Be a similarly Leisurely guy, but you'll need a little more drive and to take charge of things, without pressuring her. Speak third person when making suggestions;

> *"Some people say that camping nude is hip this year.*
> *I just copped some kick ass pot. Wanna try it?"*

She prefers a guy who will take control of situations and does all the planning in the relationship. You have to be the responsible yet laid back boyfriend, and you have to tolerate the fact that she will put minimal effort into anything. You cannot make a Leisurely girl do something she doesn't want to do. She will not change to meet your agenda and demands. Compromise is not her strong point.

In a nutshell, she is your typical lazy ass, Liberal chick. When she hears of people quitting jobs and living in sleeping bags following the Grateful Dead around, she smiles and calls them visionaries. Communes intrigue her. Doing bongs makes her smarter…just ask her. (speak slowly). The bastard employees at the DMV who make you wait 2 hours to renew your drivers license are her Idols.

She has the comically jealous mindset that people who achieve things are
**174**

just lucky. The fact they take huge risks and for years bust their ass 80 hours a week to succeed never crosses her mind. To seduce her you need to role-play her same worldly view of putting minimal effort into life and disdaining the "fortunate" people who make it. When you see an entrepreneur with a Mercedes convertible, or an average looking guy with a hot babe, shake your head, and while smirking say:

*"Some people are just born with a Silver Spoon,*
*and really don't deserve what they have."*

Practice being elitist and condescending, and snorting with disgust at the lucky sperm of the world. For advanced levels, master a bullshit accent….arrogant Brahmish Bostonian is very popular. Pontificate mindless nonsense with lengthy multiple syllable words used out of context in monotone ten minute sentences. Sure it's complete gibberish, but you'll sound sooo smart to her…(think John Kerry); that'll get her big ole dirty granny white panties even more soiled.

Brag about how you hold your own against **The Man**; blather on and on how people of authority are not to be trusted. Boast how you are an innovative individual blazing your own trail (while working for someone else). Laugh out loud at Alpha Studs with babes in Jaguars saying, *"pray tell Babs, anyone who works more than 40 hours a week is a slave."* Always stick up for the little guy and the underdog.

Whatever her passions are, join her in them unconditionally. This type is often very creative (in her mind), so show glowing admiration and support of her talent. If you are strong, driven, and opinionated, you will not be able to seduce her. Her belief systems are impenetrable. Remember to cut back on bathing more than once a week, and throw out the cologne. Before your dates, roll in the mud, rip your clothes for the proper Gen X clothing style. Pattern your look after Shaggy from Scooby Doo, I mean Dirk Nowitski.

If she's bi-sexual and supplies horny girls, it's time to really get into her soul. Become a true believer and drink the Zombie Kool Aid with crazed zeal. Sing Kumbaya on your answering machine message. Join her in sign holding protests on street corners shaming people who kill Minks for fur, then buy her a Big Mac in a place where they kill Cows for food. Hand out 10,000 flyers condemning cutting down trees in forests, printed on fancy paper made from trees cut down in forests.

## Target Conclusion

I know what you're thinking; why the hell chase some dumb liberal broad? Well, why not fuck her brains out? I mean, how long could it take?

There are few things funnier than a girl with half your IQ trying to talk down to you. Besides, the playoffs don't start till next week.

Now she better be really hot to put up with this energy-less babe. If she is, you've got yourself a zero maintenance chick who will sit at home 7 days a week. Buy her a lot of books, and put a keg in the fridge…you're going to need it. Don't expect anything more than an uninspired missionary position. If things don't work out and you're having trouble dumping her, show up wearing a suit and tell her you started a phenomenally successful business and work 80 hours a week. She'll recoil in horror.

## One Night Stand
### Difficulty Level:
### 3.5

She's easy to nail on a first date. Get her bombed or stoned and go into the vintage Us vs. Them routine. The hard part is trying to stay awake during the seduction. Also, she's not exactly a clean freak. Make her shower first. Borrow a John Deere tractor for her bush preparation. Spray Hydrogen Peroxide on your rod for a week.

— — — — — — — — —

A successful quick escape and no call back
**+ 3 points**

Make it the first week without burning itchy sensations
**+ 5 points**

Forge her signature and sign her up for the military
**+ 12 points**

Slip her a Mickey Finn,
tattoo Rush Limbaugh's face on her back
**+ 30 points**

She spray-paints "Cum see me at
anal-granny-fucker.com" on your Mercedes hood
**- 50 points**

— — — — — — — — —

"Madam, if I were your husband, I'd eat it. "
**WINSTON CHURCHILL,**

Replying to a nagging woman who said,
"If you were my husband I'd poison your food."

# CATASTROPHE QUEEN
### (Anti-Social Personality Disorder)

**Dominant Characteristic:**
Aggressive free-spirit. Life is a jungle, only the Strong survive.

**Her Greatest Fear:**
Boring safe lifestyle, being exploited, not getting what *she deserves*.

## What Makes Her Tick:
A master manipulator disguised as the sad, helpless victim. When she smells a sucker, she turns on her spunky, easy lay charm. Underneath she's a con artist with ice running through her veins. Hold on tight, this species is a ticking time bomb, with no direction, no sense of decency, no guilt, no shame, no conscience or concerns for the basic rules of society. Though sleek and seductive, she is irrational, melodramatic and dangerous. The ultimate problem child, everything is an urgency catastrophe. If her IQ reaches 50, she should sell.

She is completely devoid of emotion, except when she is conning people and gaining power by creating pain. Constant risk-seeking behavior, nymphomania and alcohol/substance abuse are her modus operandi. She has no fear. In dangerous situations her nipples will get hard. She creates problems and tragedy situations just for the turn on. She is the drama queen, laughing one second, crying the next and threatening suicide. Some have two kids from two different men, and the guys have custody. She hasn't seen them in months. There will be many things you'll never know about her. She won't even mention her kids till a month after you start dating. In a nutshell, deranged, bipolar, and an imagination that knows no boundaries.

### Personality Strengths
1. Nymphomaniac
2. Conniving, Exploitative
3. Aggression, Predatory
4. Deceitful Manipulation
5. Short term memory loss
6. Adventure, Independence
7. Getting her way at all Costs
8. Smiling while Breaking laws
8. Party Animal, never says No

# Target Profile

Coal black eyes without a soul. The sexier, advanced players will claim to be a singer, model, or aspiring actress. She's an expert fantasy storyteller, and will be well versed in every nuance of the business she is "pursuing." **(she watches E!)** A Prolific name dropper, she has the inside scoop on everything. In fact, she'll tell you she's just one break away from making it, but has the rotten luck of having entertainment lawyers not as driven as she is. She says it with a straight face despite knowing you know she's living in Motel 6 if not her car. Her 4 PM Breakfast is whiskey, blow and a cigarette. In a nutshell, she has Anti-social Personality Disorder. She's a sociopath who has no guilt about her actions, and is quite the manipulative seductress. (But goddamn, what an incredible lay). If she does work, you'll find her holding down a shameless scam career.

## Typical Careers

- MLM Sales
- Blues Singer
- Televangelist
- Telemarketer
- Internet Spam
- MADD mother
- Used Car Sales
- Parasite Live In
- All-Nude Stripper
- Aspiring Politician
- Amway Distributor
- Junk Lawsuit Solicitor
- Car Dealership Service Writer

# Sizing up the Target

## How to Spot:

Smoking hot body, why else would you be such a sucker for going on a date with her? Killer bootie in low hip huggers, washboard tummy under the midriff. Funky hat or do-rag on her head, multiple tattoos and personalities, and no tan lines. The hair looks like it got caught in a paper shredder. It's been colored so many times, it's taken on a kaleidoscope tint. Picture walking up behind her with the yard weedie and buzzing a few times across her locks. (*There, perfect!!*) She shaves her eyebrows off, and then draws them back on with a crayon. The **Tramp Stamp** tattoo on the tailbone of course, piercings everywhere, some have a dragon tattoo covering half her back. For eye makeup, it looks like she fell for the old black paint on the binocular lens trick. If she had a black eye, you wouldn't even know.

## Her Pad:
If she has one, you'll need fishing waders to maneuver in her apartment. Wear plastic gloves, and clothes you can throw away after you leave. Avoid the bathroom, and take short breaths beneath your oxygen mask. You may not want to sit down either. Don't step on the snakes.

## Positives:
19 years old, 5'4", 100 pounds of lust. She's a confident tomboy, and is great at doing off-the-wall practical jokes…at your expense. Loves being photographed….while walking naked thru Blockbuster. Initiates oral highway within seconds of every ride. Drinks like a fish, and she can't keep her hands off you. Brings her bi girlfriends on your dates. If only she were a mute. You'll laugh all the way to jail.

## Negatives:
Delusions of adequacy, extensive police record. She leaves you with funny itching sensations. May prolong affair by filing false rape charges. Ex-boyfriends named Spike appear regularly. Will definitely stalk you when you dump her. You'll get huge unexpected bills.

## Habitat:
VIP Rooms of Titty bars, Tattoo parlors, backstage at Metal Concerts on her knees, Starbucks, confessional booths, condom stores, any after hours bar where she can do the bartender for free drinks. (every bar in the city).

## Car Report:
Drives a $300 car with no insurance. The inside looks like squatters have lived in it for a month. A huge spider web crack in the front windshield, the headliner rests on the headrests. She has to drive with her head out the window to see. There's an empty keg on the rear seat. Front floor mat is a sea of burnt joints, empties, and used diapers. A 1981 inspection sticker peeling off, skipping 8-track player. Three donut tires with threads sticking out, and one regular tire that's been flat for a week now. The steering wheel violently shakes and turns to the right when you're going straight. No mirrors, no muffler, no windows, no rear windshield, no license plates, and no worries mate. She knows there's not a cop in town that'll give her a ticket, he'll give his phone number instead.

## Reality Check:
Once you let a Catastrophe Queen move in with you, reality sets in. She sleeps till 4 pm, hasn't worked in years, has no ambition, no direction and no skills. Whatever stories she tells you now will completely change on the hour. In fact, she really has no redeeming qualities at all except her ass and being promiscuous. There in lies the problem; in that department she's a 10.

# Seducing the Target

You'll find her sitting alone drinking Jack Daniels straight, in one of those lonely heart biker bars full of a frightening cast of characters; sort of like the local Star Wars Bar scene. She hates the timid and weak people of the world. Despite having a hard exterior shell though, her eyes will give away her sadness and vulnerability. The best approach is to use the Classy Bad Boy image (see chapter). Hide your Wall St. Journal and briefcase in your trunk. Practice grunting, scowling and swearing before entering the club. Apply fake tattoos, and use the traditional bottle of *Spray on Sweat* prior to your cocky entrance. Don't trip. Don't look particularly coherent.

Without saying a word, swagger on up to the bar next to her, and buy a few shots. Slide one over to her without looking at her. Raise yours and give a deep throated hate inspiring toast: *"Here's to walking all over the losers in life."* Give your best smirk, and chug it. Slam the shot glass down upside down on the bar. No gagging on the liquor, and no crying if you hurt your hangnail. Don't let her see your clip-on-tie tucked away in your pants pocket. Bad girls love bad boys. Next, you need to find out what her fantasy desired career is. It shouldn't take much; *"I bet you sing your ass off in a band, right?"* She'll let you know. In fact, she probably won't shut up from that moment on, even during the sex in the parking lot an hour later. She's the entertainment, just kick back and enjoy the show. You rarely need to speak. In fact, your sole contribution from that moment forward will be her sounding board, bartender, and walking ATM machine.

Watch yourself, the girl is an amazing actress, and oozes sex appeal. With a twinkle in her eyes, her passion for flirting and discussing her artistic skills will suck you in. **To seduce her,** just show a "sincere" interest in watching her sing (act, whatever). Assume the savior role and attitude.

*"I like your spunk, kid. (grunt) I think you're going places. Lemme tell ya something...I friggin' know people in this town that make things happen...ya know what I'm saying? Listen, The Corleones in Vegas owe me a few favors; I'll make a few calls for ya. Now turn around and show me that ass, so I know I'm not wasted my time. Fagetaboudit. "*

Tell her you want to help her career get to the next level. The close is over before the seducing begins. A little name-dropping is all it should take.

-- - - - - --

Sometimes you'll spot these edgy, wacko, alternative problem chicks at Starbucks, Borders, and retro clothing stores. The fascinated White Knight role-playing still applies, only your angle should be a more refined.

**For your interview role, choose the
Hollywood Reporter technique:**

-- - - - - --

*" Is Vogue your favorite modeling gig?"*

*"Is it a tragic curse being born so beautiful."*

*" What's it like to be up for an Emmy every year?"*

*" So how long did Brad Pitt stalk you?"*

*" How many girls are joining us tonight in bed?"*

-- - - - - --

Bring a tape recorder; this stuff will never cease to amaze you. The imaginary crisis and fantasy stories are so side splitting you'll be in awe. (**"You couldn't make this shit up."**) If you can afford good legal representation, and use 2 condoms each round, she's all fire.

# In a Relationship

In the beginning, you'll be buying her McDonald's happy meals and getting laid. Soon, your hangovers trying to keep up with her will practically cost you your job. Plus, she smokes so much pot you'll smell suspicious at work, and keep getting surprise blood tests.

You'll both lust and feel sorry for her. The girl with constant problems needs solutions, which makes you her Knight in Shining Armor. She'll make you proud of her drive and ambition at achieving her impossible goals. You'll feel sorry things haven't worked out for her. Subconsciously you try to help her turn the corner to normalcy, or be realistic about her dilemma, but her own self-hate will reject you if you push too hard. She lives for the problems; it's what gives her the bad girl identity. Underneath the tragedy lifestyle persona is a girl who wields power over men, and she knows it. There's logic behind the madness. Every week will feature multiple hairstyles, tattoos and personalities. In her world, you're also her problem, but since you're supporting her she'll let you slide…for now.

Soon you'll be loaning her money for demo tapes that you'll never hear (**I'm in management now!**). Quickly the requests escalate. Eventually she's sleeping over almost every night. She keeps hefty bags full of leather pants, lingerie, and sex toys in your living room. Within minutes, your bathroom gets smothered in makeup smears and fast food scraps. Your place takes on some horrible smell you can't seem to locate…like a dead animal. Then one day it hits you. *It's all Bullshit…*you got scammed. She has no career, and is just bleeding you dry. The stress is killing you. Now the hard part comes…trying to get rid of her. Things will spiral downward to levels you didn't know were possible.

She'll create some of the most preposterous delusional lies you can imagine in trying to keep her parasite ass in your pad. It turns out she was telling people she's carrying your baby before you even had sex. When you deny it, she'll claim she's in the hospital aborting your child, but hangs up when you ask which one. There are usually some threatened Mafia hits riding on the relationship. Your car is keyed and towed. Massive unexplained bills start to appear on your credit card statements. She files for restraining orders to try and keep **you** out of your own home. This one is a pro at all of this. You should expect and ignore the routine 3 am panicked phone calls concerning bail bondsman, imaginary life threatening illnesses, stalker ex-boyfriends, sick relatives needing cash, cops calling about self-inflicted bruises she claims you caused, stolen cars in trees, etc. Then you find out you don't even know her real name. She has multiple aliases.

-- - - - - --

*"I woke up in Montana this morning with a blue Mohawk. Can you come pick me up?"*

*"Slight problem honey, these guys were chasing me and now your car's in the bottom of a lake. Um, sorry I put the cat in the microwave last night."*

*"I accidentally set a church on fire on the way to my American Idol audition. Get your butt down her and bail me out before you cost me the part."*

*"My film is up for best picture at the Cannes Festival, so as a backup I like charged a private jet to Monaco on your Amex last night…"*

-- - - - - --

# One Night Stand
### *Difficulty Level:*
### 1.5
*You said Hi and bought her a drink. Amazing technique.*

If you can remove her from the nightclub without a bar fight, it's a done deal. Hopefully the passed out chick on her bed will wake up and join you. (Hopefully she hasn't peed on the bed already.) What is perfectly normal in the sack for these girls will be a porn star experience you'll never forget. Never sleep over, and after leaving her place, you may want to burn your clothes. Use love motels if necessary. Never give her your address. Use your standard fake name and occupation until the coast is clear.

# Ending the Relationship Cleanly

A quick exit without handcuffs, explosions, or swat teams is important. If you haven't lost your job, and don't have the law or creditors after you when she's gone, consider yourself a magician.

------------------

**Successful Exit**
**+ 6 points**

The lab tests came back negative
**+ 8 points**

She'll be out in Five to Ten
**+ 12 points**

You had a foursome on the first date
**+ 15 points**

She filmed it all and gave you a copy
**+ 20 points**

Yours buddies watch it and point out
a huge bulge in one girl's panties
**- 25 points**

You blacked out in the middle of the session,
and wake up the next day walking kind of funny...
There's a dried white streak in your hair...
**- 50 points**

--------------

Ordinarily she was insane, but she had lucid moments
when she was merely stupid."

**HEINRICH HEINE ,** *German poet, 1797 –1856*

# OLD YELLER
## (Gravitational Impaired Personality)

### Dominant Characteristics:
Tonnage, volume, odor, gargantuan appetite, Ripley's believe it or not ego, complete lack of shame.

### Her Greatest Fear:
Last call at the all-you-can-eat Buffet, mirrors, scales, tight doorways.

Big old redneck women that drink like a fish, swear like a sailor, and weigh more then your refrigerator. Now if you have even the remotest pride, skills and will power, obviously you can skip this chapter. Keep in mind though, while few men waste time chasing this breed in it's single status, countless men awake each day with one transforming into cattle right in front of their eyes. These men are collectively known as "*recently married*."

This chapter assumes that she's single, gravity impaired, and wants to get drunk and naked in the front yard at her trailer park. Believe or not, there are many single men who chase drunk beefy bimbos. Visit any Pennsylvania, or Midwest bar and it's easy to see why...that's all that lives there. Most of their night clubs are ten to one guys, and the lone available female looks like a pissed off middle linebacker.

### How to Spot:
The Floor is shaking, and your drinks are sliding off your table. When she walks by at sunset there's an eclipse. You can usually hear her first. Embarrassingly loud, foul mouthed and abrasive. That's her good points. Usually she has toilet paper hanging out the back of her green pant suit. In the middle of a 110 degree summer heat wave, she'll be wearing a coat, ("Fat Jacket"), accompanied by the standard sweater wrapped around the size 50 waist to hide the view.

Big old Bucket Head, three chins, saggy jowls, cankles (cow ankles), Five o'clock shadow, droopy granny triceps, gigantic wide feet, (**sturdy base**), and a butt that wraps around the lip of the chair when sitting down. It's hard to tell where the ass ends and the calf starts.

### Habitat:
Happy hour buffets, Troughs, Wal Mart, Country Bars, Aggie Sororities, Oklahoma Model Agencies, Divorce Courts, barns stealing feed.

# Target Profile

Fatties are as obsessive as cokeheads when it comes to satisfying their addiction. It consumes their entire life…getting a loan to buy the food, arranging the tractor-trailers to transport it, dreaming and drooling during the preparation, renting the outhouses, etc. They love to dodge the fat guilt issue with excuses like *"it's my metabolism"*, or *"it's genetic."* Yeah, right. It has nothing to do with shoveling 10,000 calories a day down the throat. *"She's so fat, she sat AROUND the house."*

# The Seduction (?!!)

There are guys out there that *have* to get laid every night no matter what. The whole ritual can be seen time and time again in Country Bars. If you're patient enough to wait till last call, it's an amazing treat to view the mating chase. It starts off with the fatties actually attempting to convince the lonely stud that she has some highly desirable traits, and that multiple evenings of high dollar courting, dinners, and events will be necessary foreplay to partake in her portly Garden of Love.

"Call me next week, buuurrrrrrrpppppppp."

The guy will mentally pontificate this nonsense for about 5 seconds, than tell her she can give 'em a courtesy blowjob in the parking lot if she shuts the hell up. Shortly thereafter comes the guy's walk of shame, along with her walk of glory. The guy will speed walk out the front door trying to throw off any hint of a connection between them. Ms. Piggy will break into a full, gross, bouncy sprint trying to show off her love struck boyfriend. **Good pull, mate ! !**

For any chance at saving face, after the conquest, the guy cannot return to that bar for a month at the minimum. Meanwhile, the livestock will strut cockily back in, looking in all directions for any credit towards her newfound goddess status. Most guys in the crowd will laugh uncontrollably and turn away quickly. Others will order up three mind-eraser shots and recognize their inevitable beefy destiny. What's really funny is listening to the guys brag about the conquest afterwards; their delusional explanations and unbelievable attempts at self-congratulations on their lucky find.

--- - - - - --

"Look dude, it's been a really long time. I know she weighs 230, but she has a really cute face and a great personality. You can laugh all you want. But when I closed my eyes in the car while she was blowing me, it felt so good, I could swear she only weighed 225."

--- - - - - --

It goes without saying that a single guy should avoid horny cattle at all costs. Go home and watch ESPN. Look at it this way; you can revisit your favorite pub in peace the next night. Remember, one harmless fat escapade isn't just an unfortunate night of drunken weakness. Oh no. NOBODY ever forgets **a good hog story**, nor do they ever tire of telling it. Exaggerating the details isn't even necessary. You'll be branded a cow lover for life. If you're shit-faced in a bar and hear yourself suddenly rating a fattie 3 or 4 points higher near closing time, get the hell out of there.

# One Night Stands
### *Difficulty Level:*
## 0

If spotted during the exit, it's all over buddy. You may as well head straight to the airport and never return. Imagine having a fat stalker in your life.

– – – – – – – – – –

### Success:
-5 points

The shocks in your car didn't collapse
**+ 3 points**

Turns out that grunt she made wasn't a fart
**-20** points

Her real name should be Hoover
**+ 2 points**

She deep throats and never looks up
**+ 8 points**

Yours buddies snuck out to the parking lot and filmed it all
**- 25 points**

Your Mom hands you a copy the next morning
**- 50 points**

– – – – – – – – – –

"Women are like elephants to me, nice to look at,
but I wouldn't want to own one."
**W.C. Fields,** *American comic actor*

# The Perfect Girl Profile

If you're serious about landing the perfect girl, there are a number of qualifying characteristics she must have. No exceptions at this level of the game. These cover the inevitable hurdles that continually ruin every marriage. This means she's a sweet, wealthy, OMG face-melting, hardbody nympho; a Bonafide Trophy.

## Sexy Athletic Tomboy

Looks mean everything to a guy, so she has to keep her perfect chiseled physique. Go for the zero maintenance tomboy who hates makeup. Find a girl who excelled in sports in school and is permanently in shape. She still thrives on competitive sports and working out. She needs the physical and emotional high, and loves how it makes her look and feel. More importantly, she loves how sexy she feels watching your lust filled reaction while doing a striptease for you. *"Oops, sorry honey, I'll move...I forgot ESPN highlights are on! Tell me when the commercial starts. Here, hold my top while I get you another beer!"* Her bi girlfriends should be in fantastic shape too, and over your house constantly competing for your attention.

## Solidified Career

**She has her desired life long career intact**. This is the job she went to school for. The only thing she ever wanted to do. The job she worked her way up the ladder to get, and now she's firmly established at what she does. Hopefully her Daddy is her filthy rich boss, owns the company, and pays you to be a stay at-home husband. That gives you time to get acquainted with your new mansion he bought. It'll also gives you time to get acquainted with the amazing racks on the live-in twin maids you just hired.

## Busy Lifestyle

**She leads a fulfilling, healthy life**. The typical marriage, the man has his career, his stock portfolio, ESPN, competitive sports, workouts, binge drinking sex vacations, guy's nights out, hobbies and much more. Women have one thing: the relationship. They're utterly obsessed with analyzing it, worrying about it, picking it apart, and creating imaginary problems putting them on the verge of breaking up at any moment. Not with your girl. Your fiancée has a busy life like you; she has her dream job, investments, her sports leagues, the gym, hobbies, her tomboy bi-girlfriends, and of course her favorite thing in life; pleasing you. Plus, she's a busy homemaker, with huge to do lists on the fridge, with all the duties assigned to her.

## Emotionally Secure

She has a permanent fun personality, a great sense of humor, strong self-esteem, and is enthusiastic and spontaneous. She supports everything you do with optimism. She doesn't seek out new things out of boredom. Her style is to keep things rock solid, as she craves stability and excellence. *One personality, all day, all night.* Deliriously happy and uncontrollably horny.

## Respects You and your Life

Whatever your area of expertise is, she should be exceedingly proud of your abilities and success. In public, as well as in private, she always praises you, your talents, and shows you the utmost respect. She values your opinion. She doesn't want to change a thing between you two, not that you'd let her. And she's rock solid in her commitment to making sure it lasts forever.

## Very Sexually Open Minded

This one is real simple. Find a girl hornier than you, who loves to experiment, especially with women. The biggest obstacle in marriage is **Men Love Variety.** You take that away and you'll never stop thinking about other women. Not in your house, buddy. The perfect girl is sexually open. Adding a girlfriend would be exciting, and letting her pick up a hottie to join you would be **her fantasy**. Every man needs some strange once in a while, and your woman knows this all too well. She should want some strange too when it comes to adding bisexual woman into the bedroom.

## Healthy Family

A trip to the out-laws is vital to your future sanity. You have to meet her mother, because that's who your fiancée is going to become. What you're looking for is complete stability in their family life. No dysfunctional crap whatsoever. The Dad is all Man, and the Mom is a positively bubbly, lean machine who is ecstatic to see you. The whole family is healthy, supportive, successful overachievers with a sense of humor. You should look forward to going over there. Her Dad should be a business and playboy mentor to you.

Here's the scene. Their castle should be 20,000 square feet. When you pull up in the circular driveway, there's a bikini team handling valet parking. Dad strolls out, spanks one of the girls and hands you with a 32 oz. umbrella drink with a wink. He's wearing a T-shirt that says "**Hustler's Barely Legal Couch Auditioner.**" He puts his arm around you and slurs something about your new 8 figure trust fund, and how you're needed out back as a ref. You try to cut through the kitchen but Mom crosses your path. She looks exactly like your fiancée, only somehow younger, and in Olympian shape. Oh, and she's topless. She plants a long, slow, wet kiss on your lips, and whispers *"I've heard all about you."* Then, with a playful stroking of your crotch she purrs *"and I mean ALL about you. Don't think I can't run rings around that little daughter of mine."* (smooch, fondle, stroke). The old man pushes her aside, and it's out back to the Olympic pool. There's 3 oiled up girls on a floating trampoline, and you're job is the hands on referee of this wrestling contest. In the distance a cheerleading team screams your name, while peeling off their thongs. *"Screw the clothes, the groom's here. Yeahhhhh!!!"* That's what we call passing the family test.

**" The perfect woman has a brilliant mind, wants to make love until four in the morning—and then turns into a pizza."**
*singer* **DAVID LEE ROTH,** *in 1988.*

# Chapter VI

# CYNICAL OBSERVATIONS
from
# DEEP IN THE TRENCHES

Dating Execution Techniques
Out in the Field

# THE FRIENDS FIRST SCAM

## Q.

*I'm friends with this sexy girl who just moved into my neighborhood, and am trying to work an angle to date her and get intimate. So far, she's lowered her barriers, and thinks I'm really nice and a good listener. I take her out to dinner, we go shopping together, and occasionally I send flowers to her at work. We talk forever on the phone. She says she wants to take it slow for now, start out as* **Friends First***. So far we just hold hands, and hug...she kisses me goodbye on the cheek. After two months, I tried to accelerate things by taking her on vacation, but she insisted on me paying for her own separate room. Every time I try to advance things, she says she's not ready. How can I tell her that I'm like ready to take things a little further? I mean I don't want to hurt her feelings, and ruin our relationship.*

## A.

What size clit are you packing? Geez, this is painful to read. When you act like a limp-wristed, purse-swinging, bed-wetting girlfriend, do you expect to turn her on? Men do not let women walk all over them. Men control the situation, not the other way around. Men do not spend money on women until they're pumping them like Gladiators. If you've gone out on three dates, and her ankles don't end up in the air by the end of the evening, she's history. Tell her you don't need any more Goddamn friends, you need Sex. Ask her if she has any horny girlfriends who actually have a sex drive and aren't game players. If you're not getting any from her after two months, it's because she's either attracted to stronger women than you, or she's not a lesbian. Bet you she blew some dude right before she kissed you good night on the cheek.

*Friend first* means no sex. Ever. It's slow motion humiliation. You wanna pay for that crap? This approach never works for the guy. It's a female ploy designed to frustrate you, ride your wallet, and laugh at you behind your back. A total waste of time. If you need a friend, get a dog. Men and women are never really friends anyway, they have different interests. Do call up a girl and discuss some new strip club, Porn star, a touchdown catch, or a hot stock tip? Hell no. Think about it. How many women can you honestly say are great friends, who you haven't nailed, or aren't angling to get in her panties? A couple at best, and they're usually fat or off-limits. Friends first means she is not sexually attracted. Get over it. By the way, aren't those new pearlized Playtex applicators to die for? Snug, yet so refreshingly airy.

# THE NUCLEAR PEACOCK

**Q.**

*I made the mistake of taking my girlfriend shopping at an upscale mall, and came quite close to putting a gun to my head. She has to loiter in every single store and sample every single makeup. She sat with 20 different facial experts who showcased 20 versions of nightmares. Primping, battering, spraying, you-go-grrl-ing, ego stroking insanity. The whole scene is maddening. You know what? Not one of the fifty items she had me buy does a thing for me. Thank God I had the sense to rent a Peterbilt Tractor trailer to carry all the crap. Is a toxic wasteland face a turn on to you?*

**A.**

Are you out of your mind? You finance that clown makeup crap! What guy wants to plant a wet one on a set of lips caked in an inch of burgundy paint? Gross. Half the chicks you see in clubs and malls look like they filled a popcorn bowl with a glob of goop and dunked their faces in it. They spend hours lopping and splattering that crap around with rolling pins and spatulas and shovels and rakes until they get the proper pinkish orange Halloween glow. Then they preen around looking like highly flammable **Nuclear Peacocks**. While they're expecting Look-at-me-Glitterati treatment, it takes you every bit of strength not to get caught doubled over in laughter.

Their entire presentation is a camouflaged disguise. Women hide behind all that makeup, jewelry and deceptive clothing because they're too lazy to get off their fat asses and workout. They don't have the faintest idea what look a guy likes. Of course if they ever bothered to ask us what we like, they'd ignore our advice anyway and *tell us we're wrong*. Women dress for other women. Never date chicks who wear tons of makeup, and dress in over the top expensive outfits. It screams of High Maintenance, attitude problems, and insecurity. If she's swinging around a $700 Gucci purse (some sucker bought), she's expecting you to finance that level lifestyle. Clearly her pussy pricing is unrealistic. The higher the maintenance, the less respect you'll receive. The higher the CPF, the lousier the lay. Remember how hot Pamela Anderson when she was discovered? She had no makeup, natural tits, and was flashing a sexy tummy in a midriff. Every guy in the world instantly fell in love. Now she's gone Hollywood, and look what happened. She's a scary looking, phony, surgical white trash caricature of herself.

You want to date the au natural, zero maintenance girl, who's confidently sexy just the way she is without disguises. You know, the lean machine California blonde who's barefoot, strolling in the ocean in her ripped, old faded jeans from high school. Nipples popping thru her $5 white midriff, exposed six-pack tummy, has whitish blonde hair to her ass, AND NO MAKEUP!! EVER!!! If you look close, her T-shirt says *Fuck Oprah*.

# The Horny Holidays Hoax

## Q.

*From October through mid November, there were a bunch of girls I pursued who were way out of my league. I had my liquid courage up, got a lot of phone numbers, but the end result was shooting blanks all over town. I worked it real hard, over complimented in person, basically humiliated myself by calling them constantly, and leaving too many messages. Result: not one date, and not a single call returned. Then, I'd see them in public, and they pretended they didn't even know me. They shot me down like I was a dog; I mean they were real cold, aloof, and pissy about it.*

*Anyway, since the first of December, five of them have suddenly started **calling ME** and asking to get together. I've seen a couple others in public and they are all smiles, complimentary, and touchy feely, and asking for dates. Yo Vinny, what da fuck's up wit dat?*

## A.

Where's your Christmas spirit? It's the Horny Holidays Hoax. Nothing says Xmas like sleazy attention whores pretending sexual interest in order to con nice guys into buying them expensive crap they don't need. What better time to manipulate your ass than the holidays? Get the hopes up while the guard is down. They lead you on for a few dates; you fall for it, and buy a high dollar Xmas gift meant for royalty, in hopes of renting their pussy. Dec. 26th she dumps you before delivery of the product. Xmas Whores scam as many men as they can each December. The only guy who has a chance of scoring is the one who drops half a grand for the black tie New Years Eve party and hotel room. Then they start the charade up again two weeks prior to Valentine's Day. Bogus pending birthdays usually provide 4 or 5 suckers buying gifts as well.

*What's a Professional Bachelor to do?*

Unless you're in a long-term relationship, dump every girl you're dating the last week of November. Then for XMAS, treat yourself to a few of the hottest escorts in town. It costs the same as those dates and gifts; and you get far superior women, who are honest, respectful, and provides toe-curling, nympho-pumping, guaranteed results.

Happy Holidays Mercedes and Bambi !!!!

# Bible Thumpers

## Q.

*This girl I'm seeing really has her shit together. She comes from a strong family, has a great job, a smoking hot body, and never complains about anything. Actually, it's all so strange to encounter such a normal girl, I keep looking over my shoulders for Ashton Kutcher to see if I've been Punk'd. I guess I shouldn't complain, but it seems lately she's bringing up religion a little bit more than I am comfortable with. What does this mean?*

## A.

Well, for starters, she's probably not supplying Ozzie Osbourne with acid. When you're in the confessional booth discussing yet another gang bang, it's nice to hear an outspoken religious orator. But it can spell big trouble in dating when it's your girlfriend. Pay close attention for the early signs of a potentially aggressive Bible Thumper (**BT**). Religion in moderation is healthy. Once a week visits to church are acceptable. It means she is somewhat grounded. Hey, it beats the hell out of a gravity impaired, holier-than-thou Enviro-bitch who worships trees and preaches horoscope drivel. But you have to pay close attention. A BT will keep her point of view carefully obscured in the background early on. If she ever asks point blank about your views, say that you feel religion is a private matter. If her eyes flare up, you can be sure this will be a big problem real soon.

Remember, this is a future life of sanity and vices we're talking about here. For starters, a certified BT hates everything fun. They're a walking censorship committee protesting against every little pleasure in the world. No binge drinking, no titty bars, no porn, no threesomes. Who can live with someone like that? Never underestimate the power of organized religion. They prey on the weak minded. It's an overpowering brainwashed fixation that defies rationality. Little old ladies surrender their life savings into a glorified tip jar, held by smooth talking ex-used car salesman with a bad toupee. If your babe is secretly drowning in the elixir, run like hell.

### Warning Signs:

Did you ever hop in your Ferrari on the way to a massage parlor, only to discover a dashboard Jesus cemented in place? When you sneak into her pad unexpectedly, do you trip over headless chickens and see spine-chilling stars etched in blood on the walls? Is she sitting in a circle of candles fixated on a televangelist, with a phone and your missing credit cards in her hand? Does she actually believe Jesse Jackson is religious and prays for anything other than whitey extortion and banging sloppy, thick jungle bootie?

As the relationship grows, eventually she will start testing your faith. You wake up from sleeping and find her staring at you with a Bible open. A common first sign is her sudden request to attend Bible study during the week, instead of your softball game. Soon she acts uninspired, to flat out disinterested in sex. To even get it anymore becomes a battle. Religious girls find the whole act dirty, and any casual sexual thoughts or vices are sinful. Next thing you know, she's going to Bible study 3 days a week. The occasional Sunday mass becomes weekend church gatherings out of town. If you're hung over and refuse to go to church one Sunday, she holds a cross in your face and screams *"Burn in the lakes of fire, demon*!!!"

You have to spot this behavior transition early on, and put your foot down. A Holy Roller is far worse than your everyday chronic nagger. You can put up a fight if you want, to see if you can turn her around. Decorate your walls with Hustler centerfolds. Come home early from work plastered, and force her to watch porn naked. Whip out a camcorder and tell her you want to send in her audition tape for *Blowjobs Gone Wild*. After sermons, during handshakes with her pastor, drop of handful of glow-in-the-dark condoms. Tell him they're hers. *"She's an animal Father."* Drag her to a strip club, and buy her dances all night. If she finds the whole thing amusing, you may be just overreacting. If you're already married, and she rolls her eyes in disgust, you're in a heap of trouble. It's too late.

Soon, you'll spend your weekends with your hair in pigtails, wearing a blue bonnet, and holding a picnic basket full of cookies and recipes. Remember the guy's nights out? Cow tipping, followed by nude twister contests with the campus cheerleaders? That gets tossed for yoga positions, séances and saying *"Ohhhhhmm"* with Aunt Mildred.

Worst of all, every damn time you turn around there's some cheese ball Slick-haired dude with a phony smile, holding out his hand for a *"Vow of $1000"* in the name of Jesus. In the name of Jesus is right.

Demons be gone

# The Poison Posse

## Q.

*I'm dating this girl for a month now and things have been almost perfect. We just clicked from the very first date. We never argue, and are both infatuated with the other. We're basically living together. We have a lot of mutual interests, and there are actual confirmed moments she has held my attention while speaking. I realize it may sound strange, but the minute I finish on her butt, I don't instinctively flip over an egg timer and tell her she has 3 minutes to leave. Anyway, she skipped our Friday date to go out with her girlfriends. Get this, it's now been 2 weeks since this Girls Night Out, and she hasn't returned a single call. What gives?*

## A.

Whenever the girlfriend posse gets together, all Hell breaks loose. Next to successful divorce extortion, complaining about men is their greatest passion in life, particularly while on their cell swerving across three lanes in the Suburban. And who better to shred to pieces than the *boyfriends of their best friends!* No matter how deliriously happy a girl is with her guy, by the time she gets finished describing how great her man is, and how great the sex is, the posse will have turned a ghostly white, shrieking in horror. An intervention is imminently critical to "save her". To think this is supposed to be her support group. They will dice and slice his ass for hours. By the time they're finished, she starts concluding he's a rapist stalker who's using her. When they complete re-programming her into refusing sex, and manipulating him for a "bigger return", the guy should consider leaving town. There may be a warrant out for his arrest for having so much fun.

No man ever passes the posse test for extended periods of time. He can suffer the humiliation of footing the entire bill for girls' night out to buy temporary approval, but in the end he'll be dumped. Chances are the posse has already arranged a new suitor for your girl. She's on date three, and you're left staring at your answering machine. The rule of thumb is as long as your girl is away from her posse; you'll have a great relationship. The minute they assemble; you're on borrowed time. Never encourage the get together, and never be in their presence. Ever. The irony is that all these beefy whiners complaining about other people's relationships are never in a healthy one themselves. They're alone and miserable, and just looking for a guy to blame it on.

# Chivalry at Gunpoint

**Q.**

*My best friend just got out of law school, and took a job at a prestigious local firm. The hours suck, but he's moving up in the ranks, tight with the partners, and the perks on the horizon are quite impressive. He moves quickly in life, and after 6 months in town, he hooked up and married the hottest cheerleader at the local university. He said it was love at first sight. The ceremony was at sunset in a beautiful flower garden overlooking the ocean. There wasn't a dry eye in the crowd. I've never seen him so happy. I stopped by their house 6 months later, and they're barely speaking. She's demanding he quit night school, buy her a Mercedes and a bigger house he can't afford, and she's refusing to have sex again unless it's to pop out a baby. He looks like he's aged ten years already. What the hell is going on?*

**A.**

Forty years ago, marriage was a sacred bond based on love, honor and respect. Companionship and trust meant something, and were cast in stone. A wife's admiration of her husband was heartfelt, and because of her honesty, he proudly gave her security, chivalry, and good deeds. He was her provider, and she'd never dream of complaining or showing disrespect. Every issue could easily be worked out, and more often than not they stayed together for life.

Today, naïve men swing their dicks around recklessly and are blindsided by the hot little *what-have-you-done-for-me-lately* brides. They rush into a marriage based on false pretenses and big tits, doomed from the start. For some bizarre reason, highly intelligent, successful young men seem to be the most vulnerable candidates for approaching life by ego, instead of logic. They're poster childs for being an Accelerated Seduction Syndrome (ASS) victim. They live in the fast lane, competing with their frat brothers to see who can be the first to get rich quick, to get a Mercedes, and to marry the hottest trophy babe around. Fast money breeds men with little street smarts, but miles and miles of ego. They ignore the advice of dozens of friends and family who've already been there, because they're smarter and better, and *"it will never happen to me."* They haven't experienced failure and pain yet, but they'll get a crash course in a hurry.

**Q.**

*So are you saying that she never really loved him?*

**A.**

The bride never loved *or* respected her groom; her goal was a big ceremony and lifestyle, and he was the vehicle. It's a miracle she even got his name right on the wedding invitations. An over pampered princess cries until her demands are met as a child, and she continues this pattern of being spoiled rotten by every adult in her life. Not getting her way is simply unacceptable. As an adult, she gets her power and kicks by seducing men. She wants constant variety. She's restless, bored, impatient, and needs a steady stream of new boys and expensive toys to keep from whining until the veins bulge out on her forehead. Many have such a shallow ego; they are banging a fleet of guys right up till the vows are taken. A lot of them don't slow down much thereafter. Let's put it this way. If your fiancée mentions in passing that she's a spokesmodel for Trojan Condoms, KY, Pocket Rocket, and Sealy Posturepedic Mattress, you may have yourself a busy little beaver…and the makings of a busy big beaver. Maybe give her the quick test; when she unzips her fly, do you hear an echo?

## It's All About the Ceremony and the Ring

Surrounded by trashy mags glamorizing extravagant weddings and bowling ball sized rings of the rich and the richer, her brain swims with jealousy to keep up with Angelina, Jessica, Britney, and reality show actresses. *"If she's bleached blonde and has bolt-on airbags, her wedding better not be bigger than mine!!"* The thought of having any obligations attached to the ring never crosses her mind. The dream wedding was her pinnacle in life, as all the eyes were on me, me, me. Now it's a fading memory. History is often our guide…the bigger the wedding, the shorter the marriage. The wedding glow wears off. The excitement and attention of being a dating player has vanished. She's jaded and pissed off to find herself in this position, trapped at home…all dressed up and no one to blow. She actually has the nerve to rail against her husband for *doing this to her*. He's forced to try and save the icy marriage by providing **Chivalry at Gunpoint**, armed with only a wallet and future income to prolong her feigned interest, and to weaken her constant threat of divorce. On the bright side, he probably knows a couple of good attorneys. He's going to need them.

## Shotgun Weddings

That little string dangling out between her thighs isn't the fuse to a bomb. Relax guys. You have plenty of time to court her before marriage. There is nothing to gain and everything to lose if you marry a girl you barely know. You have to give a relationship a few years of ups and downs to determine if you two are compatible. Until you experience the pleasure of surviving a few imaginary emotional crisis and temper tantrums, the biological clock ticking, overdrawn credit cards, rank kitty litter boxes, farts in bed, totaled cars, warts on your dick, suicide threats, 2 am calls from Biff…you don't know a thing about the elasticity of the relationship, not to mention your own levels of patience. More importantly, if you race into a marriage and don't have asset protection set up in advance, you are DOA with a shark. What young, up-and-comers don't realize is that shotgun weddings make them look like a fool. It plays entirely into the girl's hand. The men don't have the faintest idea that the cute little pampered princess has ten times your survival instincts. She has been trained for this very moment since puberty, and has a fine-tuned radar when it comes to smelling a sucker. The war was over before the battle began.

Attorneys, bankers and investment brokers are notorious for this speed wedding lunacy. No wonder we live in a lawsuit happy environment. These guys go through life divorced, angry, and cash strapped. They need a steady flow of the big bucks in order to make out all those huge monthly checks to blonde con artists they barely even rented. I mean some of these guys law ads scream of multiple divorces…

"Can't think of anyone to sue?
Bring us your Rolodex, we'll find someone."

**Paid for by Berg, Berg, and Berg.**

As for the above attorney stud in a hurry, his marriage will last maybe 30 months. After the wedding cake, he'll be rewarded with uninspired sex another dozen or so times, and then ultimately fork over a couple hundred grand, a large chunk of his 401K, his future income, his house, his sanity, and his pride. Not a very good value. That works out to a CPF of a couple thousand bucks a lay. If that pussy doesn't grip like a warm vise, shoot flames, elevate the bed, and turn sperm into gold, he needs to find a new vendor. Oops, it's a tad late.

# Holding out for "The One"

**Q.**

*The hottest girl I've ever seen works in my building. No matter how many times I flirt with her, ride with her in the elevator, walk her to her car, I just can't get her to go out with me. I make small talk, and have told her my feelings about her, but nothing seems to work. I mean not even a phone number. She just blows me off with a smile, usually without saying a word. Somehow I just know that she is The One for me. What gives?*

**A.**

Gag. You're an infatuated stalker in her mind, but you are on a roll. Try sending her a dozen roses a day, licking her shoes, and wiping her ass in the john. Don't stop now. You're on fire!!!!

If a girl is not attracted from the beginning, get over yourself and move on. It's her loss. Don't make the mistake of trying to *win her over*. Showing too much interest, being overly fixated and doubling your efforts, will only double her desire to run from you. By trying too hard, you are only compounding the situation. Obsessive behavior towards a girl screams weakness. Subservient groveling, and proclaiming your feelings too early are the kiss of death. Women are never sexually attracted to a wimp who they she can walk all over. They may keep you around for your stupid spending habits, but they won't be attracted. If she's that hot, I GUARANTEE you she's dating half a dozen guys at the same time. The driving forces in life are Sex and Power. This girl has both over you. It sounds like all you've got is an imaginary infatuation and an empty jar of Vaseline. Get hold of yourself. Oh wait, not like that.

Remember, girls tell each other everything. If she has a large circle of friends, you'll be labeled a desperate loser, and soon find yourself striking out with a lot more targets than you planned. Do not place so much value on one girl. Your ego takes over, until it becomes an emotional quest that blinds you of the masculine traits you need to attract a woman. Do a quick role reversal. Do want to date some clingy, co-dependent drone, or a girl with some spunk who has a life, and gives you a honest, playful chase?

Never bog yourself down with the train of thought of *Holding out for the One*. It has been the downfall of many men. Having an idealized image of a perfect woman is a projected fantasy that is doomed to fail, because from the beginning it is not based on reality. So what is the reality? Having to face your own insecurity in enduring numerous near misses and rejections. By proclaiming virtually every girl doesn't meet your idealized requirements, you protect the fragile ego. While sounding noble, you end up being an obsessing loner living a companionless existence. Keep it up, and even blow up dolls will shoot you down.

The traits you require in your perfect woman will only become more impossible to obtain after each girl you date. Every year the goalpost gets further away. Due to the importance imposed on each woman approached, your fears will be heightened, making the pick up that much more difficult. Your demeanor will be stiff and standoffish, thus guaranteeing even more rejections. If you only approach women you consider potential long-term girlfriends, you will simply never acquire the necessary pick up techniques that come with experience. When you do find a hot one, you will lack the ability to win her over. These skills can only be honed with numerous trial runs with lesser targets. Explore a little. Date around. There are dozens of different personality traits in women, and you will probably find out a completely different type can turn out just fine.

Women are attracted to Male Power. The next time you feel yourself falling hard and fast for a girl, be both charming and distant. Women want a man in control, but one who doesn't kiss her ass. You still have to be flirty and show interest, but come across as having a full life, and willing to walk. Let her know it would be nice to date her, but it's no big deal if you don't. With this attitude you become a dominant male; whether you are one or not. Every woman desire at a subconscious level towards the dominant male, whether she likes it or not.

Next time you hear yourself thinking you have found The One, take the Brett Tate Challenge. Go Fuck 10 other girls. When you're done, if you're still thinking about *The One*, you may have a keeper. But if you find yourself in a hotel room in Rio with a pack of them lined up in a nude football huddle, you may be mistaken. Why settle for one, when it's more fun picking off dozens of wrong ones. Next!!

# King of the Cahones

**Q.**

*I've been seeing this new girl for half a year now, and things are progressing rather quickly. The sex is great, though it's only when she is in the mood. The problem is, when we first met she used to tag along to all my guy events. She'd go to the gym with me, hang out with my friends, always act like she was having a great time. We were a couple. Now, she nitpicks and complains about everything, especially my involvement in anything.*

- - - - - - -

"You're getting too old to be playing that silly little softball"

"You're not going out tonight, you've got a drinking problem."

"Your friends are a bad influence. You'll never get rid of your drinking problem as long as you hang out with them."

"I hate going to that gym, the guys are all leering."

- - - - - -

*I rarely see my friends now, I dropped out of softball, and I stopped asking her to go to the gym. And she's still not happy! What gives? Gotta run. Have to cook dinner, clean the house, iron her blouses, and buy some Tampax before she gets back from power shopping. Then it's off to the church picnic to swap recipes.*

**A.**

This guy sounds about 6 months away from being a beaten down, submissive drone. In return for financial servitude, once every six weeks he'll be treated to an uninspired lay that could be topped by a late night visit to a morgue. Nine months after the wedding she'll weigh 180 pounds, have quit her job, and run up the credit cards. In eighteen months, she'll be in divorce court screaming "IT'S ALL YOUR FAULT!!"

Every chick in a long-term relationship tries the control freak move. They incrementally remove all your small pleasures in life, one by one, so as to restructure your life to fit their own. They do it to piss you off. They do it to make sure you never have fun. Like little kids, they push and push and push to see how much they can get away with. Frankly, most guys will give in, just to shut them up. But this is a fatal mistake, creating the beginning of the end. Naggers never shut up. By caving in, the guy now becomes a sappy wimp in the girl's mind. She is no longer physically or emotionally attracted to him. He's berated with disdain and ridicule, instead of admiration. In other words, a woman will castrate you, and destroy your life. This in turn destroys her relationship. And then she blames it all on you!

All long-term girlfriends are insecure worrywarts, with calculating minds working 24/7 to deprive you of your manhood. Guy's night out is petrifying to them. A special event out of town can bring sheer panic, ultimatums, bogus last minute hospital trips or suicide threats. You see, when you're out of the house, they fear the possibility of you meeting a girl nicer than the bug-eyed nagging control freak at home. They protect the security blanket wallet at all costs.

Fortunately, you can peer into the future if you are in this situation and contemplating marriage. Watch what comes out the doors of the local Wal Mart. See that beaten down, depressed guy carrying diapers, flowers, tampons, and a side of beef for his 250 lb. wife? She's screaming at him, while he stares at the ground wondering how it all happened. That could be you, unless you put your foot down right from the beginning. It's not tough, it just takes common sense and Cahones. Are you packing any?

## Bachelor Code 15

### Never surrender your Honor or Lifestyle for a piece of ass
-------

For a relationship to last, you have to lay down the law upfront. You are not changing one bit. Tell her you are keeping your hobbies, your vices, guy night's out, and your friends. If she has a problem with that or tries to change it, you dump her. You are not her girlfriend, you are a man. Men have Cajones. Your interests, hobbies, friends, and pleasures are what define your life and your character. When a girl presses early on in the relationship for some type of commitment, you have to sit her down and explain the facts of life. This is the only way your relationship will work. It's the only way to maintain any fun, self-esteem and sanity. Otherwise, you may as well put on a dress, hand over your wallet and cut your dick off.

Use reverse psychology in explaining it to her. Tell her that you like her just the way she is, and don't ever want her to change. You want to make sure she keeps her friends, girls' night out, and hobbies intact. A little time away from each other keeps you from getting bored of each other. Likewise, you are not going to change one bit. Then tell her exactly what you are not changing. Define your guy's night out, or your sports league night. Define what your hobbies and vices are upfront. Tell her you have known your friends a lot longer than her, and they are not going away. Ever. Tell her all these things will continue to be an important part of your life, and only you can choose to stop them. If she wants a long-term relationship, she has two choices; she can accept your life staying the same, or she can leave.
*"I can live with either decision."*

This is not selfish in the least. It's your life. No one should tell you how to live it, particularly someone you've known only 6-12 months. If she stays, expect the first test to be your guy's night out. You need to set a precedent, and show that it is cast in stone. Say your event is watching Topless Oil wrestling contests at a local college pub on Mondays. You must go out every Monday Night…no matter what. In the beginning, invite her to come. She may go once, but she won't like it. Make sure you go out every Monday at the exact same time; even if all your friends cancel. Just park around the corner if you have to, or go a strip club instead. You have to establish precedent.

Eventually a Monday will come around and you'll hear *"My mom cooked us dinner tonight, and we have to be there by 7 pm."* You simply say, "It's Monday, reschedule." If she continues with the whining, just ignore it and say "Not on Mondays." If she says *"can't you for once grow up and compromise"*, you leer at her and slam the door on the way out. If you crack just once, she'll start next week on your other fun hobbies. Nagging takes many shapes and forms, and women love to do it. They start arguments just for the sport of it. If you let them, they'll chew your butt off for hours on end, fling every profanity in the book at you, insult your job, your car, your manhood, and the next morning pretend like nothing happened. Morning honey!

There was a recent court case where an estranged husband was sentenced to nine months of in-house probation. He went back to the court and pleaded to be sent to prison. He told the judge that being forced to stay home with his obnoxious nagging wife was "cruel and unusual punishment". He wanted prison time instead, and he got his way. The judge was clearly living with this same disease at home.

Find out real early if your girlfriend shows signs of potentially being a ticking time bomb. Do red cheeks, icy glares, clenched fists, and slamming plates sound familiar? Does she read romance novels at night, or take kickboxing classes? Also, pay close attention when you meet her Mom. Girls all become their Moms. Is her Mom barely able to fake her condescending niceties? When she smiles, do you see dark cold-blooded killer eyes staring back at you? Does her old man never make eye contact, sit in a dark room, and stare off into space? Guess who did that to him? In the beginning, a girl does everything to camouflage the dark traits. Nagging is one trait you can never allow. If she starts up with a stream of complaints, you should either scream back at her, or be a smart ass. *"Nobody talks to me like that in my house."* Grab a pillow and whip it past her head, kick over a chair, and storm out of the house. One ultimatum ignored, she's gone. Hurry up about it, last call may be approaching, *"All girls up, all tops down."* Don't go home that night. Sleep at the office, or Motel 6 with Bambi. Don't call home for 2 days. Stay the King of the Cahones in your home, or get a new vendor, I mean girlfriend.

# Landing 9's and 10's with Consistency

**M**any times the odds seem impossibly stacked against you to get the opportunity to show yourself in your best light to a gorgeous woman. This can be for a host of reasons, usually beginning with the difficulty in getting past her strong bitch barriers, never being in the right place at the right time, or simply the inability to explain the value for her in spending the night chugging moonshine and screwing in your smelly, checkered polyester sleeping bag in your parents trailer park RV.

## Breaking down the Fortified Target

Landing the Great White Shark. The target here is the big scary supermodel type. Hot looking women spend their days acting extremely defensive. They experience a barrage of compliments and approaches all day long, to the point it becomes aggravating just to see a guy looking their direction. It's no surprise they can be hardened professionals at discarding men, sizing them up and spitting them out in a moments notice. They develop a deep mistrust in guys, except of course when they're vacuuming their wallets.

Contrary to popular belief though, if your game is high, these are actually some of the easier hookups, as it is easy to separate yourself from everyone else they see and hear. Since most men are intimidated by them, the approaches the girls are subjected to are pathetic at best, full of fawning, tongue-tied, barf bag filling compliments and pussy-like girlfriend behavior. The words just bounce of her bitch shield like mere pellets, and she blows off losers with just a glance.

I mean come on guys. If you're moving in on a 9.5 with your D+ skills and know your going to strike out hard, how bout putting a little fire and passion into your performance? Piss her off !! Tell her her fake tits look lopsided, and you think the left one has a flat. Brag about yourself. Ask if she'd like to audition to be a porn star. At the bare minimum, we want to see a nice public humiliation scene, dammit!

I want to see her pulse racing till she's blue in the face barking insults, throwing drinks at you, stomping her heels, and baring a little teeth. Oh, and make sure she has beautiful teeth, too. I don't want to be subjected to one of those horrid, discolored overbites…a smile that resembles a runaway horse.

## Initial Stalker Research

The smoothest step in an initial contact is to quickly remove their defenses, build some comfort level time, and leave the area quick. All done with nonchalance; there is never a hint of you appearing to make any moves on her. Get the hell out of there before you blow it. Suppose you see your target regularly, like the same building. Come up with some information that would clearly benefit her. Optimum choices here are career or business knowledge, or perhaps an important conference in her field that she should attend. Other choices could be help at a skill in a social club you both belong to, or hobby you excel at, or simply exercise tips in the gym. Something that would be of significant value to her, a selfless act on your part. Better yet, advice that saves her from something very embarrassing.

# The First Encounter

The first encounter, approach her speaking about something unrelated to anything. Create an unexpected distraction in their day; divulge some funny useless trivia, mention a curious thought or analysis that makes it seem like you are barely talking to them at all. It could be observation humor about someone standing nearby, something in the news. Make her laugh or frown. A positive distraction softens the defenses. Get a little banter going.

Nobody respects an ass kisser, so in the middle of it, playfully make fun of something about her in a teasing fashion. *"You have really tiny feet...must be hard to balance on them,"* and then change the topic. Since she only gets compliments all day, this throws her unexpectedly off, creating mild insecurity. If she's quick, she will tease back, which you ignore, as she is flexing her ego to try and win your approval. It's a mild power struggle showing you are no pushover like the nice guys of the world. Make a few more playful comments, and then start to leave...then turn back, and follow up the moment by telling her the free advice (business, work,etc) you've been waiting to share. Do it in passing, a *by the way* comment. For example:

*"By the way, I couldn't help noticing you have great blowjob lips. A lot of paralegals in this building use the new Enchantress Lip Gloss by Loreal. Their coral shade has shimmery vibrant undertones, and gives you a high glossy shine with consistency. Oh, and it won't stain the judge's robes while your under the table. Just thought you should know.*

### Then you move on.

The next time you see her, do the same routine with more helpful info, but make sure you never ask about the results of your last good deed. Ever.

- People often feel guilt receiving free things, as they feel like they're obligated to reciprocate; particularly when they're reminded of the assistance. (at least men feel guilty). You're above that. You have more in mind than silly ego stuff.

Second time, after the quick time together and new additional info or deed, as you're walking away, pick out something ornamental she is wearing and say *"I really like those earrings"*. Half smile/smirk, and move on quickly. This series of honest gestures makes it very easy for her to relax in your presence. You really haven't done much of anything, while you are slowing laying bricks of comfort. It's like walking backwards into a bar to skip the cover charge. You are just going about your business, and using a little comedy and stroking some minor ego buttons to generate her interest. People always remember their first impression of someone, and when it is done lightly and honest, it creates a positive association that is easier to build upon and maneuver from. Then, on the third meeting you have built enough comfort level time, it's time to steer the conversation in the direction you wanted in the first place. Introduce yourself and go for a close.

*"By the way, I'm Mortimer; I'm in charge of fries at the McDonald's downtown. You know, the one with the gang shootings in the news last week. I hope to make Drive Thru manager someday. Come see me. I'll spot you some extra ketchup packets... (snort, snort)"*

## First Sighting Target Approach

The next approach we'll cover is a first sighting, meet and greet. This situation is just one of the many approaches you can use to meet the 9's and 10's to grab her attention and create interest. It is quite effective in busy locations, since people are visually distracted by all the loud, surrounding stimuli and not thinking so much about themselves at the time. Plus, busy places offer up numerous targets to practice on. Like any seduction, removing the defenses is the first step. This approach itself, though effectual, is irrelevant. What you should pay attention to here is the ease of displaying the *Universal Alpha Foundation* traits, using jokes and basic misdirection conversation to remove her defenses and open the target.

## The Opening

You're in an upscale mall, trolling for models wearing your best peacock Con Kit; ie., well dressed, with the knockoff shiny designer shoes, and fake Rolex. Look for your target near a Starbucks, or a quickie yogurt, cookies and coffee shops. Stand in line behind her, and make sure she's at least 3 or 4 customers away from ordering. You'll need a few minutes. Examine her outfit for something ornamental that she's wearing or holding, be it earrings, arm bracelets, unusual rings, purse, and compliment it.

- "I really like that bracelet you're wearing. Must be nice being so fashion conscious. So what's good here? What are you in the mood for? " (plant the seed, followed by misdirection ).

- She'll reply "blah, blah, blah."
- You pause, and then say…

  "I don't have a clue about fashion. "( eye contact, big smile )

If she takes the bait, she'll look you up and down and give you a token compliment about your clothes/look. (Suck in your beer gut, and make sure the sock you stuffed in your crotch doesn't look too obvious. Also, don't get busted staring at the pink thong peeking out above the crack of her hot little ass in those designer jeans). You reply:

- "What these clothes? My mom bought me these. This is the only safe outfit I own. I normally wear a pink Tank top, leather pants, and clowns shoes."

Spend a few minutes bantering back and forth, get in some laughs and build a little rapport. Allow yourself enough time for the close before she orders.

- "If I get seen one more time wearing this, the girls are going to start calling me Blue Shirt guy. I've got an hour free before my next meeting, and I could really use some expert female advise in picking out some new clothes. How about spending 10 minutes with me in Brooks Brothers and share your expertise on what looks good on a man. Tell you what. What did you say you were getting? The cookies and decaf latte are on me. I'm not going to take no for an answer."

## Analysis

By listening to you, she determined you have a job, your confident, no insecurity, not intimidated, aggressive, got a little 'tude going, funny, you have high standards, you're stroking her ego, got in the token Mom comment, and her guard is down. Hell, you're really not even hitting on her. You did all that in three minutes.

If she says yes, you're building time with a model for under ten bucks. If she won't shop with you, but doesn't really blow you off, tell her you'll still buy her coffee if she spends 5 minutes sitting down together and *telling* you what to shop for. (2$^{nd}$ attempt). If she blows you off again, smile, and tell her if *she buys you* a coffee, the scary Blue Shirt guy will go away quietly. (3$^{rd}$ and final attempt).

## Phase Two:

Let's assume she says yes to the first attempt. You walk together to the store and shop. Be on your toes, sooner or later she will test you and try to parlay this into creating gift purchases for her. In the store, she'll pick out some guy clothes she likes. Make sure you don't agree with all of them like a pliable toy; disagree with a few, buy the others. If at any time she touches your arm or something, back off a little bit, and then put your arm around her and say "you're moving a little too quickly for me, I'm not that easy."

Then quickly point out another item. (implied sex moment, misdirection). Inevitably she will start looking at something for herself. Take note where the item is in the store and see if it's reasonably priced. Let's say she asks if you are going to buy it for her. You reply;

- "Bambi, I have to confess, I'm a reformed date-a-holic. I had to go to classes over stuff like this. If I gave away free stuff to every girl I meet I'd be broke and living in my car. I treat ladies very well *after* the sexual relationship begins, not before."

## Analysis:

Confident, a challenge, experienced, dominant, secure, nobody's fool, token body contact, funny, implied sex encounter.

Let's say she is only mildly interested in you. Checkout, and go for the number close. Suppose she's all over you and wants to blow you in the fitting room. Go to the checkout counter, and have your credit card out. Just as you're about to pay, tell the clerk to hold on a minute, and have her wait there. Then go fetch and buy your girl the item she was eyeing a moment ago. Checkmate. Race out to your car in the parking lot and pin her legs behind her ears. Call the mall in the morning and pickup the spy cam film and offer it to Blockbuster for a healthy rental licensing fee.

## Worst Case Scenario

Suppose you leave the store, only to find out that you totally misread the whole thing. She doesn't want to get together, and doesn't give you her phone number, and kicks you in the balls. No big deal. You got in good practice, and it cost you a hell of a lot less than a real date with a model would have. Go over the whole event at home, figure out where you went wrong, and take mental notes.

Regardless of the results of the pickup attempt, the next day you return the items she recommended you buy for a refund, and start all over with a different girl, in a different store. No reason to run up the tab, when you can rent that hot new Russian massage therapist for the same price. Next!

# Only Suckers Get Played

## Q.

*My girlfriend and I have a great time together, but she has this annoying habit of comparing traits about me to previous boyfriends. She also has the wondering eyes habit, continually making observation comments about guys wherever we go, while I respectively pretend I didn't notice the Swedish blonde with the amazing ass. She compliments me a lot, says I'm better looking, but she still keeps doing it. Should I say something?*

## A.

No. You should slouch, attach a collar around your neck, and hand her the rope. Try not to fidget when she pats you on the head. She is testing the bitch barriers with you and winning; also known as the beginning of the end. It shows zero class when a girl compares you to other guys or a previous boyfriend. If it's in passing once, let it slide. If it keeps happening, you have two choices; dump her immediately, or give her the dickhead treatment. She can give all the excuses she wants, say he has a girlfriend, *"we're just friends"*, whatever. The fact is he's on her mind. Remember, 99% of the time a woman is speaking, every word is calculated to provide *her* the most benefit. You hear only what she wants you to hear, or what she thinks you'll fall for. Pretend you've done this before, plan accordingly.

## The Bitchy Date

You're on a date, and out of nowhere her personality does a 180. She starts turning into a cocky bitch, and starts talking about him, or hitting on other guys right in front of you. Testing you big time.

**You:** *"Do you honestly think I'm going to tolerate this?"*
**Bitch:** "What?
**You:** *"You being rude and trying to test me. I show you respect. I expect the same in return.*

Be real serious when you say it. You've tested her, and drawn the line in the sand. Do it with charm, but be firm. Girls get a big kick out of trying to manipulate guys. If she keeps up the attitude, don't lose your temper or anything. Laugh and say *"looks like you're going to need a cab to get home."* Watch the bar TV without a care in the world.

If she does it again, excuse yourself like you barely know her, and say you're going to the john and getting a drink. If she doesn't start apologizing immediately, she's a game player and you've saved yourself from wasting time and money. Once you're out of view, exit a side door and leave her ass there. It's a lot of fun to by the way. Brett has left girls an hour from their home at concerts and sports events. It's their fault, not mine. It's not like she's inconvenienced. You leave her with dozens of other suckers just waiting to be played. The bitches don't even bat an eye. The first guy she smiles at will be buying her drinks, and giving her a ride home. The bitch charade continues.

# Field Situation

You're lying down on the bed, and she starts up again about an ex-boyfriend. In this scenario, you can assume one of two things.

1. You have no chance of nailing her, and she wants to play games and rub shit in your face.
2. **2.** You've already nailed her and she's testing you to find out if you're sufficiently pussy whipped enough to allow her to start bonking other guys on the side.

## Scenario 1:

1. The pre-dump test. Get dressed and walk towards the door...she'll ask what's wrong. You say:
   *"If he's all that, maybe you should go back to him. I'm not going to sit here listening to you dream about some other guy."*
2. She pulls you back down onto the bed and apologizes. Best move; lie there a little while longer, and then leave anyway. It makes a point. You say:
   *"The mood's gone, it's better go home before I say something else."*

## Scenario 2:

She compares you to another guy again; you get up and start getting dressed. She becomes a bigger ass and barks out even more insults. Say:

*"You know, I could sit here and tell you how much better looking my ex is, or how she has more direction, personality and class, but I won't. (you just did). You've got some serious issues to work out with this guy. When you resolve them, give me a call and **maybe** we'll try this again."*

This shows it pissed you off, you took action, and that you're not going to tolerate disrespect. Who knows, he probably had a 3 incher and was a lousy lay. That's why she's with you. Deep down though, she misses his money more than your rod. Guys with little dicks tend to be rich or spend like it, to make up for their shortcomings. They purchase attention in hopes that when the lights are down at night, she won't notice. She notices all right, but the cash is her desired goal anyway.

## Scenario 3

If she's being a total bitch, and is a lousy lay...Get up and leave, saying *"you are such a waste of oxygen"*. Pee on her cat on the way out, and the next day mail her a UPS box with some feminine deodorant and a compact rolled in dog shit. Put in a sympathetic parting note:

*"Thought I'd do your ex a favor.*
*P.S. Have you seen a mirror lately?"*

**Synopsis:** In life, you always have to show a willingness to walk, if treated with a lack of respect. When it comes to women, that's the only way to keep her sexually attracted. The person most willing to end the relationship has the control. You show social value and attitude, thus maintaining the "challenge" status. If you let her get away with walking all over you, where's the challenge? Attraction is tension based. If she was all over you in the beginning, and is now cold and vague, you gave her too much slack.

## She Cancels a Date with No Notice

**Bitch**: "My brother's fat wife got rushed to the hospital. They think it's Mad Cow disease. I'm heading over there now."
**You:** (don't say a word, just wait for her)..
**Bitch:** "Did you hear me and my ridiculous lie…I mean, are you there? "
**You:**

*"I can't believe this crap. I had tickets to the game tonight, and blew off my best friend because I made a commitment to you. You know, I have a telephone. You could have called and let me make other plans. Instead, you play games. I treat you with respect. If you can't show me respect in return, than you're just wasting my time. "* (then hang up).

Nine times out of ten they call back and apologize profusely. You called their bluff, and now they thoroughly attracted. From that point forward, she will go out of her way to be on her best behavior, and she'll be charged with excitement. If she doesn't call back, who gives a flying fuck? Next.

## Summary

If you let a girl get away with treating you like crap, she will no longer be attracted to you. In other words; women try to destroy her own relationship for kicks, and if they succeed, they will be pissed off at you if for letting it happen. A bunch of nutcases, aren't they?

None of this neurotic BS happens overseas.

# Don't get Caught with your Pants Down

**Q.**

*I've got this new chick in my life who's a real freak. I mean it's been real hot and heavy since the parking lot love on the first date. I'm not sure how the judges will rule, but it only took two weeks of sport-fucking and slamming her skull against the headboard to make a respectable sized dent. It's a clean impression, nice rounding, and smooth edges; about an inch deep. It does show a lot of hollowing in the center area, but then again, so does her brain. Anyway, we've been dating now for all of three weeks, and already I'm starting to have creepy feelings every time she speaks. She's moving way too quickly, and says things out of nowhere that frankly scare the crap out of me. She calls my pad **our place**, wants a key, wants to meet my parents, says honey and sweetheart, and I love you every two seconds, talks about her dream of having kids. Meanwhile, she has creditors calling her all day, her car was repossessed last week, and she called me the wrong name during sex last night. One big scare; I noticed her birth control box was empty, and saw her pretend to take one before sex. Also my crotch has been itching for a week. Gotta run, I hear some explosions downstairs. She's probably cooking up some crack again. . .*

**A.**

The sweet little girl next door is about to be evicted, and is looking for someone to support her ass. Your bonking skills must be high. You may be in the top 5 of her boyfriend choices. Looks as if you went in with beer goggles on; or she may have been role-playing to hook you in the first place. Not good. She told you what you wanted to hear, in hopes of catching an affluent newbie. They all want to bag the naïve, cashed up stud. Sounds like you used the *"I'm semi-retired, third generation old money"* comment to land her in the beginning. A nice touch. Yes, trouble is clearly lurking on the horizon. You may need to leave town sooner than you think. Although you're new at the game, you're starting off strong. The house hasn't been torched, your car isn't at the bottom of a lake, and your dick hasn't been sliced off. It's wise to be suspiciously horny in the beginning of a relationship. A player should always be on the lookout for sudden irrational behavior. The first few weeks with a new girl are like walking naked through a minefield. Sex sessions should performed swiftly, and with great caution. All sex should be restricted to stand up doggie style. Do not remove your pants. Leave them resting at your ankles, gently on top of your brand new track shoes. Drill her with beast velocity, and dismount with precision and speed. During your immediate exit, stay focused. Remember to raise your knees high and pump your arms while sprinting out her front door. Always park around the corner. Leave the car gassed up and running, have pending airline reservations, and keep the passport current. This tape will self-destruct in five seconds. Good luck, Jim.

# <u>Warning Signs</u> – G T F O
### (Def Con 4 - *Get the Fuck out*)

- Asks for a key to your place

- Insists on meeting your parents

- Knows cops on a first name basis

- Comes from a family of attorneys

- Crosses her fingers when she farts

- Goes to church group 4 days a week

- Thinks WWF and Televangelists are real

- Can't remember if she's on the pill or not

- Starts referring to your pad as *Our Place*

- All her talking points are quotes from the bible

- Knows the name of every doorman and bartender

- Has a VIP card at the pharmacy, visits every other day

- Charged lunch with a private investigator to your credit card

- She mentions your office answering machine code in passing

- After 2 weeks wants to know where the relationship is heading

- Used to date a sugar daddy, thinks 50 year old men are hot

- She pauses for 5 minutes in front of every diamond jeweler

- Car looks like squatters have been living in it for a month

- Talks to herself constantly, gets in arguments and loses

- Flips from laughing to fits of rage in a moments notice

- Starts calling you honey and sweetie on the first date

- Her pussy has an echo

# Deadly Warning Signs – R F Y L

### (Def Con 5 - *Run for your Life*)

- Her pierced tongue ring is clogged with dog hair
- Has the Marie Osmond Greatest Hits CD
- The face on her drivers license isn't her
- Quits Yoga classes, takes up kickboxing
- You find her rifling through your wallet
- Uncrosses her legs and the plants die
- Sends monthly checks to MADD
- Subscribes to AK-47 Magazine
- Likes Hillary Clinton
- Has unusual slice scarring on her wrists
- Casually mentions a friend's suicide in glowing terms
- First date she wants to put on a strap on and do you
- During sex, you find a butcher's knife under her pillow
- Shows up for a date with dried white streaks in her hair
- First date, her crotch bulge is significantly larger than yours
- Whenever she's not around, you swear you're being followed
- Keeps a Jack Daniels bottle in her car. Places it next to a Bible
- Her talking parrot starts grunting *Fuck me harder, ya black thugs*
- You mention a Cabo fishing trip with the guys, she fakes a heart condition, plants heroin in your suitcase, calls Homeland Security,
- She borrows your car, and returns with a bumper stuck in the front grill. The license plate starts with *State Judge*.
- Her brother gets out of prison next week, he's pissed off she's been cheatin' on him. He's wanton revenge on yo lily white ass
- Cites her favorite kiddy porn sites while surfing your computer

# Chapter VII

# IT'S ALL ABOUT THE MONEY

BULLETPROOF CONTROL OF YOUR ASSETS
**The Best Defense is a Good Offense**

# History of the Con Artist

In the late 19<sup>th</sup> and early 20<sup>th</sup> century, capitalism moved are such a blinding fast pace, it made the Dot Com boom look like a senior citizen bingo pot. Fortunes and whole new industries were being created overnight; the Gold Rush, the Oil Boom, Wildcatters, Speculators, diamonds, silver, real estate, the stock market, art collectibles; it was pure mania. Each decade brought new wealthy players into the market, who just a few years prior were making 25 cents an hour. Fast money breeds naiveté, and naiveté breeds open season for professional Con Artists.

The swindlers of these times were brilliant, well traveled men, armed with street smarts, shrewdness, and years of experience. Many were ex-businessmen, once victims of great cons themselves. Sophisticated and cultured, they knew the industry and their marks inside out. With great ease they impressed people with their street knowledge and charm. They cultivated an insider's mentality, and were masters of disguises. They played the mining engineer, banker, wildcatter, Old Money investor, down to the quiet, dumb, aw shucks employee. They had wealth, so time was of no concern for pulling off the job. Their portfolio of cons contained numerous exploitation angles beyond the grasp of the young, uneducated, new money entrepreneurs. The fresh baby-faced new millionaires welcomed them in with open arms, as they could legitimately learn a great deal of wisdom; right up to the part where the cons stole their last dime and disappeared into the sunset. Their biggest lesson was their last.

The swindlers' plot could take months to years to unfold. They first earned the mark's confidence by offering a promise; a means to make his business explode, coupled with a desire to join him and invest in his future. They'd infiltrate the mark's inner circle with fellow cons, and establish credible business references from the target's associates. They dug in deep, and left nothing to chance. Working in teams, they threw money around, and even brought the mark some healthy new business before the noose was pulled. They were so brilliant at studying a target's business and contacts, that some of the greatest successful heists came from swindling the wealthiest, brightest men in the world. In the 1920's Al Capone feared the cops and trusted no one. In the 1900's the Vanderbilts, Gould, Carnegie, J.P. Morgan, and Rockefellers feared the Con Artists.

## Satan's Sexy Swindlers

Fast forward to 21<sup>st</sup> century, and you'll find the swindling trade is alive and thriving. Elaborate undertakings, like the great ones from years gone past, at times are unnecessary. For the low level cons, all it takes are tits, high heels and a Mickey Finn. Like their mentors, these predators will blend into their surroundings perfectly, in this case donning expensive sexy attire, coupled with sophisticated hip conversation. Young bachelors in nightclubs, especially those who do frequent business travel, are quite the naïve, easy mark. After all, these guys tend to binge drink and have a dick. Those are the only two requirements a sexy shark needs to roll you. Working alone, the modus operandi is a quick score; a promise of sex, then a drug and run.

## Poison in the Panties

Occasionally the higher level sharks will appear when they smell a bigger score. They work in pairs, with one playing the horny drunk babe, while the other one has the role of surveillance, security and other background specialties. These fine young ladies are working the notorious traveling grifter con. They move from town to town working their magic, as sticking around with the loot can be hazardous to their health. They look for wealthy, famous or married marks out of town on business. The swindle technique in this case elevates to screw, drug, film, and blackmail. Here's how it goes down.

Sitting patiently a short distance from the hotel lobby bar, or at a table in a restaurant, they watch for a mark getting plastered and looking submissive. They saunter on over and get drunk with him. Inevitably, they corral the old coot upstairs to his hotel room for some good old fashion lean-over-the-balcony-railing doggie style; bonus points are registered if his toupee and teeth fall forty stories to the street. First comes the special drinks, then while the one is fucking, the other is secretly filming. After the Mickey Finn kicks in, they scoop up the loot and leave to a secure location for Phase Two.

The guy wakes up and his Rolex, cash, cards, car and laptop are gone. It's common they take all his clothes too, so he can't come after them quickly. If the room contents score is substantial, they may just leave town. If they determine the guy is very rich or seems particularly vulnerable, the next day they drop the bomb and threaten to go public, and/or send his wife the videotape. The guy quickly settles, and wires the blackmail funds. The cons are smart, and make the ransom maybe $5-10,000, something reasonable enough that he won't care. Some return the laptop as a sign of good faith. For laughs, they may leave a short mpeg of the video on the desktop. Other variations of the con are far more expensive and serious; bogus sexual assault or rape charges, with the charges dropped after payment.

## Learn to Con the Con Artist

For historical purposes, there were two men way ahead of their time controlling aggressive scamming women and the groupies of the world. In the early 1960's, Chuck Berry had a nice little technique for any girl who wanted to sleep with him. Before he would undress, he would take a couple photos posing with the horny girl, facing the hotel room mirror. She would have to be completely naked and smiling (while he is fully dressed); one picture looking at the mirror hugging him, one picture kissing him, ie, proof of consensual sex. In the 1970's, J. Paul Getty took precautions to the highest level. He had a tad more at risk, being the world's richest man at the time. Before he would sleep with a new girl, she would have to submit to a complete sex physical. Then, she had to hire an attorney and sign multiple affidavits relinquishing all future ability to file claims against him.

Today, the NBA has had to resort to requiring *mandatory con artist classes* for the players, instructing how to recognize these predatory sharks. I guess Koby fell asleep. They teach the boys all the warning flags to look for, and the self-defense methods for staying out of extortion situations. Blackmail is big business, and there are many players paying 4 and 5 figures a month in child support to a whore they knew for 3 hours…some guys write several checks a month. It's gotten so bad, sports figures, celebs and millionaires have learned it is unwise to sit alone in a room with **any** unknown American woman, or heaven forbid a small child. If you're a man, your guilty until proven innocent. Get used to it, and plan accordingly.

Now for the traveling male with money, it's always wiser to skip the freebie and get an escort. (it's not like it's hard to get referrals from fellow travelers, or find them near an expensive hotel). There are no complications. *"Nice to have you back at the Hilton Mr. Smith, will Maria be joining you this evening?"* For quickies, a call girl is the most honest girl out there, as you know the price going in. The sex is better; you save yourself a hell of a lot of money, and avoid the potential hassles and embarrassment. Ever notice how you rarely ever see the single professional sports or entertainment figures in your local nightclubs? What do you think they're doing? Paid sex is always cheaper than free sex.

## Snake Oil from the Tongue of the Serpent

Now lets move on to the most dangerous of all professional con artists; your everyday aspiring Trophy Wives. They are elaborate planners in their own right, with manipulation skills taking on the role of a fine art. In many ways, they are far more lethal their gold rush predecessors, as they have sexual favors in their arsenal. There are millions of them filtered throughout society, and they have dug in deep, creating an entire industry fleecing men. The media is their public relations firm, handling the disguise, and they have the complete backing of both the state, the legal and judicial system. The web they sew would make yesteryears con artist innovators proud to tears. That's how far they have infiltrated our culture into accepting their scandalous behavior. Every successful bachelor considering marriage is a potential mark, and if trapped unexpectedly by one of these snakes, their sting is ruthless.

## - Con Artist: - (kŏn) *slang*

- To swindle a victim by first earning his confidence, and tricking him into a false promise of gain (happy marriage and family), but ultimately conning them, and stealing all his money.

( see *Divorce Fraud* )

# You are Being Watched

In NYC, Beverly Hills, South Beach, and a thousand cities in between, the tradition of the Great Cons lives on. Western society is teeming with hot looking swindlers posing as aspiring wives longing for a family. They're on a hunt for a *level jumping* marriage lifestyle, and a quick profitable divorce. Some of them already have two or three kills in the bag before meeting you. If you currently have a higher level of income and wealth, rest assured that more than a few of these princesses are out there right now Watching You.

While some of these long legged sharks resort to using a PI to pry out financial data on their mark, most prefer to trust their own instincts at field research. Starting on the first date, while you're being the consummate gentlemen wining and dining her, she's busy analyzing your naiveté, assets, income prospects, and calculating her ease of accessing them as her own. Disguised as the corporate sexpot to the sultry girl next door, she will use her looks, seductive charm, and eventually sexual favors to lure in her mark. The successful con job generally takes several years to fully play out, from dating, to marriage, and ultimately the Big D(ivorce).

Their typical mark is the average looking, rising business star. The Male Careers include Doctors, Dentists, Investment Bankers, Entrepreneurs, Stock Brokers, Attorneys, Luxury Cars/Real Estate salesmen. Her target is in his 3$^{rd}$ or 4$^{th}$ year of high salaries, gets an annual bonus, and on his way to being filthy rich. While his first big house and the fancy cars are alluring, what make him such a perfect mark are his untamed ego, lack of street smarts, and pure gullibility. He's the unsuspecting newbie. Dating the first hottie of his life, he's fucking like a rock star every day! He falls hard to her sexual powers, living trapped in a catatonic state of testosterone overload. For months she will screw his brains out, until his mind goes blank with the addiction; like an IV attached to a pussy. All rational thought ceases. Once the trap is set, she threatens to cut him off because *"things aren't progressing fast enough"*. He panics, and buys her a big ring. She smiles devilishly, and turns away quickly before he sees her serpent like tongue flicking away at her eyebrows. It's Showtime, baby. The mark is so busy screwing and showing off his trophy babe, he never takes the time to respect the power of asset protection. His gold Cahones are out there swinging out in the breeze, just waiting to get crushed in the divorce vice. The only question is how much mercy she will show while turning the ratchet bar.

Most guys don't realize they've been had until 6 months into the marriage. Her confidence game starts to unfold. Those romantic little things you did that she loved during courtship become everything she hates about you during marriage. Her personality takes a bizarre turn for the worse, almost as quickly as her figure. Eventually, the wife looks and acts like a complete stranger compared to the gorgeous thin bride tiptoeing down the aisle. Her attitude and language towards you resembles a rude, drunken sailor.

After a year, she's quits her job, which forces you to work even more. Then she bitches you work too much. To amuse herself, she'll fill half a dozen safety deposit boxes with your cash and jewelry while you're slaving away for her. Soon, you can only delay the inevitable by large purchases. Her Mercedes buys you 6 months, the bigger house you can't afford spots you another year. Your divorced friends warn you when she demands a boob job, you have six months left till she drops the bomb. (the rack increases her marketability and pussy pricing for the next sucker she cons). But you stick with the charade and buy her the airbags anyway. On the rare moment she lets you touch them, you do so more out of curiosity than lust, since they feel like frozen grapefruits. From that moment on, the only thing that gets her nipples hard is dreaming of the divorce settlement.

- While it will appear her goal is for you to hate her so much you file, she is simply reverting back to her natural state. Everything was a con job, from the minute she laid eyes on you. Plus, they live for the torturous mind games. Watching your pride, mind, and wallet deflate are what gives them power. When you cease putting up a fight is when she pulls the plug. Like the black cat, when she tires of playing with the mouse, she always kills it.

You put together your final Hail Mary pass. On a perfect day in paradise, you sit together on an exotic beach gazing off into the sunset. After planning this special moment for a year, you get down on one knee and ask if she will make you a father. She looks at you with coal black eyes, an icy stare completely devoid of emotion. Almost without a soul. For a moment, you detect a demonic flash of red pupils. A vulture circles overhead. She gives a sigh, and announces, *"we've grown apart"*, or *"I'm bored, give me half,"* or *"Fuck off asshole,"* or some other noble pronouncement. It's a highly emotional moment for her, akin to throwing out a kitchen rag. She blames the divorce all on you, and curses the day **you** tricked her into all of this. Every little indiscretion, every imaginary crisis that ever occurred from the day you met will be hurled in your face in a steady stream of obscenities. Then she files. Thirty months of marriage usually does the trick. When the divorce documents are signed, she skips off into the sunset. But for you, it may be done on paper, but it's never over. You will continue

**220**

working for her, writing her checks, defending yourself in court, and tolerating her crap for the rest of your life. The con is complete. Next!

# The Queen Bee of Scammers

There's an even higher level of gold diggers that are exceedingly despicable. The **elite trophy wife** con artists are quite reminiscent of their idols from the 19th century. They cultivate an insider's mentality, as they've usually been married before. By having their own money, they can don an array of disguises in their peacock presentation, and buy memberships and mingle in the high dollar social networks. Sophisticated and cultured, they have miles of street smarts and charm. Their portfolio of role-playing cons and exploitation angles know no boundaries. Always the consummate actress, they can play the supportive socialite, the submissive co-dependent, the domineering housewife, the artistic drama queen, the bimbo; whatever role is necessary for the part. They dig in deep and are in it for the long haul. They leave nothing to chance.

These elite predators have been known to go to great lengths in the exploratory phase of their mating quest, employing slippery to devious tactics to gather data. Nowadays, all it takes is an internet connection, and hiring a Private Investigator. Their first goal is to narrow down and quantify the potential male targets by assets; to learn as much information about him as possible before deciding if she should pursue. The PI team creates a financial mockup. They'll map out his complete portfolio of assets; liquid, business, real estate holdings, retirement accounts, art collection, jewelry, collectibles, cars, and insurance policies. They will find out how his income and estate are structured, with particular attention to how accessible it is (Trusts, LLCs), i.e., what deeds, titles, and accounts are registered in his name. They'll research his salary, perks, bonuses, his previous divorce settlement payouts, current monthly alimony checks, and even gauge if his law firm is known to settle quickly. In the end, she'll have a nice round estimate of her love for him, I mean potential settlement. All that before the first date. His health history is also a consideration. These women are romantics after all, and would prefer a man with a heart still ticking; at least for a few months past the vows.

Like a black widow, these seasoned professionals lay low, waiting for the opportune moment to strike. They sit patiently until they have a shot at the most prized of victims; the great white whale...Ole Daddy Big Bucks. The perfect mark is the lonely older widowed man, whose wife passed away a few years back. His mourning period has recently ended. He's been spotted peeking back out in the social scene, and been known to flirt and drink a bit too much. The PI's go to work, and start prying out his surface personal information, so that she can arrange the "chance meeting."

**Here's the basic stalking info she will acquire**

1. Where he lives, where he works
2. His friends, and business associates
3. His daily rituals: locations with exact times.
4. Favorite clubs, social functions, restaurants
5. Where he goes to church
6. His habits, hobbies, vices
7. His golf course

Once she has all this information, she has no problem doing a great deal of stalking research. She will watch him from a distance for a month to dissect his personality, mannerisms, and interests. There will be intelligence-gathering conversations with his friends and business associates, disguised as mindless flirting. She will study the mark. Watch him. Get inside his skin. Come to understand what makes him tick. She'll see what women he likes, what clothes they are wearing, what hairstyle, and jewelry he prefers. She will get photos of his ex and study her look. Then, like a chameleon, she will re-create herself and become his dream target.

When the moment is getting closer, she may work in teams and send in a friend for hit and run conversations with the actual target, to test out various seduction approaches, and to gauge his readiness. In due time, when the look and attitude has been perfected, she will finally plant herself in front of him. She has him at hello. Often times she may approach first at his church, where he would least expect it. The consummate seducer, by the time she sets the trap, the mark will think *he* did the pickup, and be impressed of his own talents. "*Sonofabitch, I've still got the magic.*" Well, he's going to have a lot less magic by the time she's through with him.

Sometimes true love is only a few zeros and a comma away. In the elite trophy wife's compassionate heart, she will experience cherished moments of bliss that few women have ever felt. These moments don't occur during the marriage. When the divorce judge finalizes her 7 to 8 figure payout, the mere echo of the slamming gavel in those mighty chambers has been known to trigger multiple orgasms. That's how powerful her love was for old Broderick, er um Worthington III, or whatever the hell his stupid name was.

**Bambi**: "If it wasn't for me, my ex wouldn't be a millionaire"

**Tiffany**: "That's true, but he was worth ten million when you met."

Many men feel these women are so sleazy, they give con artists a bad name. Con Artists complete their mission, and move on. With these compassionate sweethearts, it's a whole other story. Many of them make it their life mission to destroy the ex-husband. Whenever they get bored, or hear the ex is enjoying life, they file lawsuits. If he gets a big bonus, they sue for their piece. If he makes a fuss, they use their other favorite trick. They have him arrested with a steady stream of false charges; physical assault, verbal assault, stalking, destruction of property, attempted rape, sex offender, the list is endless. They also use the kids as pawns for more lawsuits, and ultimately destroy her own kids' minds and lives in the process. When the husband dies, an ex-trophy wife will think nothing of suing his ass for a larger portion of his estate while he's still warm in the coffin.

It's just not fair to insult the con artist name by allowing the trophy wife scammers to join the club. Many men believe these women are really nothing but a bunch of classless Hookers. Well, that also can come across as a bit strong, and gives off the appearance of an unfair smear campaign. It's seems quite rude that people would make such a comparison. Why show such disrespect to the women of the oldest profession in the world? They are completely honest about their intentions and service, and their price is fully explained upfront.

## THE DIVORCE INDUSTRY

There were 1,182,000 divorces in the year 2001. The US Census lists married-couple households having a median net worth in 2000 of $91,218. Women confiscate roughly half of the family's current marital assets, regardless of how menial their contribution is. So, are you sitting down? Each year, the Divorce Industry enforces an annual *transfer of wealth* from men to women of approximately:

### $45 Billion Dollars a Year

Government census figures show annual child support payments women receive from men is roughly **$3 Billion dollars**. Throw in up to 25% of your income in alimony payments for a number of years, half your retirement account and life insurance policies, and your looking at the most profitable industry in the United States.

The lawyers who helped propagate this racket are quietly kicking some major ass as well. The average litigated divorce can easily cost as much as $20-40,000 for both parties combined. Oh, and husband has the pleasure of paying for her divorce attorney to boot. How thoughtful of you, honey! Fighting for custody in Court can bleed you dry as well, to the tune of at least $15,000-$30,000. With 1.1 million divorces a year, the lawyers are easily pulling in a cool $20-30 Billion dollars a year. This brings the grand total of this behemoth industry to close to an **annual $70-100 Billion dollars.** The Divorce industry is little more than a socialist redistribution scheme, confiscating male assets and rewarding women.

# Only the Paranoid Survive

In the courtship phase, if a hot looking girl is being overly aggressive, you should be nervous; not patting yourself on the back. Never give her a key to your place. Believe half of what you see, and none of what you hear until proven otherwise. If she pressures you to move in a few months after you meet, or suggests a what-the-hell Vegas marriage, it's a gigantic sell signal. Pull the plug, change the locks and move on. By the way, don't kid yourself; she's not on the pill.

Let's suppose you've got a very large salary and are on the fast track to being wealthy. You've been dating someone special for a year, and think you are finally ready for marriage. In the modern era, it's always wise to be on the side of caution. Protect yourself, and do a peripheral background check on her. Pay in cash. If using a PI bothers you, for a small fee, get a paid legal background search on the net. See if her life story pans out; verify her past addresses. If she's moved 5 times in the last two years, besides being unstable, she's either hiding from something or someone, and probably in debt up to your ears.

Analyze all of the liabilities she is bringing to the table. Make sure you see her tax returns are paid in full; back taxes are 18% interest a month. Don't think she is going to be upfront if she owes a ton. The same goes with massive credit card and student loan debts. Make sure she is not a party of any pending lawsuits or has any civil judgments. Separate all of these to her side in the pre-nup. Do a criminal background check. Also, find out is she has already done a quick marriage and divorce. After doing your research, ask her a few questions in passing and compare your results to her answers. Feel no guilt, you're protecting yourself. It's not like she's the Virgin Mary when it comes to knowing your financial status intimately.

# The Need to Beat the System

Everyone wants to be a winner, to have complete control over their decisions and direction in life. Money provides a more rewarding lifestyle, stability and independence. Money is the root of all power. It gives you the ability to work where you want, buy what you want, date whom you want, and it allows you to tell people to take a fucking hike if you want. If you have money, you control your destiny.

If someone else control's your money, *they* *control your destiny.* They have power over your decisions and direction, and are looking out for their own best interests, not yours. They can make you as happy or as miserable as they want, which usually means a life of servitude and mind games. When someone else controls your assets, money becomes the root of all evil. The fact of the matter is when you sign on the marriage dotted line, your documents contain three parties in the relationship; you, your wife, and the state. That means the state's attorneys, her attorneys, the judges and the law have now joined her side in controlling your money going forward. The system is entirely rigged in the woman's favor.

–––––––

## Bachelor Code 16
### Amendment 6, sub-section 12-3a
## The marriage institution is failing because women have a financial incentive to destroy it.

–––––––

Women initiate 75% of the divorces, and you can be damn sure money is a motivating factor. Their monetary rewards in a divorce are often like winning the lottery; they get half your assets, the house and car, alimony payments, child support, half your retirement, half the life insurance, your 401K, the list goes on and on. Divorce is legalized castration for a man. The man gets nothing he didn't already have. A woman can marry and divorce as many times as she wants, and will win in court virtually every time. And she can continue suing for more at will.

# It's All About the Money

Money is what separates the sexes. When a woman chooses her perfect man, it's all about his money and controlling it; success trumps looks every time. They all want a higher income man who can provide her an upgraded lifestyle without responsibility. A husband with money gives her the freedom to quit working, enabling her to do what she wants, when she wants, and of course buy what she wants. *Me, Me, Me.* Maybe even have a family if she gets around to it. The one requirement for her to obtain this freedom is she has to control the man and his money. This condition is automatic fulfilled *unless* the guy takes steps to protect himself in advance.

When a man chooses his perfect woman, her money is irrelevant. Men ignore her personal assets, status, and potential in business. **All men want is a sexy girl who's nice, loves sex, and will make pretty babies**. In fact, we find women without money are far more honest, and have a warmer personality. They don't go around with a chip on their shoulder, battling confused-gender issues, power struggles, and the typical emotional roller coaster mood swings. You can trust them and their intentions.

This glaring difference between the wants and desires of men and women creates an impenetrable wall. Marriage is set up for failure for men. Women control men because they control our money via the threat of a divorce. We literally lose all power to control our own lives, as the woman has the final word in every major decision. If she says no to our wishes, and we pursue them anyway, she can just call up the state and her attorney and tell them it's time to seize half your assets. She can micromanage your life worse than a drill sergeant, and there's nothing you can do about it. If you argue and file divorce yourself, the result is the same. You lose half either way.

As unfair as that sounds, the even bigger issue for men in a marriage is usually not the money. If we marry a sexy girl who's nice and can make pretty babies, after marriage, what's to stop her from no longer being sexy or nice? Nothing. The best scenario men can hope for is to maintain the status quo; and we all know how rare that is. When men file for divorce it's for one reason. **Women change**. Mentally, and physically. The changes in the appearance department can be quite shocking. The average weight of an American woman is, I kid you not, now a gargantuan 169 pounds; the size of a defensive back. That's just the average. Try to visualize sleeping next to ones well above the average the next time your getting the marriage itch.

## Peg – The Exploding Housewife

Husbands around the country have had to take drastic measures to afford the added expense of feeding a large animal at home. Bumper stickers are appearing on mattresses: *Sponsored by Monroe Shocks*. Front lawns advertise a cover charge to see circus acts in the backyard: *"Step right up and see the greatest show on earth. Come watch Peg the whale try to get out of a swimming pool without a forklift!!!"* Billboard companies are trying to rent out space on a thigh or two. At the very least, you'd think the wench would help out with the yard work and munch on the high grass out back. It's not like they have a job or anything. Sadly, for many men, the size is only half the problem. The bitchiness and attitude from some of these great white buffalo gives new meaning to the word evil. Like a wiseman said:

> "If you didn't have a pussy, there'd be a bounty on your head."

## The Best Defense is a Good Offense

The divorce system is rigged, and there's no way women will ever change it to benefit men. Fortunately, **you have the ability to change it in your favor**, by exercising the available options. The best defense is a good offense. The tools to control your assets permanently are available for everyone. Defend yourself from becoming one of the ten's of millions of divorce victims out there who are walked all over by women. You have insurance on your car, insurance on your house, why in the world would you marry without insurance on your assets? A Professional Bachelor sets up **Asset Protection** long in advance. If the marriage doesn't pan out, you keep virtually every pre-marriage penny in a divorce. When men have sole control of their own assets going into the marriage, all the rules change in their favor. Her monetary incentive to file is removed. A woman's attitude towards her husband returns to being one of respect. They could no longer use sex as an exploitive weapon. They would no longer be able to pull off the big con jobs, or change into something undesirable to

**226**

indescribable after the vows. The Pegs of the world would become rare. The marriage institution would return to being based on honesty instead of money, and two parents would once again raise their kids together. The mere thought of this sends panic into women and attorneys across the country, but it's the way it has to be if you want to live a happy married life.

## Cover your ASSets - Bulletproof from Divorce

Let's do a role reversal in analyzing the situation. Imagine you're about to marry a wealthy young woman. Do you think her Father who created his daughter's wealth, and the family attorneys would allow her to put herself into the subservient position the typical groom does? Do you think she would sign a legally binding financial agreement, of which she is a submissive party; subject to losing her investments, property, future earnings, retirement, and kids? Would she enjoy being a passive spectator, handing over her estate to a deadbeat husband's whims, greed, and fleet of parasite attorneys? Of course not, only a fool would do such a thing.

When a man buys his first home, he immediately pays for quality legal advice. He does lien searches, title searches, reviews zoning restrictions and easements, and buys an array of insurance policies. He consults every close friend and family member he knows for the best first hand advice they can offer. Yet when it comes to marriage, men dive in headfirst like buffoons, blindly ignoring the most important financial decision of their life.

### That my friend is the *Power of the Pussy*

Chances are, somewhere down the road the groom will learn the full effects of the poison he succumbed to. In that back of his mind, he already has a clue. Ever notice after the wedding ceremony is over, the bride is awash in a glow of giddy happiness and fulfillment? That's the face of Victory. Her quest is complete. The groom sits in the corner with an embarrassed fake grin. By the end of the day it decays into a puzzled smirk. The hairs on the back of his neck start to tingle. He will try to ignore it, but his instincts are warning him that he may have just made a terrible mistake. His wedding ushers don't know whether to congratulate him, or feel sorry for him. His divorced friends, well, they can already envision the inevitable Jaws of Life prying him from his own home and estate.

## What you don't own can't be taken from You

Twenty years ago, a pre-nuptial agreement was enough. Over time, pre-nups have been regularly challenged, and often deemed from ineffective to irrelevant. The power to control your assets is back once again in the man's side of the court, for those who intelligently exercise their options in advance. You need Financial Planning, which keeps you in control, but at he same time separates you from technical ownership. This fundamental concept is the cornerstone of solid asset protection. If it is not yours, it is also not available to your creditors. The objective of any sound asset management plan is to maintain control, while removing legal ownership from your name. **You control everything, and own nothing.**

**Asset protection** used to be a tool only for the wealthy. Creating an asset protection plan is no longer an option but a necessity. In today's litigious society, anyone with a net worth of $50,000+ or salary of $75,000 and up needs to establish asset protection. It is vital to structure one's assets in such a way to insulate them from uninvited parties or circumstances. Asset protection creates a legal shield between your assets and any potential creditors; unbalanced divorces, future judgments, frivolous lawsuits, overzealous plaintiff attorneys and ambulance chasers.

**Lowering your asset profile** is also a result of a proactive planning. While in the past this was done primarily to discourage frivolous lawsuits, it has become much more important today. With identity theft, phishing, pharming, and similar criminal schemes being rampant, it makes sense to keep valuable assets separate from your legal name or from being reported under your social security number.

By transferring assets into an LLC, Trust and business entities, the assets are no longer held or reported in an individual person's name. This makes it difficult to impossible for criminals and curious attorneys to locate or access either the account information or the assets themselves. In the case of a divorce court, if you are questioned under oath, you must tell the truth about what you own and how it is held. The proper legal structure removes the assets from your name, allowing you to tell the truth in saying no to ownership, protecting your property from claims and liens.

Asset protection plan is essentially a *pre-nuptial before the pre-nuptial.* An asset protection plan will not only protect you in the event that you are sued, it will play a vital role in **preventing you from being sued** in the first place. Proper asset protection in advance becomes psychologically intimidating to creditors, or would-be creditors. It often prevents attempts of litigation or aggressive collection against debts. Most lawyers work on a contingency basis, foregoing an upfront payment. Before they will initiate action on behalf of their client, they determine if the person they are considering suing has substantial assets. At the bare minimum, enough to cover their fees and justify their time and effort. If in the discovery phase, the litigant will either not find assets to collect (due to financial privacy measures), or he will see that these assets are effectively shielded and not worth pursuing. There is no incentive to proceed..90% percent of the cases never go to court; they either dismiss or settle for pennies on the dollar.

Attempting to pierce a sold asset program can be a very expensive and lengthy legal process. Say your ex-wife sues your FLP to try and steal your legally protected investment accounts. To win, her attorneys must prove you set up your entity in a fraudulent manner, or that you're using it as your own piggy bank. Both instances should be fruitless. You set them up legally, and leave the investment assets untouched. Use your salary, credit cards and checking account to pay for your bills and lifestyle. These funds never co-mingle with the protected assets. In other words, she not only loses the case, she has to pay both her own huge attorney bill, as an added bonus, by government law, **she has to pay your attorney fees!** Touche, beeotch.

In the rare case where they win, creditors of an LLC or FLP cannot secure anything more than a *"charging order"* against that partner's interest in the partnership. A charging order gives the creditor no rights to control or attach the assets of the partnership, but only has the right to receive the partner's distributions. Moreover, in a properly drafted LLC or FLP agreement, a creditor has no right to vote or inspect the books and records of the entity.

You win in this scenario also. Since family members control most FLP's, the general partner will usually cease or alter distributions, resulting in no money distributed to the creditor. For example, say your wife blows the 80 yr old judge and she wins the case. Because of IRS ruling 77-137, she is still responsible for all the taxes the partner would have owed, even if she does not receive a penny of distribution. Therefore, not only will she not get any money, she will owe "phantom taxes", meaning she has to pay the full tax amount on the money *she never even collected* ! She wins, and still ends up significantly poorer. This strongly dampens the enthusiasm of a creditor and attorney to pursue an LLC or FLP member's interest in the first place. In summation, before you get engaged, make sure all of your business assets, physical assets, liquid assets, retirement accounts, and home are safely protected in a multi-layered asset protection program.

**For the cashed up stud**, hot women will be pursuing *you*. Enjoy the spoils of your money and use them, just like they are using you. Eventually the time will come when you're pressed for marriage, and your feelings about a pre-nup. Answer with a role reversal, and prepare for a hilarious response:

*"Marriage? If a wealthy girlfriend asked me to sign a pre-nup, I would absolutely sign it. I mean, I'm marrying her for love, not money. There's no faster when to find out someone's true intentions than asset protection."*

She'll say crying in horror, *"what are you telling me?!!!"* You reply:

*"I believe in honesty. My assets are legally shielded layers deep in trusts and entities "for my future children." If you're considering marrying me for love, I'm interested. But if all you're after is money, you won't see dime one in a divorce. So honey, what's your honest motivation? Love or money?"*

Cold reality exposes how conniving women can be. Wait till you see how indignant and offended most act for you daring to suggest something so vile and underhanded as keeping **all of your own money**. Fists, bricks through windshields, screaming obscenities in your face, calling you a selfish A\*hole..."*how dare you not trust me...you used me*", etc. Aspiring trophy wife con artists will throw themselves off a cliff before marrying a guy with solid asset protection coupled with a pre-nup. If your babe can't accept you being smart and safe, she'll walk. Almost every girl will. If she stays, you've got yourself a special girl who is honest. After this moment has passed, let her know you will pay what you feel she deserves in spousal support if it doesn't work out, but the amount is entirely up to **you**, not her attorney. Let her know you will not reward bad behavior.

Now, a few important rules you must follow. If you do marry, go into it with a home and lifestyle *way below* what you can afford. Most marriages fail in the first few years. You want to test the waters and find out how she handles being a wife in the looks and attitude department. The odds are she will change, they pretty much all do. If she stays what you want, after year five upgrade your lifestyle. Why the precautions? If she quits her job and becomes a screeching whale, you want to make sure that when you appear in court, "*the lifestyle she's accustomed to*" is nothing extravagant. If you've got a 20,000 square foot home, she gets that, and maybe an alimony reflecting that. If a homeowner, transfer your home to a trust pre-marriage. The smartest move is budget renting for years. This is not to say that YOU have to live in poverty. Treat the old lady to a primered Yugo, while you valet park your Ferrari Convertible dining solo at the finest restaurants in town. Then switch cars at the Storage Garage on the way home to your beat up 73 Impala, change into dirty rag clothes, and bring her home TV dinners; complain about yet another late night at the office. Make sure your house is small, in fact preferably share an apartment or rented RV. For her weekly allowance give her $20; if she complains tell her to get a better paying job.

**Another thing to remember.** The con artist women who marry with the intent to divorce **will steal from you blind for years** until filing. A large percentage of the spending cash you provide her will end up stashed away. You will continually see large unexplained withdrawals via her ATM card, CC and your checking account. Take steps to prevent this. Set up separate checking and CC accounts. If you can't, make sure the checking balance is always tiny. Tell her "*Damn honey, we never seem to get ahead. Maybe you should get a second job.*" Keep her credit card limit small, with bank required phone approval from you before any large purchases go through.

Beat women at their own scams; take action from Day 1 of marriage. Every week, cash a portion of your paycheck, and establish a pattern of sizeable ATM withdrawals for your own "living expenses." Charge everything, pay by check, creating a track record and low check balance, while pocketing cash away. If pressed, say you eat out a lot and spoil yourself for working so hard. For her big $$ inquiries, claim a bad run of luck sports betting or in

**230**

Vegas. Put this cash, money orders, or loaded up debit cards (in a different name) in an out of town safety deposit box secured in a business name or someone else's name. Feel no guilt. They all do it to the husbands, so be smart and return the favor. After all, you earned the money. It's just additional intelligent asset and divorce protection. Remember, for every dollar you protect, you earn an instant 50% return if she files. In a few years, you'll be surprised how quickly it adds up to a rainy day slush fund.

(True Story verified 9/7/2006): A 65 yr old wealthy business associate's wife of 35 years died unexpectedly. He took the death certificate to his bank to close out her bank accounts, and they steered him to her safety deposit boxes that he knew nothing about. They were filled with $50 + $100 bills. On a whim, he took her death certificate to the next bank, only to find more. He spent the next few weeks and drove to banks all over the county. There was no way to determine the total of banks she used, but he found close to dozen, containing well OVER A MILLION IN CASH she stole from him. He then decided to check self-storage places and found *thousands* of brand new high dollar dresses with the tags still on them. He had to rent a gymnasium to display and sell them. Trust me; ask any male banker in the safety deposit rooms; half the boxes are filled with cash that wives steal from husbands.

# ASSET PROTECTION GAME PLAN
(created before engagement)

There are numerous levels and layers of protection an individual can utilize. Your situation depends on the diversity of the assets, and size of your estate. The more money, property, and companies, the more layers of protection needed. There's generally three layers to be concerned with. At the very minimum are LLCs and FLPs, next level is C and S-Corps (for self-employed business owners), and lastly the Trust, which is for controlling these, as well as estate purposes.

The preferred state of choice to form your protective entities is Nevada. Nevada has decades more experience, more protective case law, more privacy rules in your favor, less regulations, no state taxes, and lower formation costs. As an added bonus, if you fly into the state for the closing, they have incredible Strip clubs. You want to choose a very reputable attorney, of which there are many. This is not an area you want to skimp. Your attorney in Nevada will be the designated manager and signatory for the entities' formation. This keeps your name off all the initial formation paperwork. Your attorney is termed your "resident agent", as you need a resident in the state to receive your paperwork. (he forwards all to your address of choice.) Common practice is the day after the official formation of your entities, he resigns as the general manager, and you resume management duties. (you fund your entities after receiving the paperwork of formation, and paperwork showing his resignation). Congratulations, you are officially a ghost. Now for the details. **231**

## Stocks, Bonds, Mutual Funds, CDs.

The ex-wife's attorneys will first pursue your liquid assets; cash and securities (excluding your IRA or retirement plans). Fortunately, these are easy to protect. The preferred entity of choice is a family limited partnership (FLP), with your trust as the money manager. Assets held in an FLP are beyond the reach of creditors, meaning no creditor can attach your assets, force you to distribute your assets, or dissolve your FLP. You maintain 100% control and ownership of your FLP and the assets held by it. The asset protection benefits are effective immediately. In Nevada, costs to create an FLP range from $1500 to $2500, plus initial filing fees of $360. Annual fees to the Secretary of State for an FLP are only $85.

# Rental Property

Owners of real estate and rental properties are now finding themselves liable for environmental claims based on acts from the previous owner. With an LLC, if a tenant sues, he can't get to your personal assets, such as your house and liquid assets. Other environmental hazards, such as your ex-wife, will likewise try and steal your home. You're not getting it, sister. Owners of rental properties are wide open for litigation without an LLC. Hell, anyone can fake falling down and sue for the deed these days. Each property you own goes in it's own multi-member LLC. Each property has no ties to the next. The managing member is your FLP or Estate Trust. Your name never appears on any paperwork. Taxes flow through to the minor member, you, on your Schedule C.

## Small Business Equipment

An LLC is the recommended entity to hold medical, construction, heavy to expensive high-risk equipment. Your equipment is held in one LLC and leased to your professional corporation. This removes it as an asset to be attached in a malpractice or accident claim. It also removes it from the main business (in it's own LLC). This also creates additional protection at the corporate level, making your professional corporation a less desirable target.

## Planes, Boats, Cars, Bikes

These are all high-risk or **at-risk assets**. Remember, an LLC is just an added insurance policy that separates you from a lawsuit and your assets. For your medium valued cars and bikes, generally you do not require an LLC, simply buy a $5 million umbrella policy add on to your original policy. (around $300 annually). If you own expensive cars or bikes, and intend to keep them a while, an LLC can be used to protect them from the old lady. Have your S or C -Corp lease them from the LLC for a write off. You can also write up your LLC to allow changing to new vehicles any time in the operating agreement. Planes and boats should be kept in separate LLCs if possible. If you have an accident and lawsuit with one, you are not jeopardizing the assets of the others.

232

## IRA's, 401 (k)'s, Retirement Plans

Protect these assets prior to marriage by placing your retirement plans in a Pension Limited Partnership. If you're not getting married, it varies state by state, but under Nevada Law funds held in an IRA, SEP, 401(k), pension, profit sharing or other retirement plan are exempt up to $500,000. Funds in excess of this amount are subject to attachment.

## Primary Residence

The more sizeable asset is usually your primary residence. Each state has its own laws concerning judgment protection allowed for you home, called the **Declaration of Homestead**. The exemption varies from state to state; most offers a limited coverage of $150,000-250,000. The limits can cover certain circumstances, some a flat amount for the value of the home, some cover only a medical bill judgment. Florida and Texas exempt the entire value of the house. Your personal home should not be in an LLC. You lose your capital gains exclusion upon sale of the property, as it is no longer your principal residence, but property owned by the LLC. In addition, you will have to address the "due on transfer clause" in your mortgage in order to transfer to a LLC. Tax wise, in order to live in the property owned by the LLC you would have to pay fair market rent (income to LLC and not deductible to you) or take the value of the rent as income, deductible to LLC but income to you. In addition, your losses for the interest may only apply to your passive income, requiring you to carry losses forward.

A Declaration of Homestead offers limited protection, it prevents a creditor from foreclosing on your primary residence as long as your equity is less than $125,000. Your home can be liened immediately, thereby preventing you from (1) refinancing, (2) taking out a second mortgage, or (3) moving. As soon as the equity exceeds $125,000, your creditor can begin legal action to foreclose. One smart option is to have an unexercised home equity loan/line of credit that covers all your equity to keep it under $125k. If a situation arises, borrow the full value and invest it, or keep it in the bank. A few percent gain or loss on a loan is far better than losing the house in a frivolous manner.

## Life Insurance

A creditor can attach any cash value, which you may have in a whole life or universal life insurance policy. The entity of choice to protect these is an irrevocable life insurance trust (ILIT). Holding insurance in an ILIT not only places the cash values beyond the reach of creditors, but also removes the proceeds from your taxable estate. Most people are aware that life insurance proceeds are income tax free. Many do not realize that the proceeds are not estate tax free unless held in an ILIT. It really doesn't make much sense to own insurance individually where it thereby is exposed to attachment by creditors and will be included in your taxable estate, especially when both problems can easily be avoided. The costs of creating

**233**

The costs of creating an ILIT range from $1,500 to $2,500. It is a one-time expense. There are no annual maintenance fees or expenses.

## Protecting a High Income

If you make the big bucks, you need to shield the salary and cash from the potentially greedy wife and her alimony demands. Setting precedent before you get married is vital from a legal standpoint. Simply restructure *how* you get paid, by redirecting the money flow.

## Cramming down your Salary

ABC Corporation wants your services, and will pay $300,000 a year. Have them hire and make payments to your **Trust**. Your trust hires you directly, or an LLC or S Corp of yours, which functions as a manager of your services. You are an employee of the LLC, S Corp or Trust, and pay yourself a nominal fee of say $75,000 a year. This salary figure should be enough to pay all your regular living expenses, plus a few extra thousand a month. As the trust or LLC builds up equity, you remove these new assets and place them in your FLP that handles your liquid investments and assets. The Net Result in a divorce settlement: instead of alimony and child support based on $300,000 a year, it is based on $75,000 a year. Nice.

# Self-Employed Business Setup

Here's an example of how to set up an asset protection plan. Let's say your business model is to buy a plot of land and build a Strip Club. We will set up 3 LLC's and use your Trust for control. The goal is to reduce liabilities, protect assets, and REMOVE YOUR NAME from all paperwork.

- **LLC#1** will control the real estate and building. We transfer the deed/titling of the real estate into LLC #1.

- **LLC#2** will control the strip club business, asset and fixtures.

- **LLC#3** is set up to manage the operation of the Strip Club business. The Club LLC#2 hires LLC#3 to operate the business, and you take a nominal salary as an employee of LLC#3.

Your trust is the managing member of each LLC. All permits, licenses and public filings show the LLC is the owner of the business. The Articles of Organization for the LLC list the name of your **Trust** (Joe's Plumbing Trust Company)—but not your name. Anyone attempting to determine the owner of the LLCs (Pastor John's LLC) would find only the name of the trust. A judgment creditor cannot seize the assets of either LLC. If someone sues the club business, the management LLC is the party of the suit. The management LLC has no assets to attach; if the attorneys are persistent, you simply file bankruptcy for LLC#3, and form a new one.

As profits accumulate within the strip club business **LLC#2**, you legally redirect them away into your **FLP** (The Virgin Mary FLP), which holds

234

your liquid assets. The Trust's operating agreement allows for you to write checks per your instructions. The real estate is protected from any suit, as it is 3 levels removed. Whatever happens to the Strip Club Biz has no bearing on the real estate, as they are separate entities. Also, your business can make millions a year, but you personally only show an income of say $50,000 a year, as an employee of **LLC#3**. Now that's asset protection.

### Rule of Thumb for Your Assets

1) FLP holds all the **liquid (safe) assets**, you invest as you normally would.
2) LLC is general partner of an FLP, or the Trust is a limited partner.
3) LLCs holds **at-risk assets**: cars, boats, planes, businesses, equipment, Real Estate investments etc., the trust is the managing limited partner.
4). Life Insurance goes into an ILIT.
5) Residence protected by Homestead Trust Act.
6) IRA, 401K goes in a Pension limited partnership.

# WHO SHOULD HAVE AN LLC OR FLP?
(Limited Liability Company - Family Limited Partnership)

- DBA business owners.

- Owners of rental property.

- Owners of valuable patents, copyrights.

- Anyone considering marriage down the road.

- Owners of expensive equipment, expensive vehicles, collectibles.

- Anyone with assets and investments they do not want to lose.

- Professionals in a high-risk field: Medicine, law, accounting, securities, construction, builders, etc.

- Anyone perceived as wealthy, or who has a high profile is a frivolous lawsuit target.

- Business owners, especially sole proprietors are undefended from liability in tort cases, subject to life crippling judgments.

- Any business owner who is only incorporated, who owns more than 10% of the company. You are not shielded from massive torts or business liabilities. In an LLC, the most you are liable for is the asset amount you put into it. [The exception; you will still be liable for business debts placed into an LLC if you personally guaranteed them originally.]

- Anyone with a salary of $75K or more, or a net worth of $50K liquid or more.

- A wealthy drunk who may just kill his greedy future ex-wife rather than paying her.

# LIMITED LIABILITY COMPANIES

The Limited Liability Company (LLC) has become an influential tool for accomplishing multiple asset protection goals. It is the most versatile and convenient strategy for shielding owners from a business itself, for protecting property, insulating at-risk assets, and achieving a superior level of financial privacy. The intent of the law is to allow individuals to perform their financial and business affairs in an efficient and expedient manner without the restrictions, rules and regulations, and liabilities associated with other entities. The operating agreement can contain most any procedures and rules that the parties desire and once put in place can just sit there maintenance-free. The initial drafting of the operating agreement is important. It must comply with state and IRS regulations, so that the LLC will be taxed as a partnership and not as a corporation.

## In a Nutshell

LLCs are the perfect entity for your risky, lawsuit prone assets; an absolute must for real estate investments, businesses, boats, planes, expensive cars, patents, bikes, patents, expensive toys or collectibles. You control the LLCs with your trust or FLP as the manager of the LLCs. When properly set up, your name never appears on any paperwork, thus you're safely protected from massive tort attempts, and achieve complete anonymity.

## LLC Players

### General Partner
♦ Decided by the operating agreement, all control can be given to the general partner, or any person. Also, members can split up control amongst themselves.
♦ Liability for actions of the partnership (generally recommended is using a S or C Corp, or a Trust as the general partner)
♦ Optional Compensation for Management

### Limited Partners
♦ No Liability Exposure beyond the original financial interest in the partnership (ambulance lawyer proof)
♦ Limited Transfer Rights
♦ A Right to Share in Profits
♦ A Right to the Return of your Capital upon Dissolution

## Taxation

Unlike a corporation, an LLC is not considered separate from its owners for tax purposes. Instead, it is what the IRS calls a "pass-through entity," like a partnership or sole proprietorship. This means that business income passes through the business to the LLC members, who report their share of profits - - or losses -- on their individual income tax returns. Each LLC member must make quarterly estimated tax payments to the IRS. Tax preferences do vary, some choose to tax as an S-Corp, C-Corp, or a partnership.

## LLC Advantages

When the LLC is taxed as a sole proprietorship or as a partnership, and assets are placed in or withdrawn from the LLC, the tax consequences are those typical of the same transactions by a sole proprietorship or a partnership. This characteristic makes placing land and other appreciating assets in a LLC with sole proprietorship or partnership tax status presently e much more feasible than placing such assets in a corporation.

## Limitations

Since an LLC does not have extensive case law in place, it is advised to be used for business purposes only. Liquid assets should be in an FLP or in a trust. Single member LLCs have been challenged and the assets were lost in a bankruptcy filing recently. Multi-member LLC's should be used, with the general partner being a Corp or a Trust. Assets that have been personally guaranteed by a member are not protected in an LLC.

## Primary Residence

Your home does not go into an LLC. If it did, you would lose your capital gains exclusion when you sell your property, as it is no longer a principal residence but property owned by the business. In addition, you will have to address the due on transfer clause in your mortgage in order to transfer to a LLC. Tax wise, in order to live in the property owned by the LLC you will have to pay fair market rent (income to LLC and not deductible to you) or take the value of the rent as income, deductible to LLC but income to you. In addition, your losses for the interest may only apply to your passive income requiring you to carry losses forward.

## Charging Order Protection

Like an FLP, the Charging Order Protection is available for a multi-member LLC. The major remedy that a judgment creditor of a member of an LLC gets is a "charging order" against that member's interest in the company. A charging order gives the creditor no rights to control or attach the assets of the LLC, but only has the right to receive the member's distributions. In a well-structured LLC, the Managing Member retains the right to cease or alter distributions, resulting in no money being distributed to the creditor.

## Steps for setting up a Limited Liability Company

- **Articles of Organization**
a) Complete the LLC Articles of Organization
b) Name Search with the Secretary of State
c) File the Articles of Organization with the Secretary of State
d) Pay the Filing Fee (varies from state to state)

- **Federal Tax I.D. Number**
a) Complete the IRS: SS-4 Form
b) Telephone the IRS – get your number
c) Separate I.D. number for each LLC

- **Operating Agreement**
a) Complete the Operating Agreement:
b) Decide if member managed or Manager managed
c) Members' Rights
d) LLC's Capital Structure
e) Financing Mechanisms
f) Member's Withdrawal Rights
g) Duration of Life
h) Rights to Transfer Membership Interests
i) Complete the Schedule A
j) Signed by all members

- **Transfer of Property into LLCs**
a) Real estate deeds are filed with the registrar of deeds in the county where the property is located. Contact your insurance company for title and umbrella insurance transfers
b) Titled Property – Change the title (Cars, bank accounts, stocks, fund accounts, etc.)
c) Personal Property – List on the Schedule A of the Operating Agreement

## Annual paperwork Requirements FOR AN LLC

- State Filing fee or Franchise Tax –
  IRS Tax Return C-Corp. Form 1120
- S-Corp. – Form 1120S
  - Partnership – Form 1065
  - Sole Proprietor – Schedule C
  - State Tax Return if required

The Limited Liability Company (LLC) is a relatively new entity, legislatively created in Oregon in 1993. Prior to 1995, every limited liability company was required to have at least two members. After 1995, the legislature allowed people to do business as a SMLLC, (single member LLC). However, in a recent bankruptcy claim case a creditor was able to successfully obtain control of the assets. (*re Albright*, 291 Bankruptcy Rptr. 538 (Bkrptcy. DC Colo. 2003).

Thus, the effective means of using an LLC requires multiple partners, as the code originally intended. For a managing partner of your LLC, in real estate people generally use a Sub S Corp to take advantage of the write offs, and pay themselves a salary from the Sub S Corporation. Other options for managing partner or your LLC include your Family Limited Partnership, or a Trust. In either case, the layers of entities afford you the protecting necessary, and removes yourself from liability.

# Family Limited Partnerships

## PARTNERSHIP PLAYERS
### General Partner
- ◆ 100% Control
- ◆ Liability for actions of the partnership (generally recommended is using a lesser LLC as the general partner)
- ◆ Optional Compensation for Management

### Limited Partners
- ◆ No Management Rights (yeah right!)
- ◆ No Liability Exposure beyond the original financial interest in the partnership (ambulance lawyer proof)
- ◆ Limited Transfer Rights
- ◆ A Right to Share in Profits
- ◆ A Right to the Return of your Capital upon Dissolution

Having multiple FLP's or LLCs is common, due to the varied risk levels of assets. You must separate your "at risk" assets (boats, planes, rental properties, equipment, etc) from "safe assets". (stocks, bank accounts, bonds, jewelry, artwork, patents, collectibles), i.e., monies with a very low probability of suit. It's hard for a stock certificate to fall down and get injured. You can lump all your liquid assets in one FLP. No IRA's, retirement money or Interest in an S Corporation allowed. Never put at risk assets with safe liquid assets. The most common setup is one FLP containing liquid assets, with a multi-member LLC as general partner. You can have multiple LLCs for the at risk assets, and setup each LLC as a multi-member, with your trust as limited member. Also, a common setup is having your "estate trust" as a limited partner of your Family Limited Partnership. Get expert advice on setting up the operating agreement for your entities, and leave in a clause that allows for subsequent structures to supercede previous agreements. In other words, this is our operating agreement, unless we change it to something completely different.

## Advantages of a Corporate General Partner

1. **Liability Protection** – With a corporate general partner, the other individual partners have no exposure to unlimited liabilities. Exposure is limited to the capital of the corporate partner (which is zero), rather than the members of the partnership. "At risk assets", should have a corporate general partner. The general partner faces the unlimited liability, not the partners.
2. **Peripheral Benefits** – The Corporation is a great avenue to provide partner compensation and benefits. You pay management fees to the corporation for services rendered, and in return re-direct the money in salaries and benefits to family members employed by the corporation.
3. **Stability** – Using a corporation as a general partner continues the life of the partnership. If the general partner dies or goes bankrupt, the partnership is at risk or shut down.

## Charging Order Protection

As provided by the Revised Uniform Limited Partnership Act, the only monetary remedy of an ex-wife or judgment creditor of a limited partner is a "charging order". This is a note against the partner's share of the FLP. This charging order provides no rights to control or attach the assets of the partnership, merely a right to receive the partner's distributions. Since Family members control most Family Limited Partnerships, the general partner can cease or alter distributions, resulting in no monies passing through to the creditor. Even better, IRS ruling 77-137 requires the ex-wife to pay "phantom taxes" on the full amount of distribution, even though she never received a dime. Even if she miraculously wins a judgment, she ends up paying instead of collecting. Thus, a charging order is suitably unattractive, and individual creditors often avoid even trying to pursue assets protected in a FLP.

# Taxation of a Partnership

- **Pass-through Entity**: There are no income taxes paid by a FLP. The profits and losses pass through to the partners on Schedule K-1 and are taxed on the partner's individual 1040 form.
- **Schedule K-1:** A partnership must furnish to each partner a K-1 form by the due date of the partnership tax return.
- **Form 1065**: Every partnership must file IRS Form 1065, which is an informational return, regardless of the amount of income or loss. If the FLP has no income or expenses, no return is required to be filed.

## Steps to Set up your FLP

1. **Limited Partnership Agreement**
   1. Complete the Partnership Agreement Form
   2. Complete the Schedule A
   3. Signed and Notarized by all partners
2. **Certificate of FLP**
   1. Complete Certificate of FLP Agreement Form
   2. Names Search with Secretary of State
   3. File Certificate with the designated state agency
   4. Pay the Filing Fee (varies from state to state)
   5. Wait for the form to be approved by the State
3. **Federal Tax I.D. Number** Complete the IRS: SS-4 Form
   1. Call the IRS to receive your new I.D. number
   2. Separate number is required for each partnership
4. **Transfer Property**
   1. Real estate deeds are filed with the county recorder or registrar of deeds in the county it is located
   2. Titled Property – Change the title (bank accounts, mutual fund accounts, stocks, bonds, autos, etc.)
   3. Personal Property – List on Sch. A of Partnership Agreement

# Annual Maintenance Requirements

1. Cash distribution to partners (optional)
2. State Filing fee or Franchise Tax
3. IRS Tax Return – 1065 and K-1's, State Tax Return if necessary. (not in Vegas)

# IRREVOCABLE LIFE INSURANCE TRUSTS

## Primary Function:

The ILIT serves as an irrevocable trust that holds life insurance. You transfer ownership of your current Life Insurance policy to the ILIT, or have the Trust take out a new policy for you, and structure it such that your taxable estate is separate from the trust. For small estates beneath the maximum limitations for estate taxes, the life insurance proceeds pass to the beneficiary(s) estate tax free. The true benefit for an (ILIT) comes into play when you have a sizeable estate. It is quite common that adding the insurance policy assets to your estate launches you into hell, the taxable inheritance bracket. The trust's purpose is to remove the assets of the policy's death benefit from being included in the owner's taxable estate. Without this, you can easily lose 50% of the benefit in inheritance taxes. Upon your death, the proceeds from your policy in the ILIT can be used for medical expenses of your spouse, and is likewise not included in your wife's estate (set up in advance in the original agreement). You can use the trust assets to pay for you kids' schooling as well. The trusts assets are safe from Estate Taxes, judgment creditors, and it also avoids probate.

## I L I T Players

**Trustor, ie, the Grantor** – The person who creates the trust

**Beneficiary** – The person who receives the moneys, distributions, or benefits from the trust

**Trustee** – The Manager of the Trust assets. The trustee has a fiduciary responsibility to invest the trust assets and to follow the written instructions of the Grantor.

## Insurance Policy Choices

Most all life insurance policies can be secured/transferred in an ILIT. (or purchased for you by the trust). Name a close relative the beneficiary initially. If you are just getting married, leave it that way for a while, and inform the old bag "it's for the children." That way she won't hire Vito Bonaduce to whack you and get the proceeds. If you stay married for ten years, than you can put her name on it if you want. If you have kids, then structure the trust to maintain the old lady's standard of living, and funnel the bulk of the cash to pay the kids' education. If it's a large sum, payout the funds to the kids over time. You don't want them boozing away in Ferraris, liquidating the trust cash in the first year. The money starts getting paid out when they 21. The proceeds are tax free to the beneficiaries.

### Steps for Setting up an ILIT

1. Name your Trustee: Virtually anyone but you or your wife can be the trustee. Many people choose a bank due to the paperwork, but it's best to do on your own. Otherwise you face unnecessary management fees.
2. Sign and Notorize the agreement
3. Purchase an Insurance Policy: If it's a new policy, it is advised you apply for it through the trust. (see why next section).
4. Current policy transfer to a Trust: There currently is a 3 year overlap period before a transfer is effective. Otherwise, its is still a personal asset subject to estate taxes. After 3 years, you're good. Transfer ASAP.
5. Federal Tax I.D. Number: Not necessary until the funds are transferred over in death. Some do in advance.
6. The Premium Payments: the Trust makes the payments, since it now owns the policy. You can loan the trust up to $11 grand a year tax free, so you supply the cash to make the payments. You can loan any amount you want to the trust at any time, but above $11 grand it's subject to the annual gift tax. Policy payments can be made by the beneficiaries also.

### Trust's Annual Paperwork

1. Tax Return: None required, if you want to establish a paper trail, you can file IRS Form 1041.
2. Annual Report: After you kick the bucket, the Trustee prepare annual report and distribute it to the beneficiaries. The report shows the total holdings, and the amount of cash distributed. (expenses if requested).

# Living Trusts

### Primary Objective

Revocable Living Trusts are used primarily to control your estate beyond death, to avoid or decrease estate taxes, and avoid the process of probate. A Living Trust provides for a concealed, methodical distribution of your assets at your death, and follows your assignments and instructions in managing your assets if you become incapacitated and can no longer handle your own affairs. Also, your trust maintains anonymity via secrecy in documentation, and adds limited asset protection. Terms of your trust are entirely up to you, and can be changed at your whim.

### Living Trust Players

#### The Grantor (the trustor..aka, you)

♦ The person who funds the original assets and monies to the Living Trust. The Grantor creates the terms of goals of the originating documents and the provisions of control.

### The Beneficiary (you again)
- ♦ The recipient of the benefits and distributions of the trust.
- ♦ Optional Compensation for Management

### The Trustee (you again)
- ♦ The manager of the trust and the assets. The person responsible for the investments, and follower of the trust originating agreement terms. As you can see, this can be a one-man show, although you can assign the conditions as desired.

## Advantages of having a Living Trust:
1. Limited asset protection.
2. Avoid probate by protecting assets in a trust.
3. Instant activation, no waiting period.
4. The terms can be altered at any time.
5. Secrecy...formed without your name on papers.
6. Superior control of distributing your estate assets.
7. Reduces your estate tax
8. Allows for Spendthrift provisions
9. Attorney name on original documents, complete privacy.

## Types of Trusts Available

- **Revocable Trust** – the terms can be altered at will. A flow through entity for taxes; the trust income taxes go to your personal tax return. Limited asset protection.

- **Irrevocable Trust** – once the terms are established they cannot be changed or revoked. Income within the trust will be taxed under trust rules. Since the grantor is barred from changing the terms, the trusts assets are separated from the grantor's estate.

- **Living Trust** – A trust created while you are alive, changes are available, and the trust is immediately activated.

- **Testamentary Trust** – A trust that begins upon your death, with the terms followed in accordance to your will

## Steps for Creating a Living Trust

- Create the terms of the Trust, sign and notarize documents.
- Transfer your Assets
  Change the names on the titles of each asset, ie, cars, stock certificates, mutual fund, securities and trading, and bank accounts. File real estate deeds with the county registrar.
- Complete a new Schedule "A" tax form, attach it to the trust, complete the Articles of Organization
- Estate taxes apply upon death
- No Fed Tax ID required, just your Soc. Security #.
- Your Will, and instructions for guardianship of Children.
- Power of Attorney instructions if you become incapacitated or decapitated.
- Living Will for physicians, which provides the decision on whether a doctor should drain your assets or pull the cord.
- Final instructions for the new Trustor upon your death.
- Listing of assets and the assignment of such upon your death.

**Note**: There is only limited asset protection for Trusts as we speak, but having one more layer properly structured is a bonus. The overall purpose is the distribution of your assets from your estate once you kick the bucket. It's common for the Trust to simply hold the Member shares of your assets, which are safely shielded inside your Family Limited Partnerships and LLCs. Women and attorneys constantly sue to change existing laws to attempt to get further access to a man's assets. Trusts are now unfavorable in a number of US states due to recent court cases. Carefully chose your US state, preferably Nevada. To prevent being upended by future court decisions, what you should consider doing is setting up your trust offshore.

## No country in the world automatically recognizes US judgments.

This is one of the main benefits of moving offshore. Creditors are forced to re-litigate in a foreign jurisdiction. In most cases, a foreign country does not allow contingent fee litigation and requires the creditor to post a bond to pay for your legal fees if they lose. Moving assets offshore at first thought sounds risky, but it's really just a technical distinction. The trust holds pieces of paper from your other protective entities, not the actual assets. In normal operation mode, your trust assets will remain in the United States at a bank of your choice. Contingent fee litigators are likely to abandon protected offshore assets due to high costs and unlikely results. They harass people with the goal of settling, and offshore trusts are not designed for settling. They would require trials and expenses.

Overseas Trusts **remove the economic incentive to litigate.**

# Chapter VIII

The

# HOLY GRAIL

for

# PROFESSIONAL
# BACHELORS

Grab Your Passport Gentlemen

# The Holy Grail is Overseas

After a dozen years in the field, the Player results will vary across the board. Some flail around without a clue, quickly throw in the towel and marry the first girl who puts out: Mrs. Wrong. They enjoy a few good years before the wife lies about taking the pill and pops out an unexpected kid. She then quits her part-time job, and makes compulsive eating her full-time job. The guy tolerates a living hell with a bloated, angry life sucker who he pretends doesn't exist. Some guys play the game well, but choose impulsively. They continually marry and divorce like fools, and get taken to the cleaners each time. Many players become addicted to the chase, and find that it's more fun getting it than keeping it. The rarest group of men are those who excel at both the game and their target profiling, get extremely lucky with a wife who never changes, and enjoy a healthy family life. As far as the permanent bachelors, they choose a stress free life staying single and enjoy the fruits of the trade as best as they can. Their quantity and quality of results with women are directly proportionate to their income and net worth.

As for you players who reach age 35 unscathed and are still halfheartedly looking for the perfect girl, you will come to a crossroads of sorts. Eventually you reach the moment when the reward becomes a fading interest. You occasionally win the battles, but you're losing the war. The animal desire has lost its significance. You can't pinpoint exactly when it begins, but as it begins to wear you down, the feeling is unmistakable. *The chase becomes boring.* A dozen or two years working the field puts you in the unfortunate position of knowing too much about women. You've been honest and reasonable in courting girls, had a few great runs, but mostly been rewarded with childish cock-teasing, guilt tripping, attention-whoring, gold digging, nagging, and pathological lunacy. You can spot it a mile away, and have no intention of tolerating it anymore.

## You Reach Your Limit

Even the A-team players and studs can peak too quickly. The mindless games, and time wasting psychobabble required to enjoy the simple pleasures in life take their toll. The unexpected quickies become few and far between. The spontaneous girlfriends and uninhibited lust are fleeting memories. It's been a year since the last threesome. Hell, even potential parking lot love with the babysitter next door seems like a hassle. Happiness isn't truly appreciated until it is fading away. The occasional magic comes your way, but it is short-lived. You reach a point when even in the midst of pleasure, you battle the sinking feeling that you know it too shall soon pass. Ultimately, the fear of completely losing happiness endangers your ability to feel anything at all. Then the mind games invade the brain. You actually start reading Playboy. Some cases reach dangerous levels. An ex shows up at your door drunk and horny. She plops a porno in the DVD player and rips her clothes off. You respond by scrutinizing the lousy editing, song selection and lack of story line. You fail to make a move, and offer to psychoanalyze her boyfriend problems. She puts her panties back on and storms out. You've lost your game, and clearly have hit bottom.

You tire of even stepping up to the plate. Shivering with fear, you hear yourself pondering aloud about getting up there in the years, and how *maybe you should settle down.* The thought of even needing to **Exploit her Inner Psycho** is ominous. In the back of your mind, you try to rationalize your vanishing sex drive. Maybe if you just act normal and play the nice guy, things will work out. You get lazy, and decide you'll just lower your standards, and go for the lesser targets. Get a couple easy ones in the bag to get the spirits up. A little experiment with some horny old divorcees will do the trick! You set up a date with a previously hot MILF trying to re-live the glory years. Going in, you figure she'll have matured, and be witty, intelligent, and realistic about the current options father time has left her with. You wind up babysitting a self-centered, psychotic time bomb with enough baggage to fill a warehouse. While she's babbling on in a deep voice about requiring financial statements prior to shagging, you're staring out the window trying to guess the last time she saw a mirror. As she starts *telling you how sexy she is,* you have to cover your mouth from spitting up your beer. Out of the corner of your eyes, you see caked on makeup covering crazed, droopy eyes, shaved off eyebrows redrawn with lip liner, a slight beard, and a high rise Simpsons bouffant hairdo brushing up against the headliner. You have to bite your lip from saying out loud...

**"Nice helmet Mam. Will that be paper or plastic?"**

The date consists of you drinking yourself into a coma in silence, while she delusionally drones on about all the trust fund hunks that worship the ground she walks on and drop fortunes competing for her. As she hurls insults of how you'll never be half the man her ex was (who divorced her), you glance at her sloppy flat ass, tired tits, and scaly, saggy, wrinkled skin and wonder if she needs to borrow an iron. I mean after age 35, it's all dog years from then on. Fortunately, for the date you let the crusty old cougar drive, and on the first turn near a front lawn, you dive out of the car onto the grass going 30 mph in a navy seal body roll, and break into an Olympian dead sprint the opposite direction. Holy Shit!! That was friggin' close!! The thought of being forced to go through with the deed sends chills down your spine. Suddenly, you hear a muffled voice screaming from your crotch:

" What the heck did I ever do to you? Get some glasses, you blind fuck! I could've died in that hell hole !! "

The time comes when you reluctantly face the inevitable. Men play the role of the consummate gentlemen, and provide women respect, honesty, creature comforts and materialistic pleasures unfathomable in most of the world. In return, our search to marry the elusive nice, sincere, intelligent, sexy girl is an exercise in futility. We created this capitalist heaven, and in return women crap on our heads. We're forced to tolerate wasting time with self-centered, bipolar, sex-teasing beotches who feel they should have zero responsibilities, while being pampered and maintained like royalty because they have something between their legs of infinite value. How about some reality here, ladies? It's a hole. There's lots of 'em. They're friggin' everywhere. We just want a nice body and a fun, respectful personality attached it. One that won't change with a ring. Sorry, but you're not entitled to Rolls Royce pricing and treatment when you're a Dumb and Dumber scooter. Feminism's contribution to society comes down to this:

## Men get Fucked ... and only as a figure of speech

Some guys reach dangerous levels, when depression rears its ugly head. Unable to concentrate and devoid of testosterone, they lose any competitive edge. The libido sinks heavily. The occasional morning hard-on brings only a sense of amused regret. You lose faith in being a man. Perhaps you really are getting too old for this. Then you wake up in a fog, and there it is….the light at the end of the tunnel. You calmly start to realize that even the fear of death is unjustified. In fact, it actually is a welcomed sensation. With a heavy sigh, you whisper *what the hell*. You walk slowly towards it with a sigh of relief, and then BAMMMMMM!

Your wingman whacks you over the head with a pillow. You wake up screaming and discover the light at the end of the tunnel is actually his flashlight in your face. Once again, your stuck up excuse for a girlfriend who still hasn't put out has stood you up. You promptly got shitfaced and passed out on the floor. Your vicious hangover would make a Russian street bum damn proud. The air is permeated with a scent of death, as you have merely rented a fast food meal and decorated the walls with it in your drunken stupor. A flash of realization hits you. No. God isn't speaking to you. It's your wingman. He's screaming way too loud, but he's right on the money, and not a moment too soon.

"What the hell's wrong with you? You're barely 35 and wasting your life away fretting over some silicone bimbo who works at Burger King. Get a life! I've had it with this crap. Drastic situations call for drastic measures. I've booked us a vacation to Rio de Janeiro. We got to get you back in fighting shape if you're going to pass that Porn star audition next month."

# The Nympho Alpha Gladiator Unleashed

Things change. Men are very adaptive to evolutionary impulses. In dark corners, words are being spoken in hushed whispers about Holy Grail opportunities abroad. Eavesdroppers are leaning in Eyes Wide Open. Near suicidal husbands and potential grooms are disappearing on fictitious one-week fishing trips, and returning looking ten years younger. They have a bounce in their step, and twinkle in their eyes. They've rediscovered their Alpha, and drop kicked the beta *and* the old lady out the door. Soon, they laugh at the thought of marrying, over even dating another self-centered, neurotic American women. All thoughts revolve around the next trip.

## The Battle has Begun

Engagements are being called off after unexplained watershed moments. Fiancées and wives are hiring private detectives who return without evidence, and then vanish themselves. Gold diggers' cocky looks may reveal sweaty brows and nervous ticks. Wallets are leaving the marketplace, and men are happier and getting laid more than ever. Guys are being found with permanent smiles frozen on their face like the Joker. Viagra sales are skyrocketing. Eighty-year-old men are being spotted in gyms working out with their eighteen year old girlfriends. Overseas, the skies are filled with screeching feminists in helicopters dropping hand grenades, while frantically clicking away on spy cameras. The playing field is finally being leveled. The sisterhood of scammers are petrified. The feminist charade has been exposed and is in jeopardy, and it's reached full blown panic mode.

## Men are Getting It

Outside the US, the Latin and Asian cultures are the best-kept secret for single men looking for wild flings to passionate girlfriends to marriage. Shocking as it may sound, these women love men…even more than money! The interaction with foreign girls is frankly unimaginable to the average frustrated American male. It's complete role reversal. The girls compete for *you*. There are millions of beautiful young women who are proudly feminine and affectionate, and looking to hook up. In numerous popular cities abroad, the single women outnumber the men 5 to 1, 10 to 1, sometimes 15 to 1. Everywhere you go they are simply all over you, flaunting sexual interest, and trying to bed you and start a relationship. Constant smiling, stroking, and crotch grabbing; the girls are doing that too.

In Asia and South America, the essence of being a woman is a cherished quality. They are seductive, exotic, and erotic without moral boundaries. Wherever you go, girls stare you down like sexual stalkers, even when they are sitting with their man. They compete for your attention, hold on to you for dear life, and consider it normal behavior to be insatiable nymphos. You can approach almost any girl and interview like a champion.

**250**

You:   "Would you like to get together some time?"
**Chica: "Yes "**

You:   "Are you available tomorrow night? "
**Chica: "Yes "**

You:   "Can I have your phone number?"
**Chica: "What's wrong with right now, where are you staying ? "**

You:   "Can I buy you dinner, get no sex, and you whine to me nonstop?"
**Chica: "This ain't America big boy, let's just go to your room now."**

You:   "Will you still respect me in the morning? "
**Chica: "No, but I'll have sex with you in the morning."**

You:   "I hope your not threatened by an exceedingly endowed humble Billionaire."

**Chica: "Let me guess, Motel 6 Mr. Jones? Nice cologne, is that Budweiser?"**

– – – – – – –

The realization they're losing their pool of available divorce assets to extort has feminists horrified, and trying to censor the information. The warning shots have been fired. Political contributions are flowing heavy to shut down this cross border madness. As expected, the feminists are making wildly sick, false accusations of rampant sex with minors and illegal money transfers in an effort to hinder men. They're full throttle on the smear tactics. They use PIs to stalk high profile businessmen, actors, and sports figures on vacation, hoping to embarrass them and lose endorsements, jobs, or the old lady. Men are grabbing their passports in droves, investing in real estate overseas for pennies on the dollar, and living lives they never dreamed possible. The old saying has never been truer.

– – – – – –

## Bachelor Code 17

**Whenever you see a happy man,
somewhere nearby is a pissed off woman.**

– – – – – –

It's funny how so many American men eventually stumble on this discovery just in the nick of time. Guys around 40, particularly divorced men, often lose all interest in dating US women. Why risk your assets, or tolerate the drama and disrespect, just to get the occasional mediocre lay? You find yourself questioning your manhood, life, and career. You start wondering if sex is really just some silly little ritual that doesn't deserve such importance. All the heavy duty symbolic worrying boils down to one simple fact: Men need to get laid. It's human nature, the most basic animal instinct.

Trying to live without it affects your ability to function in business and in everyday life. By comparison, American women are just not that into sex like men. Regardless of beauty, any girl up to age 35, and under 135 pounds, can walk into any bar and get laid in five minutes. But they never do that, do they? If men could do that, in 2 weeks we'd be unemployed and unable to walk. There's no denying it. The US has become a Sex Prison.

– - - - - - –

## **Bachelor Code 18**

**Women's Power is derived from the Limitation of the Sex Supply**

– - - - - - –

Without women being able to use sex as a weapon, they simply wouldn't be able to act the way they do and generate any interest. Overseas, men can have sex any day of the week with zero effort. The productivity gains for your career are enormous, as you eliminate all the worthless time chasing game players. Imagine if sex was readily available anytime here. Unless women drastically changed their personalities, and the divorce laws were corrected, the marriage rates would plummet 50 percent overnight. Half the bars would close in a month. The other half would once again play Rock music, and the lame girly-men bands playing chick music and touchy feely alternative crap would finally be dumped into the trash where they belong.

What's even more frightening for guys in the US playing field is watching the potential targets transform in front of your eyes. Forget for a minute the bitchy, egotistical personalities. The average weight of an US woman has reached an astonishing 169 pounds; the *size of a college defensive back*. The female gene pool is literally exploding outward, while the quality of targets is imploding inward.

I write this after spending another blissfully horny afternoon strolling through the El Sambil Center in Caracas, Venezuela; packed floor to ceiling with well-dressed, classy women oozing with sensuality. This mega mall has a ratio of face-melting gorgeous women in the neighborhood of seven out of ten girls. Model looks aside, what always grabs my attention is how their eyes teasingly linger too long; they stare RIGHT AT ME, until I catch them. We both smile mischievously. The flirting is healthy, honest, and easily followed through to the finish line. Compared to US women's narcissism and weight, I have to laugh. And as I reach for my Margarita, I realize she has fallen asleep after the 3rd session with a smile on her face.

Beats the hell out of cellulite,
ten yards of attitude, and bad manners.

# Superior Culture -- 24/7 Porn Star Lifestyle

If you're independent, spontaneous, or an adrenaline junkie, world travel is like getting a new lease on life. To many it is a welcome release to leave. The US Constitution was written as a set of laws to protect the citizens from the government, but the politicians rewrite it at will. The nanny state is choking our freedom. The US is on a fast track to becoming France, yet another failed socialism experiment. Every day politicians and cops get hard-ons dreaming about a new tax and regulation to shove in your face, to help pay their ever-increasing salaries and perks. Police have gone from law enforcement to belligerent revenue enforcement officers. While illegal alien murderers freely stroll the streets with their middle fingers in the air, the banker coming home from a three beer happy hour is chased by six cruisers and a helicopter; fifteen officers all competing for the bullshit DUI arrest of a sober man, in order to collect hefty overtime pay in court. Like Thomas Jefferson said, every time you hear the word *Safety* from a lawmaker, they're going for your wallet. Pretty soon we'll have attorneys filing class action lawsuits for breathing air on someone else's property.

In the US, you turn on the TV or open a newspaper…what do you find? Screaming talking heads foaming at the mouth about lawsuit this, racism that, gays, murders, sexual harassment, victim hood, new taxes and laws, drug addicts, feminists, MADD mothers, blah blah blah. It's like fingernails on a chalkboard. Nonstop 24/7 whining, pessimism, stress and misery.

A Virtual Liberal Paradise.

Contrast this by turning on Latin America TV. It doesn't matter if they are selling you a funeral casket, you see gorgeous girls in bikinis dancing, smiling, and laughing, and the entire crowd is standing up clapping and singing along. When you visit their countries, it's the exact same attitude in real life. They have a survivor's intelligence in dealing with life's challenges with a lively sense of humor. The locals sparkle with vitality. People with college degrees make $500 a month, yet they display a cutting sense of humor, maintaining almost a childlike ability to see happiness in everything. They live for the moment. It's practically impossible to have a negative thought when such happy, beautiful people surrounding you. Particularly when every time you turn around college girls are winking and forcing you into yet another sex session…treating you like a piece of meat.

Overseas, the feeling of just being left alone is worth its weight in gold. Unless you make a complete ass of yourself or commit a major crime, the government pays no attention whatsoever to your existence. This lack of attention is the government's greatest asset. You're invisible; free to live as you wish without big brother and big feminist watching your every move. You'll find it's very difficult to return. In an impoverished culture, an American male is a prize. Just by appearing overseas it is assumed you are wealthy. In light of the drastically lower cost of living, and your elevated purchasing power, the assumption is actually spot on. With an investment income or internet business throwing off just $40-50,000 a year, you are considered very well off. With a $100,000 income you can live like a king. Your age and looks mean nothing. Girls you could only fantasize about in your 20's are now pursuing you, even though you are in your 40's, and 50's. If you take the trouble to learn to speak their language, the rewards are frankly unbelievable. Everyday can be a paradise if you know where to go.

## The Power of Sexual Freedom

Everything we desire comes with a price. What is available for free is often packaged with a psychological cost; feelings are manipulated with hidden obligations to provide something in return. When you choose to pay the full price upfront, there is no trickery, no guilt, and no concealed requirements. You maintain control of your freedom. The most powerful thing you can hold onto is your independence; being free to maneuver in life as you choose, without worries, stress, and unwanted responsibilities.

Some men prefer long-term girlfriends. Others are so busy, they'd be quite happy having quickies with multiple partners, no strings attached. US women rarely exchange pleasure for pleasure. For men, sex is the goal. For women, sex is a means to the goal. So despite women enjoying sex, there's always their hidden agenda in mind. The free ride may go on for a bit, but soon they will mentally check off the last "free sex" day on their calendars, and start aggressively pushing for a long-term commitment. A LTC starts out one way, but usually means your freedom is drained, the pleasure decreases, and the expenses accelerate. If you hesitate falling for the ploy, she cuts you off because *"things aren't progressing quickly enough."* However, if she sees you as an easy, wealthy target who is ripe for the taking, don't be surprised if her next move is to quit taking the pill and announce an "unplanned pregnancy". With complications like this occurring so often in casual relationships, you start to wonder if going back for seconds is really worth the fear of manipulation and threat of legal action.

After a dozen years of rolling the dice, experience guides you to become very choosy when considering a one-night stand, let alone a relationship. Eventually, you learn it's smarter to go home alone, than to sleep with a gorgeous psycho who assumes that by granting you admission to her pussy, you will provide a lifetime of servitude. Is a one-time free pass to her coochie really worth the reward of being stalked and getting bricks through your windshield for not returning her calls?

For the wealthy, celebrities and pro athletes, there is enormous value in paying for sex, even when free is available. The threat of false charges, bad press, and huge attorneys fees creates the potential for outrageously high pussy pricing and stress. The risk far outweighs the reward. Whether home or abroad, if all you simply want is a no strings attached afternoon of Sportfucking, it is always smarter to pay for it. There are no hidden expectations or feelings hurt when the process is crystal clear. She's knows you're in it for sexual gratification, and you know she's in it for money, or perhaps a little of both. Everywhere but the US, this is how the pleasure business has operated for hundreds of years. It works.

In the US, when you pour yourself an ice-cold beer, palm a slice of pizza, and turn on ESPN, you get instant, unconditional satisfaction. It's a gratifying moment of pure independence that is taken for granted. One of the reasons world travel is so liberating, is you can enjoy this feeling in most every facet of life. Anytime the mood strikes me in Bangkok, I pour myself a Beer, palm a *slice of pussy*, and turn on ESPN....it's instant unconditional satisfaction without the tease. Overseas there is no such thing as being sexually frustrated. To the newbie on his first trip, it's unimaginable how invigorating it feels. You walk around with a shit-eating grin, pinching yourself that it's too good to be true. With sex so easy, it's like having an extra 10 hours a day. When you remove the ability of women to control you through limitation of the sex supply, the world is yours.

Outside the US Sex Prison, any man with a modest sum of cash or income can enjoy this feeling every day. Plus, if you're a connoisseur who savors the thrill of the hunt, you can pole vault on your rod through the singles scene with endless choices. With smart coochie resource management, you can enjoy a fuck and release policy with a new squeeze every day for the rest of your life. Compare that to back home, where you waste 10 hours a day mentally consumed by sexual frustration, clubbing, stalking and gawking at women who barely give you the time a day until you empty your wallet, while she plants a stiletto heel into your pride and manhood.

## The World's Oldest Profession

Overseas, you can satisfy the urge anytime you like. Think of the gains in your work productivity and sanity. The value of unlimited sexual freedom and piece of mind cannot be calculated in dollars. Share this info with a feminist and she'll put a gun to your head. So, are you one of those guys who feels guilty even thinking about paying for sex? Wake up pal, you've been doing it your whole life, and overpaying to boot. When a girl is on her back, the meter is running. One way or another you're paying for it.

# Government Approved Sexcapades

Overseas, for a thousand years the girls in "paid customer relations" have operated **legally** in virtually every country in the world. They choose the career because they make the equivalent of hundreds to thousands of dollars a day, compared to working for pennies an hour in sweatshops or on the local farms. Contrary to the lies you hear in the media, most girls stay in the business out of greed, not need. The hottest ones live a life comparable to a millionaire, versus the poverty hell they left behind. It's not uncommon to see a few taking limos to work. In some countries, the government sponsors the occupation. The girls pay taxes to the government, and receive free health care and sex checkups in return. How common is it? In Germany alone, there are close to 400,000 registered sex workers.

# Unveiling the Feminists' Sex Slaves Scam

During the 2006 World Cup, the German Government got broad sided by the media and "Human Rights Advocates", who claimed the city was housing 40,000 illegal sex slave workers imported for the fans of the games. So the city launched a surprise raid of 48 of the largest brothels in Munich and the neighboring Red-light Districts. The result: they were unable to find a single girl forced into the job. In fact, in most cases the girls PAID the house to work there, in return for room and board.

So why do feminist advocates scream such blatant, transparent lies about virtually non-existent *sex slaves,* when it is so easily proven wrong? All the negative publicity gets the naïve bleeding hearts of the world to donate tens of millions of fundraising dollars to their tax-exempt "causes". Since the crisis is non-existent, there is nothing to solve. So guess where all the money goes? Under the disguise of administrative costs, the women line their own pockets with bulging Six Figure salaries. They hire friends and family to join in on the free money party, they lease Mercedes and SUV's, dine like elephant sized queens, and sleep away their hangovers with their middle fingers in the air, in their plush townhouses and furnished offices. The whole thing is one big scam. But they have an even bigger picture in mind. Feminists are petrified that our wallets are going overseas and leaving the extortion playground. When women can't control the sex supply, they lose their power over men. So they'll do anything to stop you getting laid, even if it means creating crippling new laws about fictitious crimes.

## Overseas Cattle Crossing – Female Sex Tourism Exposed

Naturally, feminists act all self-righteous and offended at men exercising freedom of choice. Here's some Scambuster News; women have been sex tourists for years, and are flying all over the world paying for sex.

http://www.gadling.com/category/gambia/
http://www.cdnn.info/news/article/a030830.html
http://www.caribvoice.org/Travel&Tourism/sextourism.html
http://www.smh.com.au/articles/2003/07/11/1057783358449.html

That's right, we're onto their charade; the old do as I say, not as I do. Two-ton Tina, the scowling office secretary who spends her day threatening sexual harassment charges when you accidentally bump into her, can be found on weekends flying to Jamaica to ride underage Sambo's big bamboo. Then she returns and writes her congresswoman demanding jail time for the *"disgusting men she saw exploiting poor young sex slaves."* Maybe we should start lobbying for donations posing as the **Human Rights Vision Foundation**, and send Sambo and his buddies some eyeglasses and heavy-duty scales.

# A Pay for Play Crash Course

### Nightclub Girls

Imagine going to a techno or salsa nightclub, full of gorgeous girls stylishly dressed to the nines in miniskirts and high heels, or low cut bootie pants and midriffs, or schoolgirl outfits. They're dancing so erotic, you end up leaving drool streaks from your mouth to mid-knees. The ratio of girls to guys is 5 to 1, 10 to 1 and up. Every girl is staring you down like a piece of meat, competing for your attention. Oh, there's this one little thing I forgot to mention. When the babes tire of dancing, you can go home with any of them, every night of the week. Fifty year old men can sleep twenty year old girls. Sounds to good to be true? Well in the US, it's a fantasy that will never happen. Overseas, it's just business as usual.

There's a few clubs like this in countless major cities. There's nothing sleazy or seedy at all about it. There are no victims. In return for a nominal services rendered fee, you have great consensual sex based on honesty upfront. Some of the girls are on vacation just like you are, and are just looking for an easy way to pay for the trip. The hardest part of the whole process is picking your girl, since you'll want so many of them. **The Technique**, if you can call it that: you choose one, say hi, and agree on a price in a few minutes. Then you drink a toast and spend the rest of the night partying away, till its time to go home and let the Gods of Testosterone take over. Some of the girls available will be levels of sexy beyond anything you have ever seen, and their attitude is comparable.

# Escort Agencies

There are several kinds to choose from; **freelance girls** who place classified ads in the newspaper, freelancers advertising on websites, or actual agency girls. The classified ad girls' fee is next to nothing, maybe 25% of an agency, but usually you are bound to be disappointed in the looks department. There are some lookers, you just have to make sure you inquire about the age, and go for nothing over 23. You don't want a bad experience with a seasoned pro who is long past her looks marketability. Half the time it's college girls looking for extra cash to buy clothes and crap.

**Independent escorts** on websites. The girls pay to run their own ads and place them on someone else's website to create business. The sites make considerable money without actual involvement, so it's in their best interests to *airbrush the photos* to create impulse clients for the girls. The girls tend to charge less than what an agency would, and are rated the highest in performance, since they want repeat customers.

**Agency girls**. They tend to be cold professionals, pissed off at their employer for the strict rules and taking such a large cut. Their performance ranges from decent to rushed. Many are clock watchers, and cost twice as much. (If all the phone numbers are the same on the website, you're looking at an agency.)

For whichever you choose, clarify precisely what it is you want. Yes, you should be sexually explicit on the phone. Know exactly what it is you're going to get and the cost before you spend one dime. Also, if there's a photo involved, determine if it is recent shot, and explain if it is not the same girl, you are going to send her back (with cab fare). Generally, the photos are retouched and maybe at best 75% accurate. When looking at the photos, if she appears from the waist up only, or is twisting sideways, assume she's overweight, or has baby stretch marks, and make another choice. Gauge her personality; if she's a cold fish on camera, guess what she'll be in your room? Clarify her taxi fare in advance as well.

*Independent escorts* can be an extremely efficient and enjoyable experience for the afternoon quickie. Remember, compared to the nightclub action, when you remove the cover charges and hefty bar tabs for two, it's more cost effective than you realize. Plus, afternoon sessions are far better than drunk early am romps. If you happen to be in Buenos Aires or Caracas Venezuela, many skip the nightclubs and just do the independent girls, since half of the girls are nines to flat out tens. Some are elevens. Ouch.

http://www.areavip.com.ar

For the Agency websites, if there are language choices between Spanish or English, choose the Spanish side. The prices are usually 25% lower. The Gringo tax lives on.

# Red Light Districts – Strip Clubs

Everybody loves a great Strip Club, but the difference overseas is instead of tipping your favorite performers, you sleep with them. Take out is always available. In most cases, you must pay an additional "bar fine" to the house. Many clubs also have an in-house choice, with the girls living in bungalows on site. For a nominal fee you get an hour of up close, full service, personal attention. Once you've experienced this club setup, wait till you return to the rip off Titty bars in the US. It feels like outer space that a 3-minute lap dance is $20 here, when abroad an hour of sex with a hottie is $50-60.

The advantage of using the nightclub technique is you get to see the package before unwrapping it. If you haven't learned yet it, the same rules apply overseas with women. When a girl makes vague promises about sex and then demands upfront high class treatment (money), you should hear a deafening laugh track. Sorry babe, no money before the honey. Excuse me while I dab my tears with a handkerchief. Paying afterwards maintains control of the entire situation in case something goes wrong. Any problems with the terms, offer her cab money and go choose another one. They usually change their mind. Keep all valuables in your in-room safe, particularly your passport.

# Local Freelancers and Non-Pros

The *third approach* to women on your vacation requires a little work on your part. This is for the guy who wants a short time girlfriend, or perhaps one to keep in touch with and revisit some day in the future. If you're going to be in a town for a while, grab a Motorola V180 quad band gsm phone off ebay for about $50. Go to a local cell phone accessories dealers and get a used SIM card for maybe $10. Then purchase refill cards there. Note: remember to obtain the PIN, as you may accidentally lock the card. Why the phone? Overseas, it's complete role reversal. The girls call and beg for sex.

As you stroll around town, ask the hottest girls you see for lunch dates...girls in the malls, bank tellers, secretaries, a girl walking down the street. A great angle is ask if she'll give you a tour of their city, and you'll buy lunch or dinner in return. If you plan on returning to the city soon, get her email address. Of course, have a special email account set-up in advance specifically for this activity only. You can lead a split lifestyle with quality non-pros during the day and Rock Star threesomes with paid girls at night.

Again, if you want to be a pro at this, before you travel on your vacation, do a fair amount of research on some of the cultural things of the country you're visiting. If you want to have a chica's attention, show her you're interested in more than just sex. After all, any girl can get laid anytime she wants, the object here is to make yourself intriguing to her. Don't sit there and talk about how rich and important you are. Don't cry about being fired from McDonald's last week. Ask about her life, and her family. Ask about her favorite places to go, what are her dreams, and of course, ask if she has any hot and horny girlfriends available for threesomes.

Treat her like a lady, and give compliments with a smile and you'll own the keys to her heart. El Gringo is a highly desired commodity. Show a sincere interest in her country. Know the names of some of the more famous sights, landmarks, restaurants, beaches, their style of music, and so forth. Rent a documentary video about the country, or perhaps watch a popular film shot there. If you don't know any of their language, your fun will be dramatically reduced. Buy a pocket translator, and learn at least some of their language. Ask your girl what sights you should visit. Steer away from any of her attempts to take you to the nearest mall and drop a fortune on her. Brush that idea aside, *"I can shop at home any day, I want to see more of your beautiful country."*

The shopping ploy is for amateurs and gullible tourists. The clothes prices are often higher in their malls than back home. Two outfits will cost as much as a night with a set of nympho twins. Which would you prefer? Shopping is definitely out, but slamming a dozen margaritas down her throat, that's a whole other story. By the way, in a lot of clubs they offer the option of buying the whole liquor bottle instead of drink by drink.

If your plan is inviting a girl to be your beach friend, be forewarned that they always forget their swimsuit, and they'll hit you up to buy a new one. If you're OK with that, tell her you've already taken care of that, and hand her a pink dental floss bottom and her 2 matching pink band-aids for the top. Otherwise, before the day happens, make sure you say 10 times "remember your swimsuit". If you plan to travel somewhere far the next day, make her spend the night. These girls have no alarm clocks, and are 99% of the time at least 2 hours late.

To clarify, we're talking about a potential girlfriend here, not a guaranteed lay. Establish up front there will be **no cell phones** on your sightseeing tour. Otherwise, she'll spend half the day on her phone with her sister, her girlfriends, or suddenly have an imaginary crisis she has to return home to immediately. Settle this upfront. If at any time during the day they start whining, get too drunk, or demand expensive shopping adventures, put them in a cab immediately.

If the afternoon trip involves *paid* company, agree on the exact amount upfront, and write it down on a piece of paper in front of her. Keep it in your pocket. If there are no issues, a few days of the tour guide routine will be an enjoyable girlfriend experience, and you'll see some sights you wouldn't normally view. Get her to do the talking. Be a good listener. Have no strong opinions about anything, and agree with whatever nonsense she has to say. This doesn't mean you become some limp wrist lib and waste your whole trip in museums. Just put in a few quality hours with her. Buy her some roses towards the end of the day, suck it up, and you'll be rewarded in spades later on. If for some reason you're unsuccessful, not to worry. There's plenty of time to hit the nearest club or brothel the minute you dump her. As fate would have it, Men can be even greater sharks.

## GFE – The Girlfriend Experience

Overseas, any guy with a basic Alpha Foundation (see chapter) can land a full time girlfriend within days. All your memories of self-centered, rude, immature US women will fade away within minutes of stamping your passport entry. When you re-visit the US, you will laugh at ever thinking of putting up with them, let alone dating them. You'll concentrate solely on your career and traveling again. Many regular travelers who do stay home often only dates Latin or Asian women in the US from then on. The worst you find overseas is gold diggers, but those are easily spotted and discarded. The age difference between you two is irrelevant as well. Be a gentleman and treat her well for 3 days and she's all yours. The difference how she treats you, her attitude, respect, affection and sex will astound you. It's like losing your virginity to a higher species. Welcome to the Club.

## The Language Barrier

As far as the girls overseas, in many cases, the business approach is the only method available due to the language barrier. In South America maybe 5 percent speak English, and Asia is barely better. Often you will find almost no one in the whole damn country speaks English, other than your fellow gringos. If you already know some Spanish, it would help to get Pimsleur tapes to listen to in your car to increase your level of the language. The lazy man's technique is using Spanish closed caption on your TV, or a pocket translator in person. This will give you a decided head start. Columbians, Argentineans, Venezuelans, and Costa Ricans all speak Spanish, and in Brazil most girls understand our broken attempts at Spanish, since Portuguese is a mixture of Spanish and Italian. Thailand and Philippines the girls speak the traditional "Me so Horny" English, so the language barrier is not such a problem.

## The Real Sex in the City

Latin women are in the full time in the business of attracting men. They spend a fortune on clothes, workout religiously, are impeccably clean, and openly sensual. They'll get boob jobs, dance like they're in Vegas Revues, and they learn anything that will end up giving them an advantage to snare a man. Why? In most South American countries there is such a high murder rate amongst young men, that in the locals popular nightclubs women outnumber the men often 5 to 1. The bottom line is that you are not a threat to them here, you are a treat. They are masters at feminine seduction, and will compete with other women to land your happy gringo ass in bed.

Likewise, in Asia, everywhere you turn you are approached by sweet little innocent looking nymphos who are so overwhelmingly polite you find yourself blushing. For every thank you said, some even bow towards you clasping hands. 25 year olds look 15 there. They are so irresistibly cute, respectful and horny, you find it impossible to consider them the same species. You also find it damn near kills you to get on the return flight back.

As far as the paid company, when you take an Asian girl home, an evening's pay ($45-60) provides a girl and her family a week of income. Some girls work the clubs for the dream of leaving their country, while some men go there for the dream of having a sweet untarnished young girl as his future girlfriend or wife. In reality, each party involved is using the other, with both enjoying the benefits of the situation. Consider the whole interaction a noble cause. Tell women back home you donate a portion of your hard earned money to single mothers around the globe.

Whatever country you're in, within a day you can have a girlfriend for the whole trip. The interaction time cycle is up to you. You can spend a few hours (short time), overnight (long time) or several days. It's up to you. Once you agree to go with a girl, she will consider herself your girlfriend until the arrangement ends.

## Avoid Drama, Mix up your Nightclubs

Wherever your travels take you, it's recommended you visit different clubs every couple of nights to meet women. If you keep returning to the same place, you open the door to drama and BS. The girls can become very possessive of you, your manhood and your wallet. Not necessarily in that order. Is it because you're the hottest man on the planet? Is it because they want material things from you? Is it to get a passport to the US? Maybe. The most obvious reason is she is an independent businesswoman, you are her paying client, and any other girl showing you attention is cutting into her business cash flow.

These girls get real jealous. When you're new to the game, by the fourth day you'll walk into the same club and see all your previous night's girlfriends lined up in a row, tugging at you saying *"Baby please, why you cheat on me? I'm you're girlfriend, let's go now."* While the attention is great, who wants all the drama and problems? The truth is, just like the strippers at home, they're all great actresses. They will tell you whatever you want to hear in order to hook your cash and your ego.

When it comes to paid bargirls on your trips, a reality check is absolutely necessary. You have to keep your head on your shoulders and recognize you're being provided fantasy treatment. The girls are professionals. They know everything about the tourist and his methods, and for the most part men don't know a damn thing about them or their methods. The girls know exactly what you want to hear and feel, and will smother you with it for an agreed price. Unfortunately, most men ignore that little piece of advice. Their precious little egos just can't handle the truth. Look around any club, and you'll see some old guy grinning ear to ear with a girl 35 years younger than him, grinding in his lap. If you asked, he will swear up and down that she is in love with him. Younger inexperienced guys are just as gullible.

Then again, it gets somewhat difficult analyzing the situation when every time you blink the most beautiful woman you've ever seen has your rod in her mouth. Get a grip. Keep it light, or these predators will eat you alive financially and emotionally. The pros all try to get you to send money to them overseas after you return home. Don't fall for it. You're one of twenty guys who get the same email. The girls are providing a sexual illusion for you, as well as supporting themselves. Keep it reasonable and straightforward, be interesting, and have a great time. Pretty simple.

One more thing. While you're at it, pick the hottest chicks you can find. This is no time to be settling for a 6 because she's nice and talks a good game. Be patient, and when it comes time to make your move, go for the 8's, 9's, and 10s with a great attitude.


Remember, fat and old chicks are gross.

The end.

# Rio de Janeiro, Brazil

**About** :
As a tropical resort, Rio de Janeiro is a magnificent site to behold, with its dazzling wide beaches and magnificent bay on one side, and surrounded by the abruptly rising Sugarloaf Mountain ridges and tropical forest on the other. An incomparable hedonist beach colony, the *cidade maravilhosa* (marvelous city) is one of the most densely populated places on earth, and home to the world's most famous beach, **Copacabana Beach**. Jam packed with stunning views of thongs, topless nymphos, and overlooked by the infamous open armed Christ statue looking down with tears in his eyes (and binoculars).

The 3-mile Copacabana beach on weekends has some 7 million Cariocas enjoying fun in the sun, beach sports, and socializing about the upcoming evening's festivities. Your entire vacation itinerary can be fulfilled within walking distance of this location, with its restaurants and cafes, movie theatres, bars, massage parlors, chicas, chicas, and more chicas. This is a 24/7 sin city.

Rio is renowned for two colossal events, the infamous **Carnaval**, which begins midnight the Friday before Ash Wednesday and lasts five days. The legendary **New Year's Eve & Festa de Iemanjá** is the second most important event on the city's calendar. Nowhere else in the world can you observe two million white-clad people gathering in a setting as breathtaking as Copacabana beach. The velvety summer sky is the backdrop to one of the world's most spectacular fireworks displays, with hours of fireworks exploding in the glittering sky. On the sand, white-robed believers light thousands of candles and toss flowers as offerings to Iemanjá, queen of the waters, all to an irresistible Brazilian beat. December 31 at midnight on Copacabana Beach is a magical moment every year. Thrilling, unforgettable and incomparable, it truly reflects all the facets of Rio.

**Climate** :
Rio is in the tropics, heavy rains come quick and hard. Opposite seasons of the US, summer is Dec-Mar, a range from 75 to 105 degrees, Rainy season is in the summer. Winter temperature is mild…65-85 degrees.

**Entry Requirements** : From the US, passport and temporary visa are required. The visas are 1 to 5 years long, get the longer. There's an office in Houston and NYC, obtainable by mail, takes about 2 weeks. After acquiring the visa you must enter Brazil within 90 days for the visa to be validated.

$125. Here's the Brazil link for info. ( www.brasilemb.org ) The airport departure in Brazil is currently $36.00 USD. It can be paid in US dollars or the equivalent in local currency.(Real)

## Airport to Hotel-Taxis :

After immigration and customs, it's time for your taxi. Like most airports, you'll immediately be attacked by the scammer cab touts. Here, they have uniforms and look real official. Pass them up, as they charge double. You have two choices, negotiate a cab for a slightly lesser cost; Choices are without ac, or radio cab with AC. The drivers of both do not speak English. A good rule of thumb is to write the hotel name on some paper. The cheapest choice is a yellow cab with a meter waiting in the streets. The Copacabana ride is about **$40** reais. AC in a cab is more. If you hate hassles, the fastest choice is to look for the radio cab booths, of which there are five…look for women flagging you down. You pre-pay about **$50** reais for a one-way trip, you can buy round trip now as well. All of these cabs have AC. These cabs accept US dollars as well. It's $5 more, but why start a trip with a nightmare cabbie. Copacabana or Ipanema should be about 45 minutes. Buses called frescao run by Empresa Real are parked curbside outside customs at the airport and make the same trip for about $5 US. They are an hour long+ trip into the city. The buses follow the beachfront drives and stop at all the hotels along the way. If your Hotel is inland, the bus driver will let you off at the nearest corner. Around the beach, some taxis charge by the meter, others charge flat rates. Ask for all details first.

## Money Matters :

Real is the local currency. REAL, pronounced (hey·ALL), or the plural REAIS, pronounced (hey·ICE), Bill denominations are R$100, R$50, R$10, R$5 and R$1 bills. Currently around 2.20 to $1. Cabs only take reias. Banks tend to give lousy conversion rates, the best conversion is ATM's. In Copacabana, next to the Blockbuster is one on Ave. Copacabana. AMEX has offices at the airport and or Avenida Atlantica which handle travelers checks, but expect a lousy exchange rate. For late night $, Help Disco on the beach will exchange US $100 a day. Make sure you have plenty of $R10's and $R5's. On weekends it's very hard to find anyone to make change, or convert money to Reais. Hand a taxi a $50R and he can't break it.

## Tipping :

At restaurants a 10% tip is usually included. Give a little more only if service was especially good. Taxi drivers do not expect big tips, and extra R$1 is fine. Bellboys and hotel maids expect to get at least R$1. Tips to bartenders are zero to whatever.

## Hotels :

The center of the action, it's best to stay in the Copacabana area. Most hotels either charge for overnight guests or don't allow them, so make sure they are chica friendly. Hotels run approx. $65 and up to $200 at the Marriott. They also charge 16% taxes on top of that, da bastards.

Recommended for lower cost and on the corner of the busiest block from the action is **Hotel Debret**. It features a rooftop restaurant, a popular nightclub, easy access to everything, and a complimentary breakfast. It's located right in front of the Copa beach, also known as hooker beach. Guest charge of R$35 per night. The club **Help** and many of the best daytime cafes are walking distance.

**Atlantic Copacabana** is another popular choice, just $68 a night, no chica fee, it has AC, refrigerator and a dining area. Located closer to the Copa/Ipanema border.

## Hotel Debret

Av. Atlântica, 3564 - Copacabana
Rio de Janeiro, RJ 22070-001 Brasil
Tel: 55-21-2522-0132 ( www.debret.com )

Another option is to stay in Ipanema. Just a few blocks from the tourist area,, with less scammers, touts, and crime. The beaches in Ipanema are cleaner, and much more relaxing. Just a $5 reais taxi to all the action as well. Ipanema Inn and the Arpoador Inn are clean and allow guests. The latter is located right on the beach as well. For more upscale, try the Marina Palace Hotel, also guest friendly.

## Apartments

An alternate option, an apartment offers several advantages. Most have security guards, there is no chica visitor fee, and are located close to the action and quite safe. It's also more personal and less embarrassing for the girls, assuming anything could embarrass them at this point. You're missing the maid, but you gain a refrigerator.
For furnished apartments, contact
**Ken** at : ( www.ez-riorentals.com )
**David** at: ( www.gringomanagement.com )
**Don or Rhonda** at : ( www.riotrips.com ) ( Don@riotrips.com )

Use this link for an updated feel and inside scoop on hotels.
( http://ipanema.com/rio/hotels/e/hotcopa.htm  )

## Cell Phones :

$5 a day, local calls are 33cents a minute, US calls are 45 cents. If you stay more than a week, get one. Most girls give out their numbers.

## Getting Around :

Everywhere you turn there are taxis, they cost $2.50 to start and charge from there. Only get in metered cabs. They don't speak English. Write down your destination on paper if all else fails. You can also travel quickly in the Metro subway system. It works like clockwork, is very efficient, and heads down into the Centro area near the termas. From Copa, the Metro pickup point is Praca Cardeal Arcoverde. A round trip ticket is around 3 reais, a $1. Check the metro map for upgrades and new locations for pickup.

You should be aware there is a beautiful non-tourist beach about 30 minutes from Ipanema/Copa area called Barra da Tijuca. To get here, they have small minivans running up and down the main drag. At just 3 reais, it's a true bargain, since a cab could cost you closer to 25 reais. There's also the very popular Barra Shopping mall or Rio Sul here.

## Crime and Scams :

Druggies, TV's, and thieves down to 12 years old abound. After all, Rio is a huge city, and there are a million tourist targets. For the most part you'll find your garden-variety pickpockets. If you don't know by now, no wallets in the back pocket, only carry what you plan on spending at that given moment, and only what you can afford to lose. Get yourself some pants with zippered or buttoned pockets. Always carry around a photocopy of your passport and it's smart to carry written info concerning your hotel. Often the pickpockets will work in groups, you'll see a pack of 6 kids 10-13 years old, a guy jumps in out of nowhere with a knife and the kids do the stealing. Worst spot is early AM on the corner of Miguel Lemos and Atlantica between **HELP** and **Meia Pattaca**. Take a cab.

Most of the violent crime happens in the non-tourist areas that you have no business wandering into. Violent meaning shootings and death. Stay local, take cabs, move quickly and confidently. For pickpockets, here's another common scam. Up will walk what will *appear to be* a stunning scantily clad woman (transvestite), she/it will give you a hug and grab your crotch, another one will appear, put your hands on it's chest, suddenly your distracted, your hands are occupied, and then bam, a third one will sneak up and steal away with your wallet. You won't even know it for a few blocks.

For the grossest scam, watch out for the infamous *shit flickers* in the daytime, near the **Meia Pattaca** café. If you love to wear open toe sandals, there's a very high percentage you'll get hit. The deal is, the shoeshine guys sitting down here will flick shit onto your shoes or toes, claim someone else did it, and then offer to clean it off for a fee. Whatever it is they shoot at you, it's some nasty smelly stuff that you don't want to get hit by. Another safety tip, if you love the gangsta look with tons of gold necklaces around the neck, Rio isn't for you. When you least expect it, they'll be swiped by a team. The cops will watch and turn the other way. Stay away from the beach at night no matter what. Never walk on the beach side of Avenida Atlantica late at night. Leaving **Help** in the early AM can be dangerous. Thugs have been known to hide behind cars a block away and jump you. The cabs at the door charge a few bucks more, but it's worth it. Within one block you're often confronted if alone. Cops are corrupt and look the other way. There is a high crime rate at 2 am, just like any bad part of any major US city. Again, the most dangerous place to be is walking between Help and Meia Pataca after 2 AM.

Stay away from the buses at night. When going to the beach, leave all valuables in your room. Do not try and hide your money in any clothing and go swimming, it will be gone. Fall asleep on the beach and your stuff is gone. If someone is trying to hard sell you into buying something, a little kid will sneak up from behind to steal your stuff on the beach towel. The streetwalkers in the day are stunning trannies, who double as thieves.

# The Pro Bachelor Game Plan

### Copacabana Beach
Stretching 3 miles long and just 3 blocks deep, Copacabana is the center of Rio's activity, and is home to over 160,000 residents. Avenue Atlantica is the long windy main street, known for its famous mosaic boardwalk. Copa is vibrant with action 24/7, from the fishermen yanking in their nets in the wee hours, early am joggers getting rid of the hangover, to sun worshippers in the day, to the non-stop partying at night. Copa never sleeps. Start your day in front of Rio Othon Palace Hotel to Meridian Hotel. Many of the hottest chicks from the late night HELP disco are here looking for action. If you can't tell which ones, there are touts hustling chicks, towels, and umbrellas everywhere, just ask one which girls are available for a small fee. Pricing is roughly half in the day at 130R.

### Ipanema Beach
Five minutes from Copa, the renowned hotspot has a younger group, is less crowded, cleaner and safer, and features the tiniest thongs on the planet. Here you can watch sports; beach soccer and volleyball, foot volleyball, surfing, wake boarding, and jogging. Or, you can pull up a rental chair and binoculars and get bloody shitfaced and rent yourself an afternoon chica.

### Arpoador Beach
Just southwest of Copa is home to the best surfing. Here you'll find few tourists, and you'll see where the local wealthy and pretty people hang, ie, people who can't stand watching smashed Gringos pick up gorgeous hookers for sport.

**268**

## Outdoor Cafes

After your beach and daytime action, its time to move on to the late afternoon outdoor beach cafes. There are a number of them to choose from, in the area in front of the major hotels Othon, Meridian, and Rio Palace. Just go for a stroll, you can't miss them. The most well known spot on Avenue Atlantica is **Meia Pataca,** another popular one is **Mabs.** Further down the beach is **The Balcony.** The line of restaurants is seemingly endless.

Here's the routine, grab a beer or 10, some steak and seafood, and wait for the show to begin. Around 4 pm you'll find two sets of opportunities, either the local or semi pro girls coming from the beach, or the late afternoon hotties looking for men, money, drinks, or all of the above. It's very obvious who's looking for action, if you see one you like, smile, and she'll be at your table quicker than you can say Ultra Sensitive Magnum XL. No matter how hopeless you look or how bad your Portuguese, you can get a rendezvous till the evening for around $50. If all you want is a quickie twosome or threesome, the hardcore girls are ready when you are. Be smart, avoid the hassles of the hotel Mgt., and potential theft, and ask the "ladies" to take you a few blocks to the closest short time hotel for the session.

## Red Light District

Rio has an excellent red light district, found in the center of the South Side. Head to Lido Square area, near the border of Copacabana and Leme. This the home to numerous exotic bars and nightclubs which feature erotic performances, and burlesque shows with nude dancers. The clubs have the standard neon signs outside, and the featured dancers are usually shown in picture window displays. This is actually a residential area with hotels, restaurants, and the Drugstore Farmácia do Leme, and is open 24 hours. The kingpin for talent here is **Barbarella.** There's a 50R cover, which includes 2 drinks. The club has a bar fine to take out the girls, in addition to her fee. Expect a rate of $250-300R for the girls. A little pricey, but the samba strip shows and caliber of talent is an incredible sight. Other clubs to visit in this area are **Boite Holiday, Don Juan's, Frank's Bar, La Cicciolina, Pussycat, The New Scotch Bar, Niko's,** and **Baccara.** Drinks are very expensive, and you should pay cash for each one. Padded credit card tabs have been known to rival the cost of your kids first year in college.

The girls are here to dance, gulp your drinks, and many will go home with you. These clubs are for the guys who don't like the terma brothel atmosphere and want a lower profile for their coochie shopping. Help Disco (see nightclubs) has more girls, and costs less. However, the environment reeks of being a cheesy tourist hangout, and the music is techno and played at deafening volumes. Women consider it too disrespectful for a good local girl to attend. The Boites offer a better chance to meet a local girl.

**Barbarella** (50R entrance, includes 2 drinks)
Ruao Ministro Vivieros de Castro,24 ---- 2275-7349
**Doma**
Avenue Prado Junior,60 ---- 2275-4899
**Frank's Bar** (20R entrance, includes 2 drinks)
Avenue Princesa Isabel, 185B ---- 2275-9398
**Holiday**
Avenue Atlantica, 1424 ...phone 2542-4347
**New Scotch**
Avenue Princesa Isabela, #7...phone 2275-5499

## Night Clubs :

Don't forget to check some of the local discos as well. Most local clubs the women outnumber men 5 to 1. If you dance salsa, you're 90% of the way in. In the el Centro part of town, **Club Six** is the spot on Friday nights. Great looking local chicas in the 19-24 age range, this place is a goldmine for 7's-8.5's. They play a lot of US hip-hop, top 40, house music, drum & bass, jungle, some rock, Brazilian samba, and reggae. It has 4 dance floors on 4 floors, plus a VIP area way upstairs that's not guarded by security.

Another new club stuffed with hot little 18-year-old locals is called **The Bunker**. Located down on Raul Pompeia #94, a tad before Ipanema. Non pros all over, but if you're not Brad Pitt, don't speak Portuguese or dance well, you'll likely be window shopping. Who cares, with a view like this?

Best bet for late night is always **Help Disco,** billed as South America's largest dance club. Cover charge is $7, but beers are just $3R. Since the club doesn't open until *midnight*, you can find a spectacular view just hanging out at the entrance area at the **Sobre das Ondas** restaurant next door. Show up here at 11-11:30pm. The eye candy can be stunning beyond belief. Many a pro bachelor come here and choose their girl for the night without ever going in. The menu is outrageous. Many girls are waiting outside for guys to arrive and pay their admission into the club. Inside, you'll find 150-300 girls dressed in wild provocative outfits, dancing like sex machines, and 99% are available for the evening. You would happily pay $20 at home just to walk in for this sight alone. The girls range from hardcore pros to part timers, mostly the first. Don't expect to find a classy local girl here, they hate the music and the whole tourist feel. The girls at **Help Disco** know exactly what you want, and with reasonable negotiation skills they will fulfill your fantasy, and probably enjoy the sex more than you will. There's no aura of immorality here or anywhere in Rio. You have the gold, she has the goods. Brazilian women love and brag about their sex conquests.

This is not a poser bar where you stand there and expect perfect 10's to run to you. The best looking girls know they will find someone without trying, so they will dance for a few hours first. You have to make the move. Approach her, offer a drink or a dance, and if you like her, negotiate your deal. Most likely she will want to keep dancing. Expect a nosebleed price of $300 R for an hour initial quote, counter with $150-200R all night, not hourly. It takes time to cab it to your hotel. Never negotiate in dollars. Some will take less just to get it over with. If she won't bite on your price, it's no big deal. There is no shortage or girls here. Some are truly frightening, but on any given night you'll see 50 or more that are in the 8-9 range, with a few tens. You'll find that the most aggressive are at the low end of the scale. They will freely grab your Johnson, and follow you around everywhere you turn, trying to coerce you into making a bad drunk decision. Maybe fun once or twice, but it gets annoying unless they're gorgeous. Here's a tip. The club is two floors, hop on up to the second floor. There's a great bird's eye view from there to pick out your trophy girl, without getting hassled a thousand times by girls begging to have sex with you.

If your goal is to concentrate on just the local girls, a girlfriend, or to try for freebies, Help is not your place. The club is definitely frowned upon by the proud Brazilian locals, who correctly claim it's nothing but a tourist trap for gringos and hookers. For locals, you may need some time, youth, Portuguese, and strong game to move quickly. If you have all of these, and are temporarily laid off from Chippendales, you can score on almost any night. Unless you have an extended vacation planned, don't waste your valuable time. Go to the beach at noon, termas around 3:30pm, cafes at 7-10 pm, and Help at midnight. You can't miss at any of these spots. More so than any women in the world, Brazilian women are insatiable nymphos, and during the sex it is quite common you'll find yourself thinking *who is paying whom ?* They truly love to please, or are the greatest fakers on earth. Who cares, you both win in this scenario. The girls come in all shapes, shades, and sizes, and have the best asses on the planet.

**Help Disco**
Avenue Atlantica #3432...2522-1296...
**[www.discoteca-help.com]**

Here's a regularly updated link for the latest hot spots
**[www.ipanema.com/rio/nite/e/shows.htm]**

## Termas

Now, for the in-call professional chicas. The best sex experiences in Rio are found in the Termas. Termas are the Brazilian phrase for a bathhouse. There are hundreds of chicas all over town working in termas, and there's always a new girl each night you visit, due to the very high turnover. Here's the modus operandi; you pay a cover of $30-50 reais and then change in a locker room into a Hefner robe and slippers. You're given a numbered key pertaining to your locker, which all charges will be assigned to. The bartenders ask for your number when ordering drinks, and the girls may want to see the key before entering the luv den. The number comes in the form of a wristband. Wear it on your wrist, don't pocket it. People have been known to swap yours with theirs and run up gigantic tabs. **Don't lose your key.** You get your key, your locker, you take a shower and/or sauna, then head to the bar area. Walk around to survey the place *before* sitting down, because the minute your down, you're attacked by women. Be very patient. The first few you see will blow you away, but soon you'll realize there are even better ones to be had. You will need to master smiling and politely getting rid of some girls. An easy way is to say you're waiting for a favorite girl whom you've been with before. There will be times when you have your eye on one chica, and out of nowhere another hot one will appear, have her tongue down your throat and be pumping your dick under the robe, and you'll say no thanks. Try explaining that one at home.

You have 3 decisions to make here, which girl(s), how long you want them, and a regular or upgraded room. Some upgraded rooms have mirrors on the walls and ceiling with a huge circular bed. Often they are positioned like thrones, as you have to climb a few steps to get to it. Careful, when jumping around and changing positions, it's pretty easy to step off the bed, bounce down the stairs on your back, with your dick flopping in the breeze. Cameras in here are not encouraged, but you can slip a small one in your robe, and most girls are more than happy to pose for you. When you pick a girl, she will take your key and go schedule your date, she will also change and come back with a new outfit and look. The effect and minimal time delay is quite effective, when she returns the new look will be twice as hot. What's amazing in the Brazil Termas is how the girls will not stop after the first round, they want 2 or more in 40 minutes. After your session, you hit the shower or sauna and head back to the bar and couch. If the place isn't packed, the girl you just had will come back and resume kissing and stroking, like it never happened. Slow down girl, I'm not that easy.

## Monte Carlo
Also know as Club 19, is located 1 block from Avenue Atlantica in the heart of Copacabana. After arriving on the first floor, take the elevator to the showers and spa on the 2$^{nd}$ floor, and then elevator to club and chicas on the 3$^{rd}$ floor. Hours of operation are Mon.-Sat. from 4pm-2am. Cover is 50R, prices are 200R for 40 minutes or 250R for one hour in a suite.

## L'uomo
A few blocks from **Monte Carlo.** Located on the 2$^{nd}$ floor of a shopping center, and not that easy to find without help. Same management and setup as Monte Carlo, pricing is the same, and the hours are Mon-Sun 4pm – 2am. If there's no selection at one Terma, head to the other. L'uomo gets the nod

between the two for quality of girls, although diamonds in the rough are very common at both. Another good feature is that if you're there in the afternoon, they let you return later in the evening without additional cover if you inquire at the front desk.

## Quatro X Quatro

Located in El Centro at Rua Buenos Aires 44, Quatro X Quatro has the largest selection of women, from 50 to 100 exotic nymphos...all shapes, sizes, and colors. Lately this has become the home of the brazilian blondes. This is a downtown business man's club that gets packed quickly. It's best to time it for the 3-5pm shift. At night the place is almost claustrophobic it's so crowded. The entrance is a narrow hallway, then you head up stairs to the second floor entrance. Pay the cover, then with your numbered locker key it's off to the lockers. Quick change and shower, back to the stairs and up one more level. Upon entering you'll notice a bar right in the middle of the action, which includes great stripper shows, some live lesbian acts, multiple nude synchro dances, and more. The shows last 40 minutes at a time.

There's also a third floor bar in the back area, which is more intimate for your couch interviews. The bar also serves food. Just plop your happy ass down on the couch, or sit at the bar. Within seconds, some girls will recognize you're a famous wealthy and well-hung stud, and will come up and jump in your lap, make out and stroke you, until you can't wait any longer. This can be so much fun, groups of locals come in just for this foreplay for an hour or two, and then leave. Pricing for **4X4**, a $30R entrance, beers are $5R, and one hour in a suite with your date is just $160R. Rooms are on premises, complete with bed, shower, and mirrors for your porn star experience. Finish before 5pm and they waive the entrance fee. You pay your tab when you leave. Drinks for you and the girls are same price, and cheap. The girls are in bikinis or lingerie, and often dancing salsa.

There's also a bar on the first floor below **4X4,** where you can go before or after your session. A lot of the Terma girls hang out in here to drink and dance. Here you can get the girls' phone numbers, and arrange for the two of you to meet up later that night or have her come over the next day for a quickie and hit the beach. They all freely offer up their phone numbers unless you're some a cheap Charlie or an ugly rude troll.

## Termas 65

This spa is the second most expensive next to Centaurus, entrance fee is $40R and the girl is $210R, and they have a restaurant and a great masseuse. There's a pleasant professional atmosphere here, as opposed to the balls to the wall frat party schtick at 4X4. The exotic shows, stripping and nude dances here are tantalizing. Most important are the girls, as there are many young stunning, fun, classy girls who take real pride in making you sweat 10 pounds and walk like you just got off a horse. Don't be surprised if you leave here faking your manly composure, and then end up at the hotel taking a 6 hour nap with an ice pack on your crotch.

**Termas Solarium** is roughly 15 minutes from Copa in the Jardim Botanico side of town, address Rua JJ Seabra, 21, Jardim Botanica. A sexy club located in a restaurant row as well, about a $2 cab ride from Ipanema. Entrance is $40R, a session is $120R. The upgraded hour in the Jacuzzi suite is $260R. A nice crew of hotties here, and a local manager who will point out ones he recommends. The bonus is they are open on Sundays. ( www.solarium.com.br )

**Centaurus** is the granddaddy of them all. The highest class, and highest entrance fee up front of $290 reais, which includes a 40 minute session. A second round with any girl is $215R. Upon entering, an available hostess will show you around the club and try to get you to choose her. The answer is no, you want to hit the sauna first. There's so many girls here you want to wait as long as humanly possible before you decide. Similar Terma arrangement, in that you change and shower in the locker room, and then waltz around in your Playboy robe and flip flops. The club itself is 5 star immaculate. When strutting thru the first time, tilt your head in an aristocratic way, and mumble to yourself about some imaginary billion dollar business deal. This will not only display what an important dignitary you are, it will hopefully stop you from blowing a premature load during your gawking and stupid impersonation.

Talk about eye candy. Centaurus has arguably some of the hottest women in all of Rio. Now, if you like your women thick, morena or with the bigger bubblebutts, you may not like the place. If you like a loud Animal House atmosphere, then don't come here. But if you like a Gold Club environment packed with gorgeous, classier petite college students this is your place. Mostly in the range of 8s and up, and on a good night there are fifty 9s to perfect tens. You could spend your kid's entire education fund here and feel it was entirely worth it. *"Sorry kids, looks like community college...you were so close."*

There's a huge sports bar area with TV's playing the numerous sporting events of Rio. That would be soccer, soccer and soccer. Try not to mimic the announcer if there's a goal scored. They also feature live music on certain nights, as well as girls on stage doing some sexy stripping acts. Throughout the club there are countless girls roaming and attacking you. The upgrades are 2 girls, or the mirror suite for 1 hour. In the suite there's a gigantic round bed with mirrors on all the walls and the ceiling! Practice Mr. Universe flexes while slamming your trophy hoe. **Centaurus** is a once in a lifetime experience. Or, if you're at all like me, it actually happens quite often. You're safe paying here with a credit card.

**Quatro x Quatro**
Centro district, downtown, Ave. Buenos Aires #44.
The sign says  Whiskeria. Mon-Fri 2pm - 1AM.

**Centaurus**
Rua Canning 44 in Ipanema Open 4-2am Mon-Fri, 4-12pm Saturday
2523-4088

**Monte Carlo** (Club 19) in the Copacabana District
Mon-Saturday 4-2pm…phone# 2255-4489

**L'uomo**
( Copacabana District  ) Mon-Fri 3-2am, Sat-Sun 3-midnight. 2549-4113

**Solarium**
Rua JJ Seabra 21, Jardim Botanico 2274-2741  **( www.solarium.com.br)**

**Termas 65**
Rua do Rosario 65, one block from 4X4, Mon-Fri 2pm-midnight.
**(www.termas65.com.br/index.asp)**

**Termas Rio Antigua**
Rua Joaquim Silva, 2   ---- 2224-9591
**(www.rioantigo.com.br  )**

## Escort Agency Sites :

- o   Barra Vips - ( www.barravips.com.br )
- o   Chantily – (www.chantily.com.br)
- o   CIA Plus - ( www.ciaplus.com )
- o   ClassiSex - ( www.classisex.com.br  )
- o   Company Girl - ( www.companygirl.com.br )
- o   DeStack Girls - ( www.destackgirls.com.br )
- o   Escort Girl - ( www.escortgirl.com.br  )
- o   Karla's Models - ( www.karlamodels.com.br )
- o   Malicia – ( www.malicia.com.br)
- o   Mclass – ( www.mclass.com.br)
- o   Paraiso Escort - ( www.paraisoescort.com.br/ )
- o   Rio Vip's - ( www.riovips.com.br )
- o   Scort Show - ( www.scortshow.net )
- o   Sexy Dreams – ( www.sexydreams.com.br )
- o   Sexy Hall - ( www.sexyhall.com  )

For a value, the escort sites are the way to go. There has been a significant
inflation of pricing at Help, girls asking $300R an hour is common. (not that
you pay it). By comparison, Scort Show is just 100r for two hours.

## The Bullshit Vacation Story:

Tell the old lady you went to Rio to see the parakeet zoo in the mountains.

Here are the other things you did in Brazil.

## Sightseeing:

You have to make sure you do some Mountaintop Viewing while you are down here. Sugar Loaf is home to the infamous Christ statue overlooking Rio you've seen in postcards. Take the train up to the top of Corcovado, two cable cars lift you 1300ft above Rio and the Baía de Guanabara, offering a stunning view of Rio. The two-stage cable cars leave about every 30 minutes. The infamous statue Cristo Redentor. From the city going up 2330 feet is the mountain top..the statue is 98 feet tall, and weighs 1145 tons. The mountain offers magnificent panoramas of Rio and surrounding areas. Sunset up here with a girl is worth its price in gold, especially if she's wearing no panties and backs up into you on the trolley on the way down. Make sure it's clear out if you travel up it, the storms come in a hurry, and they are monsoons with lightning you don't want to experience up there.

## Carnaval

The Carnaval in Rio began it's tradition from pagan festivals long before the middle ages and was developed over the years in Brazil as the Catholics decided to let loose before Lent. Traditionally during Lent, Catholics gave up certain pleasures such as eating red meat and drinking alcohol for 40 days, starting Ash Wednesday the last day of Carnival. The five day long celebration begins with a ceremonial handing over of the keys of the city from the city Mayor to Rei Momo, the king of carnival and Lord of Misrule.

Famous for its Samba music, partying, and packed beaches. There are parties in the streets with bands, private clubs and hotels around the city offer Carnival Balls, ranging from chic sophisticated to scandalous parties with scantily clad, or practically nude women. There are also the amazing world famous PARADES in the Sambadromo. Remember, for the tourist, during the carnaval the prices double, the density of people is worse than Mardi Gras, and crime escalates. If you're OK with this, it's located right on the beach and certainly will be a moment for the record books.

## Diving:

**Barra Squalo**
Av. Armando Lombardi, 949, shop D Phone: 493.3022
Mon-Fri, from 11am to 8pm; Saturday, from 10am to 3pm
Underwater photography and diving expeditions with equipment.
**Jardim Botânico Diver's Quest**
Rua Maria Angélica, Phone: 286.2513 Mon to Friday, from 10am to 8pm;
Saturday, 12-6pm ( www.diverquest.com ) Standard PADI courses.
Equipment hire and maintenance. Diving expeditions.

# San Jose, Costa Rica

**About :**

Costa Rica is located in Central America, between Nicaragua and Panama. The country has a population of 3.8 million, with the capital **San Jose** coming in at 340,000. The people are 96% Spanish descent. CR hosts more than one million tourists each year. National parks cover almost 12% of the country. Mountain ranges throughout, from approximately 3,000 to 12,000 feet above sea level. Beautiful beaches on the west coast, and there are several active volcanoes (Volcán Arenal, Volcán Irazú). The country has a relatively long coastline in both the Atlantic and Pacific oceans, as well as a number of rivers and streams that attract expert kayakers and rafters. Costa Rica is a tropical paradise, with exotic jungles, gorgeous beaches, world-class fishing, and some of the finest Latina chicas in Central America. CR is so popular for the sex vacation industry, chicas fly in from Columbia, Panama, Dom. Republican, even Europe, to handle the overflow of US men and their money. In addition to a sea of local discos, vacation resorts, and nightclubs, there's **30 massage parlors** and **brothels** for you to choose from. The local girls are gorgeous and dress to kill, hip huggers, midriffs, waist length black hair. You're head will be sore from constantly turning around and staring. Fortunately there are no parking meters in town, or you'd be walking into them. Here's are links to the local papers.

**( www.insidecostarica.com )  ( www.ticotimes.net )**

**Climate :**

Costa Rica's year round climate is pleasant w/ naturally occurring breezes. The rain season if from May to November. We're talking rainstorms that resemble rivers pouring down from the sky, the streets get flooded above your shoes easily. The Caribbean coast tends to be wet all year. The women in the country are nymphos and tend to only have wet seasons.

**Entry and Departure :**

A valid passport gets you 90 days there without a visa. Passport cannot expire within 90 days from your arrival date. $27 to Depart

**Airlines :**

The Costa Rican national airline is Taca International Airlines (TA) Taca International flies direct to Costa Rica from Miami, La, NY.

**Money Matters :**

U.S. currency is King. Bring crisp new bills, avoid $100 bills. The local currency is colones, around 510 to 1 dollar. Best place to transfer money is the hotels, the Morazon in San Jose pays slightly higher than the others.

**Taxis :** Airport is 20 miles from San Jose, i.e., Sin City, and it's only a $12 cab ride. Skip the rental car, in town it's a nuisance and a potential liability. Cabs are $1.25 every direction in town, most places are walking distance.

## What to Wear :

Skip the typical ugly American clothes; shorts and Hawaiian shirt. Shorts are rarely seen. The girls like a man dressed up with a little class. Or, they like a man in shorts and Hawaiian shirts with a lot of cash to burn.

## Hotels :

There are three nice affordable hotels in the center of the San Jose action.

## Hotel Del Rey

Avenida Primero y Calle 9, (888) 972-7272  (www.delreyhotel.com)
Home of the famous **Blue Marlin**, ground zero for the girls, everyone here is available. The girls are checked for ID by security, and the problem girls are not allowed entry. The del Rey is around $65 a night. It's $10 per guest in the room, but they keep her passport and papers at the front desk and check with you before releasing her (all the hotels do). Across the street is:

## Hotel Morazon

Frente al Parque Morazan
San José, San José 1017, 506 219 2470  Located one block from del Rey, the Morazan, is $45 a night, 2 star at best, but they have no guest fee.

## Hotel Presidente

Avenida Central entre Calle 7 y Calle 9, #506 221 3832  $60 to $100, including breakfast.  Located a few blocks away from the **del Rey**, the breakfast café has the best view for local chica watching seats. No hotel guest fee, but only 1 guest at a time. They have a Jacuzzi on the roof you can rent. Great master suite. ( www.hotel-presidente.com )

## The Game Plan :

The main show is the **Hotel del Rey Casino**'s lobby bar. There are very few places in the world where you will walk in and be so overwhelmed with the first site. Indescribable. It's worth going with newbies just to see their initial reaction. The OMG Jaw drop. The best way to describe it is inside a casino is a self-serve Sports bar Brothel. There are about 60 girls in here at any given time, and maybe 10 guys tops. There's a steady flow of new girls every hour. Pricing has rising quickly as of late, with most starting at $100 a shot initial offer. Best bet is negotiating in colones, and hold the line at $60-75. It's the chica Hall of Fame in Central America, with girls flying in to snare the gringo dollars. The girls are local ticas, Columbians, Dominicans, and other Central and South Americans. Most are all pro, a fair amount of part-timers as well. The hip hugger bootie pants is the style here. A few hogs, age is generally 18-25 years old. If the girl is aloof and mechanical in the bar, that won't change later when it really counts. Also, be very specific on what you want on your date, time (two hours), positions, tricks, etc.

The date is best if you pay afterwards. "Pago cuando terminar." Tell her this in the bar. A common scam is she agrees, gets back to your room, showers, and when you're both naked, then she asks for money up front again. Just stand up and get dressed and open the door. Usually she'll change her mind, if not tell her to take a hike. Try to be a gentleman and make it a pleasant experience. Most will give phone numbers and you can hook up the next day or the entire trip if you'd like. Remember, all the girls talk to each other at the DR, so if you're an ass or a scammer, none of the girls will have anything to do with you after that.

Across the street is **Key Largo**, which has a live band playing closet classics from the US along with salsa. Ten years ago this was the hot spot, and the rate was just $20. Capitalism reared its ugly head. The club is still trying to find a way to make a comeback. Grab a girl at the DR and take her here. It will lighten her up, it's a great place for the girls to dance to live music, and a great place to get drunk. The bartenders here are the hottest girls in town. They have great seafood here also.

## Discos
For meeting local girls, just north of the downtown Holiday Inn is the **El Pueblo** area, with over 100 bars, clubs, and restaurants. This is a hot spot if you're under 40, and the locals here are great looking. In fact, you won't see one overweight girl your whole trip. Here is invaluable map detailing all the hot spots as well as the hotels, clubs, and malls. Print this out.
( http://adultcostarica.net/index.htm )

### Massage Parlors
The preferred spas are **Ozona Blue, New Fantasy, Idem, 747, Cha Cha**, and **Oases**. Prices run $35-50 per hour. This includes massage, steam room, shower, and other extras. At New Fantasy, when you arrive there's a huge one-way mirror that allows you to look in at the 30+ potential dates sitting on a couch. In Thailand they call this the fishbowl. Its basically a holding pen and quite a sight. Usually peering in will be 10 other guys who haven't got laid in two years in the US, and now suddenly they are picky and have high standards. Get a grip guys. The girls are 18-22 years old, and the bang for the buck is quite a value…some very enthusiastic performances.

Next up is **Idem**, a health spa with a bar. You sit and have a beer or 10, the girls are all hovering near the bar. When you're ready, point to your date. She knows she's lucky for you picking her, and has a special room to take you upstairs to tell you all about it. There's a lot more girls here than NF, 23-35 in age, a little better looking, and the dates run around $45. The boss here is named Roberto, he speaks English and can refer you to the best performers for what you're seeking. Great threesomes can be had.

## Mountaintop Restaurant - Ram Luna
For those who spoil themselves, take a girl to this restaurant up in the mountains. In the mountains above Aserrí, south of San José. Directions for

Taxi Driver: Del centro de Aserrí, cuatro kilómetros sobre la carretera a Tabarca. Tel: (506) 230-3060 / 230-3489

Recommended Dish: "Lomito Mirador," a beef tenderloin. Dinner entrées range from $6 to $13. Wednesday-night all-inclusive "Tierra Tica" Costa Rican buffet with open bar, live music, typical dancing and festivities costs $28 per person. Fireworks display at night as well.

## Bullshit Vacation Story :

Tell the old lady you flew to Central America to take advantage of the fabulous duty free cooking spices they sell. If she gives you any lip, smack her around a little bit. Who's got time for that crap?

## Eco-Sporting :

Costa Rica is an adrenaline junkie hot spot. That's why you went there, remember? There is a fascinating canopy daytrip tour that many people take tour near San Ramon. After climbing several thousand feet up thru dense jungle, you then zip line across a steel rope from one side to the other (100 yards). It's an amazing thrill because you're flying thru the air thousands of feet above the rain forest. This is not designed for those who are afraid of heights, over weight and out of shape. Great for group trips.

On the Pacific Coast is the best surfing in Central America, and for windsurfers go to the **Laguna de Arenal**, located next to the infamous volcano. For snorkeling and diving, try the **Reserva Biologica Isla del Cano**, 12 miles west of Bahía Drake, off the northern part of the Península de Nicoya and in the **Parque Nacional Isla del Coco**.

Another favorite vacation activity here is the violent white-water rafting. Outfitters and guides can arrange trips. The **Reventazón River** (class III) is suitable for beginners, next level up is done at **Pacuare** (class IV) and the **Pascua** (class V) rivers. The best times to go are from May to November.

**Río Reventazon**, in central Costa Rica, is one of the most exhilarating and scenic rivers in Costa Rica for kayakers and rafting as well.

## Windsurfing :

**Lake Arenal** was recently voted one of the world's top windsurfing spots. Situated at 5580ft (1700m) above sea level, the lake offers its best windsurfing between April and December.

## Golfing :

For golf, there are two, 18-hole golf courses near San Jose. First up is **Cariai County Club**, the only catch is you have to stay at Melia Cariai Conference Center. The second 18-hole golf course is **Parque Valle del Sol** in Santa Ana. Most golf courses are away from San Jose.

On the west coast, at the ritzy **Marriot Los Suenos** there's a third 18-hole course carved out between lush rain forest mountains with great ocean views. Well kept, about $90. Remember, it rains often and hard. For all Costa Rican golf info, go to Costa Golf Adventures. Toll free: 1-877-258-2688 from US. ( www.golfcr.com)

## Sport Fishing :

Costa Rica coasts offer some of the best Big Game Sport Fishing in the world, with fishing on both the Pacific and Caribbean coasts. Here you can catch **Marlin, Wahoo, Tuna, Tarpon, Dorado, Snook,** and **Sailfish** all year round. Costa Rica currently holds 18 world record catches.

( www.ticotimes.net/fishing.htm ) ( http://costaricasailfish.com )

### Marlin
Caught every month of the year, with mid-Nov to March exceptional, then slowing a bit from April into early June. Peaks in August and September.
### Sailfish
May through August normally the top season. They thin out in September and the slowest months are late August through November.
### Tuna
When all else fails, there are always tuna, any time of the year. More often than not when you'd just as soon avoid them to concentrate on billfish. The yellow fin and big eye tuna are found well inside the Santa Catalina Islands, 30 minutes from the beach; schools of 12-20 pounders are usually abundant on the outside. You frequently find concentrations of 40-60 pound tuna, and there are plenty of the 200 to 400 pounders caught every year.
### Dorado
More properly known as dolphin, these colorful gamesters are most abundant from late May through October when the seasonal rains flood the rivers, carrying out debris that forms trash lines close inshore that they like to lie under. Troll past a floating log and you'll likely hook a dorado.
### Wahoo
The first showing begins about the time the rains start in May, peaking in July and August. Most are caught around the rocky points and islands, but you will pick one up offshore.
### Roosterfish
Available all year, but there are more caught in the Papagayo Bay area from November through March. That may be because more boats in the northernmost area of this region are fishing inshore during those windy months, and the roosters like the structure of the shoreline and islands where they're found in 50 to 60 feet of water. Updated fishing and charter info:

( www.fishcostarica.com/index.html )
( http://centralamerica.com/cr/fish/ )

If you're already staying in San Jose, there's a travel agency in the Hotel del Rey where you can arrange charter boats trips and shuttle to the water for ½ day, day, and multi day excursions. Going rate is about $ 600-800 for a full day per boat plus about 50 bucks for transportation.

**Jaco Beach** is about 2 hours west of San Jose on the Pacific side of Costa Rica. If you prefer the finer things in life, stay at **Las Suenos Marriott Ocean and Golf Resort.** The hotel features magnificent colonial architecture set on the Pacific Coast, (1 hour, 45 minutes from Juan Santamana International Airport) on a 1,100 acre rainforest with an 18-hole championship golf course. Some attractions include: Casino , Spa Services, Tennis Courts, Water Sports, Deep Sea Fishing, and a 250 slip Marina. It's literally jungle territory, with monkeys in the trees, and Amazon hookers in the bars as well. Twelve miles away is a crocodile safari where the beasts jump out of the water and eat out of the guides hand. He even has most of his fingers. Las Suenos is a resort area specifically designed for wealthy Americans. Some girls in lobby bar, most BYOC – Bring your own chica.

Heading out further south is Jaco Beach. For lesser expensive there's the **Hotel Cocal** on the beach, it's got a nice pool decent rooms and is $69 a night off-season. Besides the **Beatle bar,** there is **El Centro Disco,** with pro, semi-pro and non-pros late night. Jaco is a weekend only place for action. Also, there's a few strip clubs, the best being **Club Hollywood.**

The best chica bar is called the **Beatle Bar**. It's pretty much a weekends only club. Jaco is a surfer town, so the bar is full of locals, surfers, and a fair amount of friendly ladies who are dying to hear all your bullshit fishing stories, for a fee of course. The smartest approach is to bring a girl from San Jose with you for an overnight trip with you. She probably has never been to the area and it will greatly enhance your outing. Interview well. The nicest beach in the area is Manuel Antonio. Best place to stay is the Costa Verde Hotel. By the way, Grey Line Fantasy Tour bus shuttles back and forth from the Best Western Irazu. **(**www.bestwesterncostarica.com**)**

There are two towns that people go to for sport fishing, **Quepos** and **Jaco.** Jaco has average to lousy fishing, with a great outcall Chica bar full of 40 to 50 girls. Quepos is outstanding for fishing and lousy for the chicas. Last trip in 2 days our boat caught 24 sailfish…we lost track of how many chicas.

# Bangkok, Thailand

## About:

Thailand is a fascinating combination of old traditional eastern culture and frenetic paced Western Capitalism. **Bangkok** is a city of contrasts; you'll be driving in an air-conditioned taxi while an ox drawn cart pulls up besides you. Downtown you'll find dilapidated shacks next to 14th Century temples with exotic gardens, all surrounded by brand new office buildings and 5 star hotels. Traffic is a nightmare, the heat is stifling, and the women are gorgeous. Having supported the US during the Vietnam War, free trade and big business have emerged in force, leaving the monarchy and destitute poverty behind.

Electronics, textiles and tourism are the largest industries here, and Thailand is the world leader in exportation of rice. Not all of the country has adapted to capitalism. Fifty percent of its the citizens still work in the poor climate of rice production, although this represents just 12% of the country's income. Thus, you have a huge disparity of wealth between outer country folks and city people. Overall, Bangkok has evolved into a world business player in just a few short decades.

## The Adult Disneyworld

Bangkok is the neon-lit Southeastern Asian capital of the sex world, full of half million wild, sexy, young available women. The city covers 610 sq. miles, located in the middle of Thailand and it's rice fields, surrounded by a network of natural and artificial canals crisscrossing the city. Bangkok is surprisingly easy to get around with its excellent public transport systems. A new overhead rail system connects the main shopping, entertainment and business areas of the city, while river taxis and express boats link many of the older historic sites. For an easy view of the layout of Bangkok, go the observation deck on the 77th floor of the Baiyoke Sky Hotel, ranked as the second tallest hotel in the world. As far as sightseeing tourist attractions go, there is the Royal Grand Palace, Wat Pho and the National Museum. All are located west of the railway. For the fun stuff, we concentrate on the east side, the Sukhumvit Road area.

Each year, Thailand has become a vacation destination for close to 10 million tourists. This has been the case for the last 25 years or so, as it is one of the world's favorite spots for sex tourism. The origin of this came about due to Thailand being an important US ally. They became home to the US Air Force troops for their R&R breaks over the years during conflicts and wars. When there's a lot of Americans on vacation, there's alot money to spread around. So as always, capitalism forces took over.

The commercial sex industry exploded almost overnight. After the Vietnam War a lot of the US military came back to Thailand, and many of them never left. Thai girls typically are sweet sexy little spinners when compared to Westerners. As much as you may long for one, a fat, mouthy, opinionated wench is impossible to find in this city. Thai girls have beautiful long shiny dark hair, a sexy tan, gorgeous endless smiles, and a seductive femininity that can be overpowering. Few men are not affected by their shy but incredibly naughty girl next-door persona. When experiencing Thai girls, there seems nothing wrong or immoral about prostitution. The feeling is quite the opposite, more like renting a short-term long distance relationship with a girl. Whether fake or not, they offer up sensuality, happiness, and attention rarely found in the US. Sure they ar/e doing it for money, but what *you* get out of it is so much more than that. It is this experience that keeps men coming back for more and more. Since the price is almost free, any multi-girl fantasy is easy to purchase. Sure it ruins your life for a while when you return home, but you're an airport ticket away from paradise.

Here's the Local paper in English.

**( www.bangkokpost.com )**

## Climate :
Bangkok features intense heat and stifling humidity; with the evenings cooling off to merely miserable. The best time to visit is between November and February; April is generally the hottest month and October the wettest.

## Entry Requirements :
Passport required, and must be valid $13 departure tax. Passport valid for 6 months beyond intended length of stay required. Anyone intending to stay longer than 30 days must obtain a visa prior to arrival. As far as time zones, Bangkok is 12 hours ahead of New York time. $13 departure tax

**Types of visa and cost**: Tourist: £25 (single entry); Non-immigrant: £40 (single entry), £90 (multiple entries valid for 1 year); Transit (single entry): £15. Prices are subject to change.

**Validity**: All visas are valid for 3 months from the date of application. Tourist visas are for stays of up to 60 days within that period.

## Airport Taxis :
Taxis or limos from inside the arrivals hall have fares around 500-600 Baht. If you want a meter taxi (less luxurious, less expensive) join the line outside the arrivals building and get a taxi voucher from the ticket booth outside. Tell them your hotel, payment is upon arrival. Fares vary depending on the time/distance from around 200Baht upwards. Depending on your hotel location, the driver may ask if you want to take the toll way. There are two main toll roads into central Bangkok, which costs 30-40 Baht. This is an

extra separate charge from the fare and worth the extra couple bucks. Pay the driver direct as you go through the toll way. It can be much quicker to take the toll roads in standard rush hour periods.

Airport limo: (www.thaiair.com/thailand/limousine/fares.htm#Schedule)

## Getting Around :

The bus system of Thailand is sufficient, but the new overhead sky train makes a big difference with all the street traffic. You can now go from Silom Road to Sukumvit Road and elsewhere in minutes. Taxi is best to reach parts of the city not covered by the sky train. Passenger boats and water taxis are also options worth considering for entertainment.

## Money Matters :

The baht is divided into 100 satang. *Notes*: 10, 20, 50(blue), 100(red), 500 (purple), 1000 (grey)baht. *Coins*: 25, 50 satang; 1, 2, 5, 10 baht.

For today's exchange rate, go to here: ( **www.oanda.com** )

## ATM machines

Available at most banks and shopping centers throughout the city.

**Travelers Checks / Credit Cards :**

Most traveler's checks can be cashed at banks. Take your passport or ID.

**Helpful Tips :**

The temperature and humidity here is stifling, bring sunscreen and sunglasses everywhere you go. Slam bottles of water down like it's last call. AVOID drinks with ice, meaning your shorts will all have racing stripes quickly. In evenings there's killer mosquitoes. Ask the waiter to put a *mosquito coil* under the table. Wear pale slacks and mosquito repellant.

## Hotels :

A gazillion Hotels to choose from. If you have the time, travel agencies in town get you the best deals for cheap quality hotels. If not, walk up rates can be done easily, here are a few to start with.

### Baiyoke Suite Hotel Bangkok

All rooms come fully equipped with modern amenities and the upper floors provide splendid views of the city. The property is located in Pratunam, close to department stores and wholesale shops selling a wide variety of merchandise. 209 room(s), Price From Thai Baht 1120 (Approx 28 US$)

### Comfort Suites Bangkok Airport Hotel

150 well-appointed, air-conditioned rooms. All are comfortable, sound proof, and protected with security door locks. $ 1300 BHT, $ 32 a night

**Playboy Hotel** off Soi 3, 700-800 baht, short time and long time.

**Royal Asia Lodge:** 91 Sukhumvit Road, Soi 8 Just 2 minutes from the district, with a free shuttle. Right next to the sky train. 890 Baht (US$21) for a king size bed. Recommended highly.   ( www. royalasia.co.th )

**Nana Hotel  Bangkok *****

Located in the Sukhumvit area, in the heart of one of Bangkok's busiest nightlife districts, ideal for singles looking for the unique entertainment found in the Nana Plaza area. The **Nana Hotel** is conveniently placed near the Bangkok Skytrain, so travel around the city is quick and easy, with direct access to Siam Square, Silom, and other popular shopping and sightseeing areas. Although the Nana Hotel is not close to Don Muang Airport, the expressway makes access to the hotel relatively easy. One of Bangkok's most popular discos is in the hotel basement, **Angel Disco**, and picking up a freelancer or local requires simply standing in the lobby. How's that for service.

4 Nana Tai Sukhumvit Road, Bangkok 10110, Thailand

334 rooms    $29 ( www.nanahotel.co.th/html/index.html )

**The Hilton Bangkok** is a low-rise architectural retreat that merges effortlessly with the magnificent, botanical Nai Lert Park that occupies half the property. 338 room(s), Price From Thai Baht 3510 (Approx $95 )

**Marriott** on Suk. Soi 2 True 5 star hotel, great location, including breakfast $95 + 17.7% tax. ( www.marriott.com )

Complete hotel listings here:
( www. bangkoktonight.com/hotels/ )

## Electricity :

Voltage is 220 Volt AC with flat 2 pin plugs. You can buy an adapter for shavers, laptop computers, mobile chargers, etc., on arrival at most department stores. Most hotels now have Internet either from the room by laptop, or from their business center. Charges vary from around 100 Baht for the first 15 minutes with lower charges afterwards. Additional surcharges times apply, so check first. There are also Internet cafes in most shopping areas which are generally expensive.

**Map of Bangkok :**
( www. bangkok-maps.com )    ( www. royalasia.co.th/map.html )

# The Game Plan :

## Bangkok Nightlife.

Welcome to Holy Land O Smiles. Unashamed hedonist insanity is the Bangkok sex industry. Everywhere you turn are sex clubs and massage parlors, as well as restaurant and cocktail bars. Bangkok alone is home to dozens of discos, almost a 100 Go Go bars, hundreds of karaoke bars, and literally thousands of pubs and cafes. Packs of people of all types, not just the old horny men you'd expect, but mid 20's guys and girls on vacations all peering into the sea of aggressive available girls and naked strippers. The layout is real simple. The main street is **Sukhumvit Road**, and the side streets are called Soi and number in order, odd one side, even the other.

Neon Go-Go bars and people bartering goods light up the alleys. Wander on in and discover miles of girls in bikinis or topless grinding to the latest top 40 trance, western, metal, and hip hop hits. A virtual sexual Disneyland. It's an all-round mesmerizing sight to view, and knowing not a lick of the Thai language is not a problem.

The number of girls in paid customer relations in Thailand range from 300,000 to one million. (Side note: you have to be very careful about lady boys in Thailand. We're talking a complete sex change. They thrive on fooling you.)

People come to Thailand to see the beautiful architecture, landscaping, Golden Budda Temples, and of course, the clubs where girls shoot ping pong balls out of their pussies. Try to wipe that shit eating grin off your face the first time you see the nude line dances by gorgeous Thai girls who look like teenage virgins. Strangest act I've seen involved a full beer can placed inward and then with no hands, she turned it around and shot it out. Olympian talents.

There are three main sections of the city's strip clubs, and massage parlors. **Soi Cowboy**, **Nana Entertainment Plaza**, and **Patpong**. Keep in mind, the location and layout of the red light district has been a constant for some 30 years now, the names of the clubs may change, but the song remains the same. It's usually the same owners just mixing things up a bit.

## Nanaplaza Entertainment Plaza :
(Location: Sukhumvit Soi 4, use Sky train to Nana Station)

Nana is a large open air multi-story complex of Go-Go bars consisting of ground floor beer bars, as well as home to three floors of Ripley's believe it or not sleazy nightlife. Many of the clubs here will put on a show that has to be seen, and is better off not repeated. On the first floor we find **Hollywood Rock, Playskool, Rainbow 1 and 2, Voodoo,** and **Buttums Up.** The second floor is predominately the small little bars that are home to the veteran Thai customers and expats. Best one to check out is **G-Spot**, located in the far right corner. Three huge bars occupy the third floor. Right side is **Carnival**, and the left is **Hollywood Two** and **Hollywood Strip**. A great first stop for a tourist.

Here's some quick reviews of recommended bars you should visit

### Playskool
Located in the far right corner of Nana, between Hollywood and the two Rainbow bars. The traditional setup with a central stripper dance stage. It fits maybe 6 girls, but they pack in about 20 girls, all shuffling aimlessly around looking for their night's partner. Playskool is always packed with

customers, and close to 100 dancers. The hottest girls are already *bar fined* and gone for the night by 11 pm, so make your trip here early. Some of the hottest looking Bangkok girls work here. The sexy schoolgirl uniform was the mainstay outfit, but it seems to have disappeared into topless girls in thongs. That doesn't mean you can't take the girls home for some disciplining. Cheap drinks, and indoor bar/outdoor patio.

## Angelwitch

Angelwitch is hidden on the second floor of Nana in between all the small bars on the left side, close to the infamous Casanova lady boy bar. Unfortunately, there have been a lot of political crackdowns on the total total nudity here, so it's hit or miss for that aspect. Angelwitch is infamous for it's sexotic shows, and is packed to the gills on weekends. Come here to see their intricate choreographed shows starting after 10 P.M. Highlights include S&M shows as well as exotic Thai dancing.

## G-Spot

G-spot is the biggest "A-Go-Go bar" in Bangkok, located on the second floor of Nana Plaza in the far right corner. It features 3 dance stages, the entrance is next to the left stage, and sports the club's dirtiest dancers. Always nude in the past, during crackdown season they are topless. Since the stages are larger and not so packed, you'll get to see real sexy dancing, instead of the stupid stripper shuffle. The girls can really move it here. After your fifteenth beer, feel free to act like you're the choreographer.

## Hollywood Strip

Located on the left side of the third floor of Nana is the Hollywood Strip. There's a huge rotating carousel stage on the left and another stage on the right. This place was famous for it's bizarre shows in the past, and the girls were always nude. Previous favorite acts included playing *hide the live frog in the coochie*, and other great family fun. There was no level too low for debauchery here in the good old days. It's toned down currently, but these things pass over quickly and the freak shows reappear.

## Rainbow 2

The latest edition of the Rainbow bars, this club is friggin' huge. Located on the far right corner of the ground floor of Nana Plaza, next to Hollywood Rock, it is home to well over 100 dancers. If you can't find one you like here, you should pack your bags and get on home to your 200-pound nagging wife. Maybe you should try picturing her naked if you find yourself having ridiculously high standards. The typical Thai girl's body weight could be a rounding error when calculating the weight of many US women. Other clubs in Nanaplaza to visit are **Buttums Up, Carnival, Fantasia,** and **Hollywood,** as well as dozens of other smaller ones.

288

## Voodoo

One of the biggest strip clubs, Voodoo bar is located on the ground floor of Nana Plaza in the far left corner. It features a huge dance stage, with the middle section containing a rotating carousel. You get to lust after close to 100 girls, and there are many top-notch lookers here. Arrive early, the club gets cherry picked before midnight. Outside you'll find a huge bar as well, with sports on TV's and a ringside view of the action walking in the streets.

# Soi Cowboy

Section two of Bangkok playland is Soi Cowboy, located off Sukhumvit Road between Soi Asoke and Soi 23, just a short walk from the Asoke Skytrain station. It covers a 300-yard long street area, and is comprised of close to 50 clubs on both sides of the road. Here a sex tourist can find endless scantily clad Thai girls grinding to loud classic western hits, and enjoy picking up a subservient young honey for a remarkably small date fee. As you pass by each club expect half a dozen girls waving and screaming at you, trying to pull you in. If you're bored, walk up and offer them an autograph if they can give you directions to a good Irish pub in Manhattan.

Some of the namesake bars to visit here are **Long Gun, Tilac, Dollhouse, Baccara, Midnight Bar** and many others. Nestled in between these large clubs are dozens of smaller bars to pop in and out of. Soi Cowboy is known to be somewhat more laid back than the other sections, but they do have their share of exotic shows featuring a buffet of naked dancers slithering up and down acrobatically on the stage's chrome poles. Most of the bars at Soi Cowboy charge a fee (bar fine) of about 500 baht to take one of their little honeys home with you. The girls are roughly 1200-1500 baht for a short liaison of a few hours, or 1500 to 2000 for an entire evening of debauchery. In Cowboy you can move your date and your happy ass on upstairs to a private room in about half the clubs. Beer costs 60 to 85 baht during happy hour($2) in the smaller bars, a little more at the premium spots, and the girls will all pump you to buy them house drinks for a commission.

## Long Gun

Most clubs down here come and go, but for years now this one has been a mainstay in Soi. It's not the biggest club, but it's offers up some of the best feature shows in town. Come early if you expect to even get in here. Although they do offer up some great-choreographed strip tease acts, people come here for the down and dirty. Long Gun is the big daddy when it comes to vaginal trick shows. Don't expect to see a dance show when these are going on. The girls are masters of their own domain. 11pm is show time, and the naughtiest of the crew come out in their boots and bikinis and start off their shows with bananas, balloon tricks, and a unique way of opening Heinekens. Soon, the clothes come off, and they put all kind of objects into the coochie. They shoot darts 10 feet out popping balloons, aim table tennis balls into a glass, open soft drink bottles etc. Stand back at the end of the act, they like to spray the bottles over the customers up close. A word of caution, these are real darts they shoot out. Try not to get an eye gorged out when they happen to miss. It'd be a little tough to explain to the boss at home. *"there I was, ...."*

## The Dollhouse Soi Cowboy

Their newest location, with its more famous club in Pattaya. The layout on the first floor is a large pageant-like stage, with barstools surrounding it. The second floor has two smaller stages, and more of an US lap dance environment. One of these stages has a clear floor, so the first floor customers can look up and see all the way to...um Bangkok, as the girls wear see thru clothes and no thongs. The Dollhouse has plenty of sports on its 100-inch Big Screen TV, in case 100 girls running around in transparent clothes or butt naked bores you. Get used to the 50-cent tequila shots specials, the girls working here down dozens of them thru the night. How exactly can you tell whether a girl is speaking or slurring in Thai?

**( www.thedollhouseagogo.com/index.html )**

**Suzie Wongs** on Cowboy is definitely a Bangkok must. The Suzie Wong girls are well known as some of the stars of the Bangkok nightlife. Not only does the bar employ some of the best looking girls in Bangkok, but also they have that sexy and drunk attitude that makes for a great time in the bar.

Soi Cowboy has a ton of smaller more intimate bars as well. A few favorites are **Jungle Jims,** and **The Toy Bar.** The girls here drink heavily and realize you're a famous porn star and hope to have a chance to audition in your hotel room. Dates are around $30-40, as well as a bar fine of 500Bt.

# Patpong

Section Three of Bangkok, the location is Silom Rd or Suriwong Rd. Use the Skytrain. Patpong nightlife has a huge concentration of exotic bars in a tiny area. Plus, at night it's a supermarket of imitation items, such as Rolexes, jewelry, clothing, luggage and so on. Everything is negotiated in the stores and stands, and even their method of bargaining has a Asian traditional feel to it. If you buy clothes, make them look used with wrinkles make so that you don't get questioned at customs. When its bartering time, the seller will not directly tell you a price, instead he types an amount into a calculator, to which you are invited to respond.

On Patpong 1, as you try to tackle all the endless titty bar row, make sure you check out **King's Castle I** and **King's Castel II**. Patpong 2 has some specialty bars, where girls practice sword swallowing in private or do you right at the bar if you want. Take a photo for the family album! The girls have an assortment of fantasy Costumes and toys, and will perform S&M, BDSM, or virtually any act. You name it basically. Dates are 1600+ baht for 90 minutes. **Star of Light** is another popular one. Avoid going upstairs to the bars with the shows. There have been stories of people being ripped off with huge bar tabs. In fact, pay cash for all drinks at once, no tabs ever.

# Thai Soapy Massages

This is a whole other sport in Thailand that you must do at least once in life. For soapy body massages, hop a cab to Ratchadapisek Road. They are all centered here and there are also several **Karaoke Bars** in the area as well. Definitely a great relaxing experience in Bangkok, so here's the lowdown. You go in and view a pack of girls thru a glass gallery, called the fish bowl. The girls all have numbers on their shirts for identification. That way you can tell your friends how hot #217 was last night. Makes for a real personal experience. Drinks are available, you pick out your girl, pay and move to a room. You hop in the hot tub and get a sudsy bath, then onto the massage mat. Best done in a sandwich, i.e., 2 girls. Request the body massage, where they use their whole bodies instead of just their hands. Then it's onto the bed for the last part of your date. The whole thing is around 90 minutes, with the massage fare of 1300-2500 baht. Use this link for the latest up to date locations, addresses, prices, and reviews.

**( www.bangkoktonight.com/massage/ )**

# Blow Job Bars

This one friggin' takes the cake. If you don't have the time to take a girl back to your hotel, or upstairs at the local go-go bar, what do you have left that's quicker? **Blow Job Bars**. These bars provide a level of service not normally found in go-go bars, that you may find either disgusting or hilarious. You walk in, sit at the bar for a beer, and for $ 12 a girl crawls under your stool and blows you right there at the bar. If you're running low on quality money shots, maybe pour some suds over her head. Other options are BJ's sitting on the couch, or private rooms. (may not want to sit down here). Definitely different strokes for different folks, but if you are curious, it sure beats the local Wal Mart. These are all around the Patpong Soi 2.

**Star of Light Bar**  Patpong Soi 2
(on your left hand side if entering Patpong 2 from Surawong Road) Blow jobs in a private room or at the bar counter. Blow Jobs slang in Thai is called "*Smoke*", as in "*Me like smoke you long time!*"

**Lolita's Bar** on Sukhumvit Soi 8 in Bangkok near Nana
( http://www.lolitasbangkok.com )

# Local Discos

Packed with thousands of freelancers and non-pro gringo lovers.

**Concept CM2** (basement of Novotel Hotel, Siam Square)
This is a huge Bangkok club full of pros and non-pros. They feature a house band playing band 80's and 90's US music, as well as the typical *Ornamental* fast techno crap. Cover is $6 weekdays and $12 on weekends. Girls are $35-45. A lot of hot talent here, a little expensive comparatively, but more locals and most speak English.
**Angel Disco** (ground floor of Nana Hotel) **\*\*\***
**Spasso** at the basement of Grand Hyatt, (cabbies call it "Erawan")
**Rivas** at basement of Sheraton Grande Sukhumvit
**QBar** at the end of Sukhumvit Soi 11

**(** www.bangkoktonight.com/discos/ **)**

## Thailand Escort Sites

www.bangkok-escorts.com/girls.html   www.escortsinthailand.com
www.bkkescorts.com        www.bangkoktonight.com/escorts

## Vacation Cover Story :

Tell the old bird you flew 20 hours to Thailand to take your childhood seashell collection to a new level. Make her bow to you at the airport when you return.

## Golf Courses :

There are 35 courses around the greater Bangkok area, with beautiful courses and inexpensive fees. Whether you're in Bangkok for business, a gangbang, or just fancy a game of links, there are great choices here.

**The Royal Golf & Country Club**
(located southeast of Bangkok, a short taxi)
69 Moo 7, Sukhumvit 17, Bang Sao Thong, #(02) 738 0133.
18-hole championship course. B800 during week, B1600 weekends.

**The Rose Garden Golf Club**
(located 20 miles southwest of city), Tha Talad Sub District, Sampran, Nakhon Pathom , adjacent to National Highway Number 4
(tel: (034) 322 588) 18-hole championship golf course
B700 during week, B1300 (closed Mondays)

## Ocean Fishing :

Thailand takes great pride in it's deep-sea sport fishing. In fact, the most expensive rods in the world are made in Chiangmai, Thailand, which is also the home of 10 trout fly companies. Again, just head southwest of Bangkok down to **Pattaya**. Here you can break out the cigars for the abundance of trophy catches to be made, featuring **sailfish, marlin, Mahi Mahi** (dorado), **tuna**, shaved pussies, and other species. Shallow island reefs are home to many species of light-tackle game fish including **sea bass, barracuda, giant trevally, queenfish** and **mangrove jack**. Pelagic species like **black marlin** and **sailfish**, as well as **king mackerel** and **tiger sharks**. Late November is a good time to go after marlin, tuna and any number of other fighting fish such as larger black marlin, up to 300kg. Also found are **yellow fin tuna** (20kg), **Wahoo** (40kg) and numerous **barracuda, Dorado** and **skipjack tuna**. Sharks like tiger, hammerhead, bull and the occasional **Mako Shark** take the bait during day or night-fishing trips.

Here are some sites to arrange your fishing trip.
**( www.asiatradingonline.com/fishing.htm )**
**( www.asiatradingonline.com/pattayafishing.htm )**

## Casinos :
Gambling is illegal in Thailand. Guess they have high standards here. Of course, girls shooting darts 10 feet from their pussies and popping balloons is perfectly acceptable behavior.

## Horseracing :
Horseracing takes place every Sunday in the sweltering heat at the Royal Bangkok Sports Club. Betting in Thailand is illegal, but never mind, supposedly hookers are too. **Location:** Henry Dunant Road

## Bowling :
Brunswick Bowling transforms into a disco, complete with lasers, music and luminous bowling bowls. 9pm-12pm.
Location: Brunswick Bowling, RCA Bowl
3rd Floor, RCA Plaza off Petchburi Rd
Skytrain: Not available. Go by taxi and drink heavily.

## Thai Boxing :
One of the toughest martial arts, Thai boxing uses almost any part of the body; feet, elbows, legs, knees, and shoulders. The contestants undergo a rigorous training schedule from an early age and acquire cult status if they are successful. The big fights happen at the weekend amid much mayhem. Watered down simulation fights can be seen in the RLD streets for tips.)
**Main venues**: **Lumpini Stadium**, Rama IV Road
Open: every Tuesday and Friday at 6.30 -11: 00p.m. and Saturday at 5.00-8:00 and 8:30 - midnight. Price 220 - 800 Baht.
**Ratchadamnoen Boxing Stadium**, Ratchadamnoen Nok Road, (Every Mon and Wed, Thursday at 6.00 p.m.)

For the local up to date info on clubs and bar girls, visit these sites.

( www.bangkokeyes.com )  ( www.clubelectricblue.com/links.htm )
( www.bangkokbargirls.info/NanaPlaza/map.htm )

# The Hedonist

After reading about the Holy Grail for women overseas, and what these three great cities offer a Bachelor, you should be itching to sample the goods and book a trip. Take a deep breath. There's one more step you need to take. You need the tools of the trade. I've authored an underground best seller for World Sex Vacations that has become aptly nicknamed *The Sex Bible*… do yourself a favor and pick up a copy of **The Hedonist**, available at Amazon.com. The ISBN # is 0975264001. Here's the direct link: http://www.amazon.com/gp/product/0975264001/

It's a travel guide for satisfying your dreams of Jet-setting around the world for exotic women, sports and adventure. It details the top 20 affordable, vacation paradises that feature golf, ocean fishing, and sexy young girls who always say yes. (locals, escorts, full service strip clubs, RLD) Over 200 pages of extensive, concise, well-researched travel advice. After reading **The Hedonist**, you'll have a complete picture of the best vacation honey holes. Variety is the spice of life. Take a different trip every few months. Spoil yourself rotten. By the way, if you find yourself sandwiched between gorgeous little nympho Brazilians who don't speak a word of English, remember to raise your glass and toast to your buddy Brett Tate.

# Final Thoughts

The essence of being a Professional Bachelor is creating a rewarding lifestyle full of sensuous women and exhilarating experiences. Seduction is a fine art. All women love a good chase. Perfecting your profiling ability combined with time and money management is what accelerates your player skills. Ultimately, it's just a game that takes balls and attitude. In the big picture with women, make sure you're not one of the millions of men who had their lives destroyed because they never got around to Covering their Assets. Create asset protection long before getting serious with a woman. When you take care of the downside, the upside takes care of itself.

A Player is someone who sets his goals high and achieves them, time and time again. It's a statement of success. The techniques in the art of the pickup are virtually the same methods to further yourself in business. Exercise patience and discipline, shut down your ego, and study the customer using reverse psychology. In dating, give her what she wants to see, what she wants to hear, and give her the emotions she wants to feel.

Why let the cards fall as they may around you? Life is full of adversity and obstacles. Only the meek set their sails and leave the winds of chance to steer them randomly. Winds change, situations change, and women change. The aggressor sets the rules. The Alpha Male takes control in every seduction, while teasingly showing no self-interest. By controlling the timing, tone, emotions, and direction, you control the outcome. Perception becomes reality. Live life to the fullest. Live it on your terms, and be…

## A Professional Bachelor